DAYS ON EARTH

DAYS ON EARTH

THE DANCE OF

DORIS HUMPHREY

MARCIA B. SIEGEL

YALE UNIVERSITY PRESS

NEW HAVEN AND LONDON

Designed by Sally Harris
and set in Eras type by
Graphic Composition, Inc.
Printed in the United States of America by
Halliday Lithograph, West Hanover, Mass.

Library of Congress Cataloging-in-Publication Data

Siegel, Marcia B.
   Days on earth.

   Bibliography: p.
   Filmography: p.
   Includes index.
   1. Humphrey, Doris, 1895–1958. 2. Choreographers—
United States—Biography. 3. Modern dance—United
States. I. Title.
GV1785.H8S54 1987   793.3'2'0924 [B]   87–6150
ISBN 0–300–03856–9 (alk. paper)

The paper in this book meets guidelines for
permanence and durability of the Committee on
Production Guidelines for Book Longevity
of the Council on Library Resources.

10 9 8 7 6 5 4 3 2 1

Frontispiece:
Original cast of *Day on Earth.* Letitia Ide, José Limón,
Miriam Pandor, and Melisa Nicolaides. (Dance
Collection, NYPL)

Nobody knows you, no. But I sing of you
I sing for a later time, of your profile and your grace
The celebrated ripeness of your skill

—Federico García Lorca, *Lament for Ignacio Sánchez Mejías*

CONTENTS

LIST OF ILLUSTRATIONS

PREFACE

This book actually began in 1979, when I was asked to teach a course on Doris Humphrey at New York University's Graduate Drama Department (now the Department of Performance Studies). It was not Humphrey's biography I was interested in, or even her role in the development of modern dance in America; her choreography was what fascinated me. She had been dead for twenty years—normally a guarantee of oblivion for any dance artist—but because of her unusual foresight it was possible to show students the entire span of her creative output, either on films or videotape or in live performances of her dances. This kind of concentration on the work of a single artist was rare at that time; a student with literary inclinations remarked in awe, "You mean like a course in Milton?" We did the course, looking at different dances every week, and a book about the extraordinary thirty-year achievement we had examined seemed a natural aftermath.

Doris Humphrey's choreography appealed to me from my first season of looking at dance, the summer of 1962, when the José Limón company was doing Humphrey's *Night Spell* and the posthumous work *Brandenburg Concerto no. 4.* Though I knew nothing about dance, Humphrey's humanism struck me. There was something about the dignity and firmness with which dancers in her works bore themselves. You could sense their presence as people even though they weren't playing literal characters. This image of individual power held me over the years as I discovered how singular it was, even in the determinedly individualistic field of modern dance.

Dance by dance, Humphrey's repertory accumulated in my mind. Each year somebody would reconstruct one or two, or a piece of film would be unearthed. The more I learned about choreography, the more I recognized what a fine craftsman she was, and how superior was her grasp of form, music, and theatrical effects. I saw that she had applied mind as well as intuition to the job of making dances, and I didn't hold that against her.

In 1966, the distinguished journal *Dance Perspectives* published Humphrey's unfinished autobiography—a fragment, really, covering only the period of her life before she did any of her most important choreography. *Dance Perspectives* editor Selma Jeanne Cohen completed the story six years later with *Doris Humphrey: An Artist First.* For her book, Cohen drew on a collection of documents spanning Humphrey's life, a remarkable set of materials to have emerged from anyone's attic, but for a dancer, astounding. That Humphrey kept more than 7,000 items—not only letters but notes, lectures, and other manuscript materials related to her work—was an overwhelming sign of her sense of history. Fully aware of the immediacy and ephemerality of the work she was engaged in, she nevertheless wanted it to survive in some way. *Doris Humphrey: An Artist First* dealt mainly with her family life as Cohen saw it through the letters. Eleanor King's memoir of the early days of the Humphrey-Weidman company, *Transformations* (1978), and Ernestine Stodelle's description of her work, *The Dance Technique of Doris Humphrey* (1978), added to the story, but I kept feeling unsatisfied. Her dances had touched me too deeply to explain her simply as a pioneer in a wonderfully innocent phase of dance history.

One of the many paradoxes and ironies of Doris Humphrey's story is that so little is known of her today in spite of the unusual efforts she made to pass on her achievement. In fact, she is worse than forgotten; she is frequently misunderstood and misrepresented. She left notated scores of many of her dances, but these don't describe the luminous spirit of the works or tell how to capture it. Today's dancers, sleek, airborne, and academically disengaged, have neither the taste nor the temperament for comradeship, idealism, and avoidance of clutter, some of the characteristics underlying most Humphrey dances. Form is considered too restrictive and arbitrary today unless it's concealed by decorative devices or apologized for with self-conscious folksiness. Feeling has been replaced by sentimentality and theatrics. Whenever a Humphrey dance is revived, someone is sure to say it's too simple, and someone else will say it's actually deeper and more beautiful than the dancers made it seem. In modern dance today, technique supersedes everything. Dancers must be balletic in line and skill. Choreographers must provide them with tests of escalating difficulty. Audiences expect excitement and lots of action. Finding movement for oneself is still a basic premise of modern dance, but this has come to mean adapting and augmenting some proven technique or style.

The early modern dancers accepted no particular norms for the body's capabilities, no established "look" or energy level, until they had discovered their own ways of working. Moving from the inside out was their method, not only in developing movement vocabularies but in the repeated, daily work of training and performing. "You had to *feel* what Martha was feeling to be able to do her roles," early Martha Graham dancers will report. Doris Humphrey's dances were similarly organic. Even after her training exercises and vocabulary became established, the movement in her dances had to be reconceived and regenerated by the dancers, because she was unable to demonstrate it for them. She asked instead for images. "Feel the rise and fall of a wave in your own breath," she would say. "Get up from the floor as if you were a seedling reaching for the light." Those who worked with her, from the earliest days to the last, spoke of the powerful, almost cosmic energies they experienced in doing her dances and of the individual freedom this decision making allowed them. Small wonder, then, that her dances look diminished when they're learned as shapes and patterns that can be imitated externally.

Without engaging in the never-ending debate about whether a dance can exist at all apart from its living performance, I wanted to examine Doris Humphrey's dances to find out some of the things that made them admirable. I had not wished to write another biography. But in the summer of 1980, as I read through the Humphrey letters on which Selma Jeanne Cohen had drawn and many hundreds more that had been preserved separately and made available to researchers since Cohen's book was published, I realized how inseparably linked her private and professional lives had been. I perceived with increasing astonishment that Humphrey's dances were models for the ideal state of harmony and self-knowledge into which she kept trying to coax the real life around her.

Neither a fanatic nor an intellectual, a monomaniac nor a seeker after perfection for its own sake, she saw dancing and choreographing as her work, and knew no other way to do it than full-out. She needed others to do it with her, and she assumed that they were as absorbed in its possibilities as she was. She commanded neither material resources nor the charm to acquire them. She possessed the moral fiber of a Victorian, the imagination of a romantic, and the existential courage of a modernist. Had she been rich, had she been healthier or luckier, had she been a man, her story might have been entirely different, but she never speculated on what she couldn't attain. She just went on working to develop what she had. She never thought of herself as less than a major artist, but she would not complain when she wasn't treated as one. She would not make excuses if a work turned out more modestly than she had envisioned it. She was a professional when a dance profession didn't even exist. For all these reasons, she became a role model—leader and conceptualizer, teacher and mentor—for those around her. Though I never knew her, I found her a complex and elusive personality and, finally, an irresistible challenge as a subject for a book.

On completion of her biography, Selma Jeanne Cohen remarked that Humphrey's letters would probably yield several more books, and I think that is still true. I haven't, for instance, discussed the development of her technique and theory, her lectures and writings, or the composition classes she taught for years, which, according to those who attended them, were extraordinary. I haven't traced her aesthetic legacy beyond her immediate heir, José Limón, though her influence can still be seen in contemporary dance styles. And I haven't attempted to assemble systematic memoirs or anecdotal histories of any of the dances. What I have tried to do is reestablish the claim, fully validated in her lifetime but already lapsed, that she was one of America's greatest choreographers.

Humphrey herself provided the bulk of the evidence for that claim, even without the problematic revivals through which we must gain our only direct experience of her dance. But many other people and institutions have contributed to my studies for this book. First I would like to express my gratitude to Charles H. Woodford for preserving his mother's personal and professional papers and placing them in the care of the Dance Collection of the Library and Museum of the Performing Arts at Lincoln Center, New York, where they can be examined by all who wish to learn about her. Charles Woodford was also generous in supplying answers to my occasional questions and giving his encouragement to the project. The staff of the Dance Collection under Genevieve Oswald have patiently helped me through the catalogues, threaded projectors and tape machines, trudged back and forth with call slips, and brought out folders full of treasures during my four and a half years of research.

In addition to the information and background provided by the associates of Doris Humphrey listed in the Notes, I received special help from John Angelo, Dorothy Coleman Morse, and Gertrude Shurr in trying to identify the dances on a 1929–30 home movie. Ernestine Stodelle also tried to untangle this mystery and contributed many other pieces of information. Geri Nunn of the Columbia University oral history office and Gertrude Noyes, historian of Connecticut College, gave me access to archival material that was invaluable. Others who supplied information and insights into Humphrey's dance were Deborah Brandt, Tom Brown, Selma Jeanne Cohen, George Dorris, Henry Kurth, Edith Segal, and Andrew Mark Wentink. Federico Menez translated parts of José Limón's diaries for me. Norma Adler typed the final manuscript and corrected my orthographic slips and errors. Joseph Petticrew did photographic work.

I was extremely fortunate to receive financial help during the writing of this book from the Ingram Merrill Foundation, and from the Mellon Humanities Challenge Fund of New York University for preparation of the manuscript.

Time passes with unnatural speed in dance and, it seems, in dance writing. Both professions, and my situation within them, have changed considerably since I began this project. It would have been easier to abandon it or suspend it for even longer periods than I did, but friends were always there to listen and debate, enthuse over fragments in progress, encourage, prod, and keep me from spending too long on more mundane distractions. I am grateful for that sustained support to Robert Cornfield, Nancy Goldner, Camille Hardy, Deborah Jowitt, John Mueller, Selma Odom, Allen Robertson, Laura Shapiro, and Suzanne Shelton. Others who helped the book on its long road to publication are Doris Kretschmer, Patricia Brooks and Shirley Wimmer of Ohio University, Liz Thompson, and Gladys Topkis, my editor at Yale.

Most of all, I am indebted to Doris Humphrey herself—whose dances are exceptional and whose struggle to realize them was a constant inspiration—and to the dancers, past and present, who have given them life.

New York City

DAYS ON EARTH

CRETONE-PTR

1 WHAT DO YOU CALL YOUR WORK, MISS HUMPHREY?

Late in August 1931 Doris Humphrey was invited to give two lessons at the Hotel Astor in New York, where the nation's ballroom instructors, gymnastics coaches, and dance educators were assembled for the 53rd Annual Convention of the American Society of Teachers of Dancing. In the published program Humphrey was respectfully given the lead-off position, and she contributed a single page of notes—actually just a list of reminders for classes she intended to give. Her plainspoken and open-ended sketch was followed by eighty-nine pages of dance routines by the other presenters: *The Dainty Miss Milkmaid* toe number arranged by Sonia Serova, technical exercises and ballet combinations by Alex Yakovleff, Spanish and Mexican folk dances by Angel Cansino, tap dances by Billy Newsome, bird ballets, butterfly dances, a Modern Study entitled *Daybreak,* and a Grecian affair with a big silk scarf, oddly reminiscent of a scarf dance called *Soaring* that Humphrey had choreographed ten years before. After her classes, someone asked Doris, "What do you call your work, Miss Humphrey, dancing?"

She called it modern American dancing. Along with a handful of young women and even fewer men, Doris Humphrey was leading a crusade to liberate dance from triviality and prettiness, which were among the worst sins she knew. "Graceful dancing still abounds for those who are romantic. But the modern dance is for those who have progressed toward and accepted a wider interpretation of contemporary life, one which includes both dark and light. It is for those who believe that art is a revelation of the meaning of life and not an escape from it." This statement, which Humphrey framed for a presentation in Philadelphia in 1935, reflects a whole era in American dance with its idealism, its commitment to the rigors of art, and its possibly alarming rectitude.

Ballet was the chief target of these reformers. As they understood it, ballet was an outmoded and artificial form, drained of all but symbolic meaning and linked to a social system that had been irrevocably dislodged. With weakening ties to the Christian-monarchist tradition in which European culture was rooted, American society stood for egalitarianism and the drive toward technological mastery. American artists saw themselves as addressing an audience without previously defined standards or stratifications, and beginning with Isadora Duncan, American dancers felt entitled to reinvent their medium. By the 1920s, even ballet was rethinking itself, acknowledging developments in modern art though not fully discarding prescribed vocabularies and stage conventions. When ballet put out tentative roots in American soil it still carried the aura of an imported plant, exotic and slightly out of place. The first ballet schools had been founded by European expatriates, and the earliest companies were appended to opera houses. A few independents like Adolph Bolm, who teamed up with the American experimentalist Ruth Page, were searching for a modern ballet style, but what most Americans knew of ballet was imitative, overdecorated, and escapist.

Ballet was only a small slice of an enormous spectrum of recreational and artistic dance activity that had spread across the country by the 1920s. In fact, the same aristocratic cachet that eluded Americans in ballet was exuberantly welcomed in ballroom dancing, whose popularity reached craze proportions by World War I with Vernon and Irene Castle. Fully aware of the strong religious sanctions against dancing and especially social, body-to-body dancing, the Castles projected themselves as exemplars of elegance and propriety. Exquisitely and expensively gowned, Irene Castle seemed a lithe younger sister to the society matrons who were their sponsors; Vernon was tall and elegant, with impeccable manners. The dance routines they performed in nightclubs and taught to clerks and shopgirls at their school, Castle House, emphasized lightness, gaiety, and precision. They insisted on the same erect torso, associated with upper-class deportment, that underlies the technique of academic ballet. They wanted to smooth out the wiggles and bumps and uninhibited gyrations that went with jazz. Castle dancers were supposed to be transported by the infectious rhythms of waltz, ragtime, and tango, but they were never to indulge in tasteless intimacies like the tight body contact of the Bunny Hug or the "hoidenish romping of the Two Step, the swift rush of the Polka, and contortions of the Turkey Trot."

The little book of dance instructions that the Castles published in 1914 includes a chapter on manners and deportment, with notes on how to give dancing teas and dinner parties. It also offers Irene's sensible but high-fashion suggestions as to the proper clothes for dancing, and an endorsement of the healthfulness of dancing by Dr. J. Ralph Jacoby.

The Castles represented a fusion of stage dancing and social dancing. Their steps and music came from the ballrooms and cafés of Europe. These were dances everyone could do, to which the Castles added theatrical showiness and flair. Dancing was, at that euphoric point in our history, a peek at the glamorous life. The period of dress-up was brief. Social dancing relaxed into its more accustomed earthy, physical, and individual ways, and the showiest, classiest, most intricate embellishments of social dance steps were returned to the stage, where they had flourished during a century of minstrel shows, tent shows, medicine shows, vaudeville, and variety. After World War I, movies, radio, and recorded music gave the general public increased access to professional entertainment; once again we became spectators of fancy dancing rather than imitators.

The Astaires completed the sublimation the Castles had started, as carefree rich Americans larking through the stage-set opulence of the upper crust. By the beginning of the 1930s, talking pictures made the movie musical possible and the separation between the Saturday night date and the ballroom was complete. Social dancing continued to be taught to little boys and girls as a polite accomplishment that would help them to be agreeable, well-adjusted citizens and to pair off with suitable mates.

Both in the dancing schools and in the creation of civic pageantry and celebrations, a great deal of dancing for recreation was being taught in America. Most of this teaching was in the category of social dancing, but the distinctions between that, physical culture, and dancing for artistic presentation were blurred. Physical culture had always been a component of American education, and throughout the nineteenth century gymnastics and sports were subjected to a variety of uplifting modifications as bodily activity gradually became unified with the elevated business of the mind and spirit. Religious objections to dancing were battered down as educators and medical men argued its beneficial effects on thought and morals. Dancing and the related arts of singing and elocution could form a sort of bridge between the temporal and the spiritual life, as long as they didn't become a means of unleashing violent or unhealthy passions.

One way of keeping physicality in check was to systematize it into various types of patterned activities. Sport was an acceptable solution, though for women a limited one until dress reformers began to campaign against corsets, voluminous skirts, tight boots, and other encumbrances. As the layers of clothing came off, so did many false notions about women's frailness and their vulnerability to physical exercise. Restrictive codes of behavior that surrounded the display or expressive use of women's bodies began to moderate. By the end of the nineteenth century, these prejudices were breaking down, and girls were permitted the same use of their limbs and torsos as boys, for the sake of their health if not for their pleasure.

Calisthenics—regular exercises for developing the parts of the body—were practiced in schools and colleges, often accompanied by music. Instructors became interested in breathing and in the study of the human body as a living, working organism rather than as a system of bones, muscles, and viscera charted from laboratory cadavers. Often these exercise classes incorporated the five foot positions of academic ballet with their accompanying arm movements, and some basic ballet steps, like the arabesque. Perhaps this was thought to give refinement and grace to the worklike calisthenic movements—even as it does in present-day gymnastic training.

The Europeans had developed detailed systems of physical culture, and one of the most widely adapted concepts involved combining physical movements with musical analysis as practiced in the schools of Emile Jaques-Dalcroze. Dalcroze Eurythmics, formulated by the Swiss musician in the latter years of the nineteenth century, became a popular method of training, and after the founding of the Dalcroze Institute at Hellerau, Germany, in 1911, the idea of rhythmic gymnastics filtered into American schools and studios. Physical culture became an element in the prototypical holistic health movements and back-to-nature crusades that began to appear in Europe and the United States. Spiritualism, vegetarianism, dancing, and self-expression, women's liberation, free love, and radical thought often flared up together when futuristic politics intersected with a nostalgia for the preindustrial age, and scarcely any avant-garde art of the early twentieth century was left unsinged.

The dancer who most completely enacted this Wagnerian fusion of physical liberation, spirituality, aestheticism, and the supremacy of individual expression was Isadora Duncan. With her superb performing instrument, she demonstrated ideas about rhythmic and dramatic movement that seemed, to the survivors of nineteenth-century formalism and opulence, at once simpler and more basic, and infinitely more profound on an emotional level. American dancers adopted her as a pathfinder, even those who felt she was too idiosyncratic to serve as a model. Duncan's advocacy of ancient Greek ideals as a source for dancing linked her with the American utopians, especially in her native California, where various programs for a healthier life included outdoor living and simple food and clothing, as well as interpretive dancing in the Grecian mode.

Another primary influence on physical culture training and on early attempts at expressive dancing was the philosophy of François Delsarte. The French elocution teacher, who died in 1871, constructed an elaborate system for cataloguing emotions, their characteristic gestures, and the corresponding parts of the body. Delsarte's charts and diagrams were quickly adapted to the emotive needs of oratory, acting, and aesthetic dancing.

Steele Mackaye, Delsarte's American interpreter, lectured widely and taught "harmonic gymnastics" mainly for actors. Soon after Ted Shawn had embarked on his dancing career, he encountered Mackaye's disciples Bliss Carman and Mary Perry King in 1911. Ruth St. Denis had discovered Delsarte much earlier, at an 1892 lecture by Genevieve Stebbins. Delsarte's theories were so widely practiced and adapted in this country that exponents of the system became rivals. Although Stebbins had studied with Mackaye for two years, she rejected much of what she considered mystical and of doubtful value in Delsarte's philosophy. She concentrated on what she called Modern or Practical Delsartism, "an evolution of his system in accordance with American ideas and requirements." This meant a concentration on relaxation and breathing exercises, pantomime, and "artistic statue posing," the imitation of noble sculptures from Greek antiquity. She also published lesson books and manuals of instructions.

The legacy of Delsarte is only beginning to be fully understood. Americans in the nineteenth and early twentieth centuries seem to have had a tremendous longing for culture, and in lieu of either an art tradition or a unified folk culture, people of refinement went in for pageantry and posturing that we would now consider kitsch. As the century turned, Americans, like their European counterparts, looked toward classical Greece for models of ideal beauty and a humanized interpretation of natural forms. The flowing lines of Art Nouveau and the images of languid play found in the works of such popular painters as Alma-Tadema and Maxfield Parrish were appropriated for the stage and films. Classical ballet turned toward spectacle that was not only more representational but also attempted to re-create in plastic form the life of ancient and exotic times.

Even before 1916, when Diaghilev's Ballets Russes brought to America Michel Fokine's evocations of Greece (*Daphnis et Chlöe, Narcisse*) and the mysterious East (*Schéhérazade, Le Dieu Bleu, Cléopâtre*), Gertrude Hoffmann had presented her versions of Diaghilev subjects in New York. While the ballet was becoming more humanized and romanticized, art dancers, mimes, and aesthetic interpreters proliferated on the concert stage, creating characters with expressive gestures borrowed from Delsarte and copied from paintings and sculpture. Ruth St. Denis was perhaps the most persuasive of all those artists who tried to graft aestheticism onto a dancing presence. But finally for Doris Humphrey and some of her contemporaries, this didn't serve either.

None of the dancing they had learned seemed to portray what they felt or who they were. What was needed, Humphrey thought, was a kind of dancing that expressed both the twentieth century and the American experience. For a time it might be necessary to throw all their training away and discover if anything danceable remained. American modern dancing was not an isolated impulse; Germany and Eastern Europe experienced similar self-searching and creative experimentation, and there were other stirrings toward at least revitalizing the ballet art. Europe's greater benevolence toward art experimentation allowed its dance reformers to develop their schools and their styles. At the end of the 1920s the Americans faced a dual handicap: a very limited public acceptance for any art dancing, and a disregard, amounting at times to hostility, toward performance that was considered abstract, esoteric, or not ingratiating enough. The leading innovators of the modern dance and the critics who supported them patiently formulated their ideas, explained what they were doing, demonstrated their theories, and taught classes for the layman. They believed their dance expressed universal feelings and appealed directly to what all people could remember. But after all that, few people understood what it was, beyond the highly individual, momentarily captivating, and quickly forgotten performances of the artists themselves.

Self-expression was the first principle of Humphrey's generation of dancers. Gertrude Colby, a Duncan disciple who began a "natural dance" program at Columbia's Teachers College in 1918, spelled it out: "I wanted each girl to work out a philosophy and understanding of dance for herself." This was an exhilarating challenge, and it led to much experimentation and more emoting. Doris Humphrey distinguished herself from the rest of the expressive dancers by trying from the outset to understand dance not only for herself but for all dancers.

Duncan had made a start on this, investigating the components of her own physicality and trying to impart its elements to her young pupils. But Duncan's teaching relied heavily on imitation and the force of her own presence in the studio. She did not formulate any clear program for teaching her kind of dancing, and three generations later, her followers are still transforming her philosophical admonitions into differing forms of action and training. Martha Graham's dance is primarily a personal expression in the same sense and will likely have the same ambiguous consequences when she can no longer dictate how she wants it done. Humphrey, a far less ego-centered dancer, not only sought new movements, new sequences, new ways to move, but also tried to understand a movement's context. What did it mean, expressively, to go off balance? How could you intensify or minimize the effect? How would that look as a phrase? Where would you want to use that phrase in a dance progression? Probably the question of how to use a movement in choreography was no less interesting to her than how to use it in the classroom. She was not so much a didact as an organizer, a communicator. She saw choreography and teaching as two facets of the same process, and she played on both outlets with great skill.

She had scarcely begun choreographing as an independent when she had located her key ideas. She understood how the body creates drama without being mimetic, how form is achieved and manipulated in a composition that occurs in both time and space. She insisted on the integrity of these discoveries by doing without the ballet's traditional accomplices, the libretto and the musical score, as she established her approach. She was gifted in being able to use her insights theatrically and explain her methods in uncomplicated ways. The systematic thoroughness of her approach gave credibility not only to her dance, but to modern dance as a whole. She could demonstrate its principles, compare the way it worked to music and art, and convince a public that they were watching something serious and sound, not just an aberration or a private outburst that would dissolve the moment it had formed itself.

From the first, Humphrey wanted to dance as an individual but to choreograph for other people. She was the only one of her contemporaries to begin with a partner, Charles Weidman, and a group. For the entire span of her career she declined the autocratic role of the modern dance choreographer-director; she tried to give dancers status as collaborators and managers of their artistic output. She encouraged people to choreograph yet she also reassured those who had no desire to make dances of their own. She gave her dances to students, her own and those of other teachers, so that they could practice on important, demanding work. She gave advice to almost anyone who asked for her evaluation, and she taught people to choreograph in her highly inventive classes. She extended her own range by utilizing the movement capabilities of those who came to dance with her.

Doris Humphrey was not looking for a "style" or even a technique of dancing. Her dances were not so personal that only she could do them; and her training technique, from the first an amalgam of her exercises and Charles Weidman's, underwent changes in her own lifetime. What she wanted in a dancer was not a replication of her own bodily preferences and abilities. Her dance didn't have the idiosyncratic force—or the expressional limitations—of Martha Graham's, for instance. Her work had more latitude and less quick recognizability. The paradoxical nature of dance art is such that nonballetic work made this way is both more adaptable and less enduring. Graham's dances, filmed in peak moments, can stand with other art masterpieces. Humphrey's dances, even in documentations with their original casts, are less distinctive. One can't say precisely where their luminosity and fervor come from, or what one would need to re-create their intensity.

It was in this very self-effacement that Doris Humphrey provided an alternative model for the modern dance, and perhaps also a bridge into the more conventionalized, less autobiographical idiom of ballet. Humphrey's own dances never entered the ballet repertory, but she paved the way for others with an open philosophy that allowed for eclectic influences and nonnarcissistic performing. Her dances were never tortured or obscure; they went out in a direct appeal to the audience, their outward harmoniousness a natural resolution of skillfully manipulated conflict. As a creator, Humphrey possessed an absorption in the choreographer's craft that was both singular and exemplary. She thought of choreography as a long-lived organism. Alone of her contemporaries, she realized the full meaning of repertory—as a body of works that grow deeper in interpretation the more they are performed together—and she accomplished the closest thing to true repertory of any modern dancer despite her perpetually straitened circumstances. In this, as in so much else, she was ahead of her time.

But in the making of dances, she was intrinsically *of* her time. From the austerity of the early studies, through the architectural splendor of the great communitarian essays *New Dance* and *Passacaglia,* to the elegiac yet earthy portraits of the later dance-dramas, she cast in form and motion the idealism and compassion of the American dream. Born in a dying century, she was formed intellectually and morally when the modern age was young, and neither Depression, war, nor nuclear nightmare, neither hardship, personal pain, nor the underestimation of her work ever turned her faith in the future to cynicism. What she believed in was the joy of work, the strength of collaboration. She cherished a boundless affirmation of life with all its happiness, sorrow, and rationality. This is what she thought dancing was meant to communicate, and constructing a series of heavenly worlds was how she chose to spend her life.

2 PALACE HOTEL, 1895–1917

In July 1897, Julia Wells Humphrey and Horace Buckingham Humphrey moved into Chicago's Palace Hotel, on North Clark and Indiana Streets, with their twenty-two-month-old daughter, Doris. They were beginning a new career as managers of the busy transient residence, and the family's experience there for the next sixteen years might be seen as a microcosm of American social change. The Humphreys were emerging from sheltered, small-town life to a more worldly existence in the city. The close-knit family and church circles they had grown up with gave way to more far-ranging, casual acquaintanceships. They exchanged their genteel, conventional, middle-class orientation for independence and an involvement with people who adopted individualistic, creative, and even eccentric forms of expression. Doris' parents lived on the borderline of a transition; Doris achieved it. She became an artist. Yet she could never quite resolve the conflict between the nineteenth-century values that reassured her parents' generation and the libertarianism that attracted her own.

Both Julia Wells and Horace Humphrey were the offspring of Congregational ministers, and before their courtship they had both asserted a certain independence from the strictest conventions of nineteenth-century parish life. In fact, these conventions were already beginning to loosen their hold on the families, although various relatives on Julia's side, especially her missionary half-sister, Annie, persisted in their efforts to keep the young Humphreys on the straight and narrow. Christian Science was not unknown on both sides of the family, and in his later years the Reverend Humphrey sought relief from his physical ills in the water cure. For a time during their courtship Julia and Horace read scripture together, but they had both grown away from regular church going. Horace believed himself to be a nonconformist in religion as in many other things. Although he was still living with his parents at the age of thirty-four, when his courtship began, he had already engaged in several business ventures and lived for a time in St. Paul before returning home to Oak Park, Illinois.

A personable young man who enjoyed the theater, singing in a male chorus, and marathon bicycle rides, Horace Humphrey was what we would call an underachiever. He had spent most of his working life in the newspaper business, beginning as a reporter and drifting into the shop at the *Chicago Herald,* where he supervised the department of photoengraving, the new process that was changing the graphic style of American newspapers. Horace was enthusiastic about the new technology and its possibilities, though he was a bit defensive about working as a "mechanic" rather than entering one of the professions into which his college education might have led him. He said he preferred working with his hands. But actually he was rather afraid of responsibility. Whenever he became successful enough at a job to be entrusted with more demanding work, he worried about making mistakes, worked far into the night, and eventually drove himself into a state of physical collapse or hyperanxiety. He followed this pattern all his life, and success in business eluded him. Julia provided the stabilizing influence in their family and made it possible for Horace to indulge his entrepreneurial whims without doing serious harm to the upward course they intended for their daughter.

At twenty-five Julia had left her parents' home in Northfield, Massachusetts, and was living in Boston with another young woman, May Miller, with whom she maintained a sisterly relationship that lasted a lifetime. Julia was studying music and giving piano lessons. In her mind she had not yet abandoned the role of the genteel young lady of accomplishment; she had not yet admitted that music was her profession and that what she was doing amounted to work. Ten years later she did acknowledge this by joining the musicians' union, but in the intervening decade and for many years afterward, she fretfully combined her musical vocation and her domestic duties, attempting to resolve the conflict between the role her puritan conscience dictated to her and the one her emancipated instincts preferred.

Julia and Horace shared solid Christian values, a sense of responsibility toward home and family, and also a freshness and curiosity about the future, a willingness to explore the world outside their families' accepted patterns. But they possessed these qualities in different amounts and their temperaments were extremely dissimilar. Their life together was less a blending of like minds than an accommodation of divergent ones.

Unlike the practical Julia, Horace was a romantic and something of a visionary. Though there was seldom any spare cash around for gambling, he occasionally speculated in real estate, theatrical producing, and ephemeral business schemes, and he often carried deadbeats on the hotel rolls. Once he befriended an unemployed playwright who moved in with the family for a year. It was probably his ability to imagine his fancies realized that led Horace to initiate a correspondence with Julia in early 1891. They had met three years before through distant family connections—they may have been remote cousins—and when he asked Reverend Wells for permission to write to his daughter, he probably had his mind already set for marriage.

Reverend Wells agreed, and for six extraordinary months Horace and Julia were devoted pen pals, sharing lengthy and frequent observations about their lives and acquaintances. The letters grew steadily warmer, and by the time Horace made a visit to Northfield that summer, they had tacitly agreed that they might have a future together. At the end of his stay he proposed to her, on an outing to a hilltop, a scene that acquired mythic proportions in later memory. They retold it to each other many times, recalling the scenery, the weather, the obliging horse, as if Horace's declaration of love and Julia's acquiescence to it had been totally unexpected and miraculous. They corresponded for another half-year, in terms of great wonderment at their good fortune and with loving hopes for the future. Horace thought he had found the means to perfect happiness. Julia had some misgivings. She was realistic enough to know that she could never be the docile, conscientious wife her in-laws would expect, and she wondered how she would fit into the Oak Park household where she and Horace were to make their first home. She also had reservations about giving up her music although she professed a willingness to do so.

Horace reassured her. He said he didn't believe women should ruin their health with housework, or sacrifice pursuits that gave them personal pleasure, as he felt his mother had done when she immersed herself in the role of a clergyman's wife. He said their mutual love of music had been an initial bond between them, and he wanted Julia to use her talent to educate his taste, to entertain him at home. He wanted her to improve herself in the art of music as years went by. But he said nothing about her playing the piano outside the intimate circle of their friends and family, and he didn't seem to consider musicianship a money-making skill. Certainly he did not imagine that it might become a major source of the family's income.

After their marriage in January 1892, the young couple spent their first five years together living in four different places in Chicago and Oak Park. They appeared to be a carefree pair; perhaps in their early married years they were making up for the lost pleasures of courtship. Julia learned to ride a bicycle,

gave up corsets and wore tights, and took a few Delsarte lessons. They attended plays and concerts and lectures together. Horace had always longed
for domestic companionship, and after their marriage his emotional depen-
dence on Julia grew stronger. When she returned east for her father's funeral in the summer of 1892 he begged her not to stay too long. Throughout
their marriage they were often apart for long periods of time, but much as
they both enjoyed their separate holidays, the one left at home—usually
Horace—would send constant assurances of love and reminders of loneliness. Even though they were older than the typical newly married couple,
they do not appear to have included a child in their anticipations of married
life—at least, children were not mentioned in their voluminous love letters.
Julia's early pregnancy was precarious, and she suffered gynecological problems and hospitalizations for years afterward. She often observed that she
couldn't see why anyone would want to have more than one child. Neither
parent, however, had anything but love and solicitude for their daughter
when she did arrive.

   Doris Batcheller Humphrey was born October 17, 1895. Her father announced the event with a designation used by progressives of the time: "a
new woman." Through her infancy Horace's foothold in the newspaper
business became increasingly tenuous. He couldn't keep a job—always the
hours were too long or kept him away from home until late at night, or he
was looking for better pay. Possibly he was laid off in the economic hard
times of the 1890s. He tried his luck several times in other cities—New York,
St. Louis, Philadelphia—without success. Julia quietly began giving piano
lessons and, after solicitous consulations about whether Horace would mind
helping with the extra housework, started to take in boarders to supplement
the family income. Then, in the summer of 1897, after brief stints on at least
three Chicago papers, he was offered a position managing the Palace Hotel,
which became not only the source of their livelihood but their home.

Housework was a pivotal issue in the Humphrey marriage, a sort of bargaining chip between Julia and Horace, and between Julia and her conscience.
She appeased tradition by trying to be perfect at it, and defied tradition by
demonstrating that other things were more important to her. Who did the
housework and the cooking in the family at any given time was an important sign of the way the family fortunes were going. The breadwinner was
exempted from chores; the one who had time to stay home and do them
lost caste. Initially Julia had to resign herself to home responsibilities; later, as

she became more and more successful in her career, Horace kept house and was tacitly considered a failure by his wife and daughter. But his aspirations were more limited than Julia's. He had always liked being at home, and he didn't mind tending his daughter when she was placed in his care.

Julia knew she could never live up to the impossible standards of domestic spit-and-polish and impeccably regulated routine that she had set for herself. She didn't like domestic work, and she probably wasn't very good at it. Besides that, she had an increasingly important stake in her outside musical activities. Life at the Palace Hotel was flexible at best—meals weren't always on time, hours were erratic, people came and went around the family table. Yet, the more unstable their home life was, the more Julia drove herself to give it the appearance of normality. Much as she wanted to escape the dreary detail, her marriage—at least until Doris finished school—was essentially a greatly elaborated and magnified housekeeping enterprise. Horace not only ran the business end of the hotel but also hired the staff and supervised the constant repairs and refurbishing of rooms, public spaces, and concessions. Julia attended to the laundering, mending, and replenishing of the linen supply; rode herd on the maids; shopped for new furniture and rugs; and soon learned to do the bookkeeping for the establishment as well.

In addition to the comings and goings of the hotel residents, Julia and Horace were involved with innumerable relatives and friends who had to be helped, entertained, and cared for. Horace's parents and his younger brothers and sister were often ill, unemployed, or without homes, and they brought the loose ends of their lives to the Palace. There were always spare rooms at the hotel to put up distant friends traveling through Chicago, or family from the suburbs who stayed the night after a concert in town. Julia's mother lived with them before they moved into the hotel, and after her death and the loss of the Wells home in Northfield, both Julia's half-sister Annie and her fanatically religious Aunt Lizzie had to be provided for. Annie was sent back to her teaching at a missionary school in South Africa, and Lizzie moved in with the elder Humphreys until her death in 1899. Then there were the close friends, often single women, who were included in the family circle and who made long visits, shared Christmases and vacations, and whose future plans were also debated at length. Doris had several "grandmas" and a seemingly endless supply of devoted "aunts," all of whom had to be sent letters, all of whom received—and gave—small, carefully chosen or handmade presents at Christmas.

The cooking, cleaning, sewing, planning, nursing, and other housekeeping duties incurred by this extensive family intercourse fell largely on Julia. To the physical demands of this job was added the emotional energy she always invested in arranging, approving, or disapproving everybody's actions. She was also continuing to give music lessons, and she perpetually embarked on improving projects like attending lectures at the Art Institute, going to Friday afternoon concerts, reading German, and doing church work. She kept up an extensive correspondence, and of course cared for Doris. But she would take on more: one year she'd be making clothes for her ex-roommate, May Miller; another year she was writing fiction. At Christmastime or in the spring she would go through orgies of cleaning and sprucing up the hotel and the family's quarters, driving herself to physical exhaustion. Even when she was overwhelmed by these duties, she would obsessively dispose of a few letters or household chores before breakfast, or fall asleep writing to May at night.

Julia and Horace were not worldly people. They experienced most things first-hand or not at all. Even when Horace worked for newspapers, political events were of slight interest to him. The Chicago World's Fair of 1893 captivated him because he could visit it, but he and Julia seldom discussed wars, elections, the state of the nation's business, or the economy in their letters. The ideas of literature had no hold over them, nor did the debates of Christian faith. But when friends traveled out west or overseas, they would follow the route of the journey on a map and read descriptive letters avidly. Their life in the Palace Hotel brought them into contact with aspects of the world that they had never encountered before. The noise and activity of a busy downtown street were just outside the door. Pickpockets, arsonists, drunks, gamblers, and other characters of dubious virtue made their appearance in the hotel occasionally and had to be dealt with. Even the respectable inhabitants of the place—actors, magicians, acrobats, salesmen, singers, travelers—seemed rootless eccentrics, indifferent to the traditional niceties that Julia and Horace clung to.

Although they never lived on intimate terms with their hotel clients, the Humphreys couldn't shield their daughter from all bizarre influences. In an autobiography Doris started writing at the end of her life, she recalled the colorful characters and the bustle, which seemed wonderful to a shy, solitary child, even the broken-down elevator and the thieving clerks. Julia usually invited the guests and staff to a Christmas party. The invitations were hand delivered and residents who were unable to attend sent their regrets in formal notes. There were European acrobats with their children, a shady doctor who talked Horace into opening a clinic in some of the hotel rooms—he had already tried operating a Turkish bath and a barbershop. People brought the little girl presents, and there were never-ending families of cats.

Julia was not a snob or a pretentious person, but the moment she laid eyes on the Palace, she started worrying about its potentially damaging influence on her daughter. The family's rooms were above a saloon; merrymaking, and sometimes screams, went on late into the night. Julia thought it disturbing, even improper, for a child of good family to witness the raffish life of the hotel denizens. She and Horace had been brought up under strict puritanical customs which forbade dancing, considered the theater a frivolous if not a licentious pastime, and even frowned upon amateur music unless it was kept within certain bounds. As young adults they had relaxed sufficiently to engage in these pursuits for entertainment. But in the Palace Hotel their child was surrounded from infancy by professionals working in the most common branches of the theater. Doris learned to tolerate and even enjoy these extroverts and mountebanks. But as a legacy of Julia's puritanism—one that she bore all her life—Doris retained some contempt for them; it came out years later in her conflicts about working in the commercial theater.

Another in the long catalogue of Julia's worries was the health of her daughter. Doris was not an especially sickly child, but Julia tended to exaggerate the minor maladies of childhood and even to anticipate them. Tonsillitis, coughs, and "feverish attacks" occurred in the years when Doris was beginning school. Julia tried faddish diets and tonics on Doris and for a period of time she was given daily laxatives. Medicine and health were poorly understood in those days, and Julia had an almost primitive awe of the slightest deviation in her child's well being, along with a stoic disregard for the sick headaches, exhausted breakdowns, and other fluctuations in her own health. Doris repeated this pattern too in adult life, tenaciously pursuing magic diets, then living on milkshakes and coffee; compensating for the erratic care she took of herself by being overcautious about the health of her son.

Julia made up her mind that the city environment was not good for a child, and saw to it that Doris got away to the country as often as possible, especially during the summer. In 1898 she took Doris for a visit to May Miller in Dummerston, Vermont, and the next year, when Doris was not yet four, she was sent for several summer weeks to stay with one of the "aunts" in Iowa. The little girl accommodated easily to being away from her parents and after that often visited family and friends during summers and holidays. While she was away Julia bombarded her with letters of advice and admonition as to how she should behave.

The first years at the Palace Hotel, up to about 1901, constituted the period of the greatest stress in the Humphrey marriage. The hotel itself, a full-time, live-in occupation for them both, was a great responsibility that paid them a fairly predictable living though never a munificent one. They didn't know how to bring up a child—Julia was always afraid she would somehow botch the job—and they tried to be conscientious about everything from Doris' clothes and companions to the development of her mind and morals. Family responsibilities almost overwhelmed Julia during this time; it wasn't until the feeble senior Humphreys moved to a health spa at Clifton Springs, New York, in 1901 that the worst of the dependent relatives were off her hands. They came back to live at the Palace in the winter of 1901–02, but by that time Horace and Julia had passed through a crisis and come to a different understanding.

Income from Julia's music lessons was providing an increasingly important supplement to their hotel salary. Late in 1899 Horace's sister Bessie married Carl Sauter, "an unnaturalized German, who speaks broken English, smokes, drinks beer, and is a Roman Catholic," as Julia told May. She only partly disapproved of Carl—his foreignness might improve the family stock, she thought. Besides that, he was a musician, a cellist, and that asset became the means of Julia's salvation. In the summer of 1900, Carl got a job for a trio, to play at a summer resort in Lake Harbor, Michigan. He asked Julia to be the pianist. Julia and Doris received their room and board, and for providing the hotel entertainment as well as playing in church, Julia made twelve to fourteen dollars a week. For the next six summers Horace stayed in Chicago and ran the hotel while Julia and Doris went off with the musicians to another resort hotel in Green Lake, Wisconsin.

These summers were an idyllic combination of work and play for Julia. This meant, given her complex moral machinery, a substantial alleviation of domestic cares and a satisfaction of her ambitions, clouded by periods of inkblot remorse. She and Doris shared a cabin, sometimes with Bessie and Carl or other family and friends. Horace made a weekend visit or two during the summer, but as Doris needed less and less supervision, life at Green Lake could be luxuriously unrestricted. Meals were sketchy, clothes were simple, and Julia could devote her free hours to studying music or socializing. She enjoyed walks, picnics, and what she called "kiddish" escapades like moonlight boat rides with her fellow musicians and the summer people. Doris learned to swim, and got her first taste of the limelight when, at age six, she danced informally for the hotel guests.

Julia and Horace had a bitter fight at the end of the second lake summer, perhaps the severest of their marriage. They may even have thought about separating. Probably Horace complained about being neglected, and Julia, having seen the door to her domestic treadmill opening a crack, accused him of not loving her for her deeper nature but taking her for granted as the supplier of superficial comforts. The explosion was brief; he went to Green Lake and they were reconciled. After that it was understood that she would work professionally at her music as much as she could. Horace even attempted for a few years to get performance dates for Julia and her musical associates. A printed announcement from about 1905 offered "Orchestral Music of high grade" for social occasions, artistic programs, piano accompanying, lecture-recitals, and "descriptive and historical programs specially adapted for clubs and study classes." Julia could be on firmer ground now when the relatives ran out of money or needed a place to spend a few months; somebody else must take care of them if their problems interfered with her music.

Julia Humphrey never had an extensive musical career or an eminent reputation as a performer. Giving music lessons and, later, accompanying dance classes were the extent of her professional reach, except for the summer jobs which originated from her family connections. Yet she had established her right to a career, to having a talent and an identity that did not in any way hinge on her husband's activities. It was agreed between them that her work would take her away from home for months in the summer. Among their acquaintances it wasn't uncommon for people to make long visits with friends far away or travel for weeks at a time, and Doris' need for fresh country air was always a convenient added explanation for their absence. At other times of the year Horace went off on trips by himself or with friends, and sometimes he took Doris on little excursions.

Julia's emancipation was possible in part because Doris was old enough to go to school. She was sent to kindergarten in the fall of 1900 at the Chicago Institute, a private progressive school begun by Francis W. Parker. There was much debate over this matter. Julia maintained that Doris' health was too frail for public school, and the choice of Colonel Parker's school may have been based as much on its exclusivity as on its educational program. The tuition was seventy-five dollars a year, a considerable sum for the Humphreys' modest circumstances, but Julia knew that Doris would associate there with children of good families; she would learn social graces and elevated tastes if nothing else. Julia thought her little girl was every bit as refined as her wealthier schoolmates, maybe even a little more so. She dressed Doris in fancier clothes and curlier hairdos and worried because the Palace Hotel wasn't a proper place for Doris' friends to come and play.

According to Julia, Doris was superior to both the raffish hotel folk she lived with and the ordinary-looking rich children at school. But she obviously didn't fit into either the upper-middle-class world or the gypsy community, and she must have felt some alienation even then. In her autobiography, she tells, with the gentle irony that was the closest she ever came to open anger, of her mother's desperate need to keep up appearances, her willingness to sacrifice so that her daughter would have the best, and her own retreat into reading and solitary play. Whether or not her parents sent her to Francis W. Parker School for the right reasons, the education she received there for the next thirteen years was nourishment for her artistic tendencies.

During the latter part of the nineteenth century, American education was beginning to add the idea of individual creativity onto its classical base. At that time, in addition to acquiring the three R's by rote memorization and drill, students were expected to imbibe the civilized accomplishments of the past by learning to imitate the musical, literary, and graphic masters. They memorized famous texts and copied models in an academic manner, using traditional tools and materials. The turn-of-the-century pursuit of more natural expression led to a widespread interest in Greek culture—people tried Delsarte posing, modal music, folk dancing, tunics and sandals as well as studying ancient sonnets and statues. Isadora Duncan was not by any means the only dancer who skipped about in bare feet against an imaginary background of Ionic columns. Bernard Maybeck's Palace of Fine Arts, built for the Panama-Pacific International Exposition in San Francisco in 1913, is perhaps a culminating example of the flights of fantasy and form to which the immersion in Greek sensibility led American artists.

But in the work of Maybeck's contemporary Frank Lloyd Wright and other architects of the Prairie School, whose revolutionary houses were springing up all around the Chicago suburbs, another side of the American character had begun to take hold in the nineteenth century's closing years. Ralph Waldo Emerson had given philosophical legitimacy to an instinct for intellectual as well as political independence from the creeds and cultures of the

European past. "A man should learn to detect and watch that gleam of light which flashes across his mind from within, more than the lustre of the firmament of bards and sages," he said, and his call for self-reliance became a marching banner for seekers of a truly American expression in literature, the arts, and education. Emersonian nonconformity gave rise to a more pragmatic and daring experimentation with native materials and processes, a desire to meet each problem with a unique solution. It fostered a generation of crackpot brilliance in art and technology, a generation that included Edison, Tesla, Whitman, and George Ives, a bandleader in the Union Army who taught his family to sing in quarter tones and did not disapprove when his gifted son Charles tried to play the piano with his feet.

Francis W. Parker belonged to this maverick breed. By the time Doris Humphrey entered school he was near the end of his life; in fact, the establishment of the private school that familiarly bore his name was the last of his many dramatic achievements. All his life Parker had been an advocate of public education, but his controversial teaching theories kept him constantly duelling with the government authorities who controlled public school policies. He had come to the end of a stormy tenure as head of the Cook County and Chicago Normal School when a benefactor, Mrs. Emmons Blaine, offered him the chance to start a school of his own. The Chicago Institute, Academic and Pedagogic, was founded in 1899 and opened in the fall of 1900 with 195 students, including the nearly five-year-old Doris Humphrey.

Parker had developed his radical approach to teaching in Quincy, Massachusetts, during the decades after the Civil War. Rejecting the rigid, mechanical learning techniques then prevalent, he favored allowing children to find out how the verbal and mathematical disciplines worked by solving problems relevant to their own lives. In the early grades, children were taught words rather than the ABCs, practical narrative writing rather than the rules of grammar. They solved arithmetic problems before they learned any formulas and made sketches and models to find out about geography. The applied arts, like weaving and sewing; the "play" arts, like songs, dramatics, and movement; and the creative arts, like drawing and block construction—all were part of the school day. Once they entered the higher grades, Parker thought, children would have a better reasoning capacity and would be able to learn the formal structures of spelling, grammar, and arithmetic more quickly. Parker's biographer described his school as a model democracy, a place where children would learn self-control and self-government. Parker believed that children should contribute to their own educational program, that they should be encouraged to express themselves in terms of their own experiences. His curriculum was a means of bringing children into direct contact with human and natural history, and every effort was made to link the different subjects to develop integrated minds. The purpose of the Chicago Institute was to dramatize the ideas Parker had spent his life developing, including the training of teachers, which he believed was essential to the future of education. The Institute from the first was nicknamed the Emmons Blaine School for Teachers and Children. The first classes were held in temporary quarters in the Turngemeinde Building on Chicago's North Side, and in June 1901 the elementary grades moved into their permanent building, the Francis W. Parker School, on the well-to-do North Shore.

By this time, to relieve its financial worries, the Institute had merged with the University of Chicago, where John Dewey headed the Department of Education. Dewey had great respect for Francis Parker although their educational ideas differed somewhat. Dewey was to control the upper grades while Parker retained autonomy over the elementary school. But Parker's health was declining. After the first year he took virtually no active part in the school operation, and he died in March 1902. There followed a struggle for control of the school; Dewey himself left for Columbia University in 1904, and the ideals of Colonel Parker gradually dissipated and became absorbed into the widening sphere of progressive education. Francis W. Parker had resisted forming a theory of teaching; he left no curriculum or guidelines that could direct the activity of a school system. His whole approach was to bring out the potential of each individual, whether teacher or student. As teacher Willard S. Bass told the faculty in 1908: "Parker did not want teachers to think the way he did. He wanted teachers to think for themselves."

The spirit of adventure, of self-discovery, remained a part of the Francis W. Parker School throughout the years. Doris and her fellows in the class of 1913, the first pupils to go all the way through the school from kindergarten to high school graduation, were aware of their privileged circumstances. At the Parker School Doris performed in school shows and pageants, wrote stories, made sketches, and kept a diary of a trip she took on Lake Michigan with her father. She did, however, begin to make some choices among all these creative resources. Julia started her on piano lessons when she was about eight, although she could pick out tunes for herself a couple of years earlier. She liked music but didn't apply herself diligently enough to suit her mother's militant work ethic and her perfectionism. Perhaps she rebelled against Julia's old-fashioned teaching methods; she complained in her auto-biography that she couldn't memorize the sharps and flats. She and Julia were beginning to sense the extreme difference in their temperaments. By 1908 Doris was studying with another music teacher, paying for her lessons by soliciting magazine subscriptions from the family's numerous acquaint-ances in the Midwest and New England.

At about the same time she started the piano with Julia, Doris encoun-tered another of the extraordinary educators who influenced her life. Mary Wood Hinman gave dancing classes at the Francis Parker School as well as at Hull House and John Dewey's experimental school at the University of Chicago. At first Doris took classes with her twice a week after school. Later she enrolled at Hinman's own school, where she eventually began her own teaching at the age of fourteen, assisting Mary Wood. In later years Doris was ambivalent about Mary Wood, as she was about all the powerful women in her life. Some bad feelings lingered on from trivial incidents dur-ing her teaching apprenticeship. She also felt that her old teacher fell behind the reforms she and the modern dancers were trying to effect in America's dancing. But early in the twentieth century, Hinman represented the most enlightened approach to dance education, a pioneering spirit who never ceased searching for new materials and modes of teaching.

With the inclusiveness so common in those early enthusiastic days of dance teaching, Hinman's own school offered folk and English country dancing, which she traveled abroad to learn, Dalcroze Eurhythmics, panto-mime, ballroom, and ballet. Hinman's school specialized in pedagogy; by the time Doris completed the Normal course in 1914 she was teaching interpre-tive dancing for children as well as giving private ballet lessons.

Mary Wood Hinman was more than a dancing teacher. She was a hu-manitarian and a tireless explorer of the ways in which organized movement could help people to function better in society. During World War I she gave up her teaching to do volunteer work with servicemen. She organized grand pageants and outdoor festivals for laypersons, pursued her theories about the value of social dancing in helping European immigrants adjust to life in the New World, and lectured on the relationship of folk dancing to educa-tion, industry, and art.

Doris' mature account of her first dancing lessons with Mary Wood Hin-man is reserved, considering that she is reporting the discovery of her life's work. "She showed you how to move your feet and you had only to make

Doris as Titania, 1912. Collection of Charles H. Woodford.

them go just like hers. It was all easy and a delight. There was music, too.
The teacher had such great enthusiasm for her children and the dance that
the afternoon classes were nothing but a pleasure." Then she adds with as-
perity: "Mother said, 'Maybe you can learn something, even if it's only dancing.' . . . It had been a foregone conclusion in her mind that I would be a
pianist, and a better one than herself." As her lessons went on, she relates,
Mary Wood told her mother she had talent, and Doris herself gradually realized that this was something of her own that she could do, not just an
achievement that Julia expected of her. She loved the excitement, and the
recognition, of performing. For school productions she made up her own
dances, and Julia would play the accompaniment, organize the costume,
and offer copious suggestions.

As Doris advanced in her training, Mary Wood Hinman urged her to study
with other teachers, and Julia took her to various ballet masters who were
holding forth in Chicago at that time. Madame Josephine Hatlanek, an emi-
grée from the corps de ballet in Vienna, taught her the ballet vocabulary but
thought her feet too weak to go on pointe. She took some lessons from An-
dreas Pavley and Serge Oukrainsky, former associates of Pavlova, who later
created ballets for the Chicago Opera and had their own touring company
during the 1920s.

Doris had her first paid job as a dancer when she was barely fourteen, performing for the Steel Works Club of Joliet, Illinois. In partnership with Albert
Carroll, a boy in her class, she entertained for organizations and private parties. By her senior year she was arranging pageants as well as teaching and
performing after school. During this last year of school, Julia got up a little
company to make a tour out West. At that time the Santa Fe Railroad would
send entertainers along its routes to give shows for its employees. Doris was
excused from school for two weeks to be one of a pair of dancers in the variety troupe; the other performers were two singers and an actress who gave
monologues. Every day or two Doris wrote a long, enthusiastic letter home
to her father, and her descriptions forecast, in rudimentary form, the story of
what it would be like for all future dancers on the road in America.

Doris and her partner, Effie, made up their own dances, which were interspersed with the songs and recitations on the program. They began with
folk dance solos, a Polish one and a czardas. There was an "aesthetic
group," probably like the Grecian dances she had made for her Hinman students. They did a pantomime, then Effie danced a Sailor's Hornpipe in trou-

sers and middy, and Doris had a piece she called *Lindy Lee*, with a Jumping Jack encore. They finished with a Spanish number that usually met with wild approval.

The little company would be met at each stop by a Santa Fe representative and taken to their hotel, usually one of the Harvey chain, right next to the station. They would proceed, with apprehension that increased as the trip went on, to the scene of that night's performance. Sometimes it would be a high school auditorium, but more often it was a recreation room in the local YMCA or something worse. In Chillicothe, Missouri, the audience was so close that in one of Doris' aesthetic dances "my flowers scattered over the first five rows of the audience. Everybody grabbed a flower and when I was ready for the next dance there wasn't a flower on the floor. I suppose they thought it was souvenir night." Dancing was sufficiently rare in these small towns that local sponsors thought any platform would be adequate. In Las Vegas, New Mexico, the six-foot-deep stage was made of boards laid on boxes and covered with burlap. The piano blocked the entrance to the dressing room. "At first there was a wide crack between the wall and the back of the stage, but for the performance that was filled up artistically with gymnasium mats," Doris reported. "The boards were loose, you know, so we couldn't dance at all, it was mostly an exhibition of two girls trying to keep their balance." The other performers endured similar disadvantages, and "altogether it was the punkest show we ever gave. They were remarkably enthusiastic though."

Prejudice against dancing was still entrenched in some places, too. The Arkansas City, Kansas, school board cut the dancing numbers from the program and asked if Doris and Effie could do anything else. "No, we told him, we know nothing but our art." In Winslow, Arizona, the words *Opera House* on the circulars had been crossed out, and *Methodist Church* substituted. Again, no dancing. While the others looked the place over, Doris and Effie "did a clog in front of the pulpit for spite." By mistake the wardrobe trunk was left behind in Las Vegas, New Mexico, and they had no costumes they could dance in at Albuquerque, though the other performers improvised with street clothes.

Traveling by train, and sometimes treated to automobile rides by new acquaintances along the trip, Doris got her first glimpse of Indian country. At Winslow, she and Effie planned to get up and see the sunrise in the desert. "We'd be just as like as not to concoct a prehistoric dance to the prehistoric sun," she told her father. "It would be a fine addition." She also learned about the Penitentes, the Christian-Indian sect whose sacrificial Hermit Mound was near Las Vegas, New Mexico. Doris described the secret ceremonies reenacting the Crucifixion, in which three men were chosen to carry crosses up the hill, where they were flogged and nailed to crosses. She recoiled at the savagery of such practices, which were later to be transmuted into extraordinary dances by Martha Graham. Her own desert dance, *Song of the West,* emerged nearly three decades later, in 1940.

Even though the conditions were primitive, Doris was aware of keeping up standards and advancing people's taste. After performing before a "fool audience" in Seligman, Arizona, the troupe was rewarded at the end of the trip by getting to play in a real opera house in Kingman, Arizona, "with a peachy stage, real wings, bona fide dressing rooms. . . . Maybe we didn't howl for joy." The next day they visited the local school, and for the first time she experienced one of the bonuses of touring in the provinces: in the school corridor little girls were hopping around trying to do the czardas.

✳

By the time of her graduation Doris was not only a seasoned performer, but in her own mind she had embarked on a career. Her high-school chums and associates had no further hold on her affections; she had outgrown them already. It was her dance teachers and fellow performers with whom she felt the closest ties, and her future activities in the dance world took precedence over anything she had learned in school. Although both her parents had attended college, Doris appears never to have considered higher education. Her ambitions coincided with those her mother had for her, but only partly. Julia had begun to see her daughter and herself as a team, and a few months after graduation, before Doris had formulated any clear intentions, a family crisis threw them on the mercy of their combined skills.

Doris was in New York for a day of classes with Vernon and Irene Castle, on the way home from a vacation with Cape Cod relatives, when she received word that the Palace Hotel had been sold from under Horace and Julia. The family went to live temporarily with friends in Oak Park, and as a matter of course Julia set about opening dance classes to support them. Horace was completely demoralized, and his subsequent efforts to establish a commercial photography business never brought in more than a minor income. That Christmas, after seeing performances of Anna Pavlova's company, Doris began to realize that what she wanted more than anything else was to be dancing on a stage. But by that time she was thoroughly immured in teaching.

In a series of rented halls and borrowed studios, Doris and Julia gave interpretive classes to children in the afternoons and ballroom classes for adult
couples in the evening. Their work was in demand, and they traveled to
other suburbs to give more sessions. Doris still taught for Mary Wood Hinman and at a private dance studio as well. After a year, they found their own
apartment in Oak Park, where Horace tinkered with his photography business and cooked dinner for them to eat on the run between afternoon and
evening classes or before falling into bed at the end of an exhausting day.
Doris grew increasingly restive. Before the first year of this routine was over
she wrote to May Miller that she had thought about retiring from dancing
and becoming a producer of pantomimes, but Julia had objected so strenuously that she backed down. "The only aim I *can* have is . . . doing everything she wants without demur," Doris told "Auntie" May. Julia's constant
managing, and her tendency to commit them both to more work than they
could possibly accomplish, restrained Doris' tentative sense of frivolity and
exploration; she wasn't even twenty.

But the tradition of outdoor summers in the country was solidly approved
in the family, and Doris took the opportunity not only to get away but to extend her professional range, much as Julia herself had done in her musical
summers at Green Lake and afterwards, when the family acquired a cottage
in Ravinia, Illinois, the summer home of the Chicago orchestra. In 1914 Doris
taught dance and worked on a Japanese pantomime at the Outdoor Players
Camp in Peterborough, New Hampshire. That year she also performed English folk dances in a play at the MacDowell Colony.

Part Chautauquan-uplift, part summer camp, part professional showcase,
the American summer arts colony was—and is—a tradition for dancers, actors, and musicians. Adapted from the physical culture schools and prestigious music festivals of Europe, these colonies once centered around resort
hotels. Far from the steaming city streets, professional performers gathered
on an informal basis with novices, teachers, and interested members of the
public for classes, productions, and socializing.

When dance established itself as a relatively autonomous art form, its
summer centers gravitated to college campuses, where there were facilities
more suitable for classes and performances. Programs began to stress training dancers and creating new works rather than summer sports and diver-
sions. Doris spent nearly every summer of her working life in one or more of
these programs. From the first, they provided important contacts and stimulus, as well as financial return and an opportunity to try out new work.

Through her summer contacts and an affectionate, growing crowd of former students, she became interested in the wider professional world of dance. She no longer corresponded with school friends about parties and boys, but exchanged dance talk with other neophyte teachers and performers. Someone sent her a new tango routine. Someone else was on the trail of a job in variety shows. She assessed performances she had seen and classes she was giving.

By 1916 she was actively seeking to break out of her bondage. She inquired of the vaudeville dancer Marion Morgan about openings in Morgan's well-known company, which specialized in Grecian-style dancing and draperies. Morgan asked for her picture (wearing as few clothes as possible) and said Doris could come for an interview when the company played in Chicago. Doris and another girl tried out, but Morgan found Doris too balletic. She also inquired about a teaching job in Pittsburgh. Finally, in June of 1917, Mary Wood Hinman opened another door. Sending along a brochure for the

Pageant at the Outdoor Players Camp, circa 1914. Collection of Charles H. Woodford.

Denishawn School in Los Angeles, Mary Wood recommended that Doris go there for summer study. "It is so full of what one wants," Hinman advised. "I feel that [Ruth St. Denis] is in your line and she could make a lot out of you—she is of tomorrow."

3 DENISHAWN, 1917–26

For a while Doris managed to convince her family, and possibly herself, that she was going to Denishawn to enhance her teaching in Chicago. Summer training courses were as important to the professional enrichment of local dance teachers as they were to the economic survival of those who offered them. During the years before 1930, dancing teachers in America were an eclectic breed who absorbed their craft from a motley array of sources. Although her principal teacher had been unusually creative, Doris was typical in possessing a background that included basic body training, folk dancing, the elements of ballet, and assorted popular dance styles. Doris' stage experience, in variety shows and "aesthetic" presentations, had so far served to prepare her as a coach and director of nonprofessional productions. Teachers from academic schools and colleges also participated in summer courses, although dance teaching in those institutions was more closely allied to physical training and gymnastics, and performing favored the "interpretive," Duncanesque kind of pageantry over variety or balletic presentations.

Mary Wood Hinman was very much aware of the need for stimulation among dancing teachers who lived too far from large cities to see performances or study regularly with master teachers. In a prospectus for the Hinman School for 1916–17, the Normal (teachers') curriculum included lectures on aesthetics, and readings on the history of dance in relation to the culture, as well as the various dance techniques. Hinman also offered private instruction for visiting teachers; they could take up to six lessons a week. She would send members of her own faculty to give one-week courses in other towns in preparation for pageants, festivals, and country dancing displays, and she also supplied teachers to community groups in Chicago on a per-lesson basis. Like many important dance teachers of the time, Hinman published instructions for dance routines and sold them by mail order. Such programs helped to spread dance culture across America.

Ruth St. Denis had established an important reputation as a recitalist who interpreted the sacred and secular dances of foreign cultures. After a great

success among the artists and intellectuals of fin-de-siècle Europe, she returned to her own country and toured as a soloist until joining forces with
Ted Shawn in 1914. They married and the following year institutionalized
their work under the rubric "Denishawn." The Denishawn school was at that
time located in a sprawling, gracious residence near Westlake Park in Los
Angeles. Combining the atmosphere of a summer camp and a finishing
school, it followed the general trend of offering ballet as its basic technique,
stage arts with an emphasis on Delsarte, and—instead of European folk
dance—a variety of Asian styles. Denishawn aimed at "presenting the dance
as an art unity," with classes that would prepare pupils for "the most effective presentation of dances in schools, drawing rooms, ballrooms, hotels,
and cabarets as well as for the stage and film."

Denishawn was thus not only a school but a series of interlocking activities that fed on the popularity of dancing in America. St. Denis and Shawn
knew that they were training teachers, and part of their curriculum included
"franchising," the teaching, recording, and publication of dance routines.
Through the 1920s, they sold work notes, musical scores, and piano rolls by
mail, but the key to maintaining the quality of the dances, they thought, was
individual instruction. From the pool of students in their summer courses
they could select good dancers for their touring companies, place performers
in the movies and on the stage (names of these alumni always appeared in
the advertising), and develop teachers for Denishawn and its branch studios.
In addition to providing students with dances, Denishawn gave lessons in all
types of stagecraft and costume making as well as pedagogy. The announcement that Mary Wood Hinman sent Doris early in that summer of
1917 promised, in addition to lessons in dance technique, teacher training,
and stagecraft, a series of Burton Holmes travel films showing "real native
dancing" from countries around the world, and lectures on Delsarte's Theory
of Motion and Science of Gesture by Madame Richard Hovey. Shawn was
already working with special men's classes as well as teaching technique,
and St. Denis offered inspirational evening lectures and private instruction.
Denishawn, the brochure said, believed in the Individuality System. They
maintained that "the highest achievement possible is to be unique, incom-
parable, solitary," and predicted that after exposure to all the techniques and
crafts at the school, the student would "gravitate toward his own."

It's not clear whether Doris ever saw Ruth St. Denis dance before this forecast of paradise came into her hands. Independently or as a part of a vaudeville package, St. Denis had appeared regularly in Chicago. As a soloist, and

later with Shawn, she gave seasons downtown in 1909, 1911, and 1913, and at Ravinia in the summers of 1913 and 1914. The Denishawn dancers were in Chicago again three separate times in 1916. Doris said only that when it was agreed she could enroll in the summer course she thought, "These people were on the stage; this was a chance to come within the glamorous aura of the theatre." Soon after her arrival in California she took a private lesson with St. Denis, who advised her that she was wasting her time teaching and should be dancing professionally. Miss Ruth became the closest thing Doris ever had to an idol. Even in the early, starstruck days with Denishawn, Doris could be clear eyed in appraising her mentors, but she was drawn to Miss Ruth, always looking forward to chances to study and dance with her.

All her life, Doris had stood in the wings, an interested spectator of theater life. She knew how theater people lived and entertained themselves; understood their camaraderie and the riskiness of their independence. She knew about lessons and practice, and about stage magic—the allure great performers have for the audience and the transitory homage with which audiences feed performers. Until 1917 she thought she was never to experience that life for herself. From the time she escaped Oak Park, she referred to her teaching there as drudgery; in fact, she professed a distaste for all teaching even though she offered unflagging encouragement to young dancers and choreographers during forty-five years of classes. That first teaching was marred by many things. Before she had time to explore her own skills, she found herself supporting her parents; worse, she found that she was expected to go on supporting them even though they were not yet elderly (her mother was forty-seven in 1913 when they began their partnership and her father fifty-six). At least as galling as her frustrated wish to go on the stage was the oppressive yet supportive presence of Julia, playing for her classes, arranging, admonishing, and monitoring Doris' personal and professional activities. She reached the age of twenty-three before she would openly defy Julia's standards, her expectations, or her love, all of which were tied together in one efficient knot of maternal anxiety.

Life at the Palace Hotel was never dull, and her parents had taken care to provide their child with the right opportunities for travel and culture, but Julia's tight morality cast a pall of caution—if not suspicion—over every new experience. Like her mother, Doris had a limited ability to cut up, cut loose. She could relax only under certain conditions, at those times when she succeeded in entirely setting aside her work responsibilities. Denishawn was a rare vacation of the spirit for her, and it initiated the period of her greatest emotional and artistic experimentation. Photographs and descriptions of her throughout the 1920s always seem to evoke the outdoors. She's forever playing on beaches, dancing with hoops and scarves. Nude or wearing scanty garments, she embodies youth, grace, and the joyful surrender of inhibitions.

The atmosphere at the Westlake studio itself suggested leisure and expansion. The resortlike buildings, the warm climate with outdoor classes and performances, and the freedom from financial worry, must have seemed luxurious indeed to Doris after her work-obsessed adolescence in the extremes of Chicago weather. Not that she didn't work hard. Even in her first summer, as a student, she attended classes and rehearsals for most of the day. In the evenings there were lectures and programs to stimulate the mind and refresh the spirit. She was among other young people with professional aspirations, not amateurs like her fellow high-school thespians. She quickly formed a close friendship with Ian Wolfe, a young actor who wrote to her affectionately for years after abandoning the theater for films, and Margaret Suhr, who opened a Denishawn-type studio in Cleveland after the summer.

The substance of Denishawn's work was another great liberating force. Doris was well schooled in interpretive dancing before she came to Denishawn; three pastel studies and a Grecian dance of hers were published in Mary Wood Hinman's *Folk and Gymnastic Dancing* instruction book (1916). She had studied clog dancing and other European folk forms with Hinman. She could put together a variety routine or a pageant. But the purpose of knowing how to do all these things was practical: to prepare students, pass on dances to other teachers, put on shows for special occasions. At Denishawn all resources were treated seriously and shaped into entities the leaders believed to be Art. Commercial jobs were accepted for economic reasons, and were understood to be less worthy pursuits for a dancer than concert work, while the school, a necessary financial component of Denishawn, was an important means of spreading a philosophy and cultivating an audience. The repertory and the classes were built around basic ballet training and Ruth St. Denis' interpretations of Asian dances, with supplementary lessons in breathing, yoga, and Eastern philosophies. Nothing was taught at Denishawn without being given an aesthetic context, or sanctioned as a contribution to the health of body and mind. Shawn's Christian convictions formed a spiritual counterpart to St. Denis' Orientalism. He sustained a lifelong interest in sacred dance, choreographing a church service in San Francisco as early as the fall of 1917.

St. Denis and Shawn were careful to see that the pagan luxury surrounding Denishawn and its activities was cloaked in the utmost social decorum. A five-minute documentary film they made around 1915 gives a vivid picture of this curious mixture. In seven scenes, we glimpse what they must have intended as a cross-section of life at the school. "Guests at Denishawn" shows a group of civilians walking through an entryway. In "Leaving the Dressing Room," a file of young women come toward the camera one by one. Each girl takes off her robe, gives it to a turbaned black attendant stationed at the side of the frame, then continues on, wearing a tank suit and turban. The girls exhibit a rather charming mixture of little-girl shyness and exhibitionism. Miss Ruth sits cross-legged at the head of an outdoor yoga class in the next scene. After some very solemn arm and head gestures, the class is seen in a procession with baskets on their heads as if in an Eastern bazaar. Dressed in saris, they practice holding out the basket to an invisible shopper, putting it down gracefully on the ground. Then Shawn gives ballet instruction to a little girl wearing pointe shoes. Her approving parent sits just at the edge of the picture. Then we see St. Denis leaning over a garden wall talking to her pet peacock. The students are seen playing in a stone garden pool with a trickling fountain. Finally, Shawn and St. Denis are served tea on a veranda by a black servant. They're dressed in modish summer clothes and look like the curate and his wife on a Sunday afternoon, not like theatrical personalities who could possibly threaten the morals of anyone's children.

Though she was straining desperately to break the maternal bonds, Doris failed in her first attempt. Julia assumed that she would be home in a few weeks to start their 1917 fall classes, with the prestigious Denishawn course added to her credits. Julia even suggested that Doris take some classes with the Russian emigré Theodore Kosloff, who had a ballet school in Los Angeles. "You'd better add somebody with a foreign name to your string if you can," she advised after another Chicago dancing teacher returned from studying in New York with Louis Chalif. Horace's photography business was going well that summer, and Julia magnanimously urged Doris to stay in California for an extra two weeks of classes.

At the end of August, Ted Shawn was preparing to go on a vaudeville tour with a Zodiac ballet and a dance based on Botticelli's *Primavera* (to Johann Strauss' Voices of Spring). Doris auditioned and was invited to become a member of the company. Horace was delighted. Julia panicked. First she assailed Doris with questions: what would be the financial arrangements, would Doris make as much money as she could teaching at home, what would be the extent of her obligation to Denishawn, what assurances did they provide for the job continuing? She thought maybe she could train Doris' friend Carrie Bagley to take over some of the classes if Doris were away for only three months. "Of course I'm thinking too of the added reputation this episode would give when you've gotten tired of public work and want to come back." A day or two later she succumbed to gossip. She wondered whether the work at Denishawn could be considered "immoral or loose," as was no doubt assumed in church circles. "After all even such a chance wouldn't be worth accepting if it identified you with a type of work which lowers your standards in any way." She bombarded Doris with admonitions about how hard it would be, how lonely, and how suspicious she would have to be of all her companions who would be trying to steal the limelight and make her look bad.

Then she went to talk with the owners of the various schools where she and Doris held classes. They, of course, had already advertised Doris as a faculty member for the fall. She reminded her daughter of all the people who would be disappointed if she didn't return. She did not mention those, including Mary Wood Hinman, who were overjoyed with the chance and fully expected Doris to take it. Maybe Doris could stay in Los Angeles for the month of September, then come home and teach until after Christmas, when Julia would be able to go back out West with her. Or maybe she could wait until spring, when the Shawn offer might be made again. On the back of Julia's last frantic telegram, Doris drafted her capitulation, "No point in staying through September Miss Ruth and Mr. Shawn take vacation. Will leave on Wed. if can get reservations." She crossed out the sentence, "They will take me after three months" and concluded, "Will come back after Christmas. Miss Ruth says I can make as much in a year as I do at teaching now."

But she didn't go back in three months. In the winter of 1918 Miss Ruth went on the road for fifteen weeks with dancer Margaret Loomis, and Shawn was keeping the school afloat while waiting to be drafted. Doris was in Oak Park trying to make up her mind.

In its third year of existence, Denishawn was already beginning to suffer the strains of its dual proprietorship. The working relationship of Ruth St. Denis and Ted Shawn was as tenuous as their marriage; both partnerships retained their nominal unity long after they had ceased to function, and our present-day concept of Denishawn as a monolithic institution looks increasingly shaky as scholars begin to examine its actual history. The formula on which St. Denis had built her reputation as a solo dancer—an amalgam of sex and spirituality, ascetic discipline practiced in lavish surroundings—underlay all the activities of Denishawn. St. Denis thought of herself as an artist and periodically felt overwhelmed by the practical necessities of touring and teaching. She would "retire" from the exertions of vaudeville in order to work creatively with small, modest groups or appear in less taxing programs of her famous solos. Shawn was an indefatigable showman; no branch of show business was beneath his attention if it offered a chance to present serious dancing to the public. His wide-ranging eye for opportunities—together with a shrewd practicality and a gift for publicizing the work—kept money coming into the Denishawn coffers. These diverging needs came out in the open in the fall of 1917, when Shawn took the Zodiac ballet on a vaudeville stint while St. Denis and Margaret Loomis toured from Texas back to the West Coast with their own concert programs. St. Denis and Shawn did not tour again under the same billing until 1922.

After the Zodiac tour, Shawn returned to Los Angeles. He joined the ambulance corps and commuted to the school from Camp Kearney, near San Diego, until the end of the war. By early summer Doris had found her way back to Denishawn where she was dancing with St. Denis as well as teaching at the school. By good luck Doris found a young woman there, Ethel Moulton, who was looking for an opportunity to teach, and with Julia's reluctant agreement she sent Ethel to take over for her in Oak Park. At last she was a dancer, free and clear.

In addition to teaching technique and giving private instruction at the Denishawn school, she was immediately drawn into all the activities that the busy dance center generated. She danced in a movie, performed in a benefit for the families of servicemen at the Lasky Studios, and acted as St. Denis' assistant choreographer for *The Light of Asia,* a play performed outdoors for a three-week run at the Theosophical Institute. She also appeared as a nautch dancer in the ensemble for this piece, which she described to Auntie May as "very pagan of course but full of dramatic possibilities. Miss Ruth is teaching the dances, so we are all very happy to be in it, in order to have some of her." She saw St. Denis' program at the close of the Loomis tour, and thought her *Spirit of the Sea* "one of the most artistic things I have ever seen."

Best of all, she began working with St. Denis to prepare a tour. Shawn had alluded to great things in store for Doris—"the lead and management of a company" she reported—apparently as insurance against the possibility that Ruth would continue to make herself scarce after her tour with Loomis. But this offer was forgotten when St. Denis resumed her leadership, and Doris gladly relinquished any ephemeral prospects she might have entertained to work under the artist she admired so much. From November 1918 through the summer of 1919 Ruth St. Denis, assisted by Doris, Betty Horst, Edna Malone and Pearl Wheeler, with Louis Horst as accompanist, crossed the country on the Pantages vaudeville circuit. The program they carried, performed three or four times a day almost continuously except for brief intervals of traveling, included St. Denis in her *Dance of Theodora;* a set of Greek pieces in which Doris danced a solo, *Sunrise;* the *Dance of the Royal Ballet of Siam,* where she played the villain, Ravan; Shawn's *Serenata Morisca,* for Betty Horst; and a patriotic number, *Spirit of Democracy,* which involved Miss Ruth looking heroic as the others mimed wounded victims throwing hand grenades until the unseen enemy surrendered. Other Oriental numbers were substituted later for the Greek pieces.

The St. Denis act traveled as a unit to different theaters, where it would be fitted into a bill with a line-up like this (from Detroit): the Aerial Mitchells (Fun in the Air), Jack Sidney and Isabel Townley in *A Subway Flirtation,* a skit entitled *The Piano Tuner,* Sylvia Clark That Klassy Klown, and Harry Slatko's Midnight Rollickers in a Jazz Review *Dancing Around.* Often the show opened with a newsreel and a film short. On this tour they also shared programs with such comedians as Ben Bernie, Georgie Price, Frank Fay, and Fred Allen, and also with dog acts; *Little Cherry Blossom,* a Dainty Japanese Playlet; and one Olga the Modern Dancing Violinist. Doris thought she was the luckiest person in the world.

While Doris thrived in this atmosphere, by 1919 Ruth St. Denis was sure her artistry was slowly drying up. The relentless grind of these road trips, what she called "the dull business of earning an honest dollar," not only sapped her energy—she was forty by then—but afforded her no time to create anything but capable numbers to vary the act. She dreaded returning to Shawn's go-getting management. He was already contemplating their postwar enterprises when, after the Armistice, he met her on tour and they thrashed it out. They agreed to close Denishawn, though they continued to live together until their house in Los Angeles burned down a year later. Shawn sold the school at Westlake Park and opened his own studio. By fall 1919 he was producing multiple programs for vaudeville. *Julnar of the Sea,* a student production, stayed on the boards continuously for the next year and a half, for over 1,200 performances. He made an Aztec ballet, *Xochitl,* for his protégée, Martha Graham, and sent that on the road for the 1920–1921 season, and he continued to devise other pieces: *Les Mystères Dionysiaques* (a Bacchic divertissement reworked from Denishawn days), American Indian dances, music visualizations, and religious dances that could fit into vaudeville programs or Shawn's own concert tours. In the fall of 1919, Ruth announced that her vaudeville days were over and, with Doris as her assistant, began making works for the Ruth St. Denis Concert Dancers. The company of fifteen women dancers plus musicians gave its first program at the end of that year. St. Denis and Shawn billed themselves as Guest Stars.

St. Denis' restlessness—an artistic malady that recurred throughout her long, prolific career—originated in more than the rigors of commercial touring. She was always looking for ways to revitalize her art, and during the Concert Dancers tour she explored the techniques she called music visualization and the synchoric orchestra. The main sources of Denishawn work, and indeed of all nonballetic art dance of the time, were two dramatic devices. The dancer could use "character," the dance forms, costumes, decors, rituals, and ethnic traits of foreign countries, to create impressionistic scenes. Or, without benefit of program or stylistic trappings, she could simply dance out the feelings the music inspired. This kind of expressive dancing was practiced superbly by Isadora Duncan, yet St. Denis identified the impromptu quality as the one thing about Duncan's dancing that did not satisfy her. She saw Duncan at a loss when some piece of music she had been following became too complicated, saw her resort to standing still and gesturing when the music became most eloquent. This, Ruth felt, was an artistic weakness. She decided to try treating music more analytically.

As she described it in the *Denishawn Magazine* (1924), music visualization was "the scientific translation into bodily action of the rhythmic, melodic, and harmonic structure of a musical composition, without intention to in any way 'interpret' or reveal any hidden meaning apprehended by the dancer." Nonemotional music, like the Bach Inventions later choreographed by Ted Shawn, would translate into "the pure mathematics of the dance," while more coloristic works like her first big music visualization, Beethoven's *Sonata Pathétique,* contained an emotionalism that could spill over into the dance. St. Denis specified a one-to-one relationship between sound and movement: each note in the score called for a corresponding, equally weighted and timed movement. Dance dynamics would reflect the score. Even the ascend-

ing and descending direction of the melody would be materialized in the
dancer's relation to the plane of the stage, from the body lying flat to the
highest leap. If she had the resource of a full symphony orchestra to work
with—this happened all too seldom—she could assign individuals or
groups of dancers to double the instruments and ensembles within the orchestra, and to replicate the quality of those instruments both in their body
types and in their movements. This synchoric orchestra would be developed
first by assigning the individual dancers to their parts, then relating the individuals to their instrumental family, and only then putting the elements together in a total form.

Emile Jaques-Dalcroze had experimented with similar analytical processes,
breaking down the score and assigning movements to each musical event.
Ruth acknowledged that Dalcroze Eurhythmics had been taught at Denishawn before 1919 but maintained that any resemblance between her ideas
and the work of the Swiss pedagogue and theoretician was purely the coincidence of inventive minds. She insisted that her whole approach derived
from her response to Duncan. She did, however, give credit to Doris and to
musical director Louis Horst. Accompanist and champion of new music,
Horst left Denishawn in 1923 and for many years served as intellectual goad
and stimulus to Martha Graham. He probably introduced St. Denis to the
idea of rigorous musical analysis and helped her through the intricacies of
scores. Doris already had musical training and an analytical mind. Among
them they realized in fairly primitive form an American abstract choreography. St. Denis called it "the first symphonic dancing in this country."

St. Denis admitted that audiences would not be sophisticated enough to
appreciate a purely abstract dance. You might have to trick the eye, she said,
with visual devices or superficial structures like plots. Some of the music visualizations that survived, the ones that stay in a viewer's memory, relied on
scarves and veils manipulated in sensuous ripples, a whole gallery of tricks
St. Denis knew well from her skirt-dancing days in variety. Doris' biographer,
Selma Jeanne Cohen, attributes four works to her during the St. Denis Concert Dancers period (1919–21), two of them co-choreographed with Ruth.
These were the *Valse Caprice* (also called *Scarf Dance*), the Bach *Bourrée*,
and (with St. Denis) *Soaring* and *Sonata Pathétique*. She made at least another six dances before her professional apprenticeship ended with the for-
mation of Humphrey-Weidman in 1928. These were: *Sonata Tragica* (1923),
Hoop Dance or *Scherzo Waltz* (1924), *A Burmese Yein Pwe*, *At the Spring*,
and *Whims* (1926), and *The White Peacock* (1927). The true extent of the St.

Denis-Humphrey collaboration was probably much greater. Doris may have worked on the Debussy *Second Arabesque* and other dances for which she didn't claim credit. As a learning experience for her this period was ideal. She began to find out how to manipulate a group of dancers in relation to a musical structure. She was as eager to do "serious" work as her mentor, whom she soon surpassed.

We can learn much about what she was dancing at that time from the earliest of her films, made in about 1924, and from revivals that are still being performed by several modern dance companies. On the film, which also contains Shawn's *Death of Adonis* and excerpts from his *Cuadro Flamenco*, Doris performs phrases from her *Hoop Dance* and *Scarf Dance*. Today we couldn't call these anything but period pieces, and like all period pieces they tell us much about the conventions, assumptions, and images of their time.

Doris got the idea for *Hoop Dance* during a Denishawn tour and found someone on the road to make the prop for her, a seven-foot hoop painted gold. Trying out movements she could do with it, she found it gave her new possibilities by extending her body space. Although she felt the idea was revolutionary, the effect of the dance is similar to that of much post–Art Nouveau imagery, the figure prettily offset by the medallion-like frame of the hoop. On the film she rolls the hoop back and forth on a slightly sloping lawn. Dressed in the Denishawn "fleshings," or tank suit, she skips and gambols, sometimes fitting herself inside the hoop, sometimes curving around its edge. Her movement is simple, nymphlike, and "natural" as Isadora and the aesthetic dancers of the time defined that word. Kicks, backbends, leaps, and stretches are, with the runs and skips, almost her entire vocabulary. The body is never totally extended or sculpturally curved but falls into gentle lines broken slightly at the joints—a dangling foot, a drooping wrist or neck. Fingers are demurely spread, with the pinky especially prominent. *Hoop Dance* was a Maxfield Parrish design come to life.

Movements from *Scarf Dance* were filmed in slow motion, which emphasizes the flow of the body line. Today's highly trained dancers have trouble capturing the deliberately unstudied look of this kind of dancing, and even Doris looks somehow underworked, a little too mature for such trivia. She holds a long strip of silk and waves it so that it makes floating designs in the air as she runs, bends, or spins inside it. We can still see the prototype of this dance in Peking Opera performances, although Doris managed to use more of the body than the peripherally dextrous Chinese do. The dancer's freedom, her pleasure in the extra latitude for reaching and turning that the scarf

Hoop Dance. Photo by Wayne Albee. (Dance Collection, NYPL)

affords her, is at least as important as the circular and serpentine designs it describes.

The body imagery in both these films resembles what other interpretive dancers were doing in the 1920s. Dance magazines of the time are filled with photographs of wholesome young men and women breathing deeply, arms outflung, dancing in natural environments of hilltops and forest glens; and pensive nymphs and diaphanous maidens gazing into woodland pools. Parrish, in a verse that accompanied an illustration of Pan, rhapsodized: "casting the body's vest aside / my soul into the boughs does glide." The art dancers of the early twentieth century hardly wanted to dematerialize themselves, but they did express a longing to escape the confines of an industrialized world. In Doris there was a strong element of impersonality, of androgyny, that differed substantially from the sexy foreign flavor underlying Denishawn's popularity. During these years she loved to dance—privately— in the nude, and she had at least two nude photo sessions, one with the hoop and one where she draped herself in a length of fabric with a secluded rocky cove for a backdrop. Doris was only moderately successful in the earthy Denishawn works—she certainly tired of performing them—and of all the dances she choreographed during her association with the company only one, *A Burmese Yein Pwe* (with St. Denis), had an exotic theme. St. Denis, with her sensuous beauty and gift for creating character, appeared only marginally in the "pure-dance" music visualizations. Ruth thought Doris had a boyish quality and liked to cast her as fauns and cupids, but the public admired her most for pure-motion pieces like *Scarf Dance* and *Hoop Dance.*

Since the existing films of her during this period are silent, our only means of studying Doris' music visualization in complete form is to look at contemporary reconstructions. On a film of a program called "The Spirit of Denishawn," the Trisler Danscompany performs the *Scarf Dance* and two St. Denis-Humphrey collaborations, *Soaring* and *Sonata Pathétique,* under the direction of Klarna Pinska. Doris' *Scarf Dance,* performed on this film by Trisler dancer Anne-Marie Hackett, comes into clearer perspective when we can see it accompanied by the Chaminade Valse Caprice. Dancey without being musically literal, it needs no program to express its point.

Even at this distance it seems that Doris' musicality exceeded Ruth's in flexibility and motive power. Perhaps Ruth had become accustomed to using music as a prop for ethnic and folk steps; her interpretations in the *Sonata,* for instance, or in the Debussy *Second Arabesque* mimic the music to an extreme. Taking her own definition of music visualization quite literally, she had the feet step on every emphasis, the arms rise on every climax. A key principle of music visualization was to avoid the ballet vocabulary, but Ruth had a limited capacity for invention once this system was not available to her. She had little sense of the leg except to enlarge upon the gesture of walking or running, and locomotion was the main source of movement, together with large exclamatory gestures of the arms. In these reconstructions the torso follows the line of the gesture or is maintained in a neutral posture. The arms work bilaterally most of the time, stretched overhead, reaching forward or spreading to the sides; or pulling the body into a tilt. As in much Asian ritual dance, the group is treated as a unit, and all of its members do the same thing. In the *Pathétique*, six women work sometimes antiphonally with a soloist-loner, and sometimes in concert as she becomes their leader and incites them to battle. The effect of these dances is of clarity and simplicity bordering on the obvious.

In *Soaring* (to Robert Schumann's Aufschwung) the collaborators hit upon the idea of using a large silk scarf in its airborne state to carry some of the musical line. Four girls at its corners toss it up and gently guide it down filled with air; later they run with two corners, folding the scarf over itself so that it billows like a wave. In another contemporary version of the dance, taught by Marion Rice, the dancers turn the scarf into an unfurling lily, with a fifth dancer standing in its center. These tricks—accompanied by dramatic lighting—are all extensions of effects achieved by Loie Fuller at the turn of the century, but while they constitute the visual focus of the piece, the dancers making them happen are not simply waving their arms about as Fuller tended to do. Perhaps cued to the idea of suspension by the spread-out lyricism of the scarf, the choreographers varied the rhythm by setting steps only on the downbeat of Schumann's purling music. Later, when the music becomes more dramatic, the dance goes faster as the dancers run, duplicating every beat. Perhaps, too, Schumann's dual melody suggested visual counterpoint, for the balanced four-against-one group that prevails is broken when two women hold the scarf and a trio circles downstage. Although it looks at first simply like another Grecian three-Graces motif, this disturbance in the dance's symmetry introduces a hectic passage in the music and a "storm" in the pastoral mood. While the two girls shake the scarf behind them, then pass it agitatedly over their heads, the trio run confusedly as if looking for shelter. The storm passes and women and scarf resume their harmonious play.

Early in 1921, after two years of fairly easy touring, the period of indulgence in artistic experimentation came to an end abruptly in Little Rock, Arkansas.

The St. Denis Concert Dancers tour ran out of bookings and money. Doris was stranded—with $100 in her savings account, she said later. Ruth promptly became engrossed in a project to combine poetry with dancing, and went back on the road with actor Craig Ward, a musician, and Shawn, who dropped in occasionally to dance and keep an eye on her close relationship with Ward. With Shawn also occupied in vaudeville and solo concert appearances, Doris decided to try touring on her own. From then until 1927 she was seldom off the road. During those six years she had almost no time for experimental work, and the grind of traveling and performing cured her permanently of her enthusiasm for the gypsy life.

Pauline Lawrence had joined Denishawn as pianist and sometime dancer when the split occurred in 1919 and had toured with both the St. Denis Con-

Doris and the *Soaring* scarf. Collection of Charles H. Woodford.

Doris' first touring group at the Palace of Fine Arts, San Francisco, about 1921. Photo by Arthur Kales. (Dance Collection, NYPL)

cert Dancers and Shawn's production of *Xochitl.* She and Doris became close friends. Pauline's organizing abilities and her inexhaustible energy complemented Doris' talents, and together they thought they could run a small touring company. Pauline served as conductor and business manager, and the two young women with three other female dancers mounted a program that could be booked into vaudeville. It's hard to identify the precise works done by the act but they were probably a selection of the more elevated Denishawn numbers Doris had been doing for years. She performed the Bach *Bourrée* and her *Scarf Dance;* there was a *Rose Dance,* origin unknown; Shawn's *Gnossienne;* an Italian dance with a tambourine; and a group dance in which Doris wanted to use a working fountain but probably didn't because of the expense. A series of photographs was made of the group in Greek chitons, posing languidly at San Francisco's Palace of Fine Arts. Louis Horst was orchestrating music for them in the summer of 1922 at the Shawns' summer headquarters, Mariarden, in Peterborough, New Hampshire.

The venture was successful, and the group preserved its artistic integrity among the gaudier scenes of vaudeville. In fact, they were doing well enough to lend Shawn some money at the end of 1921, when his luck ran out in New York. By this time Shawn had moved the school to New York and was consolidating talents and teaching, schools, companies, and ideology under the title Greater Denishawn. He persuaded Ruth to rejoin him in the spring of 1922, and they signed a lucrative, juggernaut touring contract with the producer Daniel Mayer. Ruth exacted top billing, but the Denishawn company was an entity again, engraving its name and its repertory all over the American landscape for the next three years. By 1924, Greater Denishawn had affiliated schools run by its former dancers and students in Boston, Rochester, Minneapolis, Wichita, and San Francisco/Berkeley.

Doris had had no serious differences with the Shawns, and she gradually eased herself back into the organization. She made a guest appearance at the end of their two weeks at New York's Town Hall in April 1923, dancing the Debussy *Second Arabesque* and her *Scarf Dance.* She used this opportunity to check out the way the Denishawns were doing *Soaring,* and she didn't approve. At times during this tour, Shawn and later Charles Weidman had danced the central figure, which Doris thought was inappropriate for the girlish piece. *Soaring* came out of the repertory until Doris returned to the company. These concerts may also have been the only time Doris and Martha Graham appeared on the same Denishawn program, since Graham had worked with Shawn during the years when Doris assisted St. Denis, and Graham left Denishawn to work on her own shortly after the Town Hall dates. When the company went out again in the fall, Doris had replaced Graham at the top of the list of dancers—just below the two stars.

No matter how much Doris wanted to think of herself as a dancer, she could never escape her skills as a teacher; this aspect of her profession was a dependable if demanding source of income all her life. In the summer of 1923, she joined the faculty of the Denishawn Normal course in New York, teaching dances (including *Soaring*) to teachers. Her directing ability brought her the title of ballet mistress when the company reassembled. For the next three years, touring in the United States and the Orient, she had time for little else but performing, rehearsing the repertory, coaching replacements, and, in the summers, teaching in New York and Mariarden.

Doris did make one creative breakthrough during the remaining Denishawn years. This was a group work featuring herself and Charles Weidman, choreographed to Edward MacDowell's Sonata Tragica. Ruth St. Denis suggested after its premiere in Atlantic City in October 1923 that the dance could stand up without musical accompaniment, and from then on it was successfully performed in silence. Critics and audiences were intrigued by the powerful, primitive movement and the necessity of following the dance without any auditory clues to help them. "There was fresh interest in Doris Humphrey's *Tragica*, a test of pure rhythm without sound, as the tense group of dancers flung themselves silently, simultaneously, this way and that, a true motion picture, black and white, breathless, dumb, enthralling," was the way a *New York Times* writer reacted to it. Perhaps more significant as a forecast of where Doris was heading are the notes she jotted down about the dance.

> The Ensemble—flowering of the dance—instrument of as much depth, color and architectural capacity as the symphony although as yet possibilities have only been scratched—solo instrument always greatest importance—I believe that music and the dance are exactly analogous in the respect that the solo and ensemble bear the same relationship to each other—Technique—succession based on natural flow found in nature applied to whole body.

But she had little chance to pursue these ideas on tour, least of all during the company's one-and-a-half-year travels in the Orient. This trip, which lasted from late summer of 1925 through 1926, was considered a valuable opportunity by all the dancers, and for St. Denis and Shawn it seemed a dream come true, bringing them into direct association with the scenes and styles they had been fabricating for a decade. Along with their music visual-izations and "Americana" numbers, they showed their interpretations of Asian dances to Asians and colonials who seldom saw white performers of any kind. All along the tour, with an eye to future productions, the Shawns bought costumes, jewelry, and curios, soaked up local color, and hired local masters to instruct them in the authentic dance styles. By the end of the tour, in fact, they had added Burmese, Japanese, Chinese, Javanese, Singhalese, and Hindu dances to the Indian and North American exotica already in the tour repertory.

For Doris the tour was as debilitating as it was rewarding. The strain of traveling, performing as principal dancer, coaching, taking classes, and adapting to the extremes of climate and food took a toll on her physical con-dition. She went down with dengue fever in Malaya and suffered other ail-ments and injuries. By the time they sailed for home, she was totally de-pleted, a state she frequently reached all through her life after a strenuous, sustained period of work. Back in the States, a doctor found tuberculosis le-sions in addition to a generally run-down condition. Her exhaustion was probably aggravated by emotional stress, a result of having brought her mother along on the tour.

Doris had urged Julia to come to the Orient, knowing how much she would appreciate such an opportunity, and she arranged for Julia to assist in the company wardrobe department to keep her busy; Julia paid her own ex-penses. Whereas Doris tended to be impatient with inconveniences that would use up her limited energies, Julia was an excellent tourist, observant and adaptable to local customs, and she sent back voluminous, detailed let-ters to Horace and May Miller about everything she saw. But she had not really imagined the kind of life now being enjoyed by the thirty-year-old daughter who had left home a protected, proper young girl. Doris, too, had underestimated how removed her life had become from her mother's experi-ence, and she probably had suppressed the memory of how stern and ha-rassing Julia could be once her disapproval was incurred.

Despite the aura of rectitude with which the Shawns tried to insulate the company, composed largely of very young, middle-class girls far away from their families and engaged in what was still a doubtful profession, the moral code at Denishawn was decidedly unconventional. While Miss Ruth tried to enforce curfews and exaggeratedly modest clothing rules, permissiveness

Doris à l'Orientale. Collection of Charles H. Woodford.

quietly reigned in more serious matters. The Shawns themselves, of course, were far from an average married couple. Their separations, Shawn's homosexuality, and St. Denis' dalliances with sensitive young men were well known. Shawn was a devoted follower of Havelock Ellis, the English philosopher who advocated sexual experimentation as a way of deepening the emotional resources of the artist, and love was more than a romantic ideal at Denishawn. Homosexuality and bisexuality as well as heterosexual affairs were tolerated if not actively encouraged.

By 1925 Doris and Pauline Lawrence had been working and living together for several years. After their return to Denishawn, they annexed Charles Weidman to their team. Charles was a handsome, charming young man of nineteen when he appeared at Ted Shawn's studio in the summer of 1920. He had wanted to be a dancer throughout his teenage years in Lincoln, Nebraska, taking Ruth St. Denis as his ideal after seeing a Denishawn performance. He acquired what training he could, mainly ballroom, from Eleanor Frampton, who taught in the Lincoln High School Physical Education Department. Without waiting for his graduation, he left for Los Angeles at the end of May 1920. Shawn gave him a scholarship and pressed him into service a month later to replace an injured dancer as Martha Graham's partner in *Xochitl*. He remained on tour with Shawn's productions until joining the reconvened Denishawn for the 1922–25 Mayer tours. Although Pauline had been musical director for *Xochitl*, Doris was working with St. Denis at the time Charles arrived, and she probably didn't get to know him well until she and Pauline gave up their independent troupe and went back to the fold in 1923.

The exact nature of Doris' and Charles' early relationship is difficult to unearth, but one letter he wrote her at that time strongly suggests that they were deeply attracted to each other and that only Charles' homosexuality deterred them from becoming lovers. They had been out together, probably at a party, and at the end of the evening Charles had failed to seduce her as she must have expected. He confessed his "humiliation" at his inability to be "more or less an equal who could stimulate you with his knowledge and help you." He offered her her freedom, and added "mine I take." Assuring her that he would never understand "why you loved me," he concluded, "Your friendship I want and your love I will always cherish as the most perfect and beautiful thing I have ever possessed."

On Charles' side the initial attachment was probably very serious, though

lacking a sexual component. On Doris' side it was probably the kind of amo-
rous attraction she felt briefly for other men at that time in her life. She affected these objects of her fancy quite drastically. Though no femme fatale,
she was a beautiful and accomplished woman who had always acted independently, and there are several letters from suitors who were smitten after
some experience of momentarily basking in her favor. Charles' instinct was
to retain this formidable presence close to him in a safe and enduring relationship, and if she was disappointed at the loss of romance, she warmly accepted the alternative.

She and Pauline and Charles became a triumvirate, appropriating the nickname "The Unholy Three" from a Lon Chaney movie of 1925. Their convivial-
ity and high spirits were a fixture within the company, although their sexual
relations were less clear. Outsiders like the conventional Julia Humphrey
may have wishfully seen Charles' affectionate solicitude as a "crush" on
Doris; members of the company accepted that in the Orient her favorite
companion was Pauline. Doris also attracted serious admirers among the
lonely businessmen in those white outposts of Asia where they performed.
Julia viewed this situation very unfavorably, with what Doris later described
as "resentment and self-pity and accusations of neglect." Doris tried to include her mother on their parties and sightseeing trips, but Julia was deeply
shocked and intolerant of what she surmised was going on in Doris' sex life.

Whatever obsessive traits and guilt Doris inherited from her mother, she
did not acquire Julia's excitable temper. She consistently downplayed any
personal conflicts that would interfere with her creative work. But in the Orient her fights with Julia reverberated throughout the company. She grew
more tense under the strain of trying to mediate between her desire to treat
her mother decently and her involvement with her friends. An awestruck
teenage dancer, Jane Sherman, witnessed one hysterical scene when she
lost her temper entirely and ran to Charles' room screaming and in tears. Less
than a year into the tour, in May 1926, Julia left for home. Doris began to
bury the hatchet immediately, urging her mother to remember the good
things about the trip and assuring her that "with me the unpleasant unhappy things tend to fade." To her father she gave a cool analysis of the difference in their natures and promised to explain any wrongdoing Julia might
accuse her of: "As I think of us three it seems to me that you and I are considerably alike in apparently being tractable, but really hard to control (always) and that she has fretted her life away trying to make us do as she

thinks best, the consequence being that she—the fretter—is miserable, and you and I comparatively happy." But obviously it had been a devastating experience for both of them. After that Doris sent her parents money whenever she could spare it, wrote less and less frequently, and paid them only brief and rare visits. She was solicitous, dutiful—and distant.

4 A NEW DANCE, 1927–28

The Orient used her up without feeding her artistically. She created nothing new except the Burmese piece, which was a section of a larger company dance-drama; *At the Spring* (Liszt), which seems to have been rather pretty and plastique, and not as unusual as she thought; and *Whims* (or *Grillen*), a reworking of some Schumann music she had set for her vaudeville troupe. An abstract depiction of children's games, the last piece premiered after the company returned to the States. Now Doris wanted more than anything to stay put and work on her dances. But instead, the Denishawns set off immediately on a four-month cross-country tour, showcasing their new pageantry from the Orient along with music visualizations and older divertissements. Doris felt that *At the Spring* wasn't understood by audiences, and Jane Sherman, who danced in *Whims,* felt that it, too, puzzled viewers. By the time they reached New York in April of 1927, Doris was played out. "This year for the first time, I don't feel that I've come back bigger and better."

Shawn had been spinning his web again, intending to capitalize on the prestige and visibility all this arduous touring had brought the company. He showed Doris his new plan for the Greater Denishawn while they were still in the Orient. He wanted not only a regular theater but a roof garden theater, a school for vocational training (probably a Normal school), a separate division for the creative pupils, and many grand facilities. Soon after their return to the States, he bought a piece of property near Van Cortlandt Park in New York City, and construction was begun on a new Denishawn House, which was to house the school and its proprietors. The cost of all this was going to be enormous, and Doris, with characteristic dry pessimism, knew she would have to be one of the ones to pay. She saw that in return for bodies and a theater to count on, she would have to teach. She also thought that during the two years or more it would take to finance and carry out Shawn's plan, the company would have to hit the road again, possibly for Europe.

Despite its reputation and its appearance of stability, Denishawn did not

operate on the same basis as do professional dance companies today. Dancers were gathered together and paid only when the company was performing, and since it had no home theater, this meant touring. The economic survival of the company, as well as its public identity, depended on road
appearances. Creative work could be done only between tours, and then the
dancers had to spend much of their time teaching to make a living or find
other temporary jobs. Much of the work in the Denishawn repertory was not
choreographically new but a variation on the same few formulas with different costumes, gestures, or locales. Doris detested this expedient way of
working—doing new numbers simply to liven up a program and not to extend the choreographic art—and the history of her own career is in part a
constant struggle to find a better solution.

By the spring of 1927, another tour was unthinkable for her. Temporarily,
an agreement was reached. Doris and Charles would run the school in New
York while the Shawns took the company on a Ziegfeld Follies tour (September 1927–May 1928). But this arrangement only delayed a real accommodation, and, when the company got back to New York again, the differences
between the two factions had deepened beyond repair.

Although the company offered only small pieces and solos alongside typical vaudeville acts in the Follies, Denishawn had become the most important
art-variety attraction in America, and certainly the best paid. The years of
one-night stands had paid off. So had the efficient propaganda machine that
was kept carefully oiled. St. Denis and Shawn's quasi-religious interests extended from their dance-making into inspirational talks that students and
company members were expected to attend regularly, and a fervent prosely-
tizing for vague concepts like expressiveness and spirituality found its first
regular outlet in the *Denishawn Magazine* (four numbers were issued between 1924 and 1925). Shawn had written the first of his many books, a biography of St. Denis, during the separation of 1919–22. After they were back
at the New York home base in 1927, they started a series of "Denishawn
Dialogues," voluminous transcriptions of their conversations about art and
life, that were mailed out "to let you know as personal friends of the Shawns
what they are doing and thinking." They were thinking about art versus entertainment, about how to raise money for their projects, about critics, and, it
seems, persistently and exclusively about themselves. Somehow, almost
every issue of *The Dance,* the main magazine covering art dance of the time,
contained an article by Ruth or Ted, or about their artistic theories and triumphant achievements. When the post-Orient tour was over they presented

each of the company members with a silver pin in the Yin/Yang pattern that had been devised as the Denishawn emblem. Doris' good taste was offended. "My emotions were mixed," she reported. "Appreciation for the thought but a little annoyance with the badgelike look of the thing."

Although one of the least self-centered of all dancers, Doris must have felt some resentment at the way the company was saturated with the leaders' personalities. Billed as a leading dancer, she always received special notice from critics, but it was St. Denis and Shawn who dominated the company's image. The *Denishawn Magazine* reads as if nothing had ever been thought of or accomplished by anyone but Ruth and Ted. For instance, in a 1924 souvenir program, included as an insert in the magazine, the following caption is found, "Miss St. Denis was materially assisted by Miss Doris Humphrey, who did the actual dance writing of 'Tragica,'" making Doris seem like a sort of notator or secretary. Doris spoke of feeling "swamped" in the post-Orient show, and she worried about what the future would be like in an even greater Greater Denishawn. She must have sensed that she would be useful only so long as her choreography conformed to St. Denis' and Shawn's non-controversial, escapist aesthetic and that her ideas would quickly be subjected to the corrosive process that wears down a touring repertory. By 1927 Doris knew that she did not wish to become another Denishawn satellite.

Thin and exhausted, she recovered her strength during the early summer at the country house of a friend, Nell Alexander, in Westport, Connecticut. She planned dances in her head—she worked out the scenario for *Color Harmony* and thought about another dance based on geometric shapes. "I'm so tired of dinky little dances, and decorative or character or cute ballets, that I've gone to the extreme of abstractness I guess," she wrote her parents. By the beginning of August she was back in the city full of energy and ideas, ready to start classes at the Denishawn school. Passing up the Follies expedition was costly—the dancers received a handsome raise in salary—but the arrangement she made for the year was more to her liking. She and Charles were to be in charge of the school in New York, teaching twice a week for about fifty dollars, and sharing the profits on a sliding scale with the parent institution. Doris was to receive the highest percentage, then Charles, then Pauline, who was to play for classes, then the two other women who assisted them, Hazel Krans, the children's teacher, and secretary Olga Frye. When they left, Shawn owed them over $400, which they didn't collect until they hired a lawyer several years later.

Doris probably never again enjoyed teaching so thoroughly as she did during that year of 1927–28. The classes, held in one of the studios above Carnegie Hall, were so successful that Doris and Charles had to split them to keep them a manageable size, thereby doubling their own work. But their satisfaction came from more than the realization that they could draw students without the bolstering presence of Shawn or St. Denis. For the first time in her life Doris had no one to serve in her teaching but herself. Neither mother nor mentor, proprietor nor model was there to dictate the rules, and Doris promptly set about finding new ones. She developed choreography and pedagogy side by side, a practice that became her mode for many years. "I feel more free to do as I please now . . . and I let my imagination run— instead of teaching the old routine things," she wrote her parents.

Another singular characteristic that Doris retained to the end of her life was her awareness of other forms of dance. She wanted to be in touch with what others were doing, not to work in some isolated hothouse. In 1927, *The Dance* magazine was filled with descriptions and photographs of the German modern dance and its exponents. Although the spectacular Mary Wigman and Harald Kreutzberg had not yet made their first American appearances, there had been considerable penetration of the ideas introduced early in the decade in Europe and already highly developed there. American dance teachers had taken summer courses at the Dalcroze Institute, at the schools of Laban and his disciples, and at the centers for Swedish gymnastic training; and European modern dancers had found their way to the States. Ronny Johansson, who later founded the Swedish Dance Teachers Organization, taught and performed with Denishawn before returning to Stockholm in 1932 to open her own school. Louis Horst, who worked with many modern dancers before allying himself exclusively with Graham, had studied in Germany in the mid 1920s, absorbing the total arts climate there, and he no doubt imparted what he saw to all his associates in the States. Doris understood that a new approach to dancing had taken hold. She didn't intend to copy the German theoretical ideas, although her early work, like that of her contemporaries, bore some similarities. What she sympathized with was a certain kind of antiacademicism, different from the ballet-based free forms of Denishawn.

Confidence and enthusiasm glowed from her reports to Oak Park.

I'm putting some of my ideas into practice—although they are not unique . . . *the* idea that everybody is putting into use [is] that of moving from the inside out . . . the ballet method is way out—just an interesting old antique—I suggest to my pupils studying it as you would any other period dance . . . [the new idea is] the dominant expression of our generation, if not of the age, and ballet is as out of style as bustles and leg o' mutton sleeves.

Doris was so persuasive that Julia and her partner Ethel Moulton later took a summer course with Margaret H'Doubler, founder of the dance department at the University of Wisconsin, in an effort to modernize their teaching methods.

Along with experimenting on new ways of teaching, Doris was brimming with dance ideas. In addition to *Color Harmony,* which was probably the most important product of this period and the first real Humphrey-Weidman dance, she was working on "a sort of pantomime" based on the classical story of Penelope; a "half-woman half-cat dance"; a duet with Charles to some Scriabin études, "very heavy and dramatic"; a Sleeping Beauty piece to two sections of Ravel's Mother Goose Suite; the waltz La Plus Que Lente by Debussy, which she thought was "rather wistful and reminiscent"; a "gay and rollicking" *Rigaudon* to MacDowell; "a Slavic thing" to a piece by Slavensky; Rosenthal's *Papillon,* whose pretty title she regretted; the first movement of Grieg's *Piano Concerto in A Minor,* done as a straight music visualization; and Bach's *Air for the G String.* Most of these dances appeared on a concert the following spring at the Brooklyn Little Theater.

Doris had talked for many years as if her relationship to the Denishawn organization would last only as long as conditions were advantageous to her as well as to the Shawns. She reluctantly contemplated a more definite break during 1927–28, for she knew that she was being left alone only temporarily. She reveled in the creative work that was growing under her hands, and she knew the masters wouldn't approve. She also knew what the tour must be doing to the quality of Denishawn work, and felt she must "avoid upholding [Shawn] as an example to the pupils." By November she heard that St. Denis was trying to book a solo tour in Europe the following year; she wondered what Shawn's plans would be and started thinking about some alternatives.

The season was rushing to its culmination. In January there was a private studio recital to try out some of the new works and give the students a taste of performing. Doris included the *Sonata Pathétique* on this program as a tribute to St. Denis. Some of the company, home from the tour for a few days, attended the showing and were impressed—Ronny Johansson had tears in her eyes after the Grieg *Concerto*. In February Doris met the experimental composer Henry Cowell and began work on his eerie piece The Banshee, which was played by sliding the fingers up and down the strings inside the piano.

The partners booked the Little Theater in Brooklyn for a spring concert, March 24, and just as they were focusing all their efforts on it, Shawn got nervous. He was aware of Doris' growing assurance and the attractiveness of the modern ideas being developed in the New York classes. Ostensibly it was only the summer and fall plans he was worried about, but in fact he was desperately trying to reestablish his authority over the whole institution, when he drafted an elaborate prospectus for the group in New York to consider. He envisioned an intensive program to create American Art Dances, producing two showings a week at Denishawn House with the dancers now out on tour. Doris replied at length to the plan. She was skeptical. She thought it would be impossible to maintain a high artistic standard while

Grieg's *Piano Concerto in A Minor*. Photo by Vandamm Studio. (Dance Collection, NYPL)

producing two programs a week, unless some of the creative work was turned over to "novices." She also didn't go along with Shawn's plan for her and Charles to teach in Westport, where Shawn was planning an expanded summer course at Nell Alexander's. Doris wanted to continue their current arrangement, essentially a franchise, running the New York studio on a percentage basis with Charles.

This response only upset Shawn more, and he summoned Doris to meet him on tour only a week or two before the Brooklyn concert. She was too busy to go, and Olga Frye, whom she sent as an emissary, couldn't straighten anything out. So Shawn stormed in to New York from Pennsylvania on a Sunday and began a marathon argument with Doris in which they scratched up all the personal and professional differences that by now divided them. Doris suspected that Ruth was about to do another of her withdrawals, leaving the institution under Shawn's sole command. She also saw that he was extremely jealous of the creative wave that was rising for his former protegés and bitter that he was out of action doing one-night stands. Still trying to patch things up, Doris interrupted her work right after the Brooklyn concert—which had been so successful that a second one was scheduled for the John Golden Theater in Manhattan three weeks later—and joined the company for its performances in Bridgeport and Poughkeepsie. "Ted made such a fuss before because I wouldn't spend a single day with him prior to the concert," she explained to her parents. But the gesture backfired on Shawn. Nothing could have set Doris more firmly against continuing her association with Denishawn than what she saw in those three days with the Ziegfeld Follies.

"Every spark of life has been eaten away, they make mechanical gestures—including Miss Ruth—at twice the proper speed," she wrote. "The girls seem to be moving around in an irritable grey death—frightful." Doris was particularly disillusioned with St. Denis, who had been such an inspiration to her and a model of artistic integrity; she found that St. Denis had shortened her skirts and speeded up the tempo for her *Black and Gold Sari* to accommodate the commercial tone of the show. It was indeed the worst touring situation the Denishawns had ever encountered—Jane Sherman called it "devastating"—and St. Denis was thoroughly depressed by it. The dancers were required to understudy chorus girls, and the cherished artistic numbers had been steadily eliminated from the act or whittled down to showier versions. Doris saw the effects from out front, and she also understood what this was doing to the young dancers. She said, "I'd like to snatch them out of it—only I want them to get such a good sour dose of it they'll never be tempted again." The future was going to be hers, and she was willing to wait a few months to collect in full.

The Golden Theater concert was even more successful than the first one, and at the end of April Doris exulted, "I have at last a sense of living, instead of getting ready to live . . . and now that I've smelled blood—God help anybody who stands between me and my meat!"

But the break was messy and it took time. When she wrote her autobiography thirty years later, Doris telescoped the months of proposals and counterproposals, of hope and disillusionment, into one lengthy meeting at Denishawn House. Her memory was faulty on several counts. From the beginning of classes in the summer of 1927, she had her eye on independence, but she was realistic enough to cling to the sheltering reputation and relative stability Denishawn could provide, until she could no longer live under the same roof. She temporized so long, in fact, that she virtually forced the leaders to dismiss her.

In May 1928 she recuperated for two weeks in Westport, where Shawn was building an elegant new studio with furnishings imported from Japan. Shawn dangled the bait of an outdoor concert, planned for later in the summer at the Lewisohn Stadium in New York. Ruth wanted to do some of their old dances, and there was talk of including examples of Doris' new work. She realized immediately that either the Denishawn dancers would need a period of special training or the girls on whom she had made the work would have to be brought back from their vacations for rehearsals. Both alternatives involved extra expense that she knew the Shawns wouldn't pay. "Our ideas of values are totally different & will lead to serious difficulty I foresee that. I've had a year to get a perspective on a great many things, & the results have been—to me—revolutionary." Shawn let her know that "he is most interested in building the institution of Denishawn, which he wants to do by everybody's cooperation with himself as dictator."

These were the principal issues. Doris needed to pursue her own artistic direction in her own way; she would hear of no compromise. Her work now was to correct and refocus what she felt were lapsed standards and to discover a more indigenous dance form than the borrowed eclecticism of Denishawn. "I knew how everyone moved but I didn't know how *I* moved," she told some students in 1956. "They thought all dance was one. But I and others wanted to know what it was to dance as an American." As long as that work could go on under Denishawn, she would pursue it. But she knew it could not go on if she remained in a subordinate position. "I think the only hope of working together is through a government similar to a democracy, not an autocracy. . . . Every man [should] cooperate on the government and business, but worship as he please."

Ruth made a last-ditch effort to placate the renegades. Around the middle of June, Doris reported that they had talked, and "instead of [Ted's] being dictator of the school, she has taken the bit in her teeth at last, has made a plan for the school herself, and intends to be its instigator. The whole thing is to be directed by a board—and so is a democracy after all." Ruth and Ted had been having their art versus business argument all during the Follies tour, and by the end of it, she felt almost as strongly as Doris did about the way Denishawn was heading. However, at the June meeting she didn't indicate just how much "polluted water" would be thrown out of the repertory, and she still denied Doris the chance to present *Color Harmony* at Lewisohn, claiming that it would be too expensive. She did agree to put on *Air for the G String* and the Grieg *Concerto,* the most conservative, though most successful, of Doris' new works. "Theoretically they think they ought to keep me—but humanly speaking they're not so anxious—which is perfectly natural," Doris thought.

The only portion of Miss Ruth's plan for the school that was put into practice was the creation of a governing board. This took place at the final meeting—the inquisition, Doris called it. Doris' first account of this meeting, written to her parents a few days later on July 2, is probably the most accurate version of it that exists. She reported then that the meeting lasted seven hours, not nine, as she recalled later. The personnel included the Shawns, two of their managers, and the two Denishawn fixtures who had been teaching in New York, Hazel Krans and Olga Frye. Charles and Pauline were not invited. If the board of directors was to comprise only those present, the deck had indeed been stacked. Doris reported the argument as a contest between what "they" said and what "I" said, articulating her sense that Shawn and St. Denis were now unified in their intentions. It must have taken courage to face this formidable group. Doris summarized the main points of difference to Julia and Horace, although she didn't elaborate on what must have been a personally degrading and wracked experience.

The meeting started out on a high moral plane as it was "stated and agreed" that the Greater Denishawn was to stand for "spiritual good," which was to be expressed in "a preponderance of all the works." This did not rule out "so-called secular dances that may have a morbid or even destructive tendency, if the art form is good." The organization was to have separate heads of departments, reporting to the board of directors.

The "first snag," according to Doris, came when "they" proposed that 90 percent of the institution should be of Anglo-Saxon descent. Apparently the Shawns rationalized that this would ensure that "the art is American—and is recognized by other countries as American." Institutionalized anti-Semitism was repugnant to Doris, and she vigorously opposed this scheme. "I thought of the very talented young Jewish girls already in the school and wondered what would become of them." She had grown up without much contact with Jews, and it wasn't until this first year of working in New York that she encountered them in appreciable numbers. Through working with them in class and getting to know them as individuals, she came to reject the prevailing stereotypes. As to the quota system, "Let the immigration department keep the quota down to what they consider a salutary level, but after they're once here, why not produce art with them if you can?"

Shawn continued on his moral hobby horse and talked of monitoring the sexual activities of company members. He wanted a special committee empowered to arbitrate individual morality and determine whether to require transgressing couples to marry or dismiss them from the organization. Doris was so flabbergasted by this that she didn't reply. In her mind what Ruth and the company had been doing to commercialize the Follies act was a kind of immorality in itself, and she outlined in some detail the betrayal of art that she had seen on the tour. This provoked St. Denis to tears. Doris thought perhaps she was "the only one that ever told them anything disagreeable about their art. . . . [Ruth] calls this [commercialization] a necessary adaptation to environment." Doris called it compromise, one of the most serious offenses she knew.

They spent the rest of the meeting at odds over "my objection to yielding my individuality, if it should come to a point when I should be required to do something in which I do not believe. They consider that the welfare of the institution should be everyone's first consideration, and I consider that that should be one's sincerity to art." In her clear, reasoned way, she explained to her parents that while the Shawns believed that by "compromising the individual faith to the common good you will eventually build an organization that will produce great art," she was convinced that "after you get all through, you will produce only compromised art, as a result of habit of mind."

Doris claimed in her autobiography that the final blow came when she was asked "would I or would I not go into the Follies for a season to do my share for the Greater Denishawn" and flatly refused. If this question were asked at all, it can only have been hypothetical. Denishawn had no Follies tour planned for the next year, or any other year. In fact, after the Lewisohn concerts there were only scattered appearances under the Denishawn aegis, and in 1931–32 the whole entity was dissolved. According to St. Denis, "Since Ted's and my spiritual separation had already taken place, the going of Doris and Charles meant that the last pillar fell, and very soon Denishawn, in the form we knew it, would be a thing of the past." Doris told her parents that she had brought up the Follies debacle only to underscore her opposition to touring, but she didn't say a tour was actually proposed.

Nor did she report exactly what were the words of severance that ended ten years' work. There may, in fact, never have been anything so definite as her being "voted out of Denishawn," as she later recollected, but "it certainly was perfectly definite that if I couldn't obey I was out." Within days she heard rumors that St. Denis and Shawn might reconsider, but "I don't see how we can agree."

Even this break was not total. Doris and Charles were in the middle of teaching a summer course, and it wasn't over until August. Ruth was immediately consumed with remorse for their treatment of Doris and regret for what she saw as the inevitable loss of their "children." She lamented the blow sustained by an organization that was too inflexible to allow for new ideas. She wrote Doris after a day or two, and they started to construct a relationship that was affectionate though no longer close. She attended Doris and Charles' next concert, in October, and sent a message to Doris that she thought *Color Harmony* was stupendous. But Shawn was unrelenting. He thought Doris had been disloyal, and it took many years before they reached an uneasy truce. Years later, Doris maintained publicly that she would always be grateful for the teaching, performing, and choreographing opportunities Denishawn had offered her.

Two of the works created during this transitional period have been well documented, *Air for the G String* on film and *Color Harmony* in several detailed verbal accounts. They were both major works, and they represent, respectively, a polished expression of the sensibility Doris was putting behind her, and a sketch of the vistas toward which she was advancing.

Like many of the works from this period, *Air for the G String* is very brief, only about seven minutes long. As indicated by the array of numbers done at the Brooklyn and Golden Theater concerts, Doris had a head full of ideas and didn't feel she needed to develop any of them extensively. Martha Graham followed the same course in her choreographic infancy. It was a time for feeling one's way, for discovering the themes, energies, looks, languages that would serve for a lifetime—and discarding the things that lacked enough challenge. Yet *Air* cannot be called a throwaway dance or a study. It remained in the repertory for many seasons. The beautiful film that Doris and four other women made in 1934 shows a completely worked-out idea in cameo form, a dance that owes much to the aesthetic of Ruth St. Denis but also shows signs of disengagement.

Doris made very few religious dances in her career, or even dances with a spiritual or atavistic source. She cared more, always, for the noble qualities in man himself. This was not solely a function of her agnosticism; many other nonbelievers or nonpracticing Christians, like José Limón and Martha Graham, turned to spiritual and even ecclesiastical characters and themes in their dances. Perhaps Doris' almost total neglect of religious subjects and lore was an ingrained reaction against Denishawn's persistent use of them. Or perhaps she was too much of a rationalist to enmesh herself in questions to which she could never know the answers.

Air, at any rate, asks no questions. When she was working on the dance, Doris told her mother she had "held onto the idea of that music since I was a little girl in school." Her image was almost entirely sculptural. Five women walk as if in a procession, sway toward each other in tender transports of piety, twine and untwine their arms loosely, like tendrils of some climbing plant. Doris thought of dressing them in long shifts and very long robes that trailed after them as they walked, "to give that sustained look to the movement to correspond to the tone of the violin—but of course it must not be plastic with veils—and that's where the personality of the girls comes in." By this she didn't mean that the dancers were to "express" themselves but that, in the character of the devout Renaissance maidens she had suggested through the tipped-back postures and prayerful hand gestures, they were to look seraphic. Critic Margaret Lloyd quoted her as having directed them to think of "a long, golden ray of light moving from place to place." If Doris' earlier dances had the naturalistic line of a Parrish or an Alma-Tadema, *Air* has more artifice, like the paintings of Arthur Rackham or the Pre-Raphaelites, where waves, clouds, tree shapes, and rocks are flattened into harmonizing planes and strata, with the human form seemingly carved out of the same material and following the same grain. The idealized playfulness of *Hoop*

Dance, for instance, had been achieved through an excitation of a natural flow. Here the line is an artfully sublimated, continuous, eternally interconnected curve. She isn't exactly talking about saintliness and she isn't exactly talking about sensuality, but she's somehow suggesting both.

This duality, covert and refined as it is, brings to mind some of the less flashy mystical roles of Ruth St. Denis—the chiseled goddesses *Kuan Yin* and *White Jade;* the streaming hair and draperies of her *Spirit of the Sea,* which ten years earlier had impressed Doris so deeply. The inner serenity and visual unity of these dances must have left an indelible mark on Doris' mind. Even when she no longer needed the flatness, the fixity, she never lost the innate control of line in space that they represented.

But in another way the sensibility of *Air* is greatly different from St. Denis' spiritual portraiture, because it comes from a depersonalized group. St. Denis saw her dances as devices to set off a central figure—herself—and to radiate the divine madness or intelligence of that figure. Martha Graham adopted this model. But Doris' principal entity was to be the group. A central figure, when there was one, acquired its stature from the group and served important focal purposes in the total design, but was not considered a god-like, superhuman presence. Although we are fortunate that she cast herself in the film of *Air,* she didn't ordinarily dance the role and didn't choreograph it for herself. She saw the central woman only as a means of emphasizing the group's asymmetricality, of asserting imbalance in counterpoint groupings—three against two—and of linking divergent directional tendencies.

Color Harmony shared this sense of sculptural flow and proportion but had no preexisting score. Clifford Vaughn composed the music as Doris was choreographing. Before she started independent classes with Charles in 1927, Doris had gone up to New Haven to look at Professor George Pierce Baker's new theater at Yale. There she met his assistant, Stanley McCandless, who had once been property man and electrician at Mariarden and whose later theories influenced the sophisticated lighting techniques of modern dance in the 1930s and 1940s. McCandless suggested "coming up there with a ballet and producing it, which I think would be thrilling." She was impressed with the technical facilities and equipment she found at Yale and with the expert designers who could help her, and thought it would be an ideal place to try out a dance before showing it in New York. Apparently the collaboration never took place, but she started planning a dance immediately, and it seems likely that *Color Harmony* was inspired at least in part by her foray into this specialized world of light.

Color Harmony. Photo by Soichi Sunami. (Dance Collection, NYPL)

"What to dance about" was an important enough question for Doris to devote a whole chapter to it in *The Art of Making Dances,* but she admitted there that the problem is significant mainly to the choreographer. "For the audience it often makes very little difference what a dance is about," she wrote, arguing that trivial dances can become classics—she cited *The Dying Swan*—and that high-minded inspiration does not always transfer to performance. As she began to channel her creative energies into choreography, she tried a number of approaches to developing themes, after the first inexplicable stroke of inspiration that she believed was essential. Her most familiar method was to peg the dance to a musical source, as with *Air for the G String.* Another was to carry through intuitively after the germ of an idea or an image was conceived, as in *The Banshee.* But she consciously sought other avenues as well.

She became intrigued with the idea of color as a source for movement. Perhaps Ruth St. Denis had planted the seed. In her experiments with the synchoric orchestra she had tried color-coding the dancers' costumes to different instruments, and in "The Color Dancer," in an article published in the *Denishawn Magazine,* Ruth argued that dancers should be as sensitive to the "emotional reactions to color" as they were to music and movement, and should "find out those colors that are related by the laws of harmony" both to their own natures and as abstract values. "Eventually a color dancer will think in octaves of color," St. Denis predicted, and she mentioned "interesting books" where people could look into scientific discoveries on the subject. She herself only tweaked at the idea, but Doris seized it and went to work.

In addition to the actual movement explorations that were going on constantly in the studio, Doris researched her themes extensively at this time; *Life of the Bee* and *The Shakers* were the products of lengthy investigations. During the making of *Color Harmony* she read and thought for several months about the relation of color to human expression. In Europe numerous artists, including the composer Alexander Scriabin and the painter Wassily Kandinsky, had been seriously involved in this problem for some time, but Doris never acknowledged being influenced by them. Unlike them, she did not see the making of art as pure research. She wasn't trying to examine the properties of dancing itself but to do more with what she knew. She did research by learning what others had thought about color and figuring out how to apply their ideas to her thematic notions. She was, in other words, trying to find out how to make dance metaphors that would have significance in the modern world. Her thinking was probably also influenced by the composer Dane Rudhyar, whose music accompanied four of her dances in the next three years. Rudhyar was very active at that time, lecturing and publishing on his theories about musical perception and the spiritual effects of sounds.

In a remarkable working notebook she pencilled ten pages of speculations, plans, and observations, some drawn from the books she looked at. Pauline also scrawled a few notes there on how to see color in musical terms. "Octaves of light divided into twelve semitones of color" was a possibility. Among the fourteen titles Doris listed were an essay on symbolic colors, several books on color theory, and studies relating color to sound and light. What she wanted was "symbolically to express the idea that all art is produced by the spirit which selects and controls and harmonizes . . . or in more poetic language the surge of nature yields its beauty to the power of the spirit." It seems obvious that she was thinking about the role of the choreographer.

Yet commentators, even the sympathetic critic John Martin and the enthusiastic young dancer Eleanor King, labeled *Color Harmony* in crudely schematic terms. According to Martin, it "dramatized the Young-Helmholtz theory of light with certain philosophical overtones." Ironically, Doris left posterity so much insight into her working process, in the form of notes, explanations, and images, that she is frequently pictured as some cold superbrain, manipulating dancers to prove formulas. Selma Jeanne Cohen, who completed Doris' biography, partially quotes Doris' description of *Color Harmony* in a letter to her parents (June 22, 1927). This letter summarizes the dance in the terse, noncommittal tone Doris usually employed when writing home. She began, "Following my theory that any abstract idea can be danced, I chose 'Harmony,' although in working it out I find that closely crowded by the 'Art versus Nature' idea," giving little indication of how much this particular idea meant to her.

In her notebook, however, she wrote, "Just because color has been proven by science to be objective—that is not inherent in the object," and on a page headed by a list of far from objective words—harmony—perfection—beauty—love—and self-expression—she described the dance in far more passionate terms.

First a cool blue waltz—then a yellow rhythm, warmer and capricious—thirdly a red rhythm rich and sturdy, always attracted in turn to blue and yellow. Each time red goes by they each blow toward him like flowers—

and each time the attraction grows stronger, until one red, brave and more lustful than the rest, captures a trembling and vibrant yellow. Immediately they begin to spin, and a burst of orange, a silk scarf flames up from between them. All the rest are hardly a minute later, and all the reds and yellows are in an ecstatic whirl of orange to the horror and disdain of the cool blues. Some are vibrating so rapidly that their very ardor flings them apart, and both yellows and reds sweep down upon the blues who attempt to escape and run hither and thither distractedly. But they are caught one after the other—and immediately are encircled by flames of green or purple. The couples spin so closely together they are as one— madly, with long swoops and dips—often interfering with each other. There is no form—only vibration. Through the wild colors shoots a silver arrow—it separates the couples—it draws them one by one into form— all the flaming colors are laid down in rhythmic patterns—in a pyramidal form—up high steps to a climax, where a silver streak molds itself into a stream of light that goes up into infinity.

Under this flashing banner of optimism, Humphrey-Weidman had its beginning.

5 ECSTATIC THEMES, 1928–31

Those who ventured into new dance territory at the end of the 1920s formed a variety of self-contained alliances and working arrangements. Making dance is not like writing or painting; a choreographer with innovative ideas must have dancers sympathetic to those ideas—people who are willing to be the clay—as well as technicians, managers, and boosters who can facilitate the presentation of the dance once it has been created. Convinced that they must find their own personal ways of moving, the early modern choreographers could not depend on one another for the support systems they needed. In fact they avoided professional liaisons, and when expediency brought these about, they were tenuous.

For the mission these dancers had undertaken, the sacrifice was so great and the monetary rewards so poor that another kind of attachment was required. The leader was regarded in idealized terms by the students who collaborated in the work. The "company" was more like a family, its principal members related by sexual bonding, longstanding friendship, or unquestioning admiration. The in-group character of nonacademic dance ensembles can be seen as early as Isadora Duncan, who surrounded herself with relatives and devoted intimates, never quite trusting that outsiders could represent her even in the business aspects of her work. St. Denis and Shawn openly fostered the idea of their company as a big family, encouraging the dancers to think of them as "Papa" and "Miss Ruth," and St. Denis frequently admitted that their creative achievements and coterie of students took the place of the children they never conceived. Many American dance companies operate in a similar manner even now, though the paternalistic aspects are less overtly stressed.

The weaving together of personal and professional life had been a pattern even earlier in Doris' background. The overlapping of her parents' social and business connections had grown so acceptable to her that she could compliantly make her first approach to a career as her mother's partner. In the Denishawn family, too, coworkers shared one another's private lives. Doris

Pauline Lawrence, about 1922. Photo by Wayne Albee. (Dance Collection, NYPL)

"adopted" the teenage Jane Sherman on the Oriental tour. She arranged a company job on that tour for her mother and later, when Julia needed money, advised that Ruth's brother might be willing to help her sell some of the things she had brought back from the East. In 1924 Shawn offered Doris and Pauline an apartment, probably the back room, at the Denishawn studio (Studio 60 in Carnegie Hall). The rent was cheap and they moved in, hoping the students wouldn't bother them too much, since the place was used as a lounge between classes. There are countless examples of this kind of arrangement, and by the time the trio ventured out on their own, it must have been difficult to put living and working in separate compartments. They shared meals, holidays, clothes, and money, as well as all their creative ideas and opportunities.

Although Doris believed deeply in the individual's right to be a creative entity and did everything she could to provide a more democratic system within her own realm, Humphrey-Weidman was deeply grounded in familial ties, strengthened by the economic necessity of shared living arrangements, and was doomed when its particular mesh of allegiances wore out and its financial bases disappeared.

Humphrey-Weidman really began with Doris and Pauline. Their partnership was both personal and professional. The extent of their early intimacy is undefined, but it is clear that theirs was a complete partnership. They admired each other tremendously and by 1928 had discovered each other's strengths and weaknesses, understood how complementary their personalities were, and worked out a successful interdependent living arrangement.* They were both compulsive overworkers, but while Doris tended to fix all her energies on the immediate task, be it choreographing, teaching a summer course, or rehearsing for a concert, Pauline could function with her hands in many pies at once. Doris knew how things should go but couldn't be bothered with details. Pauline played for classes, accompanied concerts, and con-

---

*Lillian Faderman's exhaustive study of "romantic friendship" between women provides a perspective and a valuable insight into several centuries of intimate though not necessarily sexual relationships between middle-class, frequently gifted women. Speaking of the eighteenth century, when such relationships were accepted and even admired by society, Faderman says: "Romantic friends courted each other, flirted, were anxious about the beloved's responses and about reciprocity. They believed their relationships to be eternal, and in fact the faithfulness of one often extended beyond the death of the other. The fondest dream of many romantic friends, which was not often realized, was to establish a home with the beloved. To that end they were willing to make the greatest sacrifices, and were devastated if their hopes were disappointed. There is nothing to suggest that they were self-conscious about these passions or saw them as being abnormal in any way" (Surpassing The Love of Men [New York: William Morrow, 1981], p. 125).

ducted when there was an orchestra, designed and sewed costumes, kept
the books at the studio, did all the managing and publicity work, saw whatever needed attention and attended to it.

Doris had never taken a great interest in her personal appearance or
health. She would go too long without rest or medical attention, drinking
quantities of black coffee and smoking endless cigarettes without giving
thought to their ill effects until, on vacation in the country, she would try to
restore herself with round-the-clock siestas, suntans, and fattening diets.
Pauline was an excellent cook, an avid shopper and planner, and a frank dis-
penser of advice about everything from clothes to artistic policy—a born
caretaker. Doris liked to feel at home among a few carefully chosen posses-
sions, but often she was too exhausted or preoccupied to enjoy the meager
time she was able to spend with them. Pauline loved fixing up houses and
apartments, but she got restless in a place if there wasn't enough to do.

Temperamentally Doris was low-key, restrained, undemonstrative. She
tended to form close ties with people who could fill her needs without making too many demands on her, and then to sustain those relationships a
long time. Most of those nearest to her throughout her life felt neglected at
times and complained that she didn't show them enough affection. Pauline
was volatile, generous, critical, something of a nag. Even in the simplest
matters she needed to be reassured that people were as conscientious as
she was, that problems on which she had expended more than enough energy were also of great consequence to everyone else. If Doris failed to re-
spond to a question, approve a plan, choose from among the alternatives
she had elaborately laid out, she took it as a rebuff.

In the early summer of 1924, for instance, Doris was in Oak Park on a
combined parental visit and concert tour while Pauline was playing for Ruth
St. Denis' rehearsals in New York. In the example that follows—the first third
of a letter—one can see the natural, compelling quality of Pauline's prose.
Words tumbled straight from her mind onto the paper, often without punctuation or organization. Whatever happened to her was subject indiscrimi-
nately to her full enthusiasm or despair, projected in letters as effectively as in
person.

Beautiful one. Charles sends his love he is washing his clothes in the
bath room. I think we have a few things to straighten out, you and I. I am
feeling very low these days and you aren't helping me a bit, I suppose you
as all the rest will say my dear its all your own fault, maybe it is, but the
case remains the same. Possibly I will feel better after I get these off my

chest. In the first place picture this, I am very lonesome, I knew I would be. All I have heard from you is please send me this and that, half a dozen times. I don't mind sending things to help you out, ordinarily I would love to but my patience is a bit worn out, I sit at home and wait for someone to ask me to do this and that. This seems a bit exaggerated. Maybe. But I tried to get you to take things with you and I was right. Don't you want me to send you the fountains? [Probably a set for a dance Doris was doing.] I will give you a list of whys etc.

1. We haven't rose music any more, no idea where
2. You had the scarf
3. Wigs, old ones, in storage, no way to get out
4. [This list continues through six items]
   There is nothing else to ans. being as you haven't said anything else. . . .

This kind of thing went on for years. Pauline's verbal bombardments must have been fairly easy to tune out. Her ups and downs didn't have to be absorbed in all their immediate intensity since they quickly oscillated in the other direction. Nor was Doris insensitive to these effusions. In those days she was capable of passion and expressed it in succinct, almost poetic terms. Writing from Maine in the summer of 1929 to Pauline in Westport, she began,

Darling—
When you went away in the bus it seemed as though you grew heavier and heavier—and the world lighter until you seemed to be the only real thing in a world of illusion. How could one small person be so much more important than anything else? . . . My joy—that you love me and will be my critic and comfort—my pain—that it will probably come to nothing and we will both go down—or probably not as dramatic as that—we'll just peter out—But there will be strength yet awhile.
   See if you can find me a coat. . . .

There were fights. They hurt each other—Doris with her seeming indifference, Pauline with her quick sarcasm—but they always reconciled. Two or three times in their nearly forty years together there were severe ruptures between them, but even then, after shifting and reassembling the pieces of their lives, they settled back into some new symbiosis.
   There continued to be men in Doris' life throughout the period when she

lived most intimately with Pauline, although she had no desire to marry. On-stage during those years, with her red hair and green eyes, she was vibrant, physically stirring, sometimes seraphically beautiful. She naturally attracted admirers, male and female. But the romantic episodes with men were more like brief holidays—weekends in New York or in the country—when she could get away from the arduous studio and theater routine, let her hair down, and forget about her responsibilities. The men who gave her these holidays offered little more than that. Usually they were married, or imma-ture, or impossibly removed from the life to which she was committed. Within the confines of that life, there were few suitable men. The languid, poetic youths to whom Miss Ruth was attracted held little interest for Doris, and most of the others were homosexuals.

In Pauline she found a person whose interests she could share and whose emotions she could engage on a very mundane level. "With you I can be natural, say what I please and what I feel. I'm so sick of concealing," she wrote Pauline in 1924. As a creative, independent, highly gifted woman she probably intimidated men, even accomplished ones, but Pauline had chosen a similar life. She sympathized completely with Doris' goals and was willing to share her hardships to help her achieve them. Their relationship was a kind of marriage. It comfortably expanded to include Charles, who had been their comrade in Denishawn and now helped them found their own dance family.

Charles' role is harder to ascertain, since his personal letters and effects have not been released for study more than ten years after his death. Some things are obvious. With a man as codirector the company immediately showed that it had different intentions and capabilities from the all-female groups of Martha Graham and Mary Wigman. There are many economic and cultural reasons for the dearth of men in dance, especially early modern dance, where the poverty and social stigma made it all but impossible for anyone to follow such a career except people with modest financial needs and egos strong enough to tolerate being outsiders in society. Since few men were attracted to modern dance, it was seen in the public's mind as the province of women. And, since it provided insubstantial financial rewards, it was perceived as an insignificant occupation, to be undertaken only by people who probably wouldn't succeed in more consequential fields.

All dancers knew they would have to struggle. For a long time Doris wrote letters to prospective members of the group explaining her ideals and realistically promising that there would be little else in the way of compensa-

tion besides the satisfaction they would all have in working them out coop-
eratively. New dance took on the fervor of a crusade, and all-female crusades are perceived differently from crusades in which men and women
march together.

In addition, female-centered groups or female soloists inevitably danced
with a limited range and scope. Even when, as was the case with Martha
Graham, they were commenting on large social or moral issues, the projection of ideas through the person of a woman or a group of women gave
them an aspect quite removed from ordinary experience. This may have
been to Graham's advantage in an art sense—her dance *had* to become
metaphorical in order to serve the grandeur of her conceptions.

Humphrey-Weidman was from the beginning a company of males and
females dancing about males and females. The choreographers worked at
times with separate ensembles, as in Doris' *Dances of Women* and Charles'
Dance of Work and *Dance of Sport*, where they wanted to emphasize the
special qualities of each sex. Some of Doris' early large works, like *Water
Study*, were not connected with personal images, and she could use an all-
female group abstractly there. But most of the dances called for no euphemistic representation of roles or slanting of the point of view. Women did
occasionally have to take men's parts in the larger works, but only until sufficiently trained male dancers could replace them. Even when they took more
abstract ideas for inspiration, their dance was intended to be humanistic, directly expressive of people.

As a dancer and family partner, Charles provided a contrast and comple-
ment to Pauline's energy and crackling wit, and to Doris' dynamic, inspiring
persistence. Tall and good looking, he was an excellent foil for Doris' lyrical
strength onstage. Like Shawn, he was interested in reforming the image of
the male dancer, and he gave special classes for men at the studio that attracted several potential dancers. To the day-to-day functioning of the group
he brought an all-important levity. Where Doris was earnest and Pauline
practical, Charles never took things too seriously. A great humorist and the
instigator of a venerable tradition of American dance that capitalizes on the
evanescent, ironic properties of movement, he was loved by comrades, students, and audiences. Not being as possessed by the choreographic art as
Doris was, he often accepted jobs dancing in other people's productions or
choreographing for what Doris considered less than noble branches of the
theater, and the money he made on these assignments helped to underwrite
their joint efforts.

Doris turned thirty-three in the fall of 1928. Pauline was twenty-eight and

Charles was twenty-seven. Besides her actual seniority, Doris' natural leadership qualities, her tenacity, and her nearly fanatical belief in art made her initially, and kept her always, the cornerstone of Humphrey-Weidman.

In many ways, the most representative work of this early period in Doris' work was *Life of the Bee* (1929). Not a lyrical piece or an easy one to look at today, the dance was the first large-scale statement of the social ideas that preoccupied her for most of her career. As early as 1926 she spoke about wanting to do a ballet on the theme of evolution, and when she read a translation of Maurice Maeterlinck's 1901 study of bees as a paradigm of human social activity, she found that it struck many sympathetic chords in her own thinking. Maeterlinck describes the life cycle of domestic bees, with great respect and wonder for the intricate way a bee colony is organized to perpetuate its own race. He speculates about the meaning of evolution, about how such a wonderfully specialized civilization could have developed and where it might fit into a scheme of things suggested by a not yet fully understood Darwinism. Like many writers of natural history at the turn of the century, Maeterlinck spoke of his subject in anthropomorphic terms. He saw the queen—the lone individual in each hive capable of laying eggs and the one whose entire existence serves only that purpose—as "the unique organ of love . . . the mother of the city," a city, indeed, "of virgins." He marveled at "the almost perfect but pitiless society of our hives, where the individual is entirely merged in the republic, and the republic in its turn invariably sacrificed to the abstract and immortal city of the future." The program note that Doris appended to her dance restates this observation in almost identical terms.

> *Life of the Bee* (after Maeterlinck)
> In the Holy of Holies of the palace, the workers dance and beat their wings around the cradle of the adolescent princess who awaits her hour wrapped in a kind of shroud, motionless and pale, innocent alike that her kingdom has yet to be wrested from pretenders close by, and that the pitiless duty of the hive decrees the sacrifice of the individual at last to the immortality of the republic.

Like Ruth St. Denis and Martha Graham, Doris often found her dances in a literary source, but unlike them she did not look for legends or rituals to translate to the stage. (*The Shakers* was an exception that at times she regretted.) While the other two choreographers put stories into dance form in

order to illuminate for the audience some special qualities in their subjects—
the moral dilemmas of Graham's later heroines, for instance, or the spiritual
purity of St. Denis'—and not incidentally to create starring roles for themselves, Doris used stories as a point of departure, a means of illustrating a
larger theme. She wanted her audience to learn, not just to enjoy or admire.
St. Denis' characters represented the audience-everyman raised to a more
beautiful, purer, or more sensual level, a sublimation of everyday existence.
Doris portrayed fictional characters as ordinary, as substitutes for ourselves;
archetypes, universals, the general, not the particular.

This view is related to her interest in group choreography. Perhaps only an
artist with such deeply democratic instincts could have developed the ensemble to so high a level of sensitivity and expressiveness. She had the ability
to submerge her personal concerns into a larger idea, to see her work in
philosophical metaphors. So when Maeterlinck spoke of the evolution of
group society, she responded; this was the work and the aspiration in which
she too was engaged:

> In proportion as a society organises itself and rises in the scale, so does a
> shrinkage enter the private life of each one of its members.

> Transition is called for from a precarious, egotistic and incomplete life to a
> life that shall be fraternal, a little more certain, a little more happy.

> The hour of the great annual sacrifice to the genius of the race . . . of the
> swarm; when we find a whole people, who have attained the topmost
> pinnacle of prosperity and power, suddenly abandoning to the generation
> to come their wealth and their palaces, their homes and the fruits of their
> labour; themselves content to encounter the hardships and the perils of a
> new and distant country. This act, be it conscious or not, undoubtedly sur-
> passes the limits of human morality.

Doris went about composing the dance by studying the anatomy and
physical habits of bees and then devising movement that would support her
theme. Deciding that "the wings were the center of bee activity," she came
up with a symmetrical, wide body attitude for the ensemble, with motion restricted mainly to the arms fanning back and forth. For the first part of the
dance she kept the floor plan cellular and frontal, as the group clustered
around the figure of the unborn queen lying on the floor. Ringing the inert
form in two rows, they moved from the inner to the outer circle in alternation, approximating the method by which bees warm the inside of the hive,
and themselves, by taking turns at the center.

The second part of the dance, its dramatic core, was the duet between the young queen and her rival. Initially these were not named characters, and Doris adhered to Maeterlinck's account, in which the young queen is born *after* the departure of the old queen with part of the hive in a swarm, and is challenged by an intruder from outside or by potential queens born inside the hive at the time of the reorganization. Curiously, reports by dancers Eleanor King and José Limón have it that the winner of the battle was the challenger, then played by Doris, who was older than her rival Cleo Atheneos. "The bees don't interest themselves in personality," Doris told an interviewer in 1931. "One Queen is as good as another as long as she is regal." In later versions, it was the defender who triumphed. But not until she was reworking the dance in 1941 did Doris actually designate a Young and an Old Queen. The idea of a fierce physical combat between two women, however, had been in her mind from the beginning. She had fought one with Ruth St. Denis, in fact, playing the Queen of the Underworld whom St. Denis defeated to rescue her captive lover in *Ishtar of the Seven Gates* (1923).

But she insisted that "the theme is never of primary importance except as inspiration. Literary drama must always yield to what I call motion-drama. . . . Form is much but feeling is much more." In *Life of the Bee*, this motion-drama was carried by the vibrating, pulsating, organized restlessness of the group as they brought their queen to life, watched her struggle with the challenger, and then celebrated the victor before leaving the hive. The successive dispersals and reconstituting of the group into large enclosing formations, tight spectator masses, and smaller contrapuntal units, rows, and lines anticipating their flight show Doris' incipient mastery of group patterns in space. *Bee* was choreographed in silence and performed to an offstage chorus engineered by Pauline. The company members who were not in the dance hummed, buzzed, and hissed through combs and tissue paper to accompany the action.

Life of the Bee went through several additional changes. For a revival at the Juilliard School in 1955, Doris replaced the improvisatory sound effects with Paul Hindemith's Kammermusik no. 1; she had also tried a score by Jerome Moross for some performances in August 1935. At Juilliard the role of the Old Queen (the challenger) was danced by both Joyce Trisler and Patricia Christopher; Trisler choreographed her own solo. Most versions of the dance have been performed by all-female casts, but for some repertory classes, Doris put men in the three central group roles, listing them on the program as Drones. This departed considerably from the structure and functions of the bee community as described by Maeterlinck, but it lent a different dramatic tone to the dance.

Doris believed that the group was the instrument for creating a truly new dance form, and she meant this in more than a political sense. In a 1929 program note she said this about the ensemble, "Through the new conception of significance in the ensemble which was developed during the last ten years, the dance promises to come to its full stature, just as music flowered through the symphony." And in 1931 she told an interviewer: "The solo dancer is too much herself. Her dancing is too much limited by size, by shape, by the color of hair and eyes. It is too characteristic and too limited to be the great dance of tomorrow. In the ensemble the audience receives only the true impressions of movement, design, accent." She underestimated how much the size, shape, color of hair and eyes—the dancer's personality in fact—meant to the audience. She had seen the effect of real glamour on the audience in the hands of a master, Ruth St. Denis. She had also seen audiences fall for quantities of fake glamour in Denishawn and in vaudeville. Temperamentally she was not a star, but she also believed that the whole concept of star quality was unacceptable.

For her the group was not just an extension of the movement she found in herself. Nevertheless, she made many solos in the early years, some of them related to larger works, as if she were testing different notions on the same train of thought. José Limón noted in his unpublished autobiography a relationship between *Life of the Bee* and an insectlike solo she did several months later, *Descent into a Dangerous Place.* Sometimes it was easier to make solo studies of an idea and to use them in the repertory for a while. *Speed* (1929), described by Eleanor King as being done almost entirely in place, with pistonlike movement and exciting balances, was a dance that King thought went against Doris' lyrical quality but it extended the vocabulary.

The audience understandably wanted to see the company leaders in solo numbers, and until larger forms evolved, Doris complied. By the end of the 1920s a very substantial audience for solo dancing had been created by Ruth St. Denis and other performers. Many of them used the conventions of pantomime and of Oriental/Indian character dancing to create the illusion of being surrounded by exotic scenery or being in dialogue with various invisible characters. For instance, the highly acclaimed Japanese recitalist Michio

Descent into a Dangerous Place. Photo by Edward Moeller. (Dance Collection, NYPL)

Ito, who created "dance poems" to well-known coloristic compositions of Albeniz, Debussy, and Griffes, showed a Greek Warrior dance at the Civic Repertory Theater, New York, in 1928 that his biographer describes as follows: "A warrior from an ancient vase fights his invisible enemy with an imaginary spear, on foot or mounted on an invisible steed, and finally clashes his invisible weapon against his invisible shield in ringing triumph." Ito's pupil Angna Enters danced debutantes at balls, girls waiting for their lovers in crowded parks, and other contemporary portraits, as well as all manner of exotics. In her 1933 full-length work *Pagan Greece,* she played fourteen mythological characters.

After leaving Denishawn, Doris, Charles, and Martha Graham all went through periods of transition, ridding themselves of their exotic past while retaining the audience appeal of the salon tradition. In 1928 and 1929 Charles contributed a *Pierrot* solo and a *Japanese Actor,* a Singhalese dance, contrasting portraits of Savonarola and St. Francis, both to Satie, and three other character solos, in addition to his duets and larger ensemble works. Martha Graham's concerts between 1926 and 1928 were laced with solos to Debussy and Scriabin, Chinese and Mediterranean sketches, many with precious French titles. But all three of them, as well as Helen Tamiris, who gave her first solo concert in 1927, were redefining the sphere of the solo dance to bring it more in line with the modern needs they all felt. They didn't want to portray characters and act out stories so much as to translate moods and symbolic states into direct physical action, uncolored by recognizable ethnic attitudes or dance styles. Eventually larger stage forms were needed, and the solo was subsumed into the group work or dance-drama, but the solo dance form endures. Nearly all American modern choreographers start by experimenting on themselves with solos; it seems the most expedient way to define their own particular styles.

Two solos by Doris survive from this period—miraculously—on film. They may have been taken with a movie camera given to her by the students for Christmas 1928. Like all home movies, the film is crude—without sound, the indoor sequences too dark, and the continuity interrupted while the operator rewound the film or adjusted the shot. Early in 1931 Horace Humphrey was giving his daughter some pointers about how to improvise better lighting for taking movies; she had sent him prints of some of her efforts, possibly including the film discussed here. It has been possible to date the film around 1929 or 1930 and, from other clues, to guess at its subject. The first section, shot in a studio with inadequate lighting, seems the most complete choreo-

graphically and is probably one or both of the solos Doris did to Dane Rudhyar's The Call and Breath of Fire. Then Doris and two girls, probably Dorothy Lathrop and Katherine Manning, are shown in some classroom exercises
involving running and jumping. This section was filmed outdoors in someone's garden, as was the last part of the footage, a waltz solo which may be
part of her *Quasi-Waltz* to Scriabin.

The Rudhyar solos were choreographed in mid- to late-1929. From a suite
of fifteen tone-poems for piano in three cycles, *The Call* opened the first cycle
and *Breath of Fire* ended it. Doris and Charles also cochoreographed *Salutation to the Depths,* the last piece in the second cycle. Doris often performed
the solos as a set, apart from the duet, and she appended the following program note to both solos: "The Dissonant Power of Rudhyar's music fitly expresses the Call to a new vision, which is followed by a shriving of the old
body and old ideas through the purification of fire." This inscription expresses
much of what Doris was feeling about her work, or what she hoped her
work could bring to the dance as a whole. If the material on the film is the
Rudhyar dance, it bore very much the same relationship to its argument as
Martha Graham's *Lamentation,* choreographed in 1930, had to its emotional
title. That is, neither dance describes anything literally or requires the dancer
to "interpret" an idea, but each finds inner tensions, impulses, and spatial necessities analagous to its conceptual theme.

Doris stands facing the camera with her arms laced tightly across the body
at shoulder height. She lets her right arm continue its sideward direction until
it pulls her upper body with it. At a certain point, the elbow of the same arm
starts to pull her back the other way. This alternation continues, the length of
the arc growing each time, until, when she is almost off balance, the cross-
over pull leads her into a spiral turn. She runs a few steps across the space,
then pivots and runs back the other way. The space between pivots de-
creases until she is pivoting on every step. This simple device draws your attention to the turn, and just when it seems she will have to go into a spin,
she is standing still facing the camera. She lifts her arms up to the sides, flut-
tering her hands with a feeling of invocation.

She repeats the first theme, but instead of ending in pivot runs, she suddenly leaps high across the space and lands on her back on the floor in a
twisted position with her arms across her chest. Now she does the arm-
pulling phrase with which she started, but on the floor her legs aren't
needed to stabilize her, and the whole body twists back and forth in opposition to the abrupt, slashing pull of the arms. Possibly she rises from the floor

with a spiral motion, though the film is too dark at this point to see the transition. There is another running and leaping section. When she spirals back to the floor, she is lying with her side to the camera, her back arched off the floor and her arms open above her head. With increasingly percussive direction changes, she swings her upper body back and forth, then rises by arching her back and pressing up from her thighs and pelvis. From this lift she takes a few steps in the same direction, her head thrown back, one arm across her chest and the other flung back, as if to receive some great illumination. The film ends with her in the same position with which it began, arms crossed, facing front.

Many of the transition points in this film take place in the dark, so it isn't possible to tell if the camera continues operating or if there are cuts and restarts during which part of the dance is lost. But from what is visible, we can see that the dance is built of contrasts—between a straight and a twisted body, between pure directional progress and circular or spiral motion. Every movement element might conceivably lead to any other; both the spiral and the straight path are implied in the moments of stasis, and once having chosen one alternative she builds organically, letting her whole body follow a small initiation until it attains a full and irreversible statement. The movement impulse grows to where the spiral must flare out or the twist must narrow into a straight line.

This dance went against accepted conventions of what a solo dance ought to be. The performer does not try to gain the audience's sympathy by representing some play of her emotions, or tell a story, or describe any persons who aren't there. She is obviously dancing about feelings, but the feelings aren't totally internalized; whatever is happening happens both *to* the dancer and *for* the audience. This state of simultaneous engagement and detachment, of subjective objectivity, was a key element of the new art form and served Doris for her whole career. The responsive stirrings in the nervous system of the audience member have little to do with rational decoding, but link up with associative memories and thoughts to produce an overriding image in the viewer, often a highly personal one. Leading the audience with a title or a program note but not coercing him with literal meaning, the dancer aims for a certain transparency; we are to see the dance through her, not see her through the dance.

The last part of the film's footage contains Doris' waltz solo which is even more of a "pure dance" than the Rudhyar, having no philosophical pretext or image from nature to lead us beyond our immediate kinesthetic perceptions. Instead of admiring the harmony or noble emotion, as we might in an Isadora Duncan solo, which this somewhat resembles, we are drawn to make this rhythm our own, to dance it with Doris, not merely to be satisfied watching her dance it. Her body is joyfully relaxed, her placement natural, but she has lost the androgynous, spritelike spontaneity she had in *Hoop Dance* and *Scarf Dance*. She has found the basic body elements that are to become the core of her style—the swing with its release and recapture of weight, the natural rhythm based on breathing, the continuity of line as the movement impulse travels successively through the body—and she is playing with ways to control them: design, dynamics, and shape.

The dance is based on two kinds of action: the swing and the idea of a twisted versus an open shape. Developing and combining these ideas, focusing them in different parts of the body, she runs and skips, sways and turns, giving an impression of abandon by carefully planned effects. We first see her in a narrow, slightly concave pose, one arm drooping across the body and the other crooked rather affectedly toward her face. She uses this arm to initiate a swing across the body that grows into a theme of arms tightly twisting around the body and unwinding to an open and eventually far-reaching backward stretch. The other theme begins with a little leap forward that grows into a running, leaping circle in which the momentum is reinitiated by a forward thrust of the pelvis. The dance constantly accelerates and decelerates as she gains momentum, then indulgently allows the thrust to spread through the body. The energy never entirely spends itself; just as the movement begins to trickle out of the flung fingers or to wrap the center body into containment, another impulse somewhere else starts a new motif into action. Even without sound, we can see the dance is singing.

Doris was powerfully stirred by natural images, particularly at this time, when she was looking for movement. This was not unusual; both St. Denis and Duncan studied the rhythms and forms in nature and tried to fuse their own action with the larger cycles of the earth. Once Doris had converted this energy into a formal process—a system of working the body—she could dance directly about human beings; but while she was developing the technique, she wanted more primal sources. The lyrical, natural line had always been a characteristic of her own dancing, and she transferred this, in a depersonalized way, to the group in *Water Study*. This work, danced in silence, is still one of the most stunning achievements in abstract dance. It had its premiere in October 1928 at the first concert of Humphrey-Weidman as an independent group.

Unlike its immediate predecessor, *Color Harmony*, *Water Study* was not conceived at all cerebrally. Doris worked directly from her own affinity to an elemental flow. "Nature moves in succession," she noted on a scrap of paper, "usually in an unfolding succession to a climax, and a more sudden succession to cessation or death. So all natural movement must follow that law of nature—of which water is the best example to follow as it most nearly approximates the capacity of our rhythm and phrase length." From this observation she developed a dance and a technique.

Doris applied a very pragmatic and even obvious method to the problem of creating dance movement. She would take a basic idea—usually a movement motif or an image—and knead it into different forms by making it bigger or smaller, more symmetrical or asymmetrical, by interrupting or distorting its natural sequence. She would slow down or speed up the length of the phrase, make the phrase fill out identical measures of time in different proportions, change the dynamics drastically or gradually. She would turn a shape—a path, a gesture—upside down, stretch it, condense it, exaggerate it, face it in a different direction or shift it to another part of the body. Always she thought in terms of movement sequence, not frozen pictures, and always—at this stage—the movement sequence was structured out of its own necessity, not boxed into a form dictated by preexisting music. The sources of this movement were the animating life forces of the body itself—breath, tension and relaxation, balance and imbalance, stasis and flow. These forces were not immutable to her. She understood them as variable, rich, in constant play with each other, a yin/yang oscillation over which the individual has considerable control. By rebalancing and counterposing these forces, the dancer can create states of great suspense, risk, and calm. Doris thought this was the process of life and also—intensified—the process of dance.

At about the time she was making *Water Study* she sketched some experiments with forces of nature in her notebook. She probably used them to generate improvisational studies in the studio. What is interesting about them is how far she searched for the implications of her idea, where another person would have been satisfied with more commonplace and one-dimensional observations.

Ocean roll . . . two lines face two lines. Typhoon.
Coming toward each other and splash very high.
a pebble in a pond.
two pebbles—quite a distance apart—the ripples meet and splash

or one overcomes the other if one pebble is heavier than the other
whirlpool (after the typhoon)
a mountain stream falling—a whirlpool on a curve
a heavy weight crushing a fragile substance
a light, persistent erosion wears away a heavy substance
a weight crushing a growing or dynamic substance
(action depends on size and weight of each)

While the movement vocabulary in *Water Study* is simple, almost primal, the form of the dance is highly selective. We are not merely lulled by wave motion but drawn into crescendos and subsidences of excitement that manifest themselves in changing appearances, both of the dancers' bodies and of the evolving form of the stage space. That the development is organic does not mean that it lacks subtlety or range.

Three main types of water motion are suggested: the swell and draw of the tide, the cumulative force and burst of the waves, and the surging subsurface flow of flat calm. These are perceived most obviously in the rhythmic phrasing. The rise and fall of breath, attenuated or condensed, determines the time it will take to complete each sequence of movements. Performed in silence, the dance breathes of its own accord. Not only does each dancer fill out her own movement phrase with her breath, but each one moves in acute sensitivity to the rise and fall of her neighbor. Before a movement spends itself, the next one has begun. In this way each individual contributes to the continuity of the line. The overall motion fluctuates but never stops. Even when all the dancers are doing the same movements, there is no metric unison. Each dancer starts and ends according to her own sense of the right moment, contributing with her momentum to the total drive. The phrase-length is understood by all. When Doris was making the dance she used to walk up and down humming the opening rhythm to establish it for the dancers. *Water Study* is not improvisational, but it must be spontaneously created by the dancers at each performance.

The typical phrase for *Water Study* begins with a nearly neutral flow, intensifies and accelerates to a natural climax, which often is prolonged with a suspension of breath, then subsides back to neutrality again. If it were diagrammed, the energy flow would make a wave shape, the dynamic opposite of the release and gathering together of energy that constitute a swing, which would be drawn as an undercurve. If we picture the energy flow of *Water Study* as an amassing and spilling out of force, we find that pattern replicated on several other levels in the dance. As the dancers link into the group, they add their movement to the ensemble. The choral effect almost always builds to its maximum strength—where all the members of the group are in motion—just at the climax of the collective thrust. Those who began earliest sustain the peak until the last ones catch up. Only after this massed high point has been reached do the individual dancers begin to drop away. This gives the dance in its climactic moments a cumulative power quite unlike the effect of fifteen women dancing in unison on the same beat.

This basically musical way of composing is analagous to adding instruments in a musical score when you want to increase the power, subtracting them when the tone dissipates. Doris had the further resource of space, and she used it in a similar way, so that in *Water Study* the rhythm begins very slowly and expansively, the rising and sinking of the dancers from a curled-up position occurring over a long interval with just enough overlap to keep the energy line from dying out. The women are spread out in the performing space so that the audience can see each one separately. Later the impulses overlap more closely, with the forward-thrusting urgency of a wave, and the dancers gather into two facing lines and alternately rush forward and throw themselves into a jump and a sideways fall back to the floor, making a climactic explosion in the center of the stage. Both the energy and the spatial configuration of the clustered dancers have condensed to a point where they must burst out. Later the shape and the rhythm of the dance spread out again into calmness.

Over and over, in the individual action and in the group patterns, we see the theme of cresting and subsiding. Running along a diagonal, the women cluster together, turn with one inhalation, and run the other way. Half the women in a leaping group fall to the floor and are pulled to their feet by the others. The explosive leaps develop out of the initial rising/folding-forward motif on the floor. At the top of the leap the body is fully extended, even flung into a backward curve. The folding inward, always on the expelled portion of the phrase, takes the form of a curving over to pull someone else up from the floor, or a crawling forward on the knees with the body curling toward the floor, or even a somersault.

We sense the overall shape of the dance from beginning to end as a rising, cresting, flattening curve as well. The inert, breathing bodies on the floor at the start progress into fuller and more complex activity, then return to their passive state. There are two focal points in the dance: the first, at the initial series of high jumps in the center, is the most intense release of long pent-up energies; the second is a compositionally more detailed, more artful working of the same impulse. In visual and rhythmic counterpoint, the group divides, with five women running in a curve upstage while the others sink to their knees and describe a slow circle with their upper bodies bending toward the floor. The five women leap into the air one by one, taking on increasingly spiral shapes, from the first woman, who jumps almost straight up, to the last, who falls twisting to the floor and immediately spirals up again.

The compositional inevitability of *Water Study* isn't allowed to become oppressive. For one thing, the dance is very short, only about eleven minutes. The means are limited enough for the dance to make a complete and satisfying statement in this time. Doris was able to find enough alternative ways of stating her theme so that it didn't become repetitious. She had an instinct for irregularity, when and how to break the forms she was constructing. In *Water Study* the dancers make slight variations in interval as they take their cues for change, imitating the unevenness within overall pattern that prevails in nature. Doris' gift for rhythmic surprise—for syncopation, counterpoint, and variation—continued to serve her when she worked again with conventional accompaniment.

Perfect as it is, *Water Study* could not be considered a full-blown choreographic statement. It served, as its title said, as an exploration of certain basic tools. Most of all it served the group. Doris' growing skill with the ensemble was persuading her that this was her true medium, not solo dancing. "I'm perfectly convinced that the group is the flowering of the dance," she wrote in the fall of 1928, "but I know I'm laying up a lot of misery for myself in depending on people for everything—not only for the art product but for a living and for reputation—and for personal satisfaction too. However there's only one way to go and that's *on*." *Water Study* and the other works of these embryonic years had a galvanizing effect on the dancers as well. Eleanor King describes *Water Study* as "the most satisfying of all Humphrey works to perform," and Jane Sherman wrote that "The work with Doris and Charles [between 1928 and 1930] was the most fulfilling dance experience of my life."

Sherman, with several other Denishawn dancers, defected after the Follies tour to become the nucleus of the Humphrey-Weidman group. Other young people were drawn to the novel group as its concerts got talked about;

some had seen Doris or Charles with Denishawn and were attracted to study with these impressive stage personalities. José Limón arrived during the formative years, but exactly when is hard to determine. The longstanding principal dancer and eventual inheritor of the Humphrey-Weidman succession had come to New York from Los Angeles with ambitions as a painter but had grown dissatisfied with his own talent. While he was drifting, he saw the great German modern dancer Harald Kreutzberg and made an immediate identification. His roommates at the time, Perkins Harnley and Don Forbes, had known Charles in Lincoln, Nebraska, and advised José to look into the new classes. Limón has variously dated this as occurring "late in the year 1928," or on March 13, 1930, or after a Sunday performance at the New Yorker Theater, where Kreutzberg and his partner danced a Chopin polonaise and "I knew with a shocking suddenness that I had not been alive, or rather that I had not yet been born."* His official debut with the company took place in the Norman Bel Geddes production of *Lysistrata* in Philadelphia, April 28, 1930, but he was listed on a Humphrey-Weidman Concert Group program, as Jose Lemon, on April 7, 1929, at the Guild Theater in New York. He appeared as one of four male dancers in Charles' *Rhythmic Dances of Java.* Having had no prior training as a dancer, José was regarded warily at first. He obviously had great sex appeal and stage power, but no control or discipline. But he quickly overcame his late start and by 1931 was an indispensable member of the company.

In present-day terms it was hardly a company and in fact was not billed as one until the spring of 1939. The first season (October 1928) the group was billed as "Doris Humphrey with Charles Weidman and their Student Concert Group." The word *student* was dropped the following spring, and from early 1930 Charles shared equal billing with Doris. As a concert group, of course, the dancers received no salaries. They were paid by the performance or went on a weekly payroll when working in outside productions. Their rewards were intangible, but important.

First, they believed they were forging a new art form, one that was to speak for Americans as no art dance in the past had ever done. Although they devoted themselves exclusively to Doris and Charles except when commercial productions offered them a way to earn money, they knew they

*Kreutzberg's first U.S. concerts with Yvonne Georgi did open with a Chopin polonaise, but they took place at the Hudson, Fulton, and Gallo theaters between January 29 and February 10, 1929. José's conversion probably took place during this time, and he probably began classes within the next few weeks, not the morning after the concert as his publicity blurbs dramatically related.

were part of a resurgence in the theater arts. In the euphoric times that followed World War I, artists understood conclusively that the nineteenth century was over, and that to take up the serious business of art again they
would have to deal with different realities, with the effects of new national
alignments, with worldwide technological advances, with urbanization, and
with the individual's newly awakened sense of himself in relation to an expanding and intrusive universe.

   In his book *The Fervent Years* Harold Clurman described the artist's ma-
laise, his seeking for a serious response to the postwar world, in the years
prior to the founding of the Group Theatre in 1931. More than serious
themes, Clurman felt what was needed was engagement. After working for
several years with the Theatre Guild, which produced important plays in
New York, he felt "that they [the Guild] had no blood relationship with the
plays they dealt in. They set the plays out in the show window for as many
customers as possible to buy. They didn't want to say anything through
plays, and plays said nothing to them, except that they were amusing in a
graceful way, or, if they were tragic plays, that they were 'art.' And art was a
good thing." The young actors and playwrights who began working with
Clurman and his associates, Lee Strasberg and Cheryl Crawford, were looking for something more, even more than the personal outcry of a Eugene
O'Neill or the dizzying iconoclasm of the new composers. "In our belief,"
Clurman wrote, "unless the actor in some way shared the playwright's impulse, the result on the stage always remained somewhat mechanical." The
Group adopted the Stanislavsky system of training as a way to "make the actor face each of the play's situations spontaneously—that is, without the
support of the play's actual lines, which often serve merely to disguise from
himself his own lack of reaction to the basic matter of the play." The modern
dancers felt much the same way about their work in relation to the stilted,
disaffected idioms of the ballet and Denishawn aestheticism, and they, too,
formed ensembles to learn new ways to go about it. That there were elements of socialism in this way of working was initially a great asset.

   Doris even more than the other new choreographers needed the individual voice of each dancer. She was aware of the contradiction in asking them
"to move and think regardless of me or anyone else" and at the same time
to be "acutely aware of each other, so that they may move in a common
rhythm." But this duality not only became one of the strengths of her choreography, it gave the members of the group the feeling of participation. Doris
posted reading lists, asked the dancers to make contact with the same

sources she was using, so that they would understand what they were dancing about, not merely parrot some steps they were shown. From the beginning she instituted Creative Nights where students and group members showed their own compositions. Her idea was to have the young dancer "show me what you want to do and I'll tell you if you're doing it and how to go at it if you're not." This was to be her practice in composition classes throughout her life and, unofficially, with many professional colleagues who came to her for help with their choreography. Doris was not threatened by the presence of creative talent around her; she encouraged it even when it might lead to the loss of her best dancers. Ernestine Stodelle saw the Little Group, which she formed with Eleanor King, Letitia Ide, and José Limón in 1931, as an opportunity to explore "the rich creative potential of Doris Humphrey's technique."

Doris' next big project was a dance about movement itself. *Drama of Motion* had neither music nor literary precedent nor imagery from nature. The dance was lost shortly after its creation, and the only records we have of it are written ones. According to dance critic John Martin, "it was the first successful approach to the dance in what might be called a symphonic as opposed to a theatric form, treating its themes and their development more after the manner of a musician than of a dramatist." By putting together several accounts of the dance, we may get an idea of the way Doris handled a concept of this scale.

"A work done entirely without music, in sonata style, with its three movements, an opening, formal Andante; a Largo in the middle; and a spirited Finale," "it has three contrasting qualities expressed both in movement and design. The first is slow and sustained, moving with a warm strength in its curving flow. The intricate patterns weave in and out only for the purpose of pleasing the eye with an ever-changing series of lines and spaces." "The first division, for the Ensemble, was a slow and winding processional, unfolding, amplifying, varying a clear design, respacing, recurving it as in variations upon a theme. The patterning, the rhythming, invited the eye, held fast imagination." "The opening Processional was a slow-motion frieze designed for trios, entering, crossing the stage, then exiting in unison, the arms of the dancers on the outside rising in a curve to come to rest on the shoulders of the one in between, like a resolving chord in music. Letitia, Katherine [Manning] and I [King] were the opening trio. In slow motion I rose from kneeling between them, my circling arms opened their connected arms, like a gate.

Each trio had a variation so there was a continuous interest in the design, which was what this part was all about. The concentration required to balance on the toes, body arched backward, head back, eyes following one arm stretched upward to infinity, without any musical support, was prodigious."

Doris danced alone in the second section's Transition and Interlude, "introduced by a brief dance which modulates from the slow movement of the first part to the sprightly jigging of the second." "A transitional division, mainly for Miss Humphrey, began in the lines and rhythm of the slow movement; gradually modulated them into more broken motions, sharper accents, quicker pace." "This part is all sharp, surprising accents and odd quirks and jerks, with the solo keeping a remnant of the first movement through it all." "She was joined by the three lightest, swiftest dancers—Sylvia [Manning], Dorothy [Lathrop], and Evelyn [Fields]—for a study in contrasts."

In the Conclusion, "the ensemble returned, now all in black. José, the one male, appeared with us." "The third movement opens with a thundering rush of power through the bodies of the entire group. This powerful accent is reiterated in different ways until a contrasting delicate quality emerges. Rudely the first theme returns and sweeps up the softer group, bursting beyond the limits of the stage in its crude gusto." "From opposite sides, in two groups we lunged toward each other in syncopated antiphonal rhythms, eventually joining into one black mass, making a sweep of the stage, swirling to a domino fall. This final section was marked by stamping foot accents and by great rushes of power."

Critic H. T. Parker appreciated the compositional excellence of the work but voiced a serious reservation. He zeroed in on the area where Doris would most often be faulted, even up to the present time, by some of her critics. Parker called *Drama of Motion* "a considered prose rather than a glowing poetry. Nor, for the time, can she or the Ensemble strike from her abstractions the vitalizing spark that is Thrill." Many things were more important to Doris at this time than Thrill, and dancers and audiences were certainly exhilarated by the mass power she was developing in the group.

On the same program with the *Drama of Motion, Salutation to the Depths,* and *Breath of Fire* premieres (Maxine Elliott's Theater, January 6, 1930) she and Charles did the first version of the duet that became the center of *La Valse,* to the mounting decadence of Ravel's music. That work did not reach its complete form until it was performed with full orchestra the following summer, at Robin Hood Dell in Philadelphia, and Lewisohn Stadium in

New York. Even then it was misunderstood by some of the dancers, for whom it was not modern enough. They had trouble learning waltzes with variations after the rigorous abstraction of the pieces immediately preceding it.

Doris' idea was satirical; the waltzing couples work themselves up into a sort of orgy, then subside into formlessness. According to King: "The couples break away, elbows linked, whirling themselves to the floor. Through the final maelstrom, Doris and Charles, pillars of society, walk coming forward . . . suggesting poles of respectability as against society's disintegrative sensuality as an aftermath of war." In José Limón's description of the ending, "The two extricated themselves, just in time, from the orgiastic chaos which threatened to engulf them, and recovered their aristocratic 'hauteur' as the curtain fell."

La Valse sounds like some of the expressionistic dances that were coming out of Germany at around that time. Kurt Jooss' great social statements, *The Green Table, The Big City,* and others, did not surface in Europe until a year or two later, but descriptions of his earlier work, as well as the satirical dances of Mary Wigman, Rudolf Laban, Harald Kreutzberg, and others, were well known to American dancers. Doris had also been impressed with Fritz Lang's expressionistic movie *Metropolis* (1927), which dealt with the subversion of a society by the forces of mechanization. But she was less interested in pursuing social messages at this time than in translating into human terms the psycho-physical principles she had been discovering in her more abstract works.

Two great ideas possessed her from this time onward. One was the Nietzschean duality of the Apollonian and Dionysian impulses. The other was the voluntary power of the artist to control and transfigure these impulses. When working on a Scriabin Etude (*Pathetic Study*) for herself and Charles in 1928, she spoke of "the joy arising from the control of one's powers . . . that joy of the release of the spirit and that release only art can give you." And in a letter to Pauline while vacationing in 1929 she meditated on the meaning of this role she had undertaken.

> Any artist's struggle is necessary to make the art live—peace and comfort and money are death to art. It's a great paradox isn't it—probably the greatest desire one has is for that satisfied rest that comes after the successful effort. Yet that very peace if too much prolonged, kills the next art-child. So all the emotions drive one to something that the mind knows is self-destructive—and yet one must do it . . . we must struggle toward rest and security—knowing we must never get there—on pain of death.

This kind of contradiction always fascinated Doris, but playing with such concepts meant more than exercise for her mind; they could suggest movement to her, and form. The constructs of philosophy seemed as natural a process as the play of waves and tide, and the Apollonian-Dionysian dialectic was especially suggestive of action. Nothing could have been more expressive of that perpetual struggle than the subject that now came to hand.

The Shakers were a sect of Utopian Christians founded in the eighteenth century in England by Mother Ann Lee, who was thought to be a reincarnation of Jesus Christ. Its practitioners came to America in the late 1700s and built a series of small communities from New England to the Midwest. Edward Deming Andrews, the principal scholar of American Shakerism, has described its religious tenets and practice in an article and several books published after 1940, confirming Doris' earlier research and authenticating the materials on which she drew. The Shakers believed that man was essentially the victim of his own carnal desires. He could attain union with God only through denial of these desires—that is, through a strictly celibate and sexually segregated life. Industrious and simple, the Shakers lived communally, producing most of their food, clothing, and furnishings, and taking no part in the social life of neighboring communities. Doris was attracted by what Andrews called the Shakers' "exalted worship," a service that included singing, speaking in tongues, and ecstatic dancing as a testament of their "war between flesh and spirit. . . . The effect of such opposition of forces was to imbue the exercises of worship with a quality of tension, unpredictability, and meanings partly veiled. The dance was a virginal expression, but not without dynamic physical character," says Andrews.

Many other things about the Shakers drew Doris' sympathy: their communal life, so self-sufficient and so removed from worldly involvement; the equal status of the sexes within that society, allowing for women as well as men to become its spiritual leaders; and the almost sensual beauty of Shaker artifacts, unadorned, functional, and true to the natural materials of which they were made. Never having "seen or consulted with a real Shaker," Doris reconstituted some of the more formal Shaker dances from published descriptions and lithographs, weaving them into a choreographic structure resembling a Shaker service. There was even precedent for this. Although the Shakers were a closed society, they depended on converts to perpetuate the sect, and they invited members of the public to attend their services, so there was often an element of display in this extremely personal worship.

Reading the texts and music of the Shaker hymns, one cannot help but be struck by the physicality of the images. Not only did the Shakers extol God with singing and dancing, they seemed to express their whole spiritual relationship in action. Since their religion was the one pervasive force in their lives, they connected daily tasks with the godly presence; God, or Mother (Ann), was an almost visible participant in their lives, and they felt closest to this being when dancing or "laboring" the most strenuously. In their dances they simulated a state of semiconsciousness in order to set themselves free, to come as close as a human being can to being supernatural, to leaving the earth, to flying. They speak also of wanting to be pressed or bowed down

The Shakers. First version, with an all-female cast in bare feet. Collection of Charles H. Woodford

closer to the earth, the more humbly to feel Mother's love and to experience the eventual release even more ecstatically. One song, full of dotted rhythms, many melodic jumps of fourths, fifths, and more, and a tonal range of an octave and a half, tells much about the connection between the mundane and the spiritual:

> Who will bow and bend like a willow,
> Who will turn and twist and reel
> In the gale of simple freedom,
> From the bower of union flowing.
> Who will drink the wine of power,
> Dropping down like a shower,
> Pride and bondage all forgetting.
> Mother's wine is freely working.
> Oh ho! I will have it,
> I will bow and bend to get it,
> I'll be reeling, turning, twisting.
> Shake out all the starch and stiff'ning!

Above all, it was the conflict inherent in Shaker belief and observance that Doris worked with. In addition to the lines and circles, the patterns and rhythms of the dances themselves, there were many symbolic gestures that she drew upon, such as a single-file, tight step with heads bowed that represented walking the straight and narrow path. And she found in their "shaking" dance—a kind of hopping shuffle with the hands repeatedly thrown forward and down—a pointed reference to the earth and its loathsomeness. To this she opposed the openhanded, palms-up gesture through which the Shakers symbolically received God's grace. The earth and the air were poles of attraction for the dancer as well as the religious penitent, and Doris built one set of the movement themes for the dance on this polarity, enlarging and extending original motifs into powerful stamping and jumping group dances. She was also interested in the duality of balance and imbalance, which had a definite counterpart in Shaker thought and action. Like the Shakers, Doris loved physical harmony and proportion, yet found in the disturbance of harmony a vitalizing contrast. Another Shaker song celebrates this disorder:

> Why I wonder you don't laugh a little . . .
> Laugh a little and laugh a little,

Why I wonder you ain't all reeling.
Backwards, forwards, sideways and downward.
Why I wonder you can go so straight
And keep such a slick and curious shape,
For of Mother's wine I've got a small portion
And it sets me into a stagg'ring motion
Well, well, I'm willing to stagger,
Stagger, stagger away from bondage.
Well, well, I'm willing to reel,
Reel, reel, reel into freedom.

Most of the movement in *The Shakers* can be identified as belonging to one of these two dualities: earth and heaven or balance and imbalance. Although it is more devised-looking than *Water Study*, the movement is as interwoven and changes with as much organic progression. The dance is very brief, less than ten minutes, and is set as a distillation of Shaker themes in the form of a condensed visionary service. The stage space throughout the dance is divided down the center by an imaginary line which separates the men from the women and represents perhaps the holy and forbidden edge of divine balance. Only the Eldress, who is their intercessor with God, ever occupies the center. Confined to their separate halves of the stage, the men and women move in self-contained but mutually responsive choruses. Except for that line between them, they are as harmonious as if they were dancing together. And often their separate paths lead irresistibly toward the line, toward the opposite group; the closer each group comes to the other, the more it's repelled, like one of the matching poles of two magnets.

Within the groups there are two contrasting orders of movement: the struggles between sin and salvation, the physical and the spiritual, imprisonment and escape; and the states of control and abandon that precede or result from these struggles. Between those poles there is no mean, only the rising intensity of the struggle. The Eldress' spinning and her didactic pronouncements alone can bring the emotional turmoil into some centeredness for any period of time. Doris' raw materials consisted of tilting off balance, the beginning of the struggle; strict verticality as the most fixed and arduous form of control; and an erratic, almost violent twisting to get free of all control. The first statement of this last theme was described by Doris as "wrestling with the devil." People stamp and shuffle, and throw their arms toward the ground; they step springily on the balls of their feet, rise, and finally jump into the air. These movement themes are developed, interconnected, and combined in a series of episodes that build in intensity to a terrific climax of rapturous jumping and a kneeling prayer as the Eldress spins in the center.

In terms of the participants, this dance can be seen as an alternation between personal and group involvement. At the moments of greatest peril and near-possession, the movement becomes most individual, least in conformity with the others in the group. Doris even specified that the dancers improvise their own gestures at certain times. The insistent rhythms and clear-cut designs of the group always serve to bring the individual back into line, both when he or she strays into carnal thoughts *and* after each ecstatic outburst. The floor patterns range from almost sociable square dance designs to spiritual circles and dutiful lines. The line patterns themselves seem variously coercive, from follow-the-leader chains to automatonlike shoulder-to-shoulder ranks. As the dance approaches its climax, these ranks turn toward the center and the dancers, one behind the other, plunge forward toward the opposite sex and strain backwards as if locked in some desperate tug of war.

The Eldress at times joins in these group dances, but she also exhorts the group to greater struggles and leads them by introducing the forms of their exertions. After an initial period when the stamping, jumping, wrenching, and attraction-repulsion themes have all been stated in sketch form, the Eldress stands on the upstage box that serves as a bench, claps her hands, and shouts, "It hath been revealed: Ye shall be saved when ye are shaken free of sin!" Then she begins what José Limón called a "crude and possessed" motion, "where the body in its entirety was stretched upwards to a shuddering tautness, from which it fell alternately forwards and backwards, passing through the tormented vertical in transit." Starting in slow motion, this phrase contains all the elements of the dance: the below/above antithesis; the shaking out of the body as it bends, almost pushes, toward the ground; the struggle to and passage through the "tormented vertical," in which the Eldress veers slightly out around the body with a searching feeling, just starting in the direction of a spiral; and the liberated opening upwards and backwards of the body at the end.

Many people who saw early performances of *The Shakers* described it as a passionate, almost violent dance. Whether audiences actually saw spasmodic, trancelike frenzy or inferred it, the dance never actually becomes disordered. Edward Deming Andrews has noted that although the Shaker practice was initially a very individual one, "largely involuntary, charged with emotionalism and characterized by divine 'gifts'," the spiritual expression gradually became conventionalized. After the Civil War, many of the "random bizarre exercises . . . entered into the traditional ritualism. . . . there dawned a consciousness of purpose and with it a tendency to rationalize and justify, as well as to elaborate the gifts." The worship took on a more restrained, predictable, and regular form, partly so that the believers could appear less threatening to society at large. The Shaker service Doris devised would have come from these latter days. We can also draw an analogy between the development of Shaker practice and the development of Doris' own work, from the personal to the formal.

She was rereading Havelock Ellis in 1931 and found in his reasoning an echo of her own, with regard to the Shakers and to the process of choreography in general. Ellis speaks of the "auto-intoxication of rapturous movement" which is the mystic's first way of attaining temporary union with the divine. "Pantomimic dances, on the other hand, with their effort to heighten natural expression and to imitate natural process, bring the dancers into the divine sphere of creation and enable them to assist vicariously in the energy of the gods." He later discusses the necessity for rhythmic cooperation in the increasingly complex work efforts of civilization. "All great combined efforts, the efforts by which alone great constructions such as those of megalithic days could be carried out, must be harmonised." Ellis saw the group impulse and the coordination of individual action into group forms as a way to achieve a society. To José Limón the "impassioned formalism" of *Shakers* was an important lesson for his own creative work.

The Shakers was extremely successful and continues to be effective with contemporary audiences. Two years after its first performance, *The Shakers,* with *Water Study* and other Humphrey-Weidman works, was incorporated in the Broadway revue *Americana,* where it was a critical and popular hit. The dance remained in active repertory quite consistently, often gaining more attention than dances Doris thought more deserving. In 1940 the gifted photographer Thomas Bouchard made an impressionistic film of the dance, with the studio fixed up to look like a Shaker meetinghouse. Although it is not a record of the dance, Bouchard's film gives a good idea of the impassioned quality Limón spoke about. Unfortunately it is not in general circulation for present-day dancers to study.

The dance made Doris a sort of lay expert on the subject of the Shakers. For the rest of her life people sent her Shaker memorabilia, articles, clippings, titles of related books they thought she should read, and scripts they had written which they thought she could help them get produced. She herself tried to interest a Hollywood producer in her choreography in 1939, but she was told that "all things at the moment, with a pretense to quality, are in very bad repute in pictures." She was occasionally asked to advise people who were attempting to preserve the customs of the cult, which was dying out. Not long after creating her dance, Doris had momentary qualms about what she had done. "One thing I vow I will not do again: Imitate in an art form the rituals of the faithful. No more Shakers. I am ashamed of the poverty of my age that it sent me sniffing around people and things that are none of my business." But her notions of what constituted exploitation were always extreme, and the dance's persistent appeal has less to do with sensationalism than with its sound theatricality and its acute use of movement to effect catharsis. One of the last surviving Shakers, eighty-seven-year-old Ricardo Belden, saw Doris' students in a 1955 revival and found himself "enthralled." A Humphrey-Weidman dancer of the early 1930s wrote years later, "I loved *The Shakers* best for I could release something emotionally."

Doris and Pauline's relationship began to change in 1931, perhaps overstrained by the demands of a company whose poverty remained unabated as its reputation grew. The leaders decided to move from their first studio in 59th Street to less expensive quarters at 151 West 18th. At the same time Doris, Pauline, and Charles rented separate apartments in the same building, a few blocks away at 248 West 17th. In May they took separate vacations. Doris, who had been depressed about a knee injury that kept her from dancing in the spring, uncharacteristically sailed on a cruise to the West Indies. She met a new lover, Charles Francis Woodford, a young officer on the Furness ship *Dominica*. She called him Leo to avoid confusion with Charles Weidman. He was twenty-eight at the time, eight years younger than Doris, an Englishman with no formal education, who had been a seaman since the age of fourteen. Doris found him physically attractive, highly intelligent, and without psychological impediments to a deep relationship. He had no knowledge of the dance world, but he wasn't trying to pluck her out of it and carry her off to domesticity either. Doris' letters to him in the months that followed were as lyrically romantic as her letters to Pauline had been in the past. She reported their affair offhandedly to her parents, commenting, "This strikes Pauline as hasty, Charles as aggravating." Pauline went off to England with a young man named Humphrey and tried very strenuously to fall in love, but did not. After the summer, to save money, Doris and Pauline began to live together again, in an apartment on West 12th Street. In terms of her daily life and work, Doris still needed a partner like Pauline.

The things that seem superficially the least suitable about Leo were probably what made him an ideal mate for Doris. The long separations were painful, but they left her free to work. One can scarcely imagine Doris fitting into a middle-class marriage with even as erratic a home routine as her mother had had, or maintaining a social life outside her professional circle. When Leo returned for weekends in port he could give her a holiday, like her earlier weekend lovers; if she was preoccupied with rehearsing, as was often the case, he quietly sat in the studio and watched. He never became much more involved with the work than that, although helpers were always badly needed. At first Doris tried to engage his literary interests in helping her organize her movement ideas into a theory book, and he tried sketching decors for a dance or two, but he never really participated in Humphrey-Weidman on a more than peripheral level. He was loving and emotionally supportive, but also in great awe of her talents. Leo disliked his job intensely—not only because it kept him away from Doris but because, as a socialist, he hated the class distinctions in shipboard life, especially the cruise ship officer's role as a sort of glorified servant to the rich passengers. Yet he did not give it up for a shore-based job. Their arrangement must have suited him as well as it did Doris.

Both of them were opposed to marriage, although the more conventional Leo seems to have considered it more seriously than Doris did. She even had a last romantic encounter with an old flame on a visit to Chicago in September. In October she apparently had an abortion, and Leo sent her ten dollars to help pay for it. At the end of that month, on a concert at Washington Irving High School, she premiered what she later called "our love dance," *Two Ecstatic Themes.*

A solo in two contrasting parts, it was set to a short piano piece by Nicolai Medtner and another by Gian Francesco Malipiero. Doris, wearing a long white dress, did the entire dance virtually in place, riveting the audience's attention to what she was doing. The first part, Circular Descent, is essentially a fall—greatly elaborated, fragmented, almost dissected, with each of its elements examined and savored in full. There is the initial release of weight in the center of the body, the languid spread of heaviness through the limbs and head, the sinking and curving backward that describes the various arcs of a spiral. But the drop is not accomplished all at once. It is interrupted by a return to the starting upright position, again by a percussive thrust with the arm diagonally toward the ground; it is retarded and enlarged with a turn, a few steps in a semicircle, a new initiation from a kneeling position. At last she succumbs to the inevitable and sinks slowly to the floor on her back.

Pointed Ascent, the second part, is almost the exact opposite: percussive rather than smooth, rising instead of sinking, aggressive rather than acquiescent. She begins it from the same position with which she ended the first, an elbow, a knee, an arm jutting upward and leading the body in its struggle for verticality. Again the route is interrupted, segmented, set back, restarted. When she finally returns to standing, it is not to the position of stasis with which she began the dance; her arms, instead of being extended to the sides, are stretched above her head, hands clasped, symbolic of aspiration, a struggle not yet completed.

Although there is no motion picture record of Doris performing it, *Two Ecstatic Themes* has been reconstructed by Ernestine Stodelle on members of the José Limón company. The success of the dance in contemporary terms testifies to the viability of Doris' intent. On a 1935 program note she called it "a counterpoint of circular and angular movement, representing the two inseparable elements of life as well as of design." We don't see Carla Maxwell or Nina Watt emoting in the film they made in 1980, but we see a clear movement idea, detailed with fine craftsmanship and deliberate emphasis— the few important moments of symmetry that restrain the long exhaling spiral in Descent, the broken lines of the body, and the dammed-up flow of action that project impetus into Ascent. The dance is a perfectly fused meeting of passion and will.

Doris and Leo finally went off to Pennsylvania in June 1932 and got married. It was almost an afterthought. Doris continued to live with Pauline. She wore no wedding ring, and didn't change her professional name. In fact, she was half-annoyed when some provincial newspaper reporter would call her Mrs. Woodford in print. Although this behavior might be seen as cold or peculiar, it might also be seen as a protective, somewhat selfish, overcompensated way of channeling energies, ideas, and responsibilities that she might not have been able to manage otherwise. Looking at *Two Ecstatic Themes*, or at Doris' matter-of-fact word and sketch notations for it, from the vantage point of the uninhibited, sensual dancing of the 1980s, it seems almost shocking to learn that Doris connected that dance with the love of her life. But the whole point of her work, especially at this time, was to avoid "self-expression" as a direct revelation of personal experience. She felt that experi-

Two Ecstatic Themes—Circular Descent. Collection of Charles H. Woodford.

ence should be molded into more durable, meaningful art forms; the greater the experience, the greater the resulting art work.

It is undeniable that she felt passion, felt poetry. Sensuality and the effort to discipline her sensations so that they could be communicated are strikingly evident in some poetic lines she wrote in a letter to Pauline while on vacation in Maine in 1921.

> The days go by, warm and golden—we spend them on the beach and in the turquoise sea frilled with white. Take little steps in the water, high tip-toes—delay the icy ring in its ascent—enjoy the burning terror of the drop-stabs. Only half a body now—a warm shuddering top—and no bottom now—a bright agony possesses all—his frothy passion has enveloped you—his salty tongue licks at your cheek—leap high above him, he will reach you—leap for the hot joy-terror within.

Among the letters in this group she preserved a snapshot taken of her, perhaps on the same beach, in a bathing suit, tilting, reaching back as if to begin one of the falls that found their way into so many of her dances during this time, the fall that is the basis of Circular Descent. Both the dauntless resisting of an inevitable force and the pleasure of submission to it are in this fall, as they are in her verbal imagery. Not a flashy way to describe love, but one that is kinesthetically arresting, even transporting.

6 CONSOLIDATION, 1930–34

Besides their obvious ambition to make and perform dances, the young people who now began to assemble in the New York studios were seized by reformist zeal. They believed they were building a better world, and their idealism served them well, both as incentive when there were few other rewards and as a sign to the world that they were to be taken seriously.

As Doris began to think more formally about the group that was to realize her works, she set forth her aims in a long letter to prospective members. She was enlisting them in a crusade. With the extraordinary mixture of crystalline practicality and inspirational ardor that she kept all her life, she foresaw a journey that would be all the more glorious for the obstacles they would surmount together. "I am first a creative artist, thirsting to see my conceptions made visible; after that I am also interested in developing individual talent in others, in performing for audiences, educating audiences, promoting the cause of Dance, making money, and establishing a Dance Theatre in America." The order in which she set down these goals was not accidental. She wanted her dancers to understand that Humphrey-Weidman could pay virtually nothing—ten dollars a performance—and she frowned on the commercial theater as a supplementary source of income. "All group dancing in musical comedy or opera or motion picture houses" she placed in a "different class," by implication an inferior one. She demanded total devotion from her company members; they must not "belong to any other group," and they were to commit themselves to rehearsals twice a week, except when concerts were in preparation; then they were expected to clear out their lives for as many extra hours as would be required. Naturally, they would also take class regularly with herself or Charles. In return for this, the company—initially a group of sixteen women and a few men—became the elect of some sixty students enrolled in the Humphrey-Weidman school. In return she offered a credo that flared from the first brochure in brave aspiration. "To be master of one's body: to find a perfect union between the inner thought and the outer form—to draw from this a radiance and power that makes of life a more glorious and vital experience—this is to dance."

In an exceptionally articulate statement of philosophy that appeared in Oliver M. Sayler's symposium *Revolt in the Arts* (1930), Martha Graham spoke for the seriousness and simplicity of the "concert dance," not a particular style or form of dancing but a performing mode "where dance is the focal point of performance—the reason—where it possesses that integrity and vital integration necessary to any art form." The concert dancers, Graham said, were opposed to the sentimentalism of some Duncan followers, the hierarchical bias of the ballet, and the "weakling exoticism of a transplanted orientalism." She made an important distinction between the dance of "appearance"—the theatrical entertainments rooted in Europe's past—and the dance of "being"—an art which would be the "fruit of a people's soul."

"It is not to establish something that is American that we are striving," Graham wrote, "but to create a form and expression that will have for us integrity and creative force. The achievement of the concert dance . . . has stung a public into protest and curiosity; a few artists, musicians and painters, it has intoxicated by its daring and honesty and its potentialities; it has created the need for dance critics . . . it has fired musical organizations."

Many were striving in the same direction, but not all of them were sympathetic to the modernists' hopes for reform. Ted Shawn, scrabbling to hold together the remnants of Denishawn, remained deeply bitter at Doris and Charles' "disloyalty," and Doris in turn suspected him of influencing critics and sponsors against her during the next crucial years. Duncan disciples and advocates of "Greek" dancing whose training went back to Isadora's contemporaries in Europe disapproved of the new dance ideas as unaesthetic, even unnatural. There were traditionalists with ballet leanings who were beginning to think about how to establish a native ballet form. There were recitalists, each one cultivating a special identity to lure a faithful audience; and square pegs like Agnes de Mille and Ruth Page, who combined ballet training with adventurous minds and made category-defying collaborative works with modernists in other art fields. Among the other modern dancers, everyone had some dramatic new truths to proclaim, like the German-trained Don Oscar Becque, who, according to the *New York World*, "makes propaganda for the autonomy of the dance, for its emancipation from music, believing that the body creating a pattern in space is able to produce of itself rhythms significant and sufficiently clear." And always and everywhere there was

Martha Graham, whom Doris admired with the cautious fascination one accords a pet cobra.

It seems to be a rule in dance that the moments of the most profound change are the most quickly superseded and forgotten. What has come down as history in modern dance actually reflects a secondary stage of development and perhaps a less daring creative achievement. The concept that modern dance was created by "four pioneers"—Humphrey, Weidman, Graham, and Hanya Holm—emerged after the work had already been considerably institutionalized and refined. In the 1980s we don't learn about the ferment, the diversity, and the tremendous amount of activity that took place in the years just *preceding* the first organizing efforts—the Dance Repertory Theatre and the Concert Dancers League in 1930. For while these two projects focused the attention of the cultural world on the most ambitious and self-consciously "modern" of the new dancers, they also launched the inexorable process of selection that occurs in any art form when lines of development and patronage begin to solidify. Some people fell away in those centrifugal moments, never to be heard of again.

The season of 1928–29 was unprecedented in its dance activity. The writers who were given the most space to cover dance, John Martin of the *New York Times* and Mary F. Watkins of the *New York Herald Tribune*, toted up 129 concert dance events for the season, October through May, not counting private showings, studio recitals, benefits, student programs, or anything in the commercial arena, which at that time harbored almost all the ballet dancing that could be seen in New York. In addition to self-produced one-shot recitals and performances, several artists managed series of monthly events or multiple concerts on successive weekends. People fashioned studio spaces into small theaters where they could perform regularly. Sunday nights became so crowded with performances that on one occasion Martha Graham moved her evening performance to a matinee so as not to compete with the visiting German dancers Kreutzberg and Georgi, thus graciously assuring both concerts the full attention of the press.

Among the better known dancers of that season (most of them didn't make it into Anatole Chujoy's *Dance Encyclopedia* twenty years later) were Margaret Severn, Marga Waldron, Gluck-Sandor and Felicia Sorel, Doris and Cornelia Niles, Edwin Strawbridge, Miriam Marmein, Benjamin Zemach, and Helen Tamiris. This was the season when Graham worked with an ensemble for the first time, having previously done only solos and trios. Students of the late Bird Larson gave dances based on her ideas. Recitalists included the mime Angna Enters and several variety dancers trying their hand at "art." Impresario Sol Hurok organized a ten-day Isadora Duncan Memorial Festival at the Manhattan Opera House, highlighted by the first American appearances of her Moscow students under Irma Duncan's direction. Several other soloists and ensembles who claimed the Duncan inheritance were on the scene too.

Agnes de Mille staged the ballets for a production of *The Black Crook* in Hoboken. Léonide Massine became dance director at the Roxy Theater—in those days, when sound pictures were in their infancy, major movie houses offered live stage shows as part of the bill—and he choreographed and danced in a new production every week or so. Former Diaghilev dancer Alexandre Gavrilov, recently named ballet master of the Philadelphia Opera, presented his Ballet Moderne, and Michel Fokine, who had established a New York school with his wife, Vera, presented his school-based Fokine Ballet. Anna Robenne gave a program of dances created for her by Fokine.

The League of Composers staged the first American production of Stravinsky's *Les Noces,* choreographed by Russian ballerina Elizaveta Anderson. The annual production of the Neighborhood Playhouse featured Richard Strauss' *Ein Heldenleben,* with Martha Graham and Charles Weidman, on a bill with Blanche Talmud in Charles Tomlinson Griffes' *The White Peacock* and Enesco's *Roumanian Rhapsody,* featuring Gluck-Sandor.

The great interest in foreign attractions and exotica had not waned, and among the foreign visitors were Kreutzberg and Georgi on their second American tour, the sensational Argentina, and the German Hans Wiener (later known as Jan Veen), who included a Laban-style motion choir in his program. Sara Mildred Strauss, one of the Americans who had traveled to Europe to study the developments there firsthand, presented a series of lectures on Laban's work at her New York studio, and the German modern dance was also being taught at the newly opened school of Eugene Von Grona. Jane and Edward McLean, a brother and sister team from the Southwest who said their mentor was Graham, presented a program of Indian ceremonials, Mexican devotions, and rituals of the penitential Christians, a body of material that Graham was soon to explore with devastating effect.

There were programs devoted to reconstructing the ancient Greek dance and drama. There were Peruvian dances, and Spanish, Palestinian, Egyptian, and English folk dances. The Americanized Japanese dancer Michio Ito spent the year touring with his company, but he was in town long enough to choreograph a production of *Turandot* at the Manhattan Opera House and to present his work in a Broadway recital. Ted Shawn gave a solo recital at Carnegie Hall and filled it to standing-room capacity. The castanet playing of Argentina could be heard on a set of Odeon recordings, and Carola Goya danced on the radio.

The spectacular windup to this remarkable season was the third annual Charity Carnival for the benefit of the Judson Health Center. Held at Madison Square Garden, it featured a pageant called *Aztec Gold* with "100 Denishawn Dancers led by Ted Shawn," under the direction of Lila Agnew Stewart, who, according to Mary Watkins, "has probably 'put on' more pageants and kermesses than any other woman alive." A Ziegfeld revue starring Tamara Geva and the dancers from the Broadway show *Whoopee* also appeared at this spectacular event.

Of course no one attempted to see all of this except the critics, and before the season was over John Martin was complaining that there were too many recitals devoted to "technique or cavorting, posing or story telling," and that too many people with good intentions were making premature debuts. Viewing the "esoteric, pantomimic, philosophical, poetical, political, or social arguments" that he thought constituted many presentations, he was "touched occasionally by nostalgia for the good old days when dancers actually danced." Martin thought a lot of the dross would separate out if nationwide attention could be focused on the dance art as a whole. "Our dancing is beginning to acquire substance and character, and the sooner its existence as a unified entity, a national expression—if such a term can be used without chauvinistic implications—is recognized, the more rapid will its progress be," he reflected in February 1929, suggesting that the Americans institute a national dance congress similar to the ones held annually in Germany, where all denominations of dancers would come together for lectures, performances, and a public airing of philosophies. "Dancing cannot forever remain in a state of chaotic indecision," Martin asserted. Indecision was not one of Doris' or Martha's afflictions—which may have been one of the main reasons they were perceived as major figures in the concert field—but chaos and financial hazard continued to plague them both even after they achieved recognition.

Attracting students and potential company members required less effort than finding the means to keep the enterprise afloat. Doris had a very low priority for making money; she always figured that somehow she could provide for

herself. But she knew that she must keep Humphrey-Weidman's name before the public, both in order to pay the rent and to assure that there would
be an audience to look at what they were creating. Her reluctance to associate with any commercial enterprise further limited her resources. She
would—she almost had to—take on any project that didn't seem compromising. In the calendar year 1929, besides regular teaching and choreographing, Doris and Charles gave a demonstration at the studio to interest
future students; they did one-night stands in Philadelphia and Lake Placid;
they did a lecture-demonstration with the group for 1,000 students at Hunter
College and shared a program at the Community Church with Elsa Findlay
and her Dalcroze Eurythmics students. There was an engagement in Boston
in October. With their dancers they participated in the Neighborhood Playhouse annual production. Charles showed his work independently on dual
concerts with Agnes de Mille and Priscilla Robineau, and he appeared twice
with the Albertina Rasch dancers. All this in addition to their major
Humphrey-Weidman "season," which consisted of two Sunday-night performances, March 24 and April 7, at the Guild Theater, when Doris' major
premieres were *Life of the Bee* and the third movement of the Grieg *Concerto.*

Sunday night in the major New York theaters belonged to the concert
dancers. The legitimate theater went dark because of a fifty-year-old blue
law that forbade entertainments to be given on the Sabbath. Using a variety
of dodges, the dancers took temporary possession of the only real theaters
available to them. "The best is to say you're giving a sacred concert," Doris
fumed, "and even then you have to give 10 percent to charity." According to
a series of articles in *The Dance,* a committee of clergymen and moralists
monitored the Sabbath Law, rousing the police when they received a com-
plaint against a particular Sunday dance concert. They maintained that dancing was a "great peril to society" that could result in "broken health . . . evils
of the most serious character . . . divorces . . . midnight orgies," but they over-
looked all the dancing in burlesque, nightclubs, and movie stage shows,
which was protected by powerful commercial interests. The art dancers,
being defenseless, were easy targets.

Something had gone wrong with Humphrey-Weidman's license application for the Golden the year before, and the concert was saved only by an
eleventh-hour visit to the authorities and payment of a fine. At times subterfuge didn't work at all. On February 24 the visiting Gavrilov company was
raided by police at curtain time at the Booth Theater, and their performance

was cancelled. Supposedly one could not give a proper Sunday night "sacred concert" or "benefit" with theatrical costumes and lighting, although both were allowed in movie house dancing. Gavrilov made the necessary gestures to official hypocrisy and managed to book the same theater for March 10, prudently letting the press know that he intended to give a percentage of the receipts to the Lord Mayor's Relief Fund for British Miners.

Mary Watkins took the opportunity of the Gavrilov fiasco to suggest the establishment of a theater that would be devoted solely to the dance. It could then be used during the week like any legitimate theater and go dark on Sundays. "There would be no conflicts, no cancellations, the critics would stay through every performance," she predicted. "The dance world is ready and waiting for a leader and an organization to correct present evils."

To Doris the duplicity and legal red tape of getting a concert on Broadway were minor irritations compared to the inconvenience such production involved. She left a vivid description of this wasteful process in some pencilled notes she planned to use in documenting the advantages of a repertory theater.

> Early in that morning you begin struggling with the mechanical problems at the theater. You have a setting that you have never tried with your dancers—it is a very simple one, but you don't know how it is going to work—but there is no time to experiment. Put it up quickly and don't fuss. At the best this takes several hours—then begins the long lighting rehearsal. On a program of fifteen numbers, each one must have its special lighting. This must all be done as quickly as possible because a crew of stage-hands is an expensive plaything, and we simply can't lose [money] on this concert. We haven't got it. This rehearsal continues until late in the afternoon, when we tear through the dances for the sake of spacing and entrances on this unfamiliar stage and also to try the dance that involves a platform and steps that we have never had a rehearsal on. At eight o'clock with no lunch and no dinner we make-up, and present an exhausted mind and body to the gaze of an expectant audience.

Added to this prodigal expenditure of energy, the Sunday evening concerts had to be produced by the dancers themselves. They accepted the financial risk in order to gain the press coverage that the city's newspapers gave anything that appeared on their Broadway beat, and to earn a little money if they could fill the theater. Humphrey-Weidman's Guild Theater "season" in March-April 1929 was even more of a gamble than usual. Their previous one-night Broadway concerts, at the Golden Theater the year before and in October 1928 at the Civic Repertory Theater, had been sold out, bringing them a few hundred dollars over their expenses. They decided to try two nights in a smaller theater, hoping to present a larger selection of dances and still draw full houses. The scheme didn't work. The first concert fell on Easter, and for the second the weather turned unnaturally hot, keeping audiences small and the box office proceeds correspondingly thin. In her usual post-concert decline, Doris told her parents, "By the time we are well enough known to get a job somewhere, we'll all be dragged out and old-fashioned like the rest of the ones that have arrived."

✳

Dance Repertory Theatre was a first attempt on the part of the dancers to alleviate their individual burdens by making common cause. Before its debut season, Mary Watkins traced the coalition back to the busy spring of 1929, when Humphrey, Weidman, Graham, and Tamiris, as the "four focal points of the dance in America," had been named dance advisers to the Conductorless Symphony Orchestra, "an organization of recent growth whose model has been the extraordinary Russian orchestras with the communistic ideal." Intrigued as always by the possibility of working with a live orchestra, the dancers held several meetings, though the orchestra failed to add any dancing to its program. But Watkins speculated that, having been singled out in this way, the four dancers began to think they had enough strength to inaugurate a producing unit of their own, one that would present "the dance for its own sake." (Most other accounts credit Tamiris with originating the Dance Repertory Theatre idea and selling it to the others.)

According to Watkins, after several meetings during the summer, agreement was reached, leading to the initial performances early in 1930. The partners "pledged" not to have independent recitals in New York during the year outside of the Dance Repertory season, although they could appear with large orchestras and festivals. "Important and representative work will be reserved for this yearly essay into repertory." There was to be a one-week season the first year, a two-week season the second. Ultimately, with the addition of other artists, the season might run a month. Once these ground rules had been adopted, said Watkins, it remained only to raise the money, "an elementary matter of discovering the proper reception at the proper time; all responses were prompt and unquestioning."

Watkins' account is excessively sanguine: raising money was far from an elementary matter, nor were the dancer-participants so sure that they were doing the right thing for themselves and their companies. Doris had misgivings about the coalition. No doubt like all the others, she feared the inevitable comparisons that would be made, and she shrank from giving up any part of her hard-won identity to a greater concept. "Organization has come to be such a hateful thing," Doris wrote, with her recent experiences still rankling. "They simply organized the life out of Denishawn." She realized, however, that the attempt must be made. Outlining some of the advantages in her notes, she deplored the "distressing conditions under which my concerts have been presented before." The situation could "be bettered by a week's engagement, at a theater that is at our disposal night and day," where there would be a "chance of giving the same dances more than once—which is a tremendous conserving of art and energy."

Tamiris served as president and raised most of the money—about $5,000 covered the first season. In some ways far less advanced as a choreographer than the other three, Tamiris lent a certain glamour and vitality to the enterprise. Ten years younger than Doris, at twenty-five she had had an equally eclectic background, which included several years in opera ballet. Unlike the other partners, however, Tamiris was not above worldliness. Where Martha suffered in cloistered asceticism and Doris was indifferent to her penury, Tamiris liked jazz, fashion, success. When most modern dancers spoke of creating art for their time, they meant something abstract or conventionalized. The concrete experience must be transformed into a more noble manifestation. Tamiris was willing to explore all methods to attain art, and she didn't exclude the commonplace or the popular. Before starting her concert career in 1927, she had danced in stage shows accompanying movies, in nightclubs, and variety, and she later became a successful choreographer for Broadway musicals while continuing to do concert work. The Europeans use the term "popular" interchangeably with "folk," but in this country popular meant not artistic. Many who were complaining that America lacked a folk tradition automatically excluded the native forms, especially those from the black experience, which had found an early outlet in the commercial theater. The dances that resulted when Martha and Doris delved into folk sources were often so elevated that they had scant relationship to these sources. Tamiris absorbed rhythms, retained the feelings of the street, gave herself over, later, to intense political sentiments. In this sense she was a true popular artist. According to historian Christena Schlundt, "she was more modern than any in that essence of modernity: a responsiveness to the unformulated will of an epoch, a drive to do what a time required."

Shortly after her solo debut late in 1927, Tamiris was invited to appear at the Salzburg Festival, and she remained in Europe for several months, dancing, meeting other artists, and learning. All along the way she sent back glowing bulletins to the critics in New York, and on her return in the spring of 1929 she gave an exultant interview to Mary Watkins, while Doris was writing sober explanations of her upcoming work for the press. By the end of the season, after two successful Broadway evenings, Tamiris opened her own School of the American Dance. Probably she struck Doris as too flamboyantly eager to display her enthusiasm and her success—she even allowed her modest European visit to be compared to the conquests of Duncan and St. Denis. She herself defined dancing as "simply movement with a personal conception of rhythm," quite a different credo from the thoroughgoing renovation undertaken by Doris, Charles, and Martha.

Four more disparate personalities would be hard to find in the dance world of 1929, but in due course Dance Repertory Theatre's first season of nine performances at the Maxine Elliott's Theatre was accomplished. The programs, offered on January 5–12, 1930, were neatly divided—two nights for each of the participating groups (Humphrey and Weidman being considered as one), and three mixed programs: the opening and closing nights and the sole matinee. All the choreographers were anxious to present their latest and best work, and the programs were generous—some critics thought too generous. On the last evening, for instance, the combined bill contained thirteen short dances and three large works, Tamiris' *Triangle Dance*, Graham's *Heretic*, and Doris' *Drama of Motion*. Some of these programs lasted till after eleven o'clock and left the audiences exhausted. Most of the dances were repeated several times during the course of the week, with only a few changes of numbers. Although the mixed programs were well attended, only the less expensive seats filled up for the single bills. John Martin thought the individual companies didn't have enough of a following to fill the theater repeatedly; the repertory idea would need sustained support from the general public. Dance Repertory Theatre was what all of them had always wanted—a chance to perform a lot while having to produce the program only once. But they hadn't had enough experience doing this, nor could they estimate their audience's needs in order to control the opportunity to their best advantage. John Martin, summing up the season as a whole, had some stern advice. First, he considered the repertory too esoteric. The critic who is always associated with promoting the modern dance in America was at this period concerned to see that the nascent field stayed within bounds. Martin had recognized individual talent and applauded it, but he knew where he thought the field should go. He wanted modern dance repertory to draw the American dance together, so that "it may appear less as a miniature war between the holders of disparate theories and more as a unified whole made up of diversified parts." He thought the incipient public for modern dance needed to be coddled a bit. "To give an impression of the dance as a precious, intellectualized art is to present a warped view," he said, implying that even he thought his protegés were a little too austere. What he prescribed for the future was mixed programs consisting of "old and tried compositions, not too rarefied in atmosphere, as colorful and popular as possible." New works, he thought, could be premiered at individual Sunday-night concerts in the same theater and under the Dance Repertory Theatre management.

Undoubtedly responding to Martin's advice, the partners did things differently the next year. For the nine performances beginning February 1, 1931, at the Craig Theater, the collaborators had only one separate evening apiece; the remaining programs were shared. More important, Agnes de Mille was brought into the Dance Repertory organization. Her presence turned out to be disruptive, but not specifically because she was a ballet dancer—the lines of that dispute had not yet hardened. De Mille and her partner, Warren Leonard, showed sketches and genre pieces, many of them inspired by European city life, with titles like *Ballet Class* (based on Degas), *Can Can, Café Dancer, The Parvenues, The Cries of London*. They also used the nineteenth-century composers who were becoming taboo among more progressive dancers—Strauss, Offenbach, Beethoven—along with baroque and traditional music. While the others were showing dances like *Steel and Stone* (Weidman), *Descent into a Dangerous Place* (Humphrey), *Revolutionary March* (Tamiris), and *Two Primitive Canticles: Ave and Salve* (Graham), de Mille either "walked away with the show entirely or else, sandwiched between compositions of such utterly different types, often threw the whole program out of key," in the opinion of Mary Watkins. The founders had imagined a theater that would declare—consecrate—itself against frivolity; even the popular Tamiris confined herself to serious compositions in this and her subsequent concert work. Yet it was de Mille, with her light, undemanding, tasteful dances, who won over the public.

One reason for the "temporary" disbanding of Dance Repertory Theatre after this season was de Mille's insistence on being treated as an equal partner in sharing the proceeds, which can hardly have been robust. *Variety* reported that, "Following reported squabbles over distribution of profits . . . Agnes de Mille, considered the Repertory's best draw, has quit. . . . Miss de Mille's share was 10 percent, against a 30 percent cut [for] the others in the troupe." Graham, Humphrey-Weidman and Tamiris, of course, had appeared with eighteen, nineteen, and twelve supporting dancers, respectively, while de Mille brought in only Warren Leonard as her partner.

Both the repertory idea and the contributions of the independent choreographers received mixed reviews. Writing as "Terpsichorean," the New Yorker's anonymous commentator gave Dance Repertory Theatre's first season a tongue-in-cheek going-over. Finding Doris and Charles neo-balletic and dancier than their colleagues, the writer advised: "If you happen not to be in sympathy with the bodily expression of moods, music, or dramatic concepts, it all will seem like a lot of fussiness in which music is supplemented by something extraneous and dancing is reduced to posturing. If the form interests you, you will discover in the activities of the Dance Repertory Theatre, and those who are going in the same direction, a sincere endeavor to make of 'the dance' an entity capable of standing on its own legs—and what legs some of them are!" Following the premiere of Graham's historic Primitive Mysteries during the second Repertory season, a typical baffled journalist declared: "Miss Graham, a serious student of Terpsichore, is a personable young lady with ideas and a finely trained body. Miss Graham intends that they should come together through the medium of the dance. Her effort in that direction results in angular, cold, stylized movement. It exposes a mind obsessed with realism." What must have been the severest blow to the collaborators was the verdict of their mentor John Martin, that those who cared about the dance in America would "devoutly hope that a third season will not be attempted by the repertory organization until it has had a complete change of heart." Martin, who only two years before had urged the new dancers to emulate the German Dance Congress in a gathering of the clans, now charged the first enterprise to make such an attempt with "too much rivalry and factionalism," which he said had also marred the German event the previous summer. Trying to soften the blow, Martin wished he could report that the season had "advanced the cause of dancing in public opinion" and helped the individual contributors artistically or financially to present their work, but the "easier and more obvious verdict would be to pronounce the whole affair a debacle." While he still backed the cause of modern dance repertory, Martin thought the group hadn't proved they could "be united for the better performance of their art and the better understanding of the public." Once again he called for composite programs that would appeal to the lay audience, discounting the dancers' efforts to do just that as having produced a "wearying and unreasonable miscellany night after night." He thought an impartial overall director was needed to arrange suitable programs and mediate between rival camps.

Martin soon got a chance to select and present the modern dance according to his own lights, in the first annual series of lecture-demonstrations at the New School. But his criticism capped what had been a disheartening season for Dance Repertory Theatre. Doris wasn't satisfied with the management, the production arrangements, or her own work. "All I could present was a few ideas," she lamented. Dance Repertory Theatre did not mount a third season. There must have been suspicion and jealousies among its constituents—Eleanor King remembers notices posted backstage warning everyone not to talk to Graham's dancers during performances. But the dancers might have been able to carry on with the project if they had reaped greater direct benefits from it.

In a fundamental way Dance Repertory Theatre did accomplish its goal, and more. The four original choreographers found themselves immediately in demand, and for the next few years Doris worked at a wider range of projects than in any other period in her career. Not only did the Repertory performances provide the artists with a visibility previously accorded only to foreign modern dancers like Kreutzberg and Wigman, it established the idea of American modern dance as a real force in the culture, a movement, whose practitioners were doing something comparable to modernist trends in the other arts. By showing two seasons of repertory, assertively modern in spirit and high in artistic quality, the dancers had demonstrated that something cohesive but individually expressive could be discriminated out of the free-for-all that constituted the New York dance scene. The public as well as the dancers themselves could see that there was something called the modern dance, something strong and contemporary and determinedly independent of superficial beguilements; that this way of dancing was altogether different from Duncanism and the orientalist tradition and anything that was being done on the popular stage. Just what this movement was and how it was going to be carried on were still to be clarified, but there was no doubt now of its viability or of who its leaders would be.

✳

Conceived by its four originators as an ambitious move to gain credibility for themselves and their still nebulous art, Dance Repertory Theatre proved to be a milestone. The shortlived phenomenon also can be seen as a reflection of its times, for other artists too were feeling the need to seek fellow workers outside their immediate circles. In the period just before the Depression, American artists were emerging from the insularity and jazz-age escapism that followed World War I to direct their energies and their arts toward society. Intellectuals and artists began to relinquish some of their individualism in order to work more closely with colleagues, either for political change or for artistic solidarity.

Malcolm Cowley has written about the polarization of Americans during the early twentieth century, a condition aggravated by the loss or diminution of many of the institutions that had protected the individual and given him the support of others. Cowley notes the longing for "comradeship or cooperation or, to use the religious word, communion," which led many intellectuals to join groups promising a more equitable and companionable world. Cowley and many of his colleagues embraced communism. For other artists, the same discontents led to more specialized, less directly political working affiliations, like the Group Theatre; the heterogeneous League of Composers, organized to present new music and bring it to the attention of the public; and the little-theater and repertory-theater movements, which tried to give more continuity to dramatic production.

Among the economically and socially marginal dancers, the Depression had little material effect; it was felt rather as an abstract moment of historic change. Something was in the air that they could identify with, that they could work for together and not lose their cherished individual voices. Dancers traditionally are not organizers, and for modern dancers in particular, individualism was an article of faith. Dance Repertory Theatre, as a first attempt at a coalition that has not been bettered in half a century, reflected more than the desperate gropings of innovators to get established. In the years that followed, dancers, for perhaps the only time in their history, became engaged with other artists and with larger issues than their own careers. But Doris voiced the commonly held view that dance tended to get smothered among the other arts and would be better off in intramural settings like Dance Repertory Theatre, "where we can be ourselves."

By the end of the 1920s the Dancers Club in New York was flourishing as a social and educational center with its own residence and 350 members, mostly dance teachers. After a lively existence, during which it published a monthly newsletter and sponsored lectures, courses, contests, and receptions for visiting artists, the club was dissolved in 1932 as more politically and professionally oriented groups took its place. The first activist group in the field, the Concert Dancers League, was formed early in 1930. Spurred by their success in organizing Dance Repertory Theatre, Doris, Martha, and Charles joined with other concert dancers under Tamiris' energetic leadership, with the specific aim of lobbying for abolition of the Sabbath Law, which had been so troublesome to them. After two years of agitation, a committee consisting of Sara Mildred Strauss, Miriam Marmein, Sophia Delza, and Agnes de Mille finally presented the State Legislature with an acceptable bill (which was passed in April 1932), allowing municipalities to regulate concert and recital dancing for themselves. Other quasi-unionist alliances were formed, and, a few years later, dancers had their own antiwar and social-justice protest organizations, more or less communistic in ideology.

After conscientiously helping the Concert Dancers League get started, Doris engaged in little political activity. She had no love for committees or any other time-consuming occupations that didn't bear directly on her work. She was certainly not unaware of the social conditions that politicized so many other artists during the prewar years, and she held many long discussions with Leo, in fundamental agreement with his socialist sympathies. But she didn't associate herself with the left-wing groups of the 1930s like the Workers Dance League, nor did she make direct reference to her political sentiments in her choreography.

Her political disengagement was not unusual. Harold Clurman describes going through a similar process during the early years of the Group Theatre.

> Actually I understood nothing of the Soviet Union's significance. . . . There was very little political discussion among us during the summer of 1931. Of radicalism there wasn't a spark. It might be asked why, for all my talk about the need of facing our times and of finding affirmative answers to the moral and social problems of our day, politics received so little of our attention. One answer may be that my education and inclinations had been chiefly aesthetic. Besides this, however, I have always had a reluctance to delve into problems while they still remained outside the range of my actual experience.

In Clurman's candid appraisal, the Group Theatre was preoccupied initially with developing its own artistic point of view and unifying itself as a group of individuals who could work together. Political action was simply beyond the Group's concerns at that time; it would come later.

Even after the practical imperative of establishing a company and a reputation had been met, Doris probably couldn't avoid applying her characteristic rationalism to politics. She wrote to her mother in 1941: "Everybody has a right to live comfortably, and to share in the resources of the people. I believe this too, but I still can't stick the loss of individual freedom." José Limón relates in his autobiography the strenuous efforts of some company members, in a series of heated company meetings around 1936, to get Doris and Charles "to place their talents at the service of the imminent and inevitable world revolution." Doris calmly countered these agitators by saying that "her works, and those of Mr. Weidman, were first and above all works of art, not tracts of propaganda. . . . She did not want to live under any sort of dictatorship, whatever its political spectrum and orientation. She preferred not to have official sanction for her work. She demanded absolute freedom to do as she saw it."

The gulf between rich and poor was only too evident as the company's growing reputation brought its activities out into the world. While the dancers still worked as janitors and models and secretaries, Doris, Pauline, and Charles rooted among their contacts for wealthy patrons. Some private donors and commissions were found—never enough. José painted an extraordinary word picture of Irene Lewisohn supervising rehearsals of the Ernest Bloch *String Quartet* in 1931.

> Miss Irene Lewisohn's limousine would deposit her elegant person, covered in sumptuous furs, on the littered sidewalk. Her chauffeur, loaded with a large picnic basket, would follow her up the dingy stairs to the studio. There, in practice clothes, 'warmed up' and ready to work, Miss Humphrey and Mr. Weidman awaited her. She would sit, the chauffeur would open the hamper, hand her a fine damask napkin and serve her lunch, during which she would by turns direct or supervise the rehearsal.

Irene Lewisohn and her sister Alice provided work for dancers, musicians, and other stage artists in their Neighborhood Playhouse productions— Charles had taken part in Bloch's *Israel* (1928), *Ein Heldenleben* (1929), and *A Pagan Poem* (Loeffler, 1930), along with Martha Graham and her dancers. Graham and Louis Horst also taught at the Neighborhood Playhouse School of the Theater, which was founded in 1928. Doris found dancing in some of the Playhouse productions "a dignified way of making a little money," though she didn't think much of the results. Irene Lewisohn usually directed these music-dramas, leaving the specifics of movement to the dancers. Doris' role in the Bloch *Quartet* was fairly typical of several large orchestral projects she engaged in around this time, although the piece had the added prestige of being commissioned by the Elizabeth Sprague Coolidge Foundation, whose benefactions to modern composers indirectly brought several important dance works into being. The Bloch piece had its premiere at the Library of Congress on April 23, 1931, before being shown in New York at the 92nd Street YM-YWHA. The scenario was conceived as an "action interpretation" by Irene Lewisohn, and Doris and Charles did the actual staging.

Lewisohn's expressionistic plot was the sort of drama of the psyche that appealed to Doris; she might have written it herself, although she might not have worked out its psychological message so literally. "There are times in the life of each individual when he feels impelled to retire inside his being and contemplate the forces that influence his way of life." The central female figure (played by Doris) was confronted first by a group (led by Blanche Talmud) which, to José, watching it from the balcony of the 92nd Street Y, seemed to be trying to drive her to suicide. Then a man (Charles) appealed to her womanly desires. Finally she determined that "she must not be possessed by either—she must find her way as mistress of her being, meet destiny in tune with all the forces of her life, and in surrender, triumph." Not only this theme but many of the movement and stage directions indicated in a prompt book of the score echo similar ideas in Doris' work at the time— the Nietzschean dialogue between formal, collective action and less disciplined individual rapture was the basis of *Shakers*, among other dances. As José described the *Quartet:* "Doris, costumed in a simple clinging sheath the color of pale fire, symbolized this entity which animates our existence. The strange, shadowy world was that of our subconscious, and the other dancers were the fears and menaces which haunt the dark recesses of the spirit. Her dancing reached a pinnacle here."

Doris knew the value of live music, and dreamed of performing with symphony orchestras, especially when she was using existing symphonic works like the Grieg Concerto and the Ravel Valse. In fact, the modern dancers' inability to afford large instrumental ensembles in the early days was a primary reason for their commissioning chamber scores from contemporary composers like Louis Horst, Henry Cowell, and Dane Rudhyar. But besides the financial and logistical problems of working with large orchestras, there was their fixation on the idea that dance should exist on its own and not be subservient to any other art form. Certainly the most prestigious collaboration of this kind, the 1930 production of Arnold Schönberg's *Die Glückliche Hand* and Stravinsky's *Le Sacre du Printemps,* did not work to the advantage of the modern dancers' artistic freedom. Graham and Weidman starred in the *Sacre,* choreographed by Léonide Massine; and Doris set the movement, largely pantomimic, for the Schönberg. Both ballets were played by the Philadelphia Orchestra under Leopold Stokowski; Rouben Mamoulian directed the Schönberg and Robert Edmond Jones designed it. The production was given at the Philadelphia and Metropolitan opera houses. It received extensive critical coverage from both the music and the dance press, but none of the modern dancers involved felt that their contributions were true to their personal goals.

Not only dancers but other American artists were reassessing their position in the culture during the early 1930s. It was a time for combining forces to facilitate new ideas. Minds were open enough to dream of grandiose collaborations like the *Sacre* and modest ones like the music-dance event on music history that Olga Samaroff-Stokowski arranged at the Dalton School, where Doris was teaching in the winter of 1931–32, with a twenty-minute opera written for the children by George Antheil. The previous year Doris, Martha, and Edwin Strawbridge had been asked to advise the League of Composers, but there were artistic disagreements and the women pulled out, leaving Strawbridge to choreograph Prokofiev's *Le Pas d'Acier* (spring 1931). Strawbridge and Yeichi Nimura were the principal dancers in the machine-age satire directed by Lee Simonson, given on a bill with Stravinsky's Oedipus Rex staged for singers and Robert Edmond Jones' sculptured figures.

Doris could never suppress her territoriality for long. During rehearsals for *Die Glückliche Hand,* she wrote, "The thing can't possibly have any unity. It simply bears out my theory that people with entirely different ideas of motion and emotion simply cannot work together." Yet she tried again and again, for she shared the prevailing ideal of a truly democratic culture that would enlighten and uplift all classes of society, not just the rich. She believed that artists had a mission to bring this about, and she knew the dancers alone could not realize such dreams.

In *Revolt in the Arts,* Oliver M. Sayler asked a question that absorbed many conscientious artists in 1930: What is the function of the arts in the Machine Age? Sayler and the thirty-six "representative authorities" in different branches of the arts whom he canvassed for the book perceived the arts to be at a kind of crossroads. Photography, phonographic recordings, talkies, radio, and an emerging television were forcing artists to reevaluate their traditional skills and methods. If the arts could become available on a mass scale, as these technological processes seemed to forecast, would art disappear as a personal, "hand-made" expression, or were there ways in which art could adapt to and even utilize machines for its own purposes? This question, of course, had been bothering artists for half a century, but probably not since the invention of the printing press had mechanization impacted so directly upon the art work itself as well as the art process.

Through these new media, some replica of the artist's work could now reach vast numbers of people for whom it had not previously been available. Sayler thought this would instigate a relaxation of puritanical restrictions on the appropriate subject matter for art and a corresponding need for the artist to examine his values. A new figure, the arts middleman, was coming into being to act as mediator between the artist and this enlarged public. In his ensuing assessment of how these changes would affect the performing, literary, and plastic arts, Sayler thought that American dance was still in too formative a stage to have much of a problem with a burgeoning public. Aside from some disciples of Isadora Duncan, he thought St. Denis and Shawn, a few concert artists, and Humphrey, Weidman, Tamiris, and Graham constituted the entire list of significant American dancers at that moment. There were a few institutions like the Neighborhood Playhouse, a few schools, a few opera ballet ensembles, and a few "glib-toed cohorts of our light musical stage" to set standards. "And all America out on the floor ceaselessly whirling to tom-tom rhythms. America dancing, but not as Isadora envisioned! So much smoke but so little fire!" Sayler thought the only way for a true American dance form to emerge from this would be if a strong leader, an Isadora or a Diaghilev, could be found and endowed with large sums of money.

The "revolt" of Sayler's title probably had more to do with social than artistic change, for Sayler and his contributors had a fairly traditional view of the arts. Creative work would arise, according to him and to most of the spokesmen he asked for essays in the book, from strong institutions—universities, repertory theaters, or benevolent commercial enterprises. Neither he nor the majority of his contributors advocated really revolutionary art. In fact, one of the few outrageous ideas in the book was supplied—perhaps half-jokingly—by theater designer Robert Edmond Jones, who suggested, in "Toward an American Ballet," that "so far no one has arisen who not only believed in ballet, but saw how to make it relevant to America, to the way we live and think." Jones speculated, "It is possible that dancing is as irrelevant to our time as archery," and proposed that the animated cartoon might be a truer form of American ballet than anything yet created.

But it was Martha Graham who voiced the serious aims of the contemporary dancers. (The only other dance essay in the book was a contribution on the teaching of children by Isadora's sister, Elisabeth Duncan.) Graham clearly differed from Oliver Sayler in that she endorsed diversity of creative views rather than the drawing together of all dance's resources under one genius-leader. "Emancipation must come through the individual," she said. Doris, interviewed at around the same time, thought an American dance form had not yet crystallized, and as long as so many individuals were experimenting separately the form would retain its vitality. "Crystallization is always the climax, and after that comes deterioration, then death," she thought. What dancers needed was a place to dance, not a coercive common cause.

For all the talk of modernism and revolt, however, the American artists, especially the dancers, were really not working at the absolute limits of experimentation at that time. They produced few statements as momentous as the original Stravinsky-Nijinsky *Sacre du Printemps*—though possibly Graham's *Primitive Mysteries* approached it on a smaller scale—and few departures from the accepted modes of dance as radical as what had been done a decade earlier by the Ballets Suédois, the Theater of the Bauhaus, or the German modern dancers. There was no American counterpart in any of the arts to Cubism or serial music, which began with a dissection of the very matter and materials of art and proceeded to turn its focus away from content or subject matter onto the more concrete perceptual questions that have endured throughout the twentieth century. Even Graham, the most conceptually advanced of the American dancers, was concerned with individual expression. A subordination of her art to the greater force of the abstract would have been inimical to her. Born in the nineteenth century, the pioneer modern dancers were shaped by the earnest aestheticism of Ruskin and William Morris, by the form-follows-function dictates of architect Louis Sullivan, and then by the spiritual linkages established for dance by Duncan and St. Denis. The modern dancers wanted to speak for their times and their people, but they were essentially humanists and idealists. They were talking about serious art because they wanted to retrieve something respectable from what they considered the frivolous, decadent, and borrowed forms of the nineteenth century. They wanted to make dancing honorable again, not abolish it entirely.

During 1932, as her commitment to Leo grew stronger, Doris' chronic cycle of ambition-hyperactivity-exhaustion shifted into high gear. She thought periodically that big success was in sight, and she worked harder than ever to keep her name in the public eye. Then would come the letdown, the depression over her still-appalling financial condition, and, for the first time, thoughts of stopping dancing to lead a "normal" family life. Leo, naturally, couldn't help imagining what it would be like to live as a more conventional couple. He was careful not to impose any direct censure of Doris' career, but whenever she faltered he held out glowing alternatives—they could live in Bermuda, his ship's regular port, for instance. Doris was susceptible to this sort of illusion only during periods of shaky health or great professional stress. Two days after her marriage, on June 12, 1932, she wrote herself a letter in answer to what must have been a major conflict at the time. Nothing like this curious item has been preserved elsewhere among her hundreds of personal documents. Signing herself with the Eastern mystic syllable "OM," she lovingly reminded herself of all her most personal reasons for dancing.

> Don't you know that you have untouched and untold powers in you, youth and strength in your limbs, experience and imagination in your head, in fact everything necessary to make magnificent dances come to life? . . . directing and composing and writing . . . are secondary pleasures. . . . I should think you could not let a day go by, you who love to feel alive all over, without dancing. . . . You might later be able to write a book that would be more lasting, and of greater value to more people than your own dancing—but no book could mean so much to you yourself. . . . I can drop in to the studio a half an hour a day, during which time I will be the master and you the slave, and perhaps we can together save for you those realms of delight. I dare say the world will thank me too.

Perhaps she resolved to meditate, or merely to keep up her daily practice. But during the next couple of years she did dance less, overwhelmed by the combined responsibilities of pregnancy and motherhood and by the effort to balance the demands of popular success against its opportunities. Her underlying artistic problem was how to build on her initial choreographic insights, and how to attract the dancers she needed to pursue this vision. She involved herself in an almost chaotic array of outside projects and schemes, all of which she believed would in some way solidify the company's position or lead to more creative work. Not only was she struggling to maintain her personal solvency and the company's; her parents' health was declining and their situation became increasingly desperate. Although it was a comfort to think she could get help from Leo in an emergency, he could not give her anything like the sums she needed to run the company. She borrowed all the money she could, trying to send her parents regular checks for fifteen or twenty-five dollars. But there was always a backlog of studio debts and company expenses, and the potential bonanzas never quite materialized.

After staging two outdoor operas in Cleveland, teaching for three weeks at Perry Mansfield Camp in Steamboat Springs, Colorado, and giving the annual teachers' course in August at the Humphrey-Weidman studio, she spent most of the fall of 1932 on the Broadway revue that was to be called *Americana*. Fourteen girls and three men, including Charles, were dancing in the show at good salaries. Doris was paid well for her work as dance director, which consisted of rehearsing and staging the dance numbers, plus training replacements for dancers who became injured or had to leave the show. This last was a never-ending job, Doris discovered, and it spoiled the easy money she otherwise collected on every long-running show she was associated with. For a while there was talk of her dancing in *Americana* as well, but she said there were royalty problems for the scores to the only pieces she could do. She was probably apprehensive because the Hungarian-gypsy orchestra director on the show insisted on making all his own arrangements. After auditioning what seemed like every piece in the Humphrey-Weidman repertory, the Broadway producer J. J. Shubert decided that *Water Study, The Shakers,* and Charles' *Ringside* were what he wanted in the show. Doris also did a special staging of the Blue Danube Waltz.

She dubiously allowed *Water Study* to be done in a "cellophane set," which she probably loathed, but she fought with the producers over what she considered inadmissible commercialization. José recalled a scene in which she told Lee Shubert to keep his predatory hands off her work and then turned away and continued the rehearsal. According to Limón, the "tyrant of Shubert Alley" had wanted to shorten *The Shakers.* Eleanor King described the argument as resulting from Shubert's desire to change the prim *Shaker* costumes from brown to purple and white. The dance remained intact, but Doris' reputation as a team person, so essential in the Broadway theater, was not enhanced. Following tryouts in Philadelphia, *Americana* opened in New York on October 7, 1932. Doris and the company received good notices for the high caliber of their work, but the show seemed uneven to many critics. In December the Shuberts closed it and took it on the road, where they planned to make changes and rename it *American Bally-hoo.* This effectively cancelled Humphrey-Weidman's run-of-the-show contract. Although it didn't make them rich as they had hoped, *Americana* brought the modern dancers into the commercial theater. As the show came to an end, Charles was already working on *Candide,* his evening-length pantomime-comedy, which was to be produced for a week on Broadway by Michael Myerberg. But Doris' forays into the commercial stage became more selective and, to her, usually less than satisfying.

She already had a long string of grievances against commercial producers to back up her instinctive mistrust of show business. Leon Leonidoff repeatedly auditioned *Water Study* in the summer of 1930 for possible inclusion in the stage show at Radio City. He didn't sign the company, but he later produced a *Water Ballet* that Eleanor King indicates had more than a titular resemblance to Doris' work. The same year she and Charles choreographed the Norman Bel Geddes production of *Lysistrata,* which was so successful it ran a year. Doris wanted to "rehearse the daylights out of it" but was taken off the payroll when she couldn't convince the producers that weekly brush-ups were necessary. Humphrey-Weidman needed tours and out-of-town appearances that would be more substantial than the usual one-night stands, and these were often in prospect but always slipping away. According to critic Margaret Lloyd, the Shuberts offered to arrange a Dance Repertory Theatre tour after its second season, but though Tamiris favored it, Graham and Humphrey-Weidman couldn't agree to continue joint concerts beyond New York.

By the spring of 1932 the company had come to the attention of impresario Sol Hurok, who assured Doris "he wants to do for the American dance what he has for foreign artists." She perceived, however, that though the poverty-stricken condition of American dancers might be causing him pangs of conscience, it was Hurok's foreign attractions that "seize almost every available date and penny. He's particularly interested in us and *would* book us *but* he has Wigman and group coming over next year, and he would try to raise a subsidy for us, but those things are hard to believe—but believe me I like you!" Hurok finally did agree to arrange a tour for the fall of 1933. It necessitated some messy negotiating and a financially debilitating settlement to extricate themselves from an existing contract with William Gassner's Concert Guild. In the event, Hurok's enthusiasm lapsed with the birth of Doris' son.

Her cynicism about ever achieving popular success received periodic boosts from the hard-bitten but still idealistic Ruth St. Denis, who wrote Doris early in 1934, when Doris and Charles were doing one of their more elevated commercial jobs, Molière's *School for Husbands*, "all great artists have had to paint bathtubs . . . their real genius is in the standard that they maintain in the face of difficulties and discordant conditions."

Charles' easy-going temperament and his gift for characterization and humor gave him an advantage in commercial work. He liked the money, and he probably also liked being relieved of the many strains of concert work—everybody at times felt the weight of Doris' unrelenting high ideals. After *Americana* Charles did a succession of shows including *As Thousands Cheer* and *Life Begins at 8:40*. The money he earned enabled him to buy a farm in Blairstown, New Jersey, which became a holiday home for the whole dance family. With Doris also out of concert work, their professional interests so diverged for a while that the men's and women's sections of the company began to acquire separate identities, and Doris took to crossing out Charles' name when she used studio stationery. Their personal relations, however, were, if anything, closer than ever.

Doris became pregnant during the *Americana* caper. She had wanted a child and so had Leo. Although she refused to be effusively maternal—she referred to "my baby project" and "my biological composition," and hoped the little darling would make its appearance according to the schedule she had mapped out—her overall state of mind during the latter stages of pregnancy and early motherhood was very positive and even relaxed.

Through the winter of 1932 she continued to give lecture-demonstration programs with the girls in the company. She planned to write her theory book during the spring, when she thought she would be out of action, but Hall Johnson asked her to coach a company of Bahamian dancers for his play *Run, Little Chillun*. This job consisted mainly of reshaping some authentic ritual dances for the proscenium stage. Doris found this work so interesting she wrote an article for the *American Dancer* magazine (July 1933) about the original fire dances, brought to the Bahamas by slaves from East Africa. As usual, however, compromise was in order. The dancers, she wrote to her parents, "of course, are superb, in fact the most interesting feature of the whole show, but Hall [Johnson] wants them cut down to nothing almost so his rather heavy and sanctimonious drama may proceed." She was supposed to get a royalty from the show, but it barely made enough to pay the stagehands, who, by union fiat, had first claim on any earnings.

Stanley McCandless asked her to help him with a demonstration of lighting techniques at Yale, and she complied with a piece to Debussy's Nuages et Fêtes for Eleanor King. In June, Doris went to Vermont for a few weeks' vacation and visit with her parents, who had moved in with Julia's old friend Auntie May Miller. Doris saw her father only once more, when she took her son to Vermont early in 1934. Horace died that March.

From her 1933 summer stay in Vermont she returned briefly to the city in answer to an SOS from Charles, who was having trouble with *Candide*. Her help was unavailing, and José later called the production "my first taste of artistic disaster." Radio City approached her about including *Life of the Bee* in its June stage show, but "I simply could not undertake it." She also had some inquiries from RKO about directing dances for a couple of movies at this inconvenient time.

The company had signed for important performances with symphony orchestras, one at the outdoor Lewisohn Stadium and two at Robin Hood Dell in Philadelphia in August, and Doris made a plan so she could manage it so soon after her child's birth. She felt obligated to dance, but there was nothing suitable in the repertory, so she decided on a new piece, to the neoclassical Suite in F by Albert Roussel. Following Doris' scenario, Charles choreographed the Prelude as an Opening Dance of greetings and salutes. Then Doris gave herself the central role in the slow Sarabande, a "dance of seductresses, sinuous, voluptuous," according to José, and the piece ended with a Gigue around a maypole.

Doris missed what was supposed to be her delivery date, June 26, and everybody began to get anxious about what would happen to their contract if she was unable to appear at Lewisohn. (The first concert was scheduled for August 7 but was rained out and postponed till the next day.) Finally, on the doctor's advice, they induced labor by racketing around the pothole-ridden West Side streets in José's new Ford. The hilarious expedition had the desired effect, and Charles Humphrey Woodford was born at Lying-in Hospital on July 8, 1933. Pauline announced his arrival to their friends Eleanor Frampton and Helen Hewett in Cleveland by calling him "America's next greatest male dancer," and Mary Wood Hinman, when she heard about the impending birth, predicted the arrival of "the next Mordkin." But young Charles—whom the family called Pussy or Humphrey—was to show no dancing inclinations, and his parents didn't insist.

Doris danced at Lewisohn and Philadelphia, and she said the only ill-effects were strained metatarsal arches, which made it necessary for her to wear special pads in her shoes for a while and to dance in sandals rather than bare feet. The prestigious Lewisohn Stadium concert was a success. According to the *World Telegram:* "Beethoven and Brahms play to empty bleachers. But Doris Humphrey, Charles Weidman, and their concert groups drew . . . an audience of 8,000 or more." To José, however, the Roussel *Suite* was "much ado about not quite nothing, but about not very much." He thought Doris in the Sarabande came "as close to being obvious and banal as I ever saw her," and said it was the only dance of hers "that literally distressed me. I hated it." Since he and Charles hadn't much use for the "baby project," his uncharacteristic, harsh appraisal may have been colored by that. In any case, the Roussel *Suite* stayed in the repertory for some years.

Doris had been looking for an apartment or a house all spring, because the dance family—now consisting of Charles and José, Pauline, Leo, and the newest Woodford—had decided to live together for reasons of economy. Charles and José had been sleeping on the floor at Doris and Pauline's 171 West 12th Street apartment because they were having trouble with their landlord. The family finally moved into a seven-room, two-bath, third-floor-through apartment at 31 West 10th Street in the early fall. Doris hired a series of nurses and baby-sitters for Humphrey so that she could return to work. In addition to her regular teaching at the Dalton School, she and Charles were preparing the dances for the Theater Guild's production of the Molière *School for Husbands,* and they were beginning to think about company concerts again. They gave their first official New York recital in two years at the Guild Theater in April 1934 and were hoping for an extensive national tour the following season.

During all the personal upheaval and bread-and-butter work of these years, Doris pursued serious choreography, often restricted by what dancers she could garner from the various show jobs that were in progress. Although none of the dances she created between 1932 and 1935 has survived, she made at least three works of importance to her own development. Their loss may be due in part to the fact that they were all large-group works, much harder to reconstruct in later years than a solo like *Two Ecstatic Themes.* But also, none of them proved as durable for repertory pieces as *The Shakers* and *Water Study.*

Dances for Women had the additional handicap of being disliked by the dancers who had to perform it. The dance was made for the second season of Dance Repertory Theatre (February 1931), but Doris continued to work on it for another year. Finally, by January 1932, she considered it finished, "against the combined opposition of everybody connected with it." This was the "verdict of fifteen girls and Pauline who told me that this composition was not only worthless but actually a bore." In three parts, The Fruitful, The Decadent, and The Militant, to a score composed for it by Dane Rudhyar, the dance, according to Doris, was to "try to include us all—both before and after the industrial revolution." After a poetic opening section, "full of plant and flower formations, of large leaves unfolding from stem and stamen in the group patterns, of delicate unfurling of fingers like tendrils, and petal-like opening and closing of hands," the dance turned satiric, with a mincing "comment about women as objects, as dolls." Then it concluded with a black-shrouded "statement of rebellion," and Doris' "valiant solo attempt at freedom, representing woman as militant, only to be stepped over by the tide of resisters."

The seemingly incongruous assemblage of the poetic, the secular, and the abstract suggested by these descriptions and by photographs of the dance was not unusual for Doris. She was convinced by this time that some such synthesis was needed to create the serious contemporary dance form she wanted. Even before she began reading Nietzsche in the summer of 1931, she was working with oppositional forces, and The Birth of Tragedy confirmed philosophically what she already knew in movement. Nietzsche defined the early Greek tragedy as a compound of the Apollonian and Dionysian impulses, the idealistic dream state and the naturalistic state of intoxication. Both the Apollonian self-control and self-knowledge and the Dionysian release from illusion and suffering were necessary to establish the true tragic image. According to Nietzsche, the early Greek chorus was neither narrator nor the "democratic" voice of the people against the gods, as it came to be thought of later, but the embodiment of the drama itself, an abstraction that could offer the spectator the "metaphysical solace . . . that, despite every phenomenal change, life is at bottom indestructibly joyful and powerful." Nietzsche saw the chorus as composed of "satyrs, nature beings who dwell behind all civilization and preserve their identity through every change of generations and historical movement." Speaking of poetic metaphor as a set of light and dark, clear and cloudy images that blend into one another, are almost present within each other, yet retain their contrary meanings, the philosopher spoke of tragedy as "a Dionysiac chorus which again and again discharges itself in Apollonian images." This chorus he pictured as a "chorus of the transformed, who have forgotten their civic past and social rank, who have become timeless servants of their god and live outside all social spheres."

Although Nietzsche did not refer to theatrical dancing—he thought the

German operatic tradition would reanimate the tragic spirit in the modern world—his descriptions could refer, perhaps even more aptly, to the symphonic movement group as Doris had imagined it and used it for ten years. She must have found in him not only an echo of her observations about the complementary nature of life forces—fall and recovery, earth and heaven, the rational and the nonrational—but also a prescription for a choreographic scheme that would be both impersonal and universal. Unlike Martha Graham, Doris did not stage the Greek myths with heroes and villains reinterpreted according to modern psychology; instead she tried to re-create Greek theater itself, with themes appropriate to modern life. Unlike her own heir,

Dances for Women. Doris on the top box. Photo by Edward Moeller. (Dance Collection, NYPL)

José Limón, she seldom made dances about specific characters from history or literature; her dances, rather, were about the life forces that moved all persons, as embodied in choral groups or archetypal figures. Throughout her career, her most memorable dances had the quality of shifting imagery, of metaphoric dream-states merging with primordial rapture, as invoked by Nietzsche. This is the quality of *With My Red Fires, New Dance, Lament for Ignacio Sánchez Mejías, Day on Earth, Night Spell,* and her last great work, *Ruins and Visions.* It was also, probably, the quality of *Dionysiaques* and *Orestes,* the other two big works of the early 1930s.

Dionysiaques was directly inspired by Nietzsche, as well as by a book Charles had given her on the Minoan excavations in Crete. First performed at a Guild Theater concert by Doris and the "concert group" (without Charles) on March 13, 1932, the dance carried the following program note. "In a ritualistic bacchanale, the ancient practice of sacrificing a chosen one for the good of the many is celebrated again." In the bull-god cult of ancient Crete Doris reencountered the theme of social renewal that she had expressed in *Life of the Bee.* Starting from a quite literal scenario that she pencilled on the back of some glossy photos of Charles, for three years she pondered the idea of the Apollonian will to balance struggling with the Dionysian will to grow, until "I could make it true for us, and remove the look of imitation of an ancient rite." It was probably inevitable, however, and not to the dance's discredit, that John Martin thought it was "by way of being a contemporary restatement of the *Sacre du Printemps.*"

Beginning with the chorus moving in orderly formal lines, Doris as the chosen victim initiated a more and more erratic energy with impulsive gestures and turns. José described her solo as a dance of

> strange, convulsive, quivering movements of arms, shoulders and torso . . . wild, abandoned leaps, ending in astounding backward falls to the floor, from which the body would rebound in some incredible fashion and stand on tiptoe, in breathless attenuation seemingly for an eternity. Turns, drunken, possessed, would end with weight balanced on one foot, while the other would extend to the side at a high oblique angle, and from this precarious balance the torso would fall sideways to the floor and rebound instantly, with the extended leg undisturbed.

As the chorus of abandon mounted to a frenzy, Doris ran up José's "legs to my shoulders, stood poised and trembling, then fell forward in one piece into an abyss formed by a ring of girls, where Gene [Martel], concealed by them from the audience, would catch her before she struck the floor." From this point on the dance grew more and more chaotic. All the dancers had made their own twenty-seven-count phrases for this orgiastic finale. Eleanor King noted that they had all studied pictures of Minoan art, and Doris trusted them to "find individual ways of varying the falling-away-from-balance principle, not as an irresponsible free-for-all, but like everything else, expressing an idea with definite form and climax." *Dionysiaques* used an existing score by Florent Schmitt, a departure from Doris' usual practice of having music written especially for the choreography.

In 1931 Doris embarked on what many people believed was her greatest work, the *Oresteia* of Aeschylus. She had found a recording of Les Choéphores (The Libation Bearers), an early work of Darius Milhaud, which had speaking and singing soloists as well as chorus and orchestra, and she made a danced treatment in seven scenes centering around Electra and Orestes' plot to kill their mother, Clytemnestra, to avenge their father's murder. She worked on this dance for at least three years, always trying to get some sponsor interested in it, and hoping eventually to set the other two sections of Milhaud's work, Agamemnon and Eumenides. Leopold Stokowski agreed to audition it in May of 1933, and the company hoped that under his direction they might produce "one of the supreme tragedies of the Western world," according to Eleanor King. The great man decided to leave for Europe the day of the audition, however. Doris never found the backing to produce *Orestes,* though it was shown in studio performances to the recorded music. Since it predated Martha Graham's first Greek dramas by fifteen years, the fact that *Orestes* was never fully produced constitutes an imponderable loss to the development of American dance, not to mention the fortunes of Humphrey-Weidman.

Among all these disappointments and distractions there was also the problem of repertory. Even if Doris could make the advances she strived for in her choreography, at the rate of one or two big dances a year, she could not supply enough new works to keep the company a going concern. With Charles off doing shows much of the time, she filled in programs with her old pieces—*Water Study* and *Shakers* were perennial favorites, as was her solo *Two Ecstatic Themes*—and made new solos and lighter group pieces, chiefly *The Pleasures of Counterpoint.* When the first section was premiered, at the March 1932 Guild Theater concert, it was performed once at the beginning and once at the end of the program. The second time Doris took the solo role which had been shared by two other dancers initially. John Martin appreciated the chance to see the dance twice, but he didn't think it exceptional, calling it a "tried and true Dalcrozian approach to plastic counterpoint." This irritated Doris, who told her parents, "The joke is that the dance was all done long before the music was composed, and we had a devil of a time fitting them together." Two additional sections were shown in April 1934, one with music by the original composer, Joseph Achron, and one by Louis Horst.

She did duets for herself and Charles: *Burlesca* (Bossi), *Three Mazurkas* (Tansman), *Rudepoema* (Villa-Lobos), and *Alcina Suite* (Handel) co-choreo-

Orestes. Photo by Doris Ulmann. Collection of Charles H. Woodford.

graphed with Charles; and a trio, *Exhibition Piece* (Slonimsky), with Charles and José. Charles contributed small pieces and occasionally lifted something from one of his Broadway efforts, finally returning to substantial repertory in the April 1934 concerts with *Studies in Conflict; Memorials to the Trivial, to the Connubial, to the Triumphant;* and the durable, lovable dance idea for which he became best known, *Kinetic Pantomime.*

Doris knew the value of light works, and she probably could toss off a dance to Handel without agonizing a great deal over it. But it provoked her to see so much of what she considered trivia going into the company's repertory just at the time when she was having to earn her living with cellophane water ballets and hugely respectable pantomimes. By 1934 she and Charles were famous. They had their pictures in slick magazines, eminent Broadway producers were said to be looking for starring vehicles for them, and they were acknowledged, with Graham, as the leaders and spokesmen for American dance. Yet it wasn't solely for the money that she accepted the job of choreographing what became *The School for Husbands* for the Theatre Guild, which opened in October 1933 and ran for several months in New York and on tour.

The assignment was another escapist ballet interlude, *The Dream of Sganarelle*, which she set as a series of "antique dances" to Lully, Rameau, and others contemporary with Molière. The costumes were lush. She and Charles and the company did eight shows a week for a while at Broadway salaries, and they were admired for their sophistication and wit. "I wouldn't lose the contract for anything," Doris wrote to the family in Vermont. "We've been anxious to make just such a break into the best of the legitimate theater, and here it is. They need us a lot only they don't know it yet."

But instead of the beginning, *School for Husbands* turned out to be virtually the end of her hopes that serious dancing would find its rightful place in the theater, that modern dancers would be appreciated and paid as generously as tap dancers or tragedians. On the road in Pittsburgh, she was reading Vaslav Nijinsky's biography by his wife, Romola, and for a depressing moment she saw her situation with terrible clarity. She told Leo that by comparison with the work of the artists in Diaghilev's Ballets Russes,

> our artistic efforts seem impossible of fulfillment . . . so what are we doing? Giving the heart of a whole season to repetitions of a seventeenth-century ballet, the rudiments of which we learned in a haphazard way (or I did) from a ballet master here and there twenty years ago in Chicago,

Rudepoema. Doris and Charles. Photo by Helen Hewett. (Dance Collection, NYPL)

and with the rest of our time we teach a system only fragmentarily worked out to mostly people who want exercise and like it to be modern-ish. How preposterous to try to give concerts of our own under these circumstances. Yet we must, or atrophy. Preposterous to do, as we have in the past, everything for ourselves, supervise the lights, the stage set, the music, even the publicity and the advertising, and no time to lose either with forty years leaping toward me. We must have help.

7 MAKING DANCES, 1934–36

The Bennington School of Dance exerts a magical but somewhat obscure power over the history of modern dance. While the choreographic products of its nine-summer existence can be placed in the pantheon of Great Works and the performances can be fondly summoned up in memory, the ongoing business of the program and its aftereffects are hardly spoken of now. Bennington was primarily a school, "a center for the study of the modern dance in America." According to its first prospectus in 1934, "the Bennington School is designed to bring together leaders and students interested in an impartial analysis of the important contemporary trends in the dance."

Humphrey-Weidman's place in it was assured from the beginning. If the project was not to be a teaching platform for Martha Graham alone—the sympathies of its administrators leaned in Graham's direction—then Doris, Charles, and Hanya Holm were the logical next most important figures. Doris and Charles had a track record at least equal to Graham's for choreography, performance, directing a company, and teaching. They were, in addition, well known in the theater and musical worlds. Holm was less established as a performer and choreographer, but she was a gifted teacher of the important German modern dance, having headed the Mary Wigman School in New York since 1931. (She prudently severed her official connection with Wigman when anti-German feelings heated up in 1936.) Together these Big Four represented the most distinct and articulate approaches to the new dance at that time. They, or their deputies, constituted the core of the faculty for the School's entire lifetime.

The performance aspect of Bennington, while it caused great excitement among the students, actually represented a small proportion of the program, which offered full-time study for six weeks in fundamentals and specialized modern techniques, as well as dance composition, music resources, stage-craft, and other related subjects. Special workshop groups in 1935–38 enabled the Big Four to make new dances with student dancers at their disposal (Doris' *With My Red Fires* and *Passacaglia* were made with an augmented company at Bennington), and regular company members were housed on the Bennington campus during these intensive choreographic periods. The workshop group members, as quasi-apprentices, were permitted to have their meals in the faculty dining room, and many reported that they had no time after morning and afternoon rehearsal periods to attend any other classes or even get to know the other students informally. They were a privileged few; creating a dance with an eminent choreographer was not the general Bennington experience.

For the choreographers, the dances created at Bennington could be considered only partially subsidized. Both workshop members and company dancers received only their room and board, no salaries or transportation. Music was commissioned for these special works, and production facilities were provided, but since sets and lighting were designed for the makeshift college theater or the Armory in town, they usually did not serve beyond the initial productions. (Arch Lauterer's set for Graham's *Letter to the World* had to be redesigned when Graham mounted the dance in a conventional theater.) And while the workshop sessions allowed the choreographers to experiment on a large scale, none of them could ever again command the forces to build on what they had learned.

For Doris, Bennington was usually a difficult experience. She needed the work—she had been teaching in summer programs for years—and it probably made little difference to her whether she gave technique classes at Bennington or Steamboat Springs (Perry-Mansfield Camp) or Greeley (Colorado State College). She enjoyed the scenic beauties of these summer retreats, but she was always too busy to exploit the recreational advantages. At Bennington her work load was strenuous, whether it was her summer to teach only one or two weeks of master classes (during which time she would also be preparing a concert) or whether she was in residence all summer making a dance and giving regular classes. She found the atmosphere competitive, even though the administration made some effort to schedule rivalrous factions during different periods. She also had to make arrangements for her son, which usually meant a search for a suitable nursemaid or sitter at Bennington so that she could carry on her teaching and rehearsals. By the time she got to Vermont—always thinking beyond it to the dreaded August teachers course at the Humphrey-Weidman studio—she couldn't muster up much gratitude for the college's benevolence. "To think," she wrote to Leo in 1936 from a pretty little cottage where she was staying, "that after only twenty years the humble Art of the Dance has brought this home and hearth to one of its dissenters." What she really wanted, she told him a year later, "I'm afraid will never happen during my dancing days—a season here with three performances a week." Because the curriculum changed from year to year, the faculty members could not even count on a steady job at Bennington, let alone home and hearth.

What, then, was the source of Bennington's undeniable importance? First, it did create a center, a convergence of ideas that had not previously rubbed so closely against each other. The mere establishment of the program brought into focus certain questions that had only been floating at the rim of awareness during the formative years of modern dance. People were attracted to the campus who were passionately interested in exploring and discussing these questions: what *is* the modern dance, how does one prepare for it, how does one create it, and what are its proper aesthetic concerns? Philosophical debate, of course, was not the aim of Bennington College, which sought nothing more than to sponsor a sufficiently advanced teaching program as a way to bring in some summer income. Over the years, however, the debate helped formulate the curriculum and the individual courses.

At the outset there were basically two points of view about teaching the modern dance. Its greatest strength up to that point had been the adventurousness with which individual dancers pursued their art. Even the Big Four, the most highly refined practitioners, were still teaching and choreographing experimentally. People who took Doris' classes at Bennington and in New York often described them as not systematically technical, but as a series of studies or phrases from dances. She wanted to build strength and facility, but she did not teach a system of dancing. Neither did Weidman, Holm or Graham at that time.

In addition, Doris wished to encourage *individual* dance expression. This was fundamental to her whole idea about modern dancing, though over and over again it backfired on her as dancers she had trained felt the need to break away and do their own work. From her very first days as an independent teacher, at the Denishawn studios in 1927, she had provided special times in the schedule for students to work on their own compositions, and she had depended on the dancers' individual contributions to her dances, from the institution of fundamental rhythms derived from the group's breath and impulse, to the incorporation of the dancers' specific choreographic phrases. This gave most of the people who worked with her a sense of responsibility and uniqueness, a desire to be original. Dancer George Bockman remembered that Doris and Charles "didn't smother people and smother the personalities of the people. They utilized this, whereas some other companies made everybody a facsimile of everybody else." Jeanne Hays Beaman, who took technique with Doris at Bennington in 1938, had vivid memories of her asking students to go across the floor with a basic pattern such as a walk or a run, and to make their own variations on the pattern. "Now whether it was good, bad, or indifferent," Beaman told an interviewer, "I still had to generate some kind of approach, a thought process about how it was going to happen."

Once set in motion, this searching process was unpredictable. Sometimes it provoked confusion, rebellion; sometimes splendid ideas; and it was for the sake of these latent new directions that many moderns taught in this way. There were others at Bennington who had similar approaches. Arch Lauterer, the designer, who gave classes in production, used to set up a different structure of lights and architectural elements for each class. He then asked the students to go up onto the stage and move in that environment, to improvise in such a way as to explore the space and the atmosphere he provided.

In contrast to this open-ended process, there were those who wished to pin down certain principles, to arrest the process, in a sense, hone its most effective elements, and eliminate its flaws. John Martin had been deploring what he thought was the anarchic state of modern dance for some years, and he welcomed Bennington's plan to feature more generalized courses in modern techniques and composition alongside the classes of the star choreographers. He himself taught dance history and criticism courses the first four summers.

Martin felt that even the best modern styles were based on "personal necessities" and idiosyncrasies of the physique or the imagination. When these styles got passed on in individual studios, he thought, "imitation of a dangerous sort . . . will not only warp the creative talents of young artists in their formative periods, but lead directly to authoritarianism and barrenness." Recognizing that the modern dance was on the threshold of its second generation, Martin thought the way to avoid "rival academies" was to gather the best styles together and offer the whole spectrum to students at once. This was the idea at Bennington. "Only in some such fashion as this does it seem possible to teach the principles of modernism and avoid the creation of new and destructive orthodoxies. True modernism in the dance, as in the other arts, can never be reduced to a formula; it is basically an approach to art in

Harriet Ann Gray at Bennington. Photo by Fritz Kaeser. (Dance Collection, NYPL)

its relation to living, a point of view." Martin had already published the first of several books attempting to discover these principles, *The Modern Dance* (1933), text of the lectures he had given in his first course at The New School for Social Research. Implicit in this finding and codifying of principles, however, was the idea of creating standards, inevitably a subjective and more or less hazy process. Martin fervently wanted to protect the "legitimate artists" and shield the public from those he felt were fakes—he even proposed to call those who did not meet his standards by another name, modernistic. This category was to apply to the "aping of the legitimately modern." The fine circularity of his reasoning didn't seem to faze anyone; he was trying to solve an eternally contradictory set of needs, and as the critic of the *New York Times,* he carried great authority.

The other strong rationalizing force at Bennington was Louis Horst. By this time Horst's performing and composing activities were pretty much confined to working with Graham, but in his capacity as teacher he was giving dance-composition classes at the Neighborhood Playhouse in New York. In 1934 he also founded the *Dance Observer,* a journal devoted to the modern dance, which aided the process of centralizing the field by publishing serious reviews by dancers and other insider-critics. Horst's studies in Europe had brought him in contact not only with contemporary art and music—and, one must assume, dance—but also with aesthetic theories and methods of teaching modern art, which were more advanced than in America. By the 1930s he had begun to work out the composition courses that were to have a pervasive presence in American dance education throughout the 1940s and 1950s. "To compose is not an inspirational experience," he wrote at the outset of his book *Modern Dance Forms.* "Composition is based on only two things: a conception of a theme and the manipulation of that theme."

In his Modern Forms and Preclassic Forms classes, which made their first appearance in the Bennington curriculum in 1935, he used established musical and art precedents to guide and discipline the learning process. For years there wasn't a modern dancer who did not know how to make an Air Primitive study, an ABA form, or a Pavane as a result of Horst's classes and their many successors in dance departments throughout the country.

The effect of both Martin's and Horst's insistence on structure was to replace personal vision with universal, systematic rules for getting at a modern dance expression. This was also implicit in the aims of Bennington College and School of Dance director Martha Hill. Bennington School of Dance was not essentially a professional program. It was not intended to train performing dancers, and its student body consisted almost entirely of dance educators rather than would-be dancers. Particularly in the school's earliest years, before the institution of workshop programs or fellowships for young choreographers, those who studied at Bennington were teaching dance for a living, usually in physical education departments at universities or in private studios. They were adult women, usually not physically ideal dancer types, and they had gone through much the same dance experience as the artists—ballet, aesthetic dancing, folk, gymnastics, a little Dalcroze. But they were specifically education-minded, and often they had been exposed to quite advanced training in body mechanics, German modern dance, or specialized pedagogies.

Martha Hill, as director of dance at New York University, then at Bennington College, was a product of this kind of training, plus a few years' dancing with Graham. Dance in education was embedded in the college and university physical education departments, but those who taught it were avid to learn the latest methods and techniques. Many of the people who attended Bennington knew Hill and her associate, Mary Jo Shelly, through the Physical Education Association or through Hill's teaching in previous summers at a camp for educators run by New York University. At Bennington, for perhaps the first time, the need was perceived to teach modern dance technique on a large scale, without the originators of each technique being present. The need was answered by Hill and Bessie Schönberg's "Techniques of Dance Movement" courses.

The process of releasing technique from identification with a single personality was furthered by the students themselves. Studying even with Graham or Humphrey, they were looking toward their own students' needs and making a sort of synthesis of it all for their own use. As one teacher/student said, "You were beginning to think in terms of yourself, how you would do a certain thing, . . . your own basic way of moving." The effect this had on dance education in the colleges was incalculable. No longer was dance some sort of airy, self-expressive exercise, nor could it be considered purely a body-building discipline. After the Bennington years, dance in the colleges became far more well-grounded aesthetically and physically.

The other significant consequence of the large number of dance teachers going out from Bennington was the establishment of a firm new audience for modern dance across the country. According to Ruth Lovell Murray, who started the dance program at Wayne State University in Detroit in 1928: "All of these teachers in the colleges around the country . . . went back to their colleges and just pestered everybody until they brought [the artists they had met and seen at Bennington] on campus to perform. That's what caused what they call the 'gymnasium circuit,' which kept these companies going financially during the 1930s." The college and university audience served modern dance companies as a significant alternative to the expensive, high-visibility commercial theaters on the touring circuits.

✳

Ironically, while Bennington placed Doris in a position of leadership and even endowed her with greater dance-making resources than she had ever commanded, there was no letup in the year-round struggle to maintain the company, do her work, and progress artistically according to her own standards. Bennington was least taxing for her the first summer, 1934. She had only a week to teach; the Big Four's separate weeks were bracketed by Martha Hill's Fundamental Techniques course, which went on for the whole six-week session. Between Charles' and Doris' weeks, the company gave a concert of repertory, with no new works. But immediately afterwards she had to return to New York for the studio's teachers' course. That year she had almost the entire responsibility because Charles was doing another show, John Murray Anderson's *Life Begins at 8:40,* starring Bert Lahr and Ray Bolger. Rehearsals in New York kept him busy, and when the show moved to Boston for tryouts, he commuted to teach in the studio. Doris even made a trip to Boston for some last-minute doctoring on the show's choreography.

She was becoming disturbed about the "disintegrating" effect of her partner's dual career, but in fact the whole company was now thoroughly enmeshed in extracurricular projects. *Life Begins at 8:40* was a hit and ran for more than a year, including a tour. Meanwhile Doris signed to do the choreography for *Revenge with Music,* a Broadway version of the famous Massine/Falla ballet *The Three-Cornered Hat.* Perhaps she was attracted by the period flavor of the production, which was set in eighteenth-century Spain, or perhaps she couldn't resist another chance to improve on a Russian ballet. But the job ended in disaster for her personally and indirectly cost her a valuable company member, Ernestine Henoch (Stodelle).

She had completed the choreography for the first act and left the dancers, including about eight from Humphrey-Weidman, to begin working improvisationally on the second while she started her fall school teaching. But the show was not going well. Suddenly the producers brought in Theodore Kommisarjevsky, the famous Russian director, who had been working in England. According to Stodelle, Kommisarjevsky was unaccustomed to the workings of the American commercial theater. His approach was analytical: he tried to find the essence of each play and make a total production scheme to bring it out. Doris' work didn't fit his new conception of *Revenge*. Much to the dancers' disappointment, Doris was peremptorily fired and re-placed by another Russian, ballet dancer Mikhail Mordkin. It cannot have been consoling to her that Mordkin was quite unequal to the job, that Kom-misarjevsky left the show before it came into New York, and that the enter-prise closed in only a couple of months. The dancers reluctantly stayed in the show until the end; they needed the money. By spring Stodelle had left to travel with Kommisarjevsky in Europe. She married him and did not return to Humphrey-Weidman.

With half the company in *Revenge,* with other dancers scattered in *Life Begins at 8:40* and a touring company of *As Thousands Cheer,* and with mainstay Katherine Manning away a good deal assisting Martha Hill for a guest semester at Bennington, the planning of concerts and rehearsals be-came a major problem. The dancers were no happier about the situation than their leaders. John Martin, reporting on a series of meetings held over the summer, said it had become clear that "the increase of professional activ-ity was gradually breaking into the heretofore admirable relations of intimacy which existed between the two principals and the group." They drew up a plan to "protect the welfare of the company. We wanted to stay together, to be solvent, to continue to have technical training," according to Eleanor King. They gave themselves classes and made an assessment on their earn-ings to build an emergency fund. They elected officers, with Doris, Charles, and Pauline as honorary members, and they even ventured to petition for a greater voice in the direction of the company. The leaders agreed in part, re-alizing that morale might improve if the dancers had some sense of proprie-torship. Yet Doris insisted on retaining final artistic control. She was, then and always, a kind of benevolent matriarch among her dancers, putting some decisions in their hands but never giving up the ultimate authority—or the ultimate responsibility.

Somehow time was found in November for company concerts at Wash-ington Irving High School and at the Dance Theater in Baltimore. King, Sto-delle, Limón, and Cleo Atheneos (later succeeded by Letitia Ide) had formed the Little Group to perform their own choreography, and other company members were trying out their work in independent concerts and lecture-demonstrations. Doris choreographed Bach's Christmas Oratorio as a miracle play, with Lillian Gish as Mary, Charles as the Angel, George Bockman as Jo-seph, and other company members in supporting parts. Conducted by

Macklin Marrow, it was given on Christmas Eve at the 44th Street Theater.
And Doris and Charles worked during the fall on a concert of their own for
early January, at which the major premiere was *Duo-Drama,* to Roy Harris'
Concerto for String Quartet, Clarinet, and Piano. According to Eleanor King,
the dance—"in abstract form representing the struggle for supremacy between man and woman—had three sections: Unison and Divergence,
Phantasm, and Integration." José Limón described it, "First was the elemental, the primeval. It was robust, earthy. There followed a period of decadence, a rococo mincing of step and gesture, languid, crepuscular. There
was a resurgence, dynamic, looking to a venturesome future." Though it was
not well received by the critics, *Duo-Drama* became a memorable piece in
the repertory.

   What was supposed to sustain the company and repair the cracks in its

Duo-Drama. Doris and Charles. Collection of Charles H. Woodford.

tenuous unity was a national tour, the first to be made by a modern dance company, in January 1935. In fact, the tour almost destroyed the company and its financial solvency. In retrospect Eleanor King saw that a phase in the company's development had been completed. "That initial wave of selfless devotion to a cause which was greater than we were, that happiness of complete dedication to an ideal which had buoyed us up and helped us surmount all obstacles since the inception of the group in 1928, that original wave of creativity had obviously passed its crest."

In planning the tour Doris, Pauline, and Charles needed to know just which of the individual group members could be counted on. They drew up their own plan for "keeping the dancers out of shows and doing concert work all next year." Visionary, ahead of its time, and based largely on the dancers' scheme of the previous summer, the plan called for a twenty-four-week season with a set pay schedule, concerts in New York and on tour, and a festival week in the spring. The dancers would be taxed 15 percent of their earnings to provide some compensation for the nonperforming weeks of the season, insurance, and a production fund. A five-member administrative committee on artistic policy would be instituted, comprising Pauline, two group members, and Doris and Charles, who would have the final say on artistic matters.

The dancers were asked to accept the plan and to decide whether they would join the tour. If they were unable to tour, Doris asked them to state in writing what their reasons were and what they thought their position in the group then was. A flood of apologetic resignations poured in. Some dancers hoped to be reinstated after the tour or planned to come back in the fall. Others simply gave up what looked like a never-ending conflict between earning a living and the pressures of the company. Far from calming the dancers' anxieties, the leaders' insistence on a commitment at this time brought out fears, illnesses, and insecurities not even the dancers knew they had.

The tour took the company from Toronto to Chicago, Austin, Dallas, Ann Arbor, and Detroit, all during the month of January, with Doris and Charles doing a duo concert in Rochester on the way to Canada. The dancers were paid minimum Actors Equity salaries but Doris and Charles took no fees; in fact, they paid their own expenses on the trip. Still, though the audiences were "happy," according to Doris, the reviews were uncomprehending and the houses were poor. She felt positive about the tour, though, telling critic Margaret Lloyd how much the dancers needed the opportunity to do repeated performances of the repertory for varied audiences. She also was glad to have "opened up the field for other dancers."

There were some university concerts and lecture-demonstrations on this tour, but the college circuit had not yet been solidified in the large cities. The vast Chicago Auditorium was only half-filled, according to Eleanor King, and Claudia Cassidy's response in the *Chicago Journal of Commerce* probably represents the reaction of the more tolerant professional critics to this new idea that was making its first appearance on provincial stages. Trying to overcome her puzzlement at a form of dance that was determinedly neither balletic nor spectacular, Cassidy admitted that the company did whatever it was they did beautifully "on a bare stage, practically in sackcloth and picking up the ashes of theater dust on their strong, bare feet, they do vital, compelling things in the name of natural self-expression." Cassidy liked Charles' work better than Doris', though she admitted she found *Water Study* "strangely absorbing." Other press persons were not even grudgingly kind; some called the whole enterprise dangerous.

A groundbreaking accomplishment that brought modern dance to the wider American public, the tour also put the whole concert-dance field in a new light. Humphrey-Weidman presented itself as a fully professional, theatrical company and thus unavoidably set itself up as an alternative to a ballet company. While Denishawn and other groups like the Marion Morgan dancers could always be thought of as vaudevillians, Humphrey-Weidman made insistent claims to high art. Ballet purists and cultural conservatives could no longer dismiss the modern dance as an aberration confined to progressive enclaves in New York. The debate had been launched. It grew hotter in the years that followed.

Although John Martin called the tour "financially encouraging," it was far from successful at the box office. In Chicago, Doris told Leo, the house was so small "they would only give us half the money contracted for." The company had started off the year with a nagging old debt of ninety-five dollars, a considerable sum then, to their former manager, William Gassner, for his commission on *Americana*. They spent the spring following the tour trying to recoup their losses, but money earned on short out-of-town trips to Boston; State College, Pennsylvania; and Great Neck, Long Island, only filtered out again in salaries and transportation.

One financial gain turned out to be the American premiere of Glück's opera *Iphigenia in Aulis* (1774), which Doris and Charles choreographed for the Philadelphia Orchestra under Alexander Smallens' direction. As on *School for*

Husbands, Doris worked with cheerful facility; she had no peripheral production worries, no money to raise. "I love to work at it," she wrote to her mother, "just because I like to compose better than anything in spite of the fact that I would never choose a Glück opera if left to my own devices." She and Charles shared the assignment, which required nine dances and had to be done in three weeks of nonstop rehearsals. Designed by Norman Bel Geddes, the production, according to Eleanor King, was "overwhelmingly beautiful." The premiere in February was very successful, though by that time Doris felt she hadn't polished the dances enough. One critic called the dancing "the most enlivening feature of the offering."

Doris had welcomed this project originally because she thought at last she was going to see *Orestes* produced. The orchestra had first proposed *Iphigenia* in a package with three additional ballets, *Orestes,* Stravinsky's *Firebird,* and a Paul Bunyan piece that Charles would do. All of these fell by the wayside in the intervening months, leaving *Iphigenia* as the sole choreographic task. Probably the real source of Doris' eventual dissatisfaction with it was that once again she had to subordinate what she considered her real art to an essentially nondance production. What was to have been the *Orestes* premiere date became a benefit concert for the orchestra, to which Humphrey-Weidman's contribution amounted to encores of their successful orchestra pieces, *Roussel Suite* and the Ravel *La Valse,* with Doris and Charles doing their Handel duet, *Alcina Suite.*

In April Doris took nine of the girls on a one-week tour of women's colleges in Virginia, where they did lecture-demonstrations, sections of dances, and Doris' solos *Variations on a Theme of Handel* (Brahms) and *Two Ecstatic Themes.* On the way back to New York, Ernestine Henoch and Eleanor King capped the season's defections by telling Doris they had other plans for the summer and would be leaving the company.

Doris had already started working with an understudy group, which numbered five or six girls by that time. In return for free classes, they learned the repertory and performed when an "augmented" group was required. Members of this group graduated to become valued and long-standing company members, including Sybil Shearer, Katherine Litz, and Beatrice Seckler. But as classes finished at the studio in May, Doris felt far from confident about the forces at her disposal. Bennington was bearing down on her. That year Martha Graham was to inaugurate a three-year workshop program, creating a work for Festival performances (it turned out to be *Panorama*), and Doris, not to be outdone, would offer a big premiere, *New Dance,* on the Humphrey-Weidman concert set for August 3. She began the summer with what was for her a most precipitous and rash act—she fled for a vacation she couldn't afford.

She needed to think about the new dance, and she was exhausted from the long and harried spring. At first she planned a visit with Auntie May Miller in Vermont. She would then take Pussy to Charles' farm. But the combined prospect of looking after an active, noisy two-year-old and rusticating among family and friends in Vermont suddenly seemed impossible to her. She couldn't leave Pussy on the Blairstown farm alone because she was sure Charles and José couldn't stand his early-morning "whoops, bird cheeps, and vocabulary rehearsals . . . and go through a day with him. . . . Of course he's lots of fun too, but I'm just not built to enjoy it and think of nothing else." At the last minute she cancelled all the arrangements it had taken her several weeks to make, borrowed money on her insurance, and took Pussy on a two-week trip to Bermuda. Though they returned on Leo's ship, she saw very little of her husband—officers were not encouraged to mingle with the passengers, even their own families—and dancer Katy Manning went along to keep her company. Back in New York she sent Pussy and his nurse to board with a family on Long Island. Leo left for a long cruise to South America, and Doris began rehearsals. She must have found the serenity she needed, because the dance she produced turned out to be not only her most important choreographic achievement to date, but a tremendous affirmation of her faith in the healing, inspiring powers of group action.

✳

If there were any specific literary ideas that contributed to *New Dance,* Doris didn't acknowledge them. According to Joan Levy (Bernstein), she just began making steps, first to some music of Chabrier, and later to the Roy Harris variations on When Johnny Comes Marching Home. Wallingford Riegger, the composer of the dance, came in and wrote his score after the choreography was completed. Norman Lloyd, who with Ruth Lloyd served as musical director for Humphrey-Weidman from 1936 to 1938, has made the interesting observation that in *New Dance* and possibly some other large works, Doris gained structural coherence by setting the dance on an existing score, then erasing the score and applying another musical form. He noted, however, that the *New Dance* Variations, with their complex rhythmic counterpoint, were set on Doris' own scheme. These variations were the work of individual company members. Doris assigned all the dancers to choreograph one, and then she chose what she considered the most appropriate for performance.

The overall scheme for *New Dance* was tight, supremely logical—and kinesthetically arresting. The dance starts with a central couple (Doris and Charles) who greet each other and dance harmoniously yet individually while the members of the group watch them from tiers of boxes placed at the sides of the stage. The female leader gradually draws the women off the boxes and into a resonant percussive dance that ends with a flurry of propulsive rushes toward the center of the stage and whirling exits. This is followed by a men's dance, choreographed by Charles, which establishes a similar idea. The four men advance toward a central meeting ground where they can address each other with comradely though aggressive gestures. Repeatedly they regroup, as if to redefine the possibilities of the simple dancing-space. The female leader draws the men's and women's groups together in a slow diagonal procession, and they celebrate their unification with a series of exclamatory advances toward the audience and some anticipatory circular runs.

Up to now the dance has made continual reference to center stage as some nearly-mystical focus or holding-point for the group, if ever the group should become strong enough to occupy it. The curtain is lowered long enough for the boxes to be moved—when it rises again, the dancers are found ranked around a central, stepped structure. In shoulder-to-shoulder groups of two or three, they begin circling with a running hitch-step, to a lively syncopated rhythm. When the music comes to a cadence, the groups coalesce to form a spokelike line that addresses a single group member, who then dances his solo while the group continues to circle the boxes. Finishing, he steps onto the boxes. There are now to be three distinct but complementary elements going on—solo dancers, the ever-diminishing group circling the boxes, and the ever-growing group on the boxes. When all the dancers have ascended the boxes, each soloist comes down to recapitulate his individual statement in capsule form. With the male and female leaders in front, the dance ends as all spin right, then left, then right, giving off a tremendous, condensed, joyous energy.*

One thing that marks Doris as a romantic beneath her modernist intentions is her frequent use of dances to show humanity in an idealized state. "Comment on our times through group dancing has always been my sole aim," she wrote around 1936 in one of two drafts for a lecture on *New Dance*, and it seems that in her most despairing moments she gave herself over most completely to a vision of a better world. She responded to an im-

---

*About six dancers could fit on the boxes. The others performed the concluding sequence of turns on the floor.

pending World War II with the ordered lyricism of *Passacaglia*, to the collapse of Humphrey-Weidman and her own dancing career with the idyllic
Day on Earth, and to her final illness with another Bach piece, *Brandenburg
Concerto no. 4*. These dances were sometimes criticized as escapist, but eva-
sion was never one of Doris' tactics. Rather she saw in dance action a way
to state positive social forces, and when she met adversity she countered it
with faith and renewal.

Her sense of the ensemble as realized in her own dance company was almost tribal, and nowhere is this better shown than in *New Dance*. The art
historian Robert Farris Thompson has noticed in African dance a strong sense
of social identity and has described the interrelated roles of soloist and
group, leader and ensemble, in arriving at "moral perfection." It seems that
this is what Doris was aiming for, though she made no direct use of existing
tribal forms or iconography. In *New Dance* she tried to create ritual and atavis-

Variations and Conclusion from *New Dance*. Photo by Sidney Bernstein.

tic power through the concrete act of dancing, searching out ways to reconcile the conflicting demands of the frontally focussed proscenium stage and
the inward-facing communality of folk dance. Against the long, persuasive
phrases of the gathering-together sections and the celebratory outbursts of
the final variations, some members of the group are constantly making percussive, throbbing movements, beating time and urging on the action in the
same way that African drummers do. The converging group keeps reassert-
ing its unity with circle and cluster formations, then announcing its force
more presentationally by addressing the audience straight on. The leaders
keep their membership in the group, even when for theatrical reasons they
are set apart, by demonstrating movement patterns that the group can share.

   With the analytical thoroughness of a critic, Doris discussed her compositional tools and processes in her extraordinary lecture on *New Dance,* noting
that she chose what she called a "Broken Form"—"an unfolding continual
change, with contrast but very little repetition"—to convey the sense of in-
completion that is the problem of the piece. As the leaders begin to per-
suade the group to merge, she used the "Cumulative Form by which only
gradually by accretion the whole group comes to perform the theme." As
she knew from experience, "a group never accepts immediately en masse."
In the Variations and Conclusion the united group creates a basso ostinato in
"Repetitional Form" that supports and controls the solos, which are in Broken
Form. She not only understood these elements as distinct forms with predictable effects but was able to account philosophically for their dramatic sequence in the dance. As to the limitation of body parts in the movement, she
said foot and leg gestures were more elemental, more often used in folk
dancing, so she reserved active use of the torso, arms, and head for the closing passages, when she considered this society to have evolved to a more
sophisticated state. She said the boxes were placed at the sides initially to
create an arena in which the leaders began their lobbying while the "uncon-
vinced but interested" group looked on as an audience. She gave reasons for
the rhythms, the sections of symmetry, the interplay of soloists and group.

   Artists in more recent times—the minimalists, for instance—have believed
that exposing their working process to public view was a perfectly acceptable thing to do, but in the 1930s perhaps the public wanted them to be
more mysterious, more intuitive. Doris may not have actually worked any
more consciously than her contemporaries, but perhaps she had a more
highly developed verbal sense than others, or perhaps she was less willing
to cover her tracks, to interpose any degree of doubt or opacity between her
idea and her audience.

New Dance was a self-contained statement, several self-contained statements, as it turned out, since sections of it, most often the Variations and
Conclusion, were performed as separate dances. It was also the culmination
and resolution of a larger idea, the New Dance Trilogy.

In her projected talk, Doris explained the genesis of the trilogy and the reason for making the last part first:

> I had an accumulation of things to be said which could no longer be con-
> fined within the limits of a short dance. There was the whole competitive
> modern world in upheaval; it must be expressed and commented upon
> and it was too large a theme for fragments and episodes. Whether it was
> my personal life within this world or my sense of technical sureness that
> impelled me into these three dances is difficult to say. I believe it was
> both. In almost the entire dance world I had seen nothing but negation.
> Anyone could tell you what was wrong but no one seemed to say what
> was right. It was with this mental conflict that I approached New Dance
> first, determined to open up to the best of my ability the world as it could
> be and should be: a modern brotherhood of man. I would not offer nos-
> trums and I could not offer a detailed answer. It was not time for that, but
> it was time to affirm the fact that there is a brotherhood of man and that
> the individual has his place within that group.

She conceived each of the three sections as stating a different part of her argument. Having drawn the joyous blueprint that would be its goal, she
"could return to the theme of life as it is: in business, in sport, in the theater,
and in personal relationships. This I did in Theatre Piece. When I had finished
these two, the first in symphonic form, the second in dramatic form, . . . there
still remained the theme of love, of the relationship of man to woman. . . .
This I treated in With My Red Fires." One of the most striking aspects of this
sweeping idea is that it was choreographed in three different expressive
modes: choral, satiric, and abstract-dramatic. The three parts were never performed together; they were thought too strenuous for the dancers—and
probably for the audience—to tackle in one evening. During 1935–36 and
1936–37 New Dance and Theatre Piece were sometimes given as a double
bill, and in the summer of 1936 this coupling alternated evenings at Bennington with the premiere of With My Red Fires, which shared a bill with
Charles' big piece of that summer, Quest. Perhaps because it never was seen
as a whole, the New Dance Trilogy has seldom received critical consideration. Its separate parts got their due accolades, but it made no cumulative
impact in its own time, and any attempt at a general assessment we make

now must be handicapped by the loss of *Theatre Piece*. It is in fact a tribute to Doris' range that these three works, created within little more than a year's time, are remembered for entirely different reasons: *New Dance* for its superlative handling of group composition, *Theatre Piece* for its nonrealistic satire, and *Red Fires* for telling a story powerfully in the modern dance idiom.

With written accounts and a few photographs to guide us, we can make

Theatre Piece. Photo by Martin Harris. (Dance Collection, NYPL)

a guess at what *Theatre Piece* looked like. Although its critics didn't stress the connection, it appears to have been a cousin of some of the Cubist and Bauhaus theater pieces that were done in Europe in the 1920s. Not for another twenty years would an American choreographer—Alwin Nikolais—use architectural elements and half-concealed bodies as part of a total, nonnaturalistic comic-fantasy world. After its premiere at the Guild Theater on January 19, 1936, Margaret Lloyd described *Theatre Piece* vividly in the *Christian Science Monitor*. The dance was set in the standard Humphrey-Weidman decor of "square and oblong platinum colored blocks and tall, columnar screens." By invisible means, "blocks become dislodged and form unexpected openings. The action creeps or plunges in and out of the openings, mounts over the varying planes and levels." Lloyd saw "something almost surrealistic about the trunkless head and shoulders gliding uncannily above one plane, while in an opening below disconnected legs or bodiless arms seem to carry on an unrelated conversation." To her this "strange, elusive phantasmagoria . . . makes all but the greatest dancing I have seen look banal. It is not literal. It is not obvious. It suggests rather than outlines. But it is amazing, provocative, and potent in its implications of modern turmoil and restless dissatisfaction."

By the time Lloyd recollected the dance for her 1949 history, *The Borzoi Book of Modern Dance,* she had subordinated these visual effects to the programmatic events of the dance indicated in its section titles and copious program notes. There she tells it in terms of the raucous, self-serving antics of contemporary characters Behind the Wall, In the Open, In the Stadium, and In the Theater. Doris, once again the lone dissenter, "maintains a circular theme, sometimes in active protest, sometimes in repose, lying prone across the floor or poised on a perilous edge of one of the higher levels—a tragic figure in gauzy yellow, a fragile, ethereal figure embodying delicate strength, courage, and high purpose." Here as in some of the more optimistic moments of *With My Red Fires,* the movement anticipated the Utopian cadences of *New Dance.*

In coming so close to modern-day behavior, in presenting a social comment so overtly, Doris for once won the approval of the political activists. Elizabeth Ruskay in the radical *New Theater Magazine* hailed *Theatre Piece* for its "condemnation of our present society." She praised the dance for being close to the audience's experience and seeming to "indicate a yearning and demand for a better world." On the other hand, the dancers considered the work avant-garde for its day, according to George Bockman. John

Martin saw it as an anti-Utopia, "Its satire has such tang and its fantastic approach to the life of the day is so inescapably devastating, that one is moved
to place it in something of the category of a choreographic Erewhon."

Doris had another special purpose in *Theatre Piece*. Aware that her work
was sometimes criticized as being too serious, she wanted to prove that she
had a sense of humor. And since this dance was to be a cautionary excur-
sion on the way to a loftier vision, she could relieve the largely abstract seriousness of the *Trilogy* without seeming frivolous. Perhaps, too, a subtle element of competition was entering her relationship with Charles. They often
pursued similar choreographic ideas. Charles' *Lynchtown* of 1936, for instance, given as part of his suite of Atavisms at the same New York concert
that saw the premiere of *Theatre Piece*, was an extended meditation on the
theme of scapegoating and the mass instinct for violence. Doris worked with
the same ideas in the second part of *With My Red Fires* later that year. Until
Theatre Piece, however, Charles had been the group's master of comedy. It
seems apparent too that Doris' comic style was influenced by Charles' kinetic
pantomime.

Partly because of increased touring and performing activity, the modern
dancers were coming out of obscurity in the second half of the 1930s. Acces-
sibility became a pervasive problem for all of them. Audiences could no
longer be counted on to understand instinctively the abstract language of
modern movement or to sympathize with arcane experiments and dowdy,
earnest tracts. New critics were coming onto the scene who could not be
expected to nurture and protect them as their earliest mentors had done. For
instance, Walter Terry had joined the *Boston Herald* in 1936, and from the
first he voiced a demand for theatricality, for less ugliness and intellectualism,
and for a move out of the ivory towers of self-expression toward more
broadly appealing stage work. Doris herself, in a radio talk given in the
spring of 1937, recognized the "great danger that the new dance would remain an intellectual pursuit about as vital to American life as Esperanto."

In *With My Red Fires* for the first time she introduced recognizable characters, two lovers and a matriarch, who enacted scenes from a familiar human
situation—maternal disapproval of a daughter's mate. Though Doris devised
these roles more as types than as individuals, and though their conflict was
embedded in a larger dance-drama of communal passions and ritual fulfillment, people tend to remember the dance as a story, a romance. Doris herself contributed many explanations of the dance couched in narrative or dramatic terms, and a lengthy synopsis was supplied by Paul Love for the New

York premiere program in January 1937, concentrating on the literal effects of the action. For instance, after the lovers elope, "The Matriarch raises the alarm. She gathers the group, molds it to her opinion, and sends it in pursuit," and so forth. This is to describe the dance in the most reductionist terms. If we consider the piece entirely on its own evidence, it emerges as a far more unusual achievement, a continuation of Doris' experiments with modern settings of Greek tragedy.

There are many indications that she was working in the same line of Nietzschean aesthetics as in *Dionysiaques, Iphigenia,* and *Orestes.* While she was at work on it at Bennington, she described *With My Red Fires* to Leo in a letter as "a hymn to Aphrodite, or Priapus or Venus . . ." She speaks of a voice issuing from the temple, summoning up the mass sexual urge that is to be satisfied through the selection of two lovers—an almost sacrificial rite by

With My Red Fires. Doris as the Matriarch. Photo by Sidney Bernstein.

which the chosen individuals execute the will of the group and vicariously relieve its deepest longings. The first part was described by Paul Love as a "primitive love-ritual." With the Bennington Workshop group at her disposal, Doris was able to choreograph on a huge scale—for forty-four dancers, plus Charles and Katherine Litz as the lovers and herself as the Matriarch. *With My Red Fires* was the largest production ever mounted at Bennington or probably anywhere else in modern dance. Doris never had so many dancers again. She kept having to diminish the scale, and in its most recent revival (a 1972 reconstruction from a Labanotation score made when she directed it for Juilliard students in 1954) the cast numbered only twenty-three. In filmed documents of this latest production, the importance of the choric patterns becomes clear; but we can only guess at the impact they must have made with twice the volume.

In Doris' most advanced use of counterpoint, the group first surges across a three-level platform spanning the back of the space. Divided in constantly changing subunits, the fourteen women and six men (originally thirty-three and eleven) build an increasingly active, insistent crescendo of movement. The groups come together only occasionally in full unison, but their developing sense of purpose seems to evoke more and more complex rhythmic patterns and contrapuntal designs. Underlying their percussive jumps and impatient flutterings of hands and feet, their sudden monolithic halts, there is a slow, inexorable momentum as members of the group press forward, sliding their flexed feet along the ground. When it was premiered at the Bennington Armory, Arch Lauterer designed an arrangement of side panels that allowed Doris to use masking effects similar to the ones in *Theatre Piece*. Here, the disembodied limbs and torsos added to the depersonalized quality of the chorus. They must have seemed overpowering and superhuman indeed, a true realization of Nietzsche's dithyrambic chorus.

Eventually the groups draw together in a cluster and their energy subsides as they fall away to reveal a couple standing face to face, embracing at arm's length. The group then hails its protegés with percussive jumps and large running leaps of exhilaration as the chosen pair dance together. Forming a long line, the group exits across the top of the platform with small, compact running steps, and the couple lie down together.

Conceptually this part of the dance bears a certain similarity to Bronislava Nijinska's *Les Noces*, which was given for the first time in America just before Doris started choreographing *Red Fires*, during the week of April 20, 1935, by Colonel de Basil's Ballet Russe at the Metropolitan Opera House. It's not inconceivable that Doris saw this production, which John Martin hailed as "assuredly one of the great works of our time." His review was one of the few nonfamily items preserved in the company scrapbook. Doris was interested in new developments in the ballet and would have been attracted by this work, which was so advanced and severe that de Basil dared not show it in the provinces, where the Ballet Russe was adored for *Aurora's Wedding* and the character ballets of Léonide Massine.

Les Noces and *With My Red Fires* both depicted a ritual mating celebration, both were abstract group compositions in which the central characters were neutral, almost depersonalized, as if they could have been any one of the group members, and, having been singled out, became the product and target of the group's wishes. Nijinska, however, achieved her power primarily through translating the violent rhythms of Stravinsky's score into spare, thrusting steps with iconic gestures and poses for further emphasis. Stravinsky was just the sort of composer Doris stayed away from. Like the other modern dancers, she avoided music so powerful that it might influence or overshadow the dance. Whatever texture and vibrancy was to be found in her dance came not from Wallingford Riegger's spare underpinnings but from her own ability to infuse rhythm with space, so that her groups were not only dramatizing a pulse but forming body shapes and traveling designs that reinforced the pulse. No hint of folk characterization determined her rhythms or visual designs either, so that this tribe she was evoking looked like nothing familiar to the audience. The body shapes and gestural ideas derived organically from the intensities of the ritual.

The dramatic "story" of the dance is told in two succinct scenes right in the middle. Labelled "Drama: Summons" and "Coercion and Escape" by Paul Love, they depict the possessive mother's efforts to prevent her daughter's marriage. In the original production, two symbolic robed figures acted as emissaries from the chorus to summon the girl back to the maternal doorstep, an action that was later absorbed into the ensuing Matriarch's dance. Appearing from behind a tall box, she leans out and "beckons" to the daughter in a grotesque, gesture-derived phrase—hands splayed over her eyes and cheeks, she thrusts her head forward and undulates her whole body in a lamenting call, accompanied by a wordless soprano singing two-note sequences of descending half-tones. The girl leaves her lover and, giving in to the mother's nervous harangue, goes behind the box construction. The boy returns and calls her out with slow, outstretched sliding steps, and she reluctantly allows him to carry her off on his shoulder.

After the lovers' departure, the furious mother brings back the group and, thrashing her exaggeratedly long skirt like an angry snake, she incites them to punish the rebellious pair. Their movements become more predatory and more circular. They hop stiffly on two feet. They run crouched over as if gathering their strength to strike. And when the couple are dragged in, the group watch with slow acquiescing pulsebeats as the mother excoriates them by running up and down the steps shaking her whole body and head violently at them. She finally rolls offstage as if in a demonic trance, and the couple are physically beaten, dragged, and thrown on the ground by some of the group members while others begin an elated series of jumps with the arms flung up. The chorus leaves, and slowly the lovers revive, rising to their feet and at the same time ascending the steps, moving in a circle, always retaining the clasped arms that stand for their enduring bond. The dance ends with their triumphant pose at the top—a pose that recurs in the first duet of *New Dance*.

Critical attention for *Red Fires* was and is always focused on the dramatic situation, even though all the action except for the two central scenes is expressed in choral terms. Doris' superb command of group forms had achieved its most definitive results. She was trying to go beyond *Orestes*, not only by enlarging the size and expressive province of the group but also by making her protagonists more contemporary instead of basing them on classical models. Some of the classical elements were eliminated entirely or altered after the first performances. These and other changes subtly redirected the force of *Red Fires* from the group to the soloists. In its own evolution the dance imitated the course of Greek tragedy as Nietzsche saw it, toward an "anti-Dionysiac, antimythic trend in the increased emphasis on character portrayal and psychological subtlety from Sophocles onward." Why Doris revised her original intentions is open to conjecture: perhaps the more abstract early version seemed too ambitious to set before audiences in Rochester and Fort Worth. As a matter of fact, narrative was more chancy in terms of the art she identified herself with. As John Martin pointed out, up to this time romantic love had been shunned as a theme for modern dance.

Before *Red Fires*, Doris had played symbolic figures, the Leader, the Chosen One, the Outsider, but never had she given herself so specific an identity as the consuming, avenging Matriarch. It was seen right away as a star part, so much so that years later Lucia Chase, director of American Ballet Theatre, tried without success to acquire the dance as a possible vehicle for the great dramatic ballerina Nora Kaye. People close to Doris suspected she was making a portrait of her own mother, who was with her at Bennington that summer, or at least was drawing on her intimate knowledge of domineering women. She made a startling success in the role, though the Matriarch's piercing suspicion, her incensed twirling of her long skirt, her paroxysms of fury, were so different from Doris' usual reserve.

The personal drama of the three central characters is countered and finally overwhelmed by the allegorical power of the group, which personifies larger forces not amenable to human logic or persuasion. The ending is curiously Victorian, a turn of events justified by wishful morality that believes in reward for the suffering righteous. Perhaps Doris could not resist making it come out this way because of her own desire for justice and her goal of showing that society could be nobler through a faith in love. After she composed the dance she found the inscription from William Blake that gave her its title:

> For the Divine Appearance is Brotherhood, but I am Love
> Elevate into the Region of Brotherhood with my red fires.

This too seems to point to the overriding importance of the group rather than the particular significance of any one romantic act.

Even the most sophisticated audiences love stories, they love characters, and they love a happy ending. Up to this time Doris had denied herself these ingratiating devices. In some ways the duality of *With My Red Fires* sums up her own ambivalence as an artist. It came at a crossroads in her career—and in the history of modern dance. Up to this time, everyone shared the same roots, the naturalism and Grecian idealism stemming from Isadora Duncan; the desire to find indigenous, non-European and nonacademic ways of dancing; and the unacknowledged debt to the work in basic movement expression that the German modern dancers had investigated before them. Martha Graham had also read Nietzsche, she had made Greek ritual dances and tried to give epic voice to the group. In *Red Fires* the ideas of Graham and the ideas of Humphrey came closest to intersecting. Graham, after this period, placed the group more and more at the service of character. After a series of "Americana" works, she returned to Greek tragedy in the 1940s, finding in the literature an abundant store of material she could make into psychodramatic dances centering around her own extraordinary performing presence. Doris pulled back from the demonic theatricality she had uncovered, almost in spite of herself, in *Red Fires.*

8 ON THE ROAD, 1936–39

After the great surge of composition represented by the *New Dance Trilogy* and *Quest,* Humphrey-Weidman took to the road in earnest. From 1936 to 1940 the first five months of the year were spent in rigorous touring to all parts of the United States. In the absence of subsidy, endowment, or institutional sponsorship, it was the only way the company could survive. In February, March, and April 1937, for instance, there were some twenty-seven performances and lecture-demonstrations on a trip that went to the Midwest as far as Kansas, swung back to New York, down South, back to New York, and into the Boston area. The next year, after three major appearances in New York and one in Philadelphia in January, they set off on a ten-week, forty-performance marathon to the west coast, booked by the indefatigable Pauline, that was capped, after only two weeks at home to catch their breath, by another New York concert. On these tours, the company would accommodate the number of dancers to the size of the sponsor's budget, and great flexibility was possible because the repertory contained solos, duets, trios, and ensemble works for up to twelve dancers. Sometimes the company would split into smaller units so they could do more.

All this touring had a strong educational component to it. Whenever there was a day or two of interlude between concertizing and traveling, Doris and Charles would give master classes and workshops at the local university or YMCA. But even more than training dancers, they felt they were developing audiences. For several years the advocates of modern dance had been trying to explain their art to anyone who would listen and, out of their appearances in John Martin's courses at the New School, Humphrey-Weidman had devised a very sophisticated lecture-demonstration format. This could be adapted to almost any number of dancers and performing situations, and could be combined in different ways with regular concert material. For instance, in 1938 most of their college dates were billed as lecture-recitals. They would begin with a talk by Doris on "The Individual Approach to Movement and Choreography." She would then present three or four of the women in technique studies, followed by Charles and men in composition studies. These studies showed how the elements of design, dynamics, rhythm, gesture, and basic motor activity could be given choreographic shape.

The second half of the program would be four short dances drawn from a very limited repertory—touring works that year included the Brahms *Variations* (on a Theme of Handel), *Exhibition Piece*, the Variations and Conclusion from *New Dance*, Charles' *Traditions*, *The Happy Hippocrite*, a section from his longer work *This Passion*, and two new pieces by Doris, *To the Dance* and *Race of Life*. In larger theaters and cities where they had appeared before, they did a regular concert, with some short works and *Theatre Piece* or the whole of *New Dance*. *To the Dance* and *Race of Life* were explicitly aimed at entertaining the audience. *To the Dance*, which won the choreographic award from *Dance Magazine*, in the same year, ironically, as the premiere of *With My Red Fires*, was nothing more than a curtain-raiser, "an opening dance in which motifs of many of the dances are woven together to form a spirited and engaging introduction to the modern dance." It was done on almost every program, even the blockbusters like the one at the Chicago Auditorium Theater in February 1937, where it was followed by *Theatre Piece*, *New Dance*, and *Quest*. Doris, who stoically accepted the hardships of touring as a necessary if not enjoyable labor, grew tired of *To the Dance's* "unvarying mood," which she said was "hard to hold night after night." She said it became "senile" after two years because "the technique is not challenging enough to make each performance a game for improvement."

The comic *Race of Life* was based on a series of James Thurber cartoons and carried a quotation from Dorothy Parker: "This sequence represents the life story of a man and his wife; or several days, a month, or year in their life and in that of their child. Anything may be read into it or left out of it without making a great deal of difference." Doris played the mother, "the most unnatural part I could possibly have chosen." José said: "She completely made herself over. She became a gross, strident harassed female; no longer young or attractive. Me she made into a fat fool of a husband: stupid, dull. Charles Weidman took to this piece like a duck to water. He became a mischievous, noisy unruly brat of nine years old." Beset by Indians, Night Creatures, and a Beautiful Stranger, the family finally succeeds in climbing a mountain, representing material success, made of the ever-useful boxes, to plant an Excelsior banner on the top. *Race of Life* was a natural outgrowth of the satirical *Theatre Piece,* and Doris connected it to the larger progression of her visionary works that began with *Shakers,* sharing what she said was "the motivation behind all my dances . . . that 'ye shall be saved, when ye are shaken free of sin.'" Sinful though it may have been, the audience enjoyed it, and it served the touring repertory well.

Relentless scheduling wasn't the only hardship of touring, but it was a major one. During the worst of these times, the 1938 tour arranged by the fanatical, hectically efficient Pauline, in the first two weeks of February alone they played Washington, D.C., Cleveland, three colleges in Ohio, Toledo, a college in Michigan, Chicago, and the State Teachers College at Milwaukee.

Race of Life. Doris cradles Charles, José provides support. (Dance Collection, NYPL)

Many of the college dates were not even in theaters, but in the gymnasiums that were the headquarters of the physical education department sponsors. Pauline would have to simulate a theater by hanging drapes across one end of the gym, putting up some lights strategically, and trusting that the faithful boxes would complete whatever illusion was needed. No matter how bad the stages were, or how inadequate the spaces on the gymnasium circuit, Doris did not complain. "She thought you were being paid to dance like that and should be able to adapt to anything," according to Norman Lloyd. After the show, there would be costumes to pack, the boxes and lights to disassemble, and everything to be loaded on a truck for the railroad station, where a late train would take them on to the next stop. Sometimes the dancers stayed overnight in a hotel and left early the next morning, while Doris, Pauline, and Charles took the night train so they could set up in the next town or be interviewed before rehearsal. Pauline seems to be the only technical person who traveled with the company; other helpers might be theater stagehands, willing students, or sometimes just the tired dancers.

The tours yielded a great deal of press coverage, some of it predictably jingoistic. Under a headline that promised "Troupe of Dancers to Translate Stories," the *San Francisco Examiner* began an advance story in March 1938 as follows: "Take the Big Apple [the popular social dance]. Put it through a rigorous college training, give it a postgraduate course to polish off the rough edges and decorate with a Ph.D. The finished product will be something like *With My Red Fires* or *The Happy Hippocrite*." Doris and Charles somehow found the time to submit to the interviews and receptions that were essential in wooing the local populace. In Cleveland a society item reported that the wife of a prominent banker agreed to be a sponsor for a recital if Miss Humphrey would teach her husband the rhumba. Doris posed in a lunge for an article on weight reduction, to which she contributed an exercise in twisting, done entirely in relevé. In those days of the great newspaper syndicates, cuteness was retailed the way crime is today. A picture spread of four-year-old Charles Woodford in a cowboy getup gushed that the youngster's famous mother was quite human though an artist; her son even made up dances about cowboys and Indians. This copy—written by a Humphrey-Weidman press agent—ran in dozens of newspapers across the country, as did pictures of the choreographers in action and a fashion story in which Doris was seen as sacrificing her all for art because she admitted to wearing sensible shoes.

Even New York's *Daily News* columnist John Chapman took a potshot at the new dance in general when he remarked: "Years before Martha Weidman came over here and began sliding the back of her lap along the floor we struggled with the phrase 'interpretative dancing.' But now it's 'interpretive'—much simpler and cleaner, but just as goofy as ever." A few days later he backhandedly repented his irreverence: "Oop! Couple of columns ago there was a reference to Martha Weidman the dancer. Well, it was a rough estimate anyway. There's Charles Weidman and there's Martha Graham and they are partners, but I really meant Mary Wigman."

Everywhere the company went there were reviews, of course; some appreciative, some uncomprehending. And in New York and Boston there was the balm of understanding approval from John Martin and Margaret Lloyd. Doris never stopped believing she was opening up the field for her own dancing and for others. "Pioneering exactly says it in one word," she observed. "Forcing your way, with Indians and the elements to battle with and the uncertain rewards of soil which may be fertile or barren but in either case will have to be cultivated strenuously after you win your right to it."

Life was scarcely easier at home. After the spring tour there would be one or more late-season appearances in New York, a rest for a few weeks in May, then summer teaching. There were always at least two jobs, Bennington, the Humphrey-Weidman teachers' course, a summer school such as Perry-Mansfield camp in Colorado. A rest, then fall classes leading up to the year's big New York concert, usually around the first of the year, where a major new work was expected. Doris' year-round teaching commitments alone were formidable. For a few years the company gave classes at the Academy of Allied Arts on West 86th Street, keeping their 18th Street studio for rehearsals. Here Doris was committed to intermediate and professional technique classes one night a week from 6 to 10 P.M. There were stints at various New York City colleges, and one year she also taught one night a week at Temple University in Philadelphia. She gave a class at Friends Seminary beginning in 1937 to pay for Pussy's tuition there.

In 1936 she and Charles began teaching for the Federal Dance Project of the WPA, which also paid some of the dancers a rehearsal salary to prepare for a performance. Given the Dance Project's rocky political history, it never became a fruitful opportunity for Doris, only another job. For the first year, when Charles restaged his *Candide*, she revived the Prelude and Celebration from the 1933 *Roussel Suite* (omitting the section she had danced herself), and her old Tcherepnine *March*. Now thoroughly resigned to indoctrinating a novice audience, she retitled the latter piece *Parade* and added a program

note in keeping with the patriotic times, "The reaction of a crowd to a parade." She didn't have a piece at all for WPA in 1937; *Candide* was given
again, on a double bill with Helen Tamiris' *How Long, Brethren,* and it ran
most of the summer. In the fall of 1938 she redid *Red Fires* for a reduced cast
of twenty-five; after many scheduling and budget problems, it ran for a week
at the Nora Bayes Theater in January 1939, with *To the Dance* and *Race of
Life.* (She had hoped to revive *Theatre Piece* and the Ravel *Valse,* probably
counting on an orchestra, which didn't materialize.)

　　Like many other things Doris involved herself in, the WPA was mostly a
matter of gaining some exposure for her work while annexing some wages
for company members who would serve as her assistants. The situation itself
was far from ideal for her creative purposes. Humphrey-Weidman played
many benefit performances for the same reasons—often for less return. They
got to do *Red Fires* and *Quest* for 5,000 people at the New York Hippo-
drome with an orchestra of twenty (January 15, 1937), but the proceeds
above their small fee went to the International Labor Defense fund. Sometimes the effort turned out to be a drain on their always low resources. *New
Theater Magazine,* which sponsored a benefit performance of *New Dance*
and *Theatre Piece* in April 1936, rented an ill-equipped theater; without
knowledgeable stagehands or adequate set-up time, the company had to
go on with a "hysterical stage manager" after only a brief spacing rehearsal.
Doris knew the company didn't appear to its best advantage in these situations, but she thought it was either this or not appear at all.

　　In 1936 they received an invitation to take over the dance department of
Temple University for five years. In return for teaching, the university would
give the company a home. Doris declined to undertake what looked to her
like even more teaching than she was doing. If she seriously considered this
proposal at all, she must have forseen starting the company over again, because she could hardly ask the dancers to move to Philadelphia. But in any
case, Philadelphia in 1936 could never have supplied a professional modern
dance company with the audiences, critical response, or creative stimulation
it needed. At least so Doris must have guessed in turning down this gamble.

The relentless life was taking its toll on Doris choreographically. After the
prolific, ground-breaking activity of the first eight years, she now began to
have trouble realizing her most ambitious ideas. She had always been able
to make minor but serviceable dances when the occasion demanded, and
responding to the rising tide of nationalism, she made *Square Dances* (1939),

which she described as "social and ballroom dances done in a modern style," to a score by Lionel Nowak, who was then serving as Humphrey-Weidman musical director.

A more ambitious work, *American Holiday*, was so badly received at its in-progress premiere at the Guild Theater on January 9, 1938, that she never completed it. This was probably the only piece of Doris' entire career that didn't get a single good review. Even the staunch Margaret Lloyd, who appreciated the novel ways in which Doris was trying to combine disparate theater elements, had to admit that the experiment didn't work. Composed half a year before Graham's *American Document*, which also used the spoken word to expand on various hallowed American themes, Doris' dance was one of those inspired but unlikely mixtures of ingredients that might have been brilliant if she had found a way to make them come together. Satire and celebration, pageant and ritual, it had, in addition to Doris and twelve dancers, an offstage singing chorus (from Allied Arts school), an actress (Mary Morris) who spoke lines written by Doris, and spoken parts for

Square Dances (Dance Collection, NYPL)

the dancers to chant. Morris Mamorsky wrote an orchestral score which was played at the premiere in a two-piano reduction.

The dance was to have three parts. Death of the Hero "celebrates the Death of the Hero in the American struggle for independence and proclaims the causes of freedom and justice for which he died." In part two, Dance for the Living, the hero, around whose coffin Doris had danced, revived as a spirit and circulated among a crowd, spreading his ideals. Margaret Lloyd was most impressed with the rhythmic and tonal effects that were achieved when words and music were "rhythmically intertwined with the action, sometimes underlining it, sometimes pitted against it. . . . One astounding sequence, in which rhythmic motion first supports the rhythmic verbal phrase, spoken by the dancers as they move, and is then repeated as rhythmic pattern in movement alone, indicates the union that can be wrought between words and movement." The projected third part, Fourth of July, was to be "a

American Holiday (Dance Collection, NYPL)

modern celebration of the cause for which the hero died." Had this been completed, according to Lloyd, it "might have pointed up the work. It was to have combined marionettes and dancers with banners and bunting and pompous oration to show the hollow mockery, the rowdiness, and revelry" of the heroic legacy.

The *New York Sun* found the first two parts little more than "formal group-ings and pageantlike progressions," while the *New York Herald Tribune* called it a "futile exhibition . . . with its childishly and tiresomely applied ide-ology." John Martin thought Doris was making "an experiment in clarity," and to him the effort resulted in platitudes. *American Holiday* was listed in the company's press book for the 1938–39 tour, but it was never given on the road. The fact that Doris was unwilling to complete or revise the piece, or even to let it grow on the company and the audience, indicates how hard-pressed she must have been at this time.

The one fully achieved work of the period was the Bach *Passacaglia in C Minor*. She made the dance at Bennington in the summer of 1938, with a workshop group of eleven women plus twelve company members led by herself and Charles. Obviously the concentrated six-week period without ex-tra worries allowed her to work thoroughly and creatively. It must be said, however, that the score, musically extended and detailed though it was, rep-resented the kind of choreographic challenge Doris worked with most easily. She didn't pose any ideological, compositional or theatrical problems for her-self that she hadn't tackled before. Perhaps this, more than the music, was the real source of what few reservations the critics had about the dance.

Doris made several program notes and explanations of *Passacaglia*. The phrase which most simply describes it—and almost all her nondramatic dances—was "an abstraction with dramatic overtones." She also called it "my most mature dance" in a 1939 *Dance Magazine* interview. Once more she showed a harmonious group that gave rise to contrasting individual and small-group statements, as the music unfurled its twenty variations on a ground-bass theme. *Passacaglia* can easily be seen as a relative of *New Dance*. When she was choreographing it, Doris told Margaret Lloyd that it contrasted with *New Dance's* vision of "the ideal of that perfection desired and demanded by youth. Well, in maturity you come to learn that perfection is not immediately attainable, but that there is still happiness, a measure of harmony, to be found while working toward that goal." Years later Charles remembered that *Passacaglia* sought to correct the "unrealistically Utopian" conclusion of *New Dance*. In musical terms, Doris was attracted to the various needs—delicate, heroic, lighthearted, tragic—that she found in Bach, seeing them all as a source for dramatic plotless movement. She said the ostinato theme underlying all of the *Passacaglia*'s musical developments stood for "man's reiteration of faith in his ideals, despite the struggle of attaining them." According to Claudia Moore (Read), a member of the augmented group at Bennington on whom Doris made the dance, she told the dancers, "It's time we go back to the past . . . every now and then we have to go back and stand on solid ground." Read felt that the lift of the arm to the side, which was one of the primary movement phrases of the dance, stated "her whole belief that man, basically, in spite of all his meanness and destruction and horrible behavior, really is basically an heroic person or soul, and that's what she was trying to say."

Revivals of the work in which the dancers can catch this spirit are rare, and this raises the question that can be asked about all Humphrey dances: is it dated? If "dated" means that its outward appearance is no longer in fashion, *Passacaglia* is dated. So is Bauhaus architecture, or a Frank Capra film. An art work's creative value, however, does not lie in the familiarity of its silhouette or the durability of its sentiment. *Passacaglia*'s distinction lies in the assurance with which the dancers move through and divide up the stage space. They're more than forthright—they're grand. Whether stepping to a new position or changing the shape of their arms, they extend the gesture over Bach's long phrase, making the simplest movement seem important. Since there are no virtuosic steps, what we have to be absorbed in are the evolving forms and progressions of the members of the group—a visual harmony and counterpoint that corresponds to the music and creates images of solidarity, spirituality, acquiescence, and assertion. Their movement isn't released in a continuous flow; rather, they move deliberately or with calculation, even when moving fast, giving a weight to each phrase. Although the dancers are not at all balletic, the movement is large, emphatic, and musically clear, almost like the massed, framing structures of the ensemble in a big classical ballet. Where the corps de ballet exists to set off the more important designs of the soloists, Doris takes the corps as her main attraction.

Passacaglia was universally recognized as a moving and brilliant composition. Beyond that, however, the reviews must have been disconcerting. Her faithful mentor John Martin, who had never before shown himself to be especially fussy about music, suddenly developed an ear. He took an immediate dislike to the use of Bach, which he held to for years whenever Doris used that composer again. When *Passacaglia* was premiered in New York, with Charles' dance-mime *Opus 51,* Martin attributed to it "moving power and imagination and great nobility," and thought it "eloquently confirms Miss Humphrey's position as the first of American [dance] composers." However, he felt the dance won this distinction "at the cost of fighting off the independent effect of the music," which he considered so great that it "leaves no room for choreographic treatment." Walter Terry—missing Doris' philosophical point—praised the dance because it made no heavy demands. "It is theatrical, for it has sweep and suspense, serenity and exultation, and it is stimulating to the senses." Doris and Charles, Terry thought, were "not afraid to let profundity of theme and social comment rest for a moment while they encourage their audience to escape into the unreality of theatrical entertainment." And the Left press chastized her for the same reason, "Audiences expect something more significant from the Humphrey-Weidman combination."

Passacaglia represented the state of Doris' world even more than she consciously knew. Humphrey-Weidman was ostensibly at the peak of its success, but Utopia was not without its flaws. There was a challenge in the wind, and Doris either didn't see it or couldn't meet it.

The challenge was to say something to the world beyond that loyal band of modern-dance believers. The new dance had indeed reached a moment of maturity. By the last part of the decade the initial discoveries had been made, the excitement that surrounds any icon-breaking had died down, and the basic truth as perceived had been organized in some teachable form. What the modern dancers needed across the board was to become less isolated from the traditional culture they had renounced.

Theatricality was a persistent imperative, and Doris insisted that her work was theatrical. But she neglected the most obvious appearances. Terrified of cheapness and vulgarity, she was appalled one summer at Bennington when the word was going around—started in the Graham camp, she suspected—that Humphrey-Weidman was no better than Denishawn, jazzing up their dances so they would be successful on tour. Since this obviously was not true, Doris' overreaction is curious. Some glamour would have helped. Not that Doris had ever affected the "Long Woolens" look that identified some of the early modern dancers. She initially designed her own dancing costume, which became a basis for the Humphrey-Weidman rehearsal outfit: a simple long-skirted sheath with a slit to allow freedom of movement for the bare legs. Beginning about 1932, however, Pauline did the costumes, and style seems to have rated quite far down in her priorities. The dancers claimed that her clothes moved well, but their main virtue must have been economy. At least, they looked homemade. The cut was often unusual without being chic. They often came in drab colors and had an unattractive tendency to wrinkle.

Then there were the indispensable Humphrey-Weidman boxes. Designed initially by Erika Klein, they incorporated features of the new-theater designs of Adolphe Appia, Gordon Craig, and Leopold Jessner. The boxes gave a stark, architectural quality to the dance space and provided the extra choreographic dimension of height above stage-level. They could be taken apart and folded flat for transporting from one theater to another. And of course they covered the necessity of having different scenic designs for each new dance, because they could be arranged in an unlimited number of ways. But after the initial goal of correcting decorative excess had been established, they began to look sterile and makeshift.

The slightly homemade look of Humphrey-Weidman was accepted by its audiences and its critics. However, in retrospect we can see that values were changing. Over the first decade, the modern dancers had made their point. One *could* do serious, artistic dance work without resorting to unseemly decorative displays, mechanical virtuosity, or exploitation. But Doris never could relinquish the missionary attitude. She always believed she was preaching to the ignorant; that she had to explain everything patiently and never risk obscuring some point or leading people's minds a bit off the track with too much superficial attractiveness. Martha Graham recognized that she no longer needed to press the point; around this time she began to move in the direction of more stylish production, and during the 1938–39 season she toured the United States appearing only in regular theaters, avoiding the college circuit entirely. Through the 1940s Graham perfected the staging, costuming, musical and scenic devices that made her dances a theatrical as well as a choreographic adventure.

As it became increasingly sophisticated, Graham's dance was able to appeal to new audiences of intellectuals and art lovers. Humphrey kept giving her earnest lecture-demonstrations and doing her idealistic dances in their impoverished settings, and was gradually eased onto a sidetrack, along with many lesser modern-dance artists. Of the modern dancers, she was in front. Of dancers, of theater, of the wider world of the arts, she was a diminishing force.

This distinction began to be made in the very places Doris had always counted on for support. Composer Dane Rudhyar wrote a reflection on the 1937 Bennington summer for the *Dance Observer*, in which he saw Martha Graham as the spearhead not only for "purposefulness and direction" in the contemporary modern dance but for the future "a new type of body-awareness is necessary, a new sense of body-response to the impact of modern life's experiences, if the American dance is to develop in a significant and vital manner," and Graham had found it. Stung by this, Doris evidently wrote him that she felt slighted, and Rudhyar answered with a long letter that was meant to be reassuring and probably was not. Graham had developed "a new and definite [nonballetic] *technique* to express the modern individual in the modern psychological sense," while Doris was potentially the developer of the ideal of "dance-drama." "You have a highly objective, clear and constructive mind, a real sense of social values and needs, and a great power of transferring those in dance moments and choreographic-dramatic organization." He urged her to "take steps to hasten the development of that seed [which he saw planted in the *Trilogy*], by proclaiming in a book your vision."

What Rudhyar saw in philosophical terms was echoed more concretely by the *Dance Observer's* Henry Gilfond in summing up the 1938–39 season. He discerned among the modern dancers a division between those who sought to illuminate contemporary and patriotic themes and "those who would turn their faces from their environment to go in for the psychological explorations of the inner man and the abstract pattern." In the first category he cited Graham's *American Document* and Eugene Loring's *Billy the Kid;* in the second *Passacaglia.* "One goes forward; the other retreats. There can be no question, however, as to which direction the American people will support. And there can be no question, at all, as to which direction spells development and progress for the art; and which does not." Gilfond completely ignored Doris' attempts to deal with the contemporary world, her conviction that she was doing so. She was perceived as an abstractionist, and in those literal times, this looked like retreat.

Another blow, this time from almost within the family, was an article, "The Modern Dance is on the Skids," written by Maxine Cushing (Gray), which Doris learned about from Betty Horst when the company was performing in San Francisco in the spring of 1938. Cushing was trying to get the article published and had sent it to several magazines. Doris was devastated. Cushing had studied with Humphrey-Weidman and had even started to collaborate with Leo on another version of the projected theory book. Doris sus-

pected the article was Cushing's revenge because she hadn't been taken
into the company. But there was obviously something to Cushing's disen-
chantment, because the next year she was working as an advance agent for
Massine's Ballet Russe de Monte Carlo.

Any defection to the ballet camp was taken very seriously. The real com-
petitors for the attention of the theater-dance audience were the newly
emerging ballet companies, and internal rivalries among the modern dancers
began to heal as the field aligned itself in opposition to its original enemy,
now making a comeback in stylish and deliberately updated form. The death
of Diaghilev in 1929 had left the contemporary ballet scene in disarray, but
within a few years elements of the original Ballets Russes reorganized themselves into various companies and began touring. At the same time, some
determinedly American efforts were being put forth here: Catherine Little-
field's Philadelphia Ballet, Ruth Page's group at the Chicago Opera, Willam
Christensen's in San Francisco, and, most importantly, George Balanchine's
School of American Ballet in New York had all made a start on capturing an
audience for classical dancing with native themes and rhythms. During one
of Balanchine's early periods of discouragement en route to a permanent
company, his patron and partner Lincoln Kirstein had organized the Ballet
Caravan, which ironically gave its debut performances in the modern dancers' own nest at Bennington College in the summer of 1936. ("A nightmare,"
Kirstein called that occasion.) This company continued to operate for a few
years while Balanchine worked in Hollywood and on Broadway shows. The
ballet had the aristocratic appeal and the glamour to overtake the modern
dance in popularity, and its voluble, argumentative spokesman, Kirstein,
would gladly have snuffed out the whole tribe if he could.

Always overdefensive about Balanchine's then-misunderstood genius, Kirstein took on not only the modern dance and its critic-supporters but the
very visible "Russian" ballet of Massine and the post-Diaghilev Russe companies in his 1937 pamphlet "Blast at Ballet." Kirstein's book, provocative even
today, must have been a red flag to the modern dancers, clinging to their
modest audiences and hard-won choreographic gains. He paid Doris the
snob's ultimate insult by not even mentioning her name, except as having
composed a dance to a passacaglia that served to illustrate what Kirstein
considered the moderns' inconsistency in accepting preclassic forms and rejecting classical ones. Kirstein conceded that despite Martha Graham's
"frightening originality, her independence of *any* tradition whatsoever," she
had "much to offer." He somehow managed to appropriate Graham for his

side: "I can find nothing inimical to the developed classical dance as ex-
pounded, for example, by George Balanchine's *Apollon*. . . . her sense of a
projected physicality, her spinal integration, her sense of controlled entrance,
and the deep human color of her dancing style, is a purer and frequently
deeper repository of essential classicism, even if it may be a narrower one
than the easily accepted and much more superficial idiom of school-ballet."

The eccentricity of Kirstein's aesthetics can be laid to his bias for Balanchine; he felt it necessary to attack not only the modern dance but the more
conservative and more successful balletic rivals like Massine, and at the same
time to assure Balanchine's place as a classicist—*the* classicist.

Meanwhile Doris found that her work wasn't becoming any easier to get
on. Pauline did all the managerial arranging, but Doris did the worrying and
planning. What they needed, among other things, was a professional manager, but even if they could have afforded one, there were those who
doubted Pauline would relinquish control. So the ill-advised gambles kept
happening, such as allowing themselves to get booked into large college
theaters on a percentage basis: the house would be only partly filled, and
the ticket sales would net the company nothing for its trouble except the familial praise of the "several hundred enthusiasts" who could always be
counted on to show up.

When she allowed herself to think about the state of affairs, Doris knew
there was something wrong. On the 1938 tour she could look objectively at
Theatre Piece, which they did in Cleveland with Charles' *Happy Hippocrite*,
and see that it "suffers badly from lack of an orchestra," and that Charles'
piece was "too out and out entertaining and more than a little frowzy in appearance. The program lacks dignity." Later that year, Sybil Shearer, who had
left the company after three years as a principal dancer, watched the Guild
Theater performance of *Passacaglia*, Charles' *Opus 51*, and three parts of
New Dance and electrified everyone by asserting at a company meeting that
besides looking shabby and technically uneven, the company lacked conviction, which to her made the meaning go out of the dances. Doris wrote to
Leo while on tour, "I think there are lots of things wrong with us—and that
our particular contribution is progressing much too slowly and that we must
take a bold step toward subsidy—but that's not being on the skids."

Doris was trying to do something about the financial condition of the company. It seemed to her that the lack of a stable income or reliable benefactors was at the root of their struggle. She could not carry out her most imagi-

native projects without finding sponsors to subsidize them, and as she learned with *Orestes,* few of the supporting institutions she needed were willing to put their resources into a dance venture not of their own making. A dance company cannot work from one production to the next, reorganizing for each reappearance, as commercial theater companies do. It derives its identity from the projection of a repertory and a common style, and these—in the oral tradition of dance—must be carried on by dancers continuously rehearsing and reinforcing the work. Humphrey-Weidman could not offer dancers a salary during the all-important periods when they were making new dances in New York. During those times, if the dancers had no husbands or families to support them, they had to take menial jobs and fit rehearsals around them. They were paid on the road, but no choreographing could be done then. Touring, the company's only salvation, was a creative liability.

For Doris personally, touring was a flawed benefit. Like many of the dancers, she enjoyed being on the road because it allowed the company successive performances of the work. For all its hardships, touring brought about a true repertory system, something that was impossible in New York. She had none of the dreary teaching and studio work to do on tour—and she didn't have to take care of a lively little boy at the end of the day's work. The long train or bus rides afforded time for unaccustomed rest and socializing. For the duration of the tour she could forget about money problems and just concentrate on dancing.

Nevertheless, tours were hard on her conscience, for even though she always left her son (now called Humphrey) in the best care she could arrange for him, and even though Leo continued to be absent much more of the time than she was, her husband made her feel that she was abdicating her responsibilities as wife and mother every time she embarked on a trip. *She* was leaving *him,* which proved she didn't love him, didn't belong to him entirely. He taxed her with this repeatedly in long, self-pitying letters when she was hundreds of miles away from New York, often adding regretful comments about how she was missing out on her son's growing up. These letters must have scorched her and given her tremendous pangs of guilt. She even dreamed once that Leo left her when she undertook one trip too many. From Ohio in 1938, she wrote him: "Bitter sweet to know that I could mean so much to any one human being and yet deliberately take myself away. . . . I suppose you can bear to hear a few details of my hateful career." Sometimes she would tactfully urge him to get a job on shore, suggesting once that he could help the company if he would "bend every effort toward a permanent dance theater in New York." But this issue was long past contention with them, and he never willingly arranged his life to help her or be nearer to her, though their separations gave him so much pain.

Doris was not the kind of personality others rushed to protect and take care of. Maybe something in her indomitable will and stamina discouraged this, and certainly some exaggerated ideal of self-sufficiency made her reluctant to ask for it. She had no taste for going to teas and buttering up rich dowagers, as dancer Claudia Moore thought Martha Graham was able to do. But this seemed almost the only way to cover the perpetual deficits of the company. Both Doris' and Leo's families were poor, and they had few rich friends, although over the years one or two modest benefactors were cultivated. Max and Adele Brandwen and Dorothy Luckie, the mother of one of the dancers, could be called on in emergencies. But the sums available from these sources couldn't sustain the work, only come to the rescue when studio renovations were needed or costumes had to be made for a new dance.

Support of the arts through corporate foundations did not become widespread until the 1960s, and the few private foundations that were active in arts funding during the 1930s often developed long-term arrangements with artists or projects they were particularly interested in, to the exclusion of everything else. There is heartbreaking evidence that Doris tried for years to attract one of these patrons, Mrs. Dorothy Whitney Straight Elmhirst, with only minimal results.

The heiress to the trolley-car fortune of William C. Whitney had married an agronomist and social reformer, Leonard Elmhirst, and they had established a model community of farmers, craftsmen, and artists at Dartington Hall in Devon, England. Ecstatic reports began appearing in the American press early in the 1930s, that told of theatrical productions in which farmers and villagers became actors, and artisans from the estate shops built the sets and worked as stagehands. The Elmhirsts imported Louise Soelberg and Margaret Barr from the innovative Cornish School in Seattle to direct a Dance-Mime school and put on creative dance productions in Dartington's fourteenth-century manor house. After a trip to England in the summer of 1932 John Martin reported on Dartington as "a venture which not only in its magnitude but in its idealism and practicality is truly modern . . . a many-sided social experiment in which a little world is being created along broadly humanistic lines." Two years later Hallie Flanagan described the flourishing community of potters, farmers, fruit growers, furniture manufacturers, and artists for *Theatre Arts Monthly,* commending the Elmhirsts' belief that "if people work together productively and play together creatively a good life is bound to result." This utopian combination of arts-and-crafts aesthetics and modern community planning coincided perfectly with Doris' ideas. In 1934 the Elmhirsts offered asylum to the German choreographer Kurt Jooss, with his school and company, and later took in Jooss' teacher Rudolf Laban, remaining their sponsor until the early 1940s. But Doris couldn't give up hoping that these patrons would also find a way to help Humphrey-Weidman.

Apparently it was John Martin who first recommended that she approach the Elmhirst Foundation's American secretary, Anna Bogue. In 1933 Doris tried to interest the Foundation in her theory book, which would be published by Macmillan if a subsidy could be found for writing it. This would have given her some respite during her pregnancy and after Humphrey's birth. Bogue said the foundation wasn't very interested in publication projects and suggested she apply for a Guggenheim Fellowship. Two years later Doris requested a general grant of $1,000. It was 1935, the year of *New Dance,* and an "Elmhirst Committee" was maintaining a somewhat mysterious presence at Bennington. After the *New Dance* premiere, Doris and Charles interrupted the studio teachers' course in New York to return to Bennington for a day-long forum on the aesthetic and social implications of the Modern Dance, run by the Elmhirst group for the entire staff and student body. Soon after this, Humphrey-Weidman was awarded $750, which came just in time to cover the deficit of the fall Guild Theater concert where *New Dance* made its New York debut. But this was never to be repeated.

In 1936 Doris asked for general funds, support for a production of *Orestes,* and help on another of her ongoing projects, an attempt to develop a workable dance-notation system. Bogue requested a budget for *Orestes,* and in the next months Doris contacted both Lehman Engel and the Westminster Choir College about collaborating on a production, but nothing came of it. In 1937, in response to Doris' request for $5,000 to support new works, Bogue replied that the foundation was supporting the American School of the Dance (possibly a Bennington brainchild that didn't materialize) and was not able to help individual dancers. Mrs. Elmhirst reorganized the foundation at the beginning of the war, and despite increasingly desperate pleas, Doris was told in the fall of 1939, in 1940, and again in January of 1941 that no funds were available to meet her petitions.

Finally, she came to the conclusion that the company must get off the touring treadmill whether or not they could count on subsidy. Repertory in a New York theater had always been a desirable solution, and from the first Dance Repertory Theatre season in 1930 Doris had thrown every effort she could into bringing such a situation about. One scheme after another to team up with other dancers was tried and abandoned. By the end of the decade, she was trying to figure out how Humphrey-Weidman could acquire a theater, perhaps by joining with a theater group that would occupy the place part-time.

What she did not realize, or refused to admit, was that the company was deteriorating at an even more fundamental level than its economic welfare. Human relations had been its activating force and its salvation for a decade of poverty. Now the love, the energy, and the mutual aspiration that had powered the enterprise began to diminish; money became the prime issue because the rest of the machine was ceasing to work. Even Doris' personal resources were failing. She accepted more and more of the burdens of the organization and had less and less ability to meet them. Why she held on so long to the idea that there was a viable consortium, a family, called Humphrey-Weidman is an impossible and tragic question.

9 STUDIO THEATER, 1939–44

By 1939 the problems that were to prove more serious than chronic poverty began to fester. Personal ambition was one of them. Dancers had always left the company, and the most valuable of them moved on to pursue their own choreographic careers. This built-in hazard was acknowledged, and even encouraged, in Humphrey-Weidman. Around 1937 and 1938 George Bockman, together with his former associate Fe Alf, began doing independent concerts; sometimes they constituted themselves the Theater Dance Company and called on other Humphrey-Weidman dancers for special jobs in summer stock and night clubs. Bockman felt that he would always be "third banana" in the company, after Charles and José, and by 1938 Theater Dance Company had attained strong enough prospects for him to resign. Sybil Shearer was also drawn into this group, on her way to doing concert choreography.

Dancers who could not be provided for during the summer as Humphrey-Weidman emissaries and teaching assistants found work at camps like the famous Tamiment, where they choreographed shows and sometimes met influential people in the Broadway theater. The precedent for accepting work in show business had been established in the earliest days of Humphrey-Weidman, but the possibilities were growing more attractive. No longer were the shows simply a means of earning a living, only slightly less distasteful than sweeping floors. People like Eleanor King discovered early that they rather liked performing steadily in lush costumes for big audiences and good pay, and hoped they could continue as serious choreographers even if their work at times became fused with plays, operas, or revues. Jack Cole, who had studied with Denishawn and briefly with Doris and Charles, was making an important name as a choreographer of outright showbiz dancing, and he too seduced dancers away, for stints at the Rainbow Room and other clubs with a group he called Ballet Intime.

Charles and José continued to do major Broadway musicals, and José's handsome, dynamic presence especially attracted attention. After ten years in the closest intimacy with the dance family and featured status in the company, José began to grope for an independent future. He was turning thirty, at the peak of his physical powers. His early compositional efforts were recognized when he was named, with Anna Sokolow and Esther Junger, a Choreographic Fellow at Bennington in 1937. When the Bennington session was held at Mills College in California in 1939, José and Katherine Manning did the main Humphrey-Weidman teaching and appeared in the season's only concert, a program of faculty works that included his ambitious *Danzas Mexicanas* as well as three of his other pieces. José taught part time at Bennington during the 1939–40 academic year, sharing the work with Martha Hill, who was still commuting to her other job at New York University. Toward the end of the spring semester he got released from his contract* to appear as a featured dancer in the Ray Bolger-Ilka Chase-Jimmy Durante show *Keep Off the Grass,* choreographed by George Balanchine. The show flopped in a few weeks, reinforcing José's vehement and long-standing guilt feelings about accepting commercial work; and by summer he was off to California again. Bennington School of Dance was going back to Vermont, but he had been invited to teach in a dance program at Mills headed by Marian Van Tuyl.

During this summer of 1940 he danced for the first time with former Graham dancer May O'Donnell, who was also teaching at Mills. To a script by Humphrey-Weidman colleague William Archibald with original music by Esther Williamson (one of the musicians at Mills), and with Doris' movement from *Orestes* as a model, he choreographed *War Lyrics.* In his autobiography, which is less than candid at times, José asserted that the escalating war had been on his mind constantly, filling him with sadness and frustration; he was devastated first by the Spanish disaster, then by Hitler's advances into Europe. By the end of the summer of 1940, with the invasion of France, he said his world was in a shambles. He had hit bottom. "I saw that my association with Humphrey-Weidman was ended. We had quite simply outgrown each other." Not quite so simply. José had been pursued for some months by a slightly dubious manager, William Neill, who was based in Buffalo. Neill lured José to perform gratis for a conference of concert managers in Ohio and finally signed him to a tight contract, with grandiose promises of spectacular bookings. Fortified by Neill's flattery and the good notices for

*Humphrey-Weidman dancer William Bales was appointed to fill out the term for him and stayed for twenty-seven years.

War Lyrics, José proceeded to New York, where the company was preparing for a fall tour. Doris was pleased with his "glowing reports" of his summer achievements and expected to put *War Lyrics* into the repertory. A month later she curtly reported to her mother that, among various other harassments, they had lost three dancers who would have to be replaced before the tour, Harriet Ann Gray, Eva Desca—and José.

Clearly in his own mind he had been preparing for a break, as he remembered the events of that chaotic month. Not only his career but also his personal life was at stake. José's relationship with Charles had been established almost from the beginning of Humphrey-Weidman. He had, in fact, been introduced to the young experimenters by one of Charles' more flaming old friends, Perkins Harnley, whom José had met in art school in Los Angeles. When the family moved in together at 31 West 10th Street in 1933, José was one of the permanent tenants, as firmly rooted there as Leo. He helped Charles buy and modernize the Blairstown farm, and like all the family members he took responsibility in the city and country for household chores, baby sitting, driving, and financial upkeep. He frequently shared teaching jobs with Charles, and the two of them were important role models at a time when there were few professional male dancers at all. They taught special men's classes and were the nucleus of the male Humphrey-Weidman contingent that performed separately on occasion. Both men were highly attractive and liked to have a good time; both were probably susceptible to extracurricular affairs. But up to this time, José had no reason to think his partnership with Charles would not continue indefinitely.

In the summer of 1939 they had met a young man from New Jersey named Charles Hamilton Weasner. (He later dropped the name Weasner.) They were teaching at Perry Mansfield, and Hamilton was a math teacher, discovering dance for the first time. Hamilton was impressed by the glamour of the scene—he didn't get to meet people like that in Trenton. In the fall he had begun taking classes at the studio, becoming more and more ensconced in the company and the family. While José was at Mills in the summer of 1940, Peter Hamilton (all Charleses in the family were given alternate names to avoid confusion with the original) lived at the farm with Charles, Doris, and the rest of the entourage. When José returned from the West Coast, already chafing to embark on what everyone was assuring him would be a glorious career, he and Charles had a disastrous fight that ended in a total break. José crept away, hiding out for a few weeks with a friend in

New York, then returned to San Francisco, where he began a new dance
family with May O'Donnell, her husband, Ray Green, and dancer-teacher
Gertrude Shurr.

Doris at this moment was as physically and emotionally undermined as at
any time in her life. For more than a year she had been beset with cares. The
1939 Mills session was a great trial. As in Vermont, whenever the Big Four
were together on the same campus, the rivalries upset her. At Mills, more-
over, there was extra pressure because this was the first time so much modern dance power had gathered on the West Coast. A filmmaker from Hollywood was on campus making a movie about them all, and Doris wanted
Humphrey-Weidman to make a good showing.

In addition to her four-and-a-half hours of daily teaching, she was deeply
involved with José's concert. By this time she was known and trusted by all
her associates as a choreographic adviser. Musical director Lionel Nowak remarked that he thought she enjoyed editing Charles' and José's dances just
for the pleasure of seeing that a dance was well formed and meaningful,
not because she wanted to manipulate people. "She would be too honest to
indulge herself in somebody else's dance," Nowak thought. José needed a
rigorous disciplinarian, and *Danzas Mexicanas,* his first big piece for Mills,
began as an effusive outpouring of everything he felt about the heroes and
peasants of his native country: Indio, Conquistador, Peon, Caballero, and Re-
volucionario. According to Margaret Lloyd the finished dance was "like a
five-word history of the country."

But Claudia Moore, who was at Mills, recalled the excruciating process by
which that economy was achieved. José had made the suite of solos during
the first part of the summer when he and Katy Manning were giving the
classes at Mills. The music was by Lionel Nowak who, with Pauline, was accompanying classes. When Doris arrived from Colorado, a few days before
the performance, she slipped into a rehearsal. José asked for her opinion,
and she started taking the dance apart. She cut the work from two-and-a-
half hours to thirty or forty minutes. José screamed as if she'd killed his baby,
said Moore, but when Doris would get up to leave, he'd beg her to stay and
continue. "Every other [idea] could be cut out and when you got through he
had nice little short pieces; then they had to be built back up again. . . . He
learned his choreography the hard way." It was, of course, hard on Doris
too, though a great satisfaction when the work succeeded—"a distinctive
contribution to the American dance," Margaret Lloyd called it.

Humphrey was with Pauline most of that summer. She took him along to
Mills while Doris taught at the New York studio and at Colorado State College in Greeley. After Mills, Pauline and Humphrey visited her family in Los
Angeles while Doris taught another week at Perry Mansfield and one at a
summer camp in Minnesota. For the first time a note of crankiness entered
Doris' letters during the spring tour that preceded this summer of protracted
teaching. She allowed herself to complain about unappreciative audiences,
about the lack of interest their Physical Education sponsors showed in the
dancers. In Greeley, she had to teach at one end of a huge gym with acrobats working out at the other end. She knew there were interesting people
on campus there but felt isolated as a guest of the "despised" Physical Education Department.

At Mills, in addition to the movie and José's dance, she fretted about the
last-night student demonstration that took the place of company performances. This had the usual competitive air among the various partisans. Doris
thought the Humphrey-Weidman students did well, but decided that in the
future Charles' teaching would have to be kept in check. His "messy, illogical
technique" was too confusing for students, though his lovable personality
charmed them. She disliked the "rigidity and frigidity" of everyone else's
teaching. The campus at Mills turned out to be inconvenient. The heat in
Greeley was excessive, and the Gilbert and Sullivan opera she was taken to
see in Central City, Colorado, was superficial—another bitter demonstration
to her that entertainment could thrive while her art was still grubbing along.

With the group scattered around the country, she spent a lot of time doing
studio business by mail and arranging schedules, finances, and future company activities. From all evidence, Doris was the long-range planner and organizer from whom the others took their cue. Pauline's managerial talents
tended to run amok unless a very clear framework was laid out in which she
could function. Charles was flighty; as the 1939 season ended he had no
Broadway shows in prospect and was talking about possibly giving up the
apartment to cut expenses and living in a furnished room so that he'd have
to pay rent only when he was in New York. This may be an indication that
he was already trying to loosen the family ties that were to break so violently
a year later. Doris had to consider what she and Leo would do if the communal family ceased to exist—how would the housework get done, the
cooking, the baby-sitting? How would the rent get paid? In Humphrey-
Weidman and in the dance family, Doris was the dreamer of possibilities—
and unfortunately also the one who could visualize how the little pieces

were going to fit together. She said once that she had been cursed with her mother's ticketing and sorting instinct. She was a natural tidier-up, though she knew she ought to spend her time on more creative things.

The 1939 living problems were temporarily solved after the Bennington-Mills summer, when José moved in with Charles, allowing his room to be rented to a family friend, Betty Joiner. But Doris' troubles got worse. Leo was agonizing about the war in Europe. As a British subject he had to face the impending question of military service, and he would claim conscientious objector status if it came to that, although his occupation as a seaman qualified him for noncombatant service. Doris refused to believe there would be a war at all, until the Nazis actually invaded Poland in September 1939. At the end of the summer the *Queen of Bermuda* was ordered to leave its Caribbean tourist route and return to England. Leo didn't know when the ship would get back to America, so he hastily resigned, at the same time applying for U.S. citizenship papers.

Their mounting depression wasn't alleviated by his enforced stay at home that fall. The company wasn't touring, and it was probably the longest period Doris and Leo had spent together since their marriage. Doris told her mother he was trying everything he knew to make a start in a "new profession," but he was always careful to stipulate that any new job would have to be suitable—meaning that he really didn't want to stay ashore. The shipping business wasn't doing well, but workers were desperately needed in factories and shipyards as the United States tooled up its war machine. This was not for Leo. His fantasy picture of shore life had Doris and Humphrey tucked neatly in a suburban cottage, whiling away their days until the magic moment when he would step off the train at night. Instead, Doris went to the studio and he took Humphrey to school, worked a little on her book, did some chores around the apartment—and brought in no income. When a job as third officer on a United Fruit Line boat came up in December, he grabbed it and fled, leaving Doris to cope with finding another way to take care of Humphrey, a short tour to the South, teaching and informal concerts at the studio, Christmas, and—right after the holidays—the company's January New York concert, this year at Washington Irving High School. On New Year's Eve she left Humphrey with Letitia Ide's baby-sitter and went to a party. Not that she cared about parties, she told Julia, but "I would like to do something besides work all the time." Yet she felt this was less than noble, "I asked for it all, and must pay the price."

For the January concert, *Danzas Mexicanas* was taken into the repertory.

The company also did Doris' *Square Dances,* which she had premiered in
November, *Race of Life,* and a revival of *Shakers.* Nothing of Charles' was on
this program. More touring was in store for the balance of the winter; a
heavy three-week trip, with only six dancers in addition to Doris and Charles;
and Doris was having a hard time coaching a new man, Bill Matons, who
she felt wasn't ready to go into the company.

Doris' mother was having troubles too. After some unprofitable seasons,
Ethel Moulton was planning to close down their studio, and Julia would be
without work at seventy-four. For her, the feeling of uselessness was almost
as potent a blow as the loss of the little she had been earning as Ethel's
manager and accompanist. Doris, as usual, sent what small amounts of cash
she could spare, and offered suggestions she knew wouldn't be much help.

Gnawing away beneath all these personal and professional difficulties
was a problem that no amount of hard work, clever scheduling or self-denial
was going to solve. It began, Doris told people, with a fall down some stairs
in Lynchburg, Virginia, while the company was on the December 1939
Southern tour. She had set off on this tour out of shape. The accumulated
stresses of the summer, the brief respite with Leo home in the fall, then his
precipitous departure and its harried aftermath had left her no time to go
into the studio and practice. For any dancer this is a situation ripe for injury,
and Doris was forty-four, hardly resilient after years of poor nutrition, skimpy
practice, and general neglect of her physical condition. She scraped her shins
in the Virginia incident but wrote Leo that she had been lucky not to have
broken something, which would send her to the hospital or make her miss
performances. The irony of this report soon became apparent. One of the
wounds didn't heal properly, and she began having pains in her back and
left leg. She continued to dance—about ten performances in early March in
the Midwest and New England.

There was no question of her not dancing. She was convinced that her
presence onstage was necessary. She and Charles were the stars, and the
audience expected to see them. Two years before, in January, she had set
off on the long cross-country tour with a bad knee—she called it a "lame
duck," as if it were some malevolent enemy that didn't really belong to
her—and admitted two gruelling months later that it was "still far from perfect" and, if she didn't dance regularly, gave her trouble. Whether this earlier
injury contributed to her later problems none of the doctors seemed to
know, but it is clear that ignoring pain and dancing in less than top condition were habitual with her. So was blotting out discomfort with painkillers;

she took aspirin regularly on the 1938 tour. Other dancers often marveled that she was so limber she could go on without even stretching or warming up. But the most responsive of muscles are subject to aging, especially if called upon for the arduous suspended falls, twisted turns, and forceful use of the lower body demanded by the Humphrey-Weidman style.

By the spring of 1940 Doris was still in pain and still refusing to slow down. Returning from the tour, she became absorbed in the problem of what to do about the summer. A scheme to go on a tour of summer theaters instead of teaching was not working out. Five or six offers had come in, but they were all based on percentage deals: the company would have no guaranteed fee but would share in box-office receipts. Humphrey-Weidman had had plenty of experience with this kind of arrangement—not only did the company stand to take a financial beating, but the effect on morale was devastating when houses were poor. Doris felt that they could accept such a contract only if a subsidy were found to pay the dancers' salaries. She went to see what few potential patrons she knew, with no results. Now it was April, and she had turned down the most lucrative of her usual summer teaching jobs, including Bennington.

The original scheme for the Bennington School of Dance had run its course. After the first, joint summer, each of the Big Four had a sort of featured year, when they created new workshop pieces with commissions from the college—Humphrey and Weidman's year had been 1936, with *Red Fires* and *Quest;* Graham's, 1935 with *Panorama;* and Holm's, 1937 with *Trend.* In 1938 the leaders all gave new works. (*Passacaglia* and *Opus 51* were Doris' and Charles' contributions.) Then the enterprise migrated to Mills for a year. In 1940, with war jitters and other financial worries looming up, Bennington decided to incorporate the School of Dance into a larger venture, a School of the Arts, where music and theater would be equally stressed. Again only one dance artist a year was to be in residence, with the others doing shorter visits, and again Graham was to inaugurate the plan. Hanya Holm had removed herself from the Bennington scene, starting what became a longstanding summer program at the Colorado Women's College in Colorado Springs. She and Humphrey-Weidman were to be represented at Bennington in technique classes taught by assistants.

Doris had not wanted to go to Bennington even before this new scheme was worked out, and as it happened, she was in no condition to teach every day that summer. But the loss of the salary frightened her; and seeing Graham given precedence again, however reasonable that seemed to the proprietors at Bennington, hurt her at a time when she could have used some

positive feedback. She had no other source of income for the summer now
except teaching at the studio and a one-week job at the University of Maryland, which she ended up sharing with Katy Manning because she didn't
feel well enough to do it all herself. She wondered, if she were to stay in the
city, who would take care of Humphrey, since all the family would be
away—José at Mills, Pauline playing for classes at Bennington, and Charles
going between the farm and various independent jobs. Leo's new ship was
carrying cargo to Central America, and it was based in Baltimore instead of
Brooklyn, so his visits home grew further apart. Looking beyond the summer,
she was trying to decide whether to invest everything in a new, larger studio, where Humphrey-Weidman could perform modestly in New York and
not have to tour. And if she could swing it, then she must find company-
related summer jobs for the dancers, or risk losing them over the summer
layoff. Doris felt she was "turning in the squirrel cage."

By this time her leg and back pains had become serious—the business
pressures can't have helped—and she was trying various doctors and treat-
ments. It was not until a year later that arthritis of the hip was conclusively
diagnosed from some X-rays, and by that time no one could isolate the
cause. Doris' early complaints centered on her leg, not her hip, and one possible route the illness could have taken is that in continuing to dance with an
injury or repeated injuries she began favoring one side, gradually throwing
her whole body out of line. Putting weight constantly the wrong way on her
leg could have caused a chronic displacement of the all-important hip socket
and triggered an arthritic inflammation. Arthritic hip joints are common
among dancers—probably for similar reasons of improper alignment and
unusual stress.*

All her life Doris had believed in self-medication, citrus diets, and quick
remedial programs like sleeping late and eating rich foods for a few weeks.
The long, corrective regimen of physical therapy was not for her, although
there were outstanding practitioners in the United States at that time. She
could not have adhered to the discipline, nor could she admit that something was happening to her body that she wouldn't ultimately surmount
along with all the other problems besetting her.

Although she had hardly any teaching to do, the summer of 1940 was far
from restful. Before everyone scattered, the company made a film of *Shakers*
in the 18th Street studio, with photographer Thomas Bouchard climbing up

*Among the early modern dancers, Jane Dudley and Bessie Schönberg of the Graham company
and Hanya Holm herself have had serious arthritic conditions and undergone hip replacements.

into the rafters for some of his dramatic effects. Doris helped him edit the film in the city after she returned from Maryland in early July. In August she gave a summer course at the studio for about a dozen girls and a few men. But her main preoccupation was with the new studio.

She had found a place at 108 West 16th Street that was large enough (fifty by twenty-five by fifteen feet high) for a decent performing space with an audience on risers. A former artist's studio, the place needed major renovations, and by midsummer Dorothy Luckie had pledged $2,000, which would cover the installation of a steel beam in the ceiling to replace supporting pillars that obstructed the sightlines. In a rare impulsive moment, Doris spent some of the money on 300 used chairs from the Metropolitan Opera House—then she had to figure out how to store them until it was time to take possession of the new space.

In fact, the decision to move to 16th Street produced a whole new series of interlocking problems, and she spent weeks coming into town from the farm to talk to contractors, real-estate agents, appraisers, and landlords about the relocation. Charles apparently took little part in these negotiations; as Leo observed around this time, Charles seemed to be "disrobing himself of the garments of a partner and putting on the overalls of an employee." Pauline's eccentrically kept books were another mystery, and Doris' letters to Bennington grew irritable. Leo, ever ready with good advice suited to more conventional enterprises, warned her that she was risking failure if she continued to run the studio "from 31 West 10th Street," meaning that Pauline's homemade business methods were inadequate. But there wasn't much alternative. By the end of July, Doris was urging Pauline, without success, to come down for a couple of days and help her. Finally she wrote in exasperation, "I think it's hell for me to be left with all this, while you play for exercises—but at that I don't think you would know a bit more about values of real estate than I do."

She did have one great consolation, in the person of a devoted, intelligent woman her own age named Helen Mary (Hay) Robinson. A Coloradan with a husband and two daughters a little older than Humphrey, Hay had also grown up in the eclectic dance climate of the early twentieth century, learning a hodgepodge of skirt dancing, scarf dancing, ballroom, ballet, and exotica from assorted teachers, and had run her own dancing school for children until disapproval from her husband's law firm forced her to close it. After that her passion for dance had to be satisfied by attending whatever touring performances passed her way.

She had been captivated with Doris since a performance of *Soaring* in the 1920s, which made her want to study at Denishawn. Later she became an intensely loyal fan of Humphrey-Weidman, convinced that this was the only kind of dancing for her. At last, when the company was passing through Denver on tour in the spring of 1938, Hay gathered up her courage and tele-phoned Doris, introducing herself and offering to drive the dancers to their next date. This was characteristic. Gifted with a quick mind but convinced that she was one of the ordinary people of the world, Hay had directed her energies to creating an inspired, lively atmosphere for her children and to the endless tasks bright women find to do in small-town society. But to her, dancers were special, and after she had met *her* dancers, who immediately included her in the family, she took the greatest pleasure in thinking up un-obtrusive ways to help them.

She wrote many amusing letters to Doris, never really expecting frequent answers, indecently grateful when she received any at all. She sent thought-ful gifts—books she thought Doris would enjoy, stationery, cigarettes during the wartime shortages—and she traveled long distances to be with the company, sometimes just to see a few performances of a tour. She didn't want to embarrass her friend by offering financial help—she and her hus-band were well off but not rich. But she provided links to potential sponsors in the Denver area and made herself available as driver, baby-sitter, and pro-vider of little holidays for Doris when there would have been no other way to manage these things. Hay's husband frowned on her infatuation with the dancers, and—perhaps partly because of this—he divorced her in 1947. She was taken totally by surprise. Her mental health was precarious for years after that, and she had only intermittent contact with Doris, Pauline, and the others. In the breakup of her household, Doris' letters were unaccountably lost—Hay insisted she would never have parted with them willingly. But her letters to Doris were saved—evidence of an extraordinary, if lopsided, friend-ship. Doris, undemonstrative, distracted, ill, knew what a treasure Hay was although she may never have been able to tell her directly, and the unas-suming Hay frequently wondered why Doris liked to have her around.

In 1940 she drove east and stayed at the farm, driving Doris into the city and up to Bennington to see Graham's performances and check out the way things were going under the new School of the Arts setup: After she went home, Doris wrote to her mother: "I miss her terribly, really she is wonderful, the very best friend I ever had, and the only one who understands about everything. . . . You know I have very few friends—and not one of them is her equal." Hay demanded nothing of her, emotionally or creatively, and when Doris would withdraw into her thoughts for long silences, she accepted this as the privilege of "genius" and simply talked to Pauline or whoever was around until Doris came back from her reverie. She didn't feel personally excluded as Leo did. She didn't criticize as Pauline did or take her role lightly as Charles did. Above all, she was never so busy with her own problems that she couldn't sympathize with Doris' difficulties, insisting with a fine sense of outrage that an artist such as Doris deserved to be treated better by the world.

All during the fateful summer of 1940, Doris acted to stabilize Humphrey-Weidman although she was deeply pessimistic about the company's future. It wasn't unexpected when José wrote from Mills warning that he might not come back. Charles thought things could be patched up; Doris felt their personal problems were too serious. Yet, against her impulse to give it all up, she put a deposit on the new studio.

In August Pauline began to talk of going to California and rescuing José from his despair, by marrying him if he would have her. Pauline had been in love with José for years, ineffectually trying to conceal her feelings behind a screen of antagonism. To Doris she had made no secret of her determination to snare him some day, and she had apparently also made some overtures to him at unguarded moments. José recalled that "an understanding" existed between them before he left for California. They did maintain a warm correspondence, but if their relationship ever went beyond hugs and kisses, no serious commitments were made. During the 1940 summer of doubt, when his involvement with Charles appeared over, Pauline was determined to seize her chance and "make a new man of him." She wrote him a long, extravagant letter admitting her love and offering to be his helper, companion, wife, on any terms he named. Doris felt her "passion for reforming" and her critical admonitions would only drive him away. She cautioned restraint. José had been deeply hurt, and he needed "a rock to lean on" rather than the prodding into new directions that Pauline had in mind. He took no action on Pauline's declaration but returned to New York undecided about his future. He and Charles affected their last brief truce, and they all settled down uneasily to see what would happen. Writing to Leo in September, Doris reported, "we are still living over a volcano, but we are supposed to be joining forces."

As soon as the summer course at the studio was over, Doris had sent Humphrey to stay with a former nurse while she went to a sanitarium in the

Poconos run by Dr. William Hay, author of a radical diet that she imposed on herself and the family intermittently for years. She needed a rest and medical attention, but all she got was some palliative treatment and orders to "drink your orange juice." Her back was twisting badly by this time, and the staff at the "home for the moribund" did advise her to see an osteopath. There was no time for this. She was going ahead with her new plan, and to her list of worries, which she gave as "debt, health, child education, teaching, composition, and a repertory theater," she added the necessity to make the company strong enough to be self-sufficient if she should have to quit dancing. Leo chose this time to develop a new anxiety about Humphrey. He worried

Song of the West—Desert Gods. Photo by W. H. Stephan. (Dance Collection, NYPL)

that the boy didn't have enough traditionally masculine role models or friends his own age. Incredibly, he hit on the idea of taking a European refugee child into the family as a companion for their son. Doris hoped he was joking, and fortunately he backed off.

By the end of September, Charles and José had made their final break—they did not speak to each other again for years. But the lease on the new studio had been signed, and construction work was going ahead. With Lee Sherman in José's roles (José was listed "on leave of absence") and Peter Hamilton pressed into service, Doris, Charles, and a company of ten dancers made another difficult college tour—doing sixteen dates in about five weeks, and traveling as far as Texas. They returned to New York with just two weeks to spare before the Christmas holidays and the opening of Studio Theater. The tour repertory was the same for virtually all performances: *Square Dances, Shakers,* Variations and Conclusion from *New Dance,* and two new works, Charles' autobiographical *On My Mother's Side* and the first two parts of *Song of the West.*

Doris started work on this dance early in 1940. Like other dances she made in periods of stress, it was a quest for composure in nobler, calmer worlds. In this case, her inspiration was the American Western landscape, across which she had trekked many times by train and in which she had lived for refreshing months of summer teaching. In the spring of 1939, en route to Ogden, Utah, she described her feelings to Leo.

> The marvelous west rises up again, vast, somber, strong—It really makes you feel wider, bigger as a person. It is more difficult to think small, to be involved in pettiness, or resentment, or fear. . . . I wonder how you would react to it. . . . You couldn't possibly care so much or fear so much about Europe where all this heavenly space frees you entirely from your wretched human warmongers. Of course it might be too endless to you and lonely like the sea, nothing about it is charming or comforting or enfolding—about as remote from an English garden as possible.

The Green Land and Desert Gods (sometimes called Desert), got their titles from lines by Archibald MacLeish and initially carried descriptive program notes: "The first dance expresses the quiet joy and rolling sensuality of green fields in the sun. The second has for its theme the desert in which the sun shines with a magical intensity. Bounding the scene are mountains, rocks, great slopes and the enormous bowl of the sky. The figures moving in it are symbolic of the burning light and are also sometimes people of the des-

ert moving in a ritual hymn to the sun." The Green Land began as a group
dance but Doris later did it as a solo. Another section, Rivers, was finished in
January 1942 and was then given as the first of Song of the West's three
parts. Roy Harris wrote the music to the first and third sections, and Lionel
Nowak the middle section. The score incorporated recorded sections for
voice and flute, an experiment that Doris hoped would extend the company's musical resources. In these days before tape recording, long-playing
records, or decent electronic amplification in theaters, the music on
Humphrey-Weidman tours was limited to what could be played by two
pianists.

Somehow, Song of the West never gelled as a dance, although it had
many admirable features. Doris kept changing it but, according to Harriet
Ann Gray, she never could get it to work. The only part that survives is the
Desert Gods section, which Doris taught regularly in repertory classes
through the 1950s, and which was filmed in at least three student versions.
Perhaps it is not too conjectural to assume she was still undergoing a crisis
of inspiration, one that had begun with the completion of New Dance Trilogy and that deepened steadily with the ceaseless demands of touring and
the threatened disruption of the whole working setup of Humphrey-
Weidman. The problem she set herself in Desert Gods, and evidently in Song
of the West as a whole, was to make a descriptive dance without even a
subliminal organizing principle like a musical structure or an unacknowledged plotline. Not since her first choreographic essays had she attempted to
dance about purely metaphorical subjects or to represent the dancer as other
than the actual persona he or she was. She had shown abstract ideas as the
products of human behavior—the communal lessons of New Dance, the
movement-dialectic in Two Ecstatic Themes and Duo-Drama. But in Song of
the West she had no philosophical themes to propose, and yet she wanted
to go beyond pure-dance entertainment like Square Dances.

She solved the problem in part by a device that was quite far ahead of its
time: without preparation or any sign other than a change in movement
quality, the dancers took on different identities at different times in the
dance. With even fewer mime signals than, for instance, Merce Cunningham's collection of animals in his 1973 Solo, the dancers suggest rock-
hugging lizards, wheeling hunting birds, and other creatures. About midway
through the dance, the linear traveling patterns, the straight, intense focuses,
the tightly massed groupings, all characteristic of animals, begin to serve as
ritual formations in some sort of worship ceremony. Possibly Doris intended

a transition to the supernatural through some human behavior—horses and riders are indicated, and also possibly Indian dances—but that wasn't fully developed.

In the later part of the dance, the group clusters around women who have been singled out to be lifted and carried like icons. The group arrangements are flat, monolithic, and inevitably recall Graham's *Primitive Mysteries,* which drew on some of the same source material. The deliberately nonnaturalistic movement also brings to mind *Life of the Bee.* On these films, what is striking is the use of group patterns—appropriate and varied as always. But one doesn't get much sense of atmosphere except in the astute filling and clearing of the stage space, which creates a sort of visual clangor and resonance. The dance ends with everyone gone except two figures who revert to the first image, flattened on the ground and peering around the empty stage.

Studio Theater opened on December 26, 1940, and was a great success. For the first three months of 1941 there was a different bill every weekend, drawn from a repertory of about fifteen dances spanning a decade of creative work. Titles were about equally divided between Doris' and Charles' works, with a couple of pieces by company dancer Lee Sherman. *Song of the West* was premiered, along with the endearing first installment of Charles' autobiography, *On My Mother's Side.* Revivals were undertaken of *Passacaglia, Life of the Bee, Opus 51,* two Atavisms (*Bargain Counter* and *Lynchtown*), *The Happy Hippocrite,* and *Alcina,* with choreography now credited entirely to Charles. Charles put in some of his numbers from Broadway shows under the collective title *Raymond Scottiana,* and he did his parody solo *Portraits of Famous Dancers.* The other dances, freshly rehearsed from the touring repertory, were Variations and Conclusion from *New Dance, Shakers, To the Dance,* and *Square Dances.* Changing the bill every week, the directors were able to try different combinations of dances and position them different ways on the programs. Some combinations were especially aimed at a "popular" appeal, and in April there was a series of children's matinees, with a revival of Charles' *Marionette Theater* (1931) and a piece Doris put together with the help of the dancers called *Dance-ings.* This was a sort of demonstration of the basic action steps: leaping, running, falling, and turning.

Studio Theater's 150 seats were practically sold out for the entire season; John Martin described the rush for tickets as a virtual stampede. A rather elaborate system of "memberships" was devised, with subscriptions available

at $5 for six concerts and rising through several categories to $100 for a participating member. A subscriber could purchase additional single tickets for
$1.25 (reserved) or $1.00 (unreserved) per performance, and special group
rates were available. This not only assured an income and an audience in
advance but permitted the company to circumvent city laws governing the
operation of theaters. According to Martin, Humphrey-Weidman was "not
attempting to open an unlicensed theater by subterfuge," although that, of
course, is exactly what they were doing. Impoverished dancers had been
getting around the prohibitive cost of performing in New York since the pre-
tend sacred gatherings at Broadway theaters on Sunday nights in the early
1930s, and they would continue to do so as off-Broadway and all its permu-
tations developed after the war. Studio Theater stood firmly in the tradition of
the noncommercial repertory theater which has sustained creative life on the
New York stage for much of the twentieth century. In dance it anticipated
the loft culture of the 1970s and 1980s.

The project received much approving coverage in the press, and Martin
was especially supportive, devoting several Sunday columns to both the repertory and the producing philosophy. Pointing out that Humphrey-Weidman
"have once again sensed the progressive direction to take in a difficult period," Martin surveyed the declining activity of American dance companies in
the face of approaching war. Sympathy for the plight of European performers in exile, he said, was diverting funds he thought should be used to support native work. The recently formed Ballet Theatre was the only major
American company with strong financial backing, Martin asserted, and neither its repertory nor its personnel were exclusively American. The only thing
for creative dancers to do was to "follow Miss Humphrey and Mr. Weidman
into self-erected bomb shelters until sanity returns."

As usual, moral success did not bring any loosening of the economic bind.
Doris immediately began talking about the need to raise more money, because even with sold-out houses, the box office didn't cover expenses; and
in March she was complaining that "the first year is hell." Leo meanwhile
was recommending that they set aside a "percentage of the profits" against
slack periods and ongoing costs of the theater operations. There were no
profits. One source of income was another impoverished group of noncommercial players, the American Actors Company, a cooperative whose members included Agnes de Mille, Joseph Anthony, and Jerome Robbins. The
group rented Studio Theater in April and May for rehearsals and performances of *American Legend* and *Texas Town*, two plays by Horton Foote, di-

rected by Mary Hunter. The trouble with this kind of arrangement was that it kept Humphrey-Weidman out of its own space when the outside group was on the scene. Bennington was faltering too, and although Doris was committed to make a new work for the 1941 festival, the college could guarantee no teaching salaries. During that summer the faculty received only expenses, and the income from tuitions and other sources was to be pooled and divided among all the teachers. They didn't receive the money until fall.

For her new work, the last to be commissioned from her by Bennington, Doris decided once again to make a dance about her own situation and to paint the prospects with an optimism greater than what she must have been feeling. *Decade* was a retrospective evening-length work, using excerpts from her dances and Charles'. Described as "A Biography of Modern Dance from 1930–1940," the piece blended the techniques of the stage revue and the documentary. Its twenty-seven "numbers" were held together by a narrative structure (by Alex Kahn) that served the dual purpose of unifying the dance material and giving an ironic, fictional twist to what was essentially the true and all-too-earnest story of Humphrey-Weidman itself. Doris and Charles had been theatricalizing their social concerns for several years. For instance, the program note for Charles' *Quest* (1936) declares, "The artist, in his endeavor to find or create conditions under which he may achieve full and free expression, encounters many obstacles, in many lands." *Theatre Piece, Race of Life,* and *This Passion* also dealt with issues of contemporary life—materialism, competitiveness, injustice, and oppression—and with the artist's involvement in a society where these things prevail. *Decade* set forth the problems again, but this time Doris didn't try very hard to disguise or objectify the characters of the protagonists. Another unacknowledged influence on the piece was the Living Newspaper plays of the Federal Theatre, in which allegorical characters called the Financier, the Sharecropper, Professor, Consumer, and so forth dramatized current events and problems, with the intent of informing and to a certain extent radicalizing the public.

Decade's theatrical device was a modern-day *deus ex machina* called Mr. Business, a relative of the Stage Manager in Thornton Wilder's *Our Town,* which had conquered Broadway three years before. In fact, Doris approached Wilder for a script but he sent regrets, saying he couldn't write well for other people's projects. As Alex Kahn originally scripted the interlocutor figure, he had different names that identified him even more specifically with various managers, producers, and agents, who offered Doris and Charles what always turned out to be an illusory good fortune. This character, distilled by the time of the premiere into one chameleonlike exploiter, was the only speaking role in the dance—it was actually mimed by a dancer and spoken offstage by actor Edward Glass. Doris and Charles mimed their end of all the dialogues.

Mr. Business becomes in turn a representative from a movie company, an opera manager, a Broadway producer, and a booking agent. They all seem to be seeking what the dancers have to offer, but they all demand unacceptable compromises and concessions to popular taste. Each encounter cues off appropriate dances or parts of dances, set as rehearsals, auditions, performances on various stages, or cinematic montages. Some of the reprised favorites were *Air for the G String, Kinetic Pantomime, Water Study, Ringside, Circular Descent, Shakers* and excerpts from newer, longer works. Finally, after many disappointments, the directors give up their first studio for a bigger one. In the script Doris speaks for the first time, telling Mr. Business—now posing as the building superintendent—that they are moving into a place of their own where they will not be "subject to outside influences . . . we intend to let all the doors that have been closed to us remain closed, and ourselves to open a new one. The door to the Future."

Decade was innovative in several ways, yet it struck the avatars at Bennington as a retreat for Doris instead of an advance. No one could decide how to view the piece, and, being fixated on the unique properties of their own art, critics and colleagues failed to notice how consistent it was with trends in the contemporary theater and the popular arts. Doris herself could not admit that her instincts, for the moment, were taking her into dramatic areas rather than choreographic ones, and *Decade* was persistently condemned for failing to push ahead in terms of dance composition. Some critics thought the excerpted dances could be meaningful only to afficionados—though that should have suited the Bennington audience perfectly.

There were technical problems—stage waits while the company changed costumes, switches of mood that were sometimes bewildering, strong passages given out of context like Doris' Matriarch solo from *With My Red Fires.* Lionel Nowak was charged with piecing together a score from composers as disparate as Riegger, Scriabin and Gluck, with Aaron Copland's Music for the Theater as a prologue and conclusion. He felt that the dance never gelled but that it was "kind of a wonderful failure." Unsympathetic writers, like the *Nation's* Sherman Conrad, objected to the idea of a dance about the dancers' own difficulties, even though Doris meant for Humphrey-Weidman's problems to exemplify and perhaps illuminate the larger problem of how the art-

ist can survive in the modern world. Like *Song of the West, Decade* remained under construction for months after its initial negative reception, and
Doris made substantial cuts and revisions for its New York premiere at Studio
Theater in December of 1941, but it still didn't entirely satisfy. Curiously, years
later, when Humphrey-Weidman had expired, critics remembered it with
nostalgia.

Once again, Hay spent part of the summer with Doris. From Bennington
she drove Doris to see a doctor in Albany, who diagnosed arthritis of the hip
and gave Doris an elastic appliance that was supposed to help her keep the
weight more evenly distributed. Hay later said the doctor told her Doris
wouldn't be dancing much longer, but she kept this from Doris. Fall activities
were as heavy as ever. After returning from a visit with her mother—Hay
drove her to Chicago on the way back to Denver—there was the usual
teaching, a month-long tour of colleges spread thinly across the map from
Texas to Connecticut, and revisions of *Decade* to get ready for the Studio
Theater opening after Christmas. But her personal problems were seriously
aggravated as well.

The communal apartment at 31 West 10th Street had become unworkable
with José gone and the resident population less stable than ever. An assortment of friends and young dancers came and went, to rent the empty room
and to take care of Humphrey when the others were away. Leo pressured
Doris to find a place of their own, and she concurred guiltily with his appre-
hensions about the atmosphere in which their son was growing up. Doris'
relationship with Pauline had grown increasingly strained after José's departure and during the difficult process of establishing Studio Theater. But in
fact, so interdependent had the family become that the addition or subtrac-
tion of one person caused everyone's position to shift. Pauline's volatile, intense personality now became a sort of negative center around which Doris
struggled to keep things coherent and from which Charles simply retreated.
The disparity among the attitudes of the three partners quickly rose to the
surface. Pauline's loyalty belonged passionately to Doris and Humphrey-
Weidman—as long as she felt they appreciated her. When spurned, she
could become a passionate enemy. Charles was willing but weak—at this
point he was the most realistic of the three; he had no exaggerated com-
punctions about taking life-saving commercial offers. Doris refused to admit
that her dream was going to fail.

On September 17, 1941, the dance family ceased to exist. Charles and Pete
moved into Devonshire House, further east on 10th Street, and Doris rented

a two-and-a-half room apartment at 145 East 22nd Street. Left behind at 31 West 10th, Pauline wrote a desolate letter to José in San Francisco, full of her anguish at "being dumped" and bitterness at what she saw as the end of everything she had worked for. For once, for the moment, she didn't have a plan of action or even enough anger to propel her into the next day. She saw herself not only abandoned by her family but also somehow shunted aside in the working structure where she had been indispensable. José's response was to wire and ask her to come and marry him. Scarcely waiting for his confirming letter, she took the train west. Her sudden departure stunned everyone. Doris sent warm wishes after their wedding on October 3; "I'm sure they'll both be happier people," she told her mother.

But studio business lapsed into near-chaos. Doris and Charles tried to share Pauline's various jobs, but there was much they didn't even know how to do, let alone have time for. Pauline was persuaded to rejoin the company briefly to keep the tour together, but then she returned to the Coast, leaving her arcane systems and plans to be deciphered by Doris and the office workers. Through the winter "surprises" kept turning up—Pauline had forgotten to tell them to withhold Social Security payments from the tour receipts, for instance, and months later when the error was discovered, the tortured finances had to be stretched to cover it. Urgent pleas for missing information went unanswered until Doris became frantic.

When she returned from the tour just before Thanksgiving, to her complete surprise and dismay Doris found herself pregnant. During the next harrowing weeks, as she was trying to decide what to do, Hay wrote her almost every day, offering advice, sympathy, and loving support for whatever course Doris chose. Hay had always favored legalized abortion; now she was indignant that someone so dear to her would be forced to undergo the danger and humiliation of terminating a pregnancy in those days. She was shocked when Doris told her she had thought about having the baby. "It is at a tremendous price and I hate to have you pay it. . . . To lose what you can give artistically for one person, is a poor bargain for mankind. All of which is *extremely* noble and the truth is, for me the only consideration is your health and safety."

After what seemed an eternity of doubt, Doris had an abortion on Wednesday, December 11. Pauline stayed with her for a few days while she recovered at home, then returned to José. Doris went back to the studio the following Monday to begin rehearsing *Decade* in its revised form. The studio opening was two weeks away. She told her mother she'd had a miscarriage.

After the United States entered the war on December 7, Leo's ship was routed into southern ports to avoid suspected enemy submarines around New York, and his visits home became even more infrequent. So Doris was left with eight-year-old Humphrey in a lonely apartment, her closest comrades physically and emotionally separated from her, and her health slipping. She had always lived among lots of people whose comings and goings had provided her with amusement and social life and whose fluctuating availability made for an improvised but successful system of keeping house. (After two years in 22nd Street, which she never did succeed in making homelike, she and Humphrey moved to a more congenial place at 132 East 16th Street—a bit closer to the studio, though she traveled back and forth by bus rather than walk the long blocks across town.)

The second Studio Theater season ran through April 1942 with two performances each weekend. For the first time Doris began to spare herself dancing assignments, and Charles' work was more prominent than hers. Beatrice Seckler took over some of her former roles. After the *Decade* revision failed to appeal to the critics, the company began doing some of the numbers they'd reconstructed for it under the catchall title *Dances from Decade.* These varied but included Air Gai from *Iphigenia,* the *Scriabin Etude, Ringside,* and *Circular Descent.* Charles created one of his most popular dances, *Flickers,* a spoof of silent movies. It premiered on January 2, with Doris in the uncharacteristically comic role of a Theda Bara-ish vamp. It was mostly mime, and she was a great hit in it. *This Passion* was revived in March on an all-Weidman program that included *Alcina, On My Mother's Side,* and two Atavisms. The season wound up with a revival of *With My Red Fires,* its power and sweep diminished not only by the reduced cast but also by the compact size of the studio space. John Martin nevertheless thought "the work had never seemed more beautiful or more intensely moving. Certainly it has never been so superbly danced."

Humphrey-Weidman was unable to sustain the box office success of its first season, and finances were so bad that some performances had to be cancelled. Doris found that in order to fill the theater, new or revival pieces had to be instituted every few weeks, but rehearsing and mounting them were a drain on the production budget and the dancers' energies. Once again the studio was rented to outside acting and dance groups, but a battle with the city zoning board developed over Humphrey-Weidman's right to contract out their space. During the litigation one play was raided by the authorities, creating bad publicity and scaring off other potential users. Doris tried to get Ted Shawn to repay a longstanding loan of $1,000, but he was busy establishing Jacob's Pillow and regaled her with a long tale of his own financial woes. The only real source of income at this time was Charles' nightclub dates. He had initiated a successful act at the Rainbow Room with Katherine Litz and Peter Hamilton early in 1942, and he undertook this kind of work more and more frequently in the next few years. Doris' personal finances, for the first time, were not in jeopardy because Leo was receiving extra pay for his hazardous war-convoy duty.

As 1942 wore on, the draft became an all-important issue. Several of the company men were called up, but many tried to get exempted from military service. For a dancer, especially one in his thirties, protracted absence from studio practice would almost certainly mean an end to his career. José's marriage to Pauline, in the nervous days before Pearl Harbor, might have been influenced by rumors that only single men would be drafted. In any case, as artists, many dancers felt they could contribute far more to the war effort by doing what they were superb at doing, aiding the morale of the troops. After months of uncertainty and reclassification, Charles was given 4F status, a medical exemption. José was called up, deferred, then finally drafted in 1943. José's life was particularly chaotic during this time. His partnership with May O'Donnell was well received, but somehow the relationship went sour. After Pauline arrived on the Coast, her abrasive personality further unsettled the collaboration. José's association with Buffalo manager William Neill proved a mistake. Energetic but ineffectual, Neill had produced virtually no bookings, and José had to extricate himself from a punitive contract with the aid of a lawyer. When this situation was resolved, in early 1942, Pauline was free to take over management of her husband's career. She was determined to push for success and was willing to get jobs for José even if May wasn't included. This put her in direct conflict with May's husband, Ray Green, who was serving as the duo's business agent as well as its composer-musical director. By April 1942, it looked as if O'Donnell-Limón was breaking up, and José had some discussions about the possibility of a collaboration with Louise Kloepper, one of the leading modern dancers of the time, who was about to leave Hanya Holm's company.

There was one last tour with May, including a concert at New York's 92nd Street YM-YWHA in June, and one at Studio Theater. The big number of this series was a new version of *War Lyrics,* which José revised as a duet and retitled *Three Women,* eliminating the sections for a women's group that had been in the 1940 Mills production. Ray Green supplied a new score. On

STUDIO THEATER, 1939–44   208

the basis of the New York concert, which also included *This Story Is Legend,* an allegorical dance-drama about the discovery of the Mississippi River; and a heavy farce, *Three Inventories on Casey Jones,* Margaret Lloyd found "two beautiful dancers sadly in need . . . of a choreographer." Lloyd thought the program a waste of good dancing. It may have thrilled the West Coast, she reported, but "silence was the answer in New York." O'Donnell and Green returned to San Francisco, and a discouraged José stayed in New York. During the summer he began working with Doris in the studio again, ending what he called "my fling at independence."

Doris gave up dancing for the summer and fall, confining herself with considerable bitterness to teaching. She wondered now whether it had all been worthwhile; "what I have is a piece of real estate and some classes," she lamented to her mother. Bennington was now finally over. Apprehensive over money, college officials had cancelled the Festival altogether and relegated the School of Dance to the status of just another program in a summer session that offered government and economics, graphic and plastic arts. There were Humphrey-Weidman and Holm representatives teaching technique as usual, but the company in residence was Martha Graham's. Once again, Graham was given a no-strings opportunity to compose, and during the summer of 1942 she reworked *American Document* and began a new piece, which became one of her most extraordinary dances, *Deaths and Entrances.* Besides showings of student works, the only performances were by Graham dancers Jean Erdman, Merce Cunningham, and Nina Fonaroff, and by the newly formed trio of William Bales teamed with Graham's Jane Dudley and Sophie Maslow.

So Doris gave classes at Studio Theater while Humphrey went to Blairstown in the care of a former camp counselor. Hay came to spend the summer in New York—she had been facetiously hoping for years that Bennington would "burn down" and thought Doris would be in better spirits without its annual pressures. But it wasn't a good summer. Pauline was also staying at the 22nd Street apartment, while José taught in Greeley, and a dismayed Hay tried with little success to alleviate the frictions between the two old friends. Pauline's mercurial and divided allegiances were close to the surface at this time, and Doris' reserves of patience were low. Finally in the fall Pauline took a place on 13th Street, where she waited out José's army service in solitary but far from silent discontent.

After José returned from Greeley, Doris suggested that the two of them work on a joint concert to fill in the time until his army status was resolved.

Charles was choreographing musicals at a summer theater, the Paper Mill Playhouse in New Jersey, and in July he signed for a six-week engagement at the Rainbow Room with Beatrice Seckler, Katherine Litz, Lee Sherman, and Peter Hamilton, doing a condensed version of *Flickers,* among other numbers. Doris had declined his invitation to do her vamp role. Charles took the company alone on a mini-tour in late October, and Doris didn't even dance in the opening concerts at Studio Theater in early November. Doris and José's project, a concert of dances to Bach, was scheduled to open right after Christmas.

Under the circumstances, it was a most felicitous work to undertake. Both of them were devoted to the great composer, and at a time when neither one was able to make long-term commitments, the task was a joy and a challenge. Doris planned a revival of *Passacaglia,* with José and herself in the leading roles, and two new works, *Four Chorale Preludes* and the *Partita in G Major.* José was also doing a solo to the Chaconne in D Minor.

Despite her growing disability, Doris still functioned best when she had a lot to do. The worst periods of her life were always postseason vacations and the—up to this time—rare intervals of illness or disruption, when she didn't have to solve multiple problems and think about several people's futures at the same time. José's return—even though it had to be temporary—brought new creative possibilities and kept her from brooding about the stalemated company and family situation. The Bach evening was also important for José. In his own mind it signalled his coming-of-age as a choreographer. He wrote in his autobiography: "I was once again under the discipline of a great master, and I saw Doris in a new light. . . . I was being treated no longer as a disciple but as an equal."

José's admiration for Doris, his acknowledgement of her position as his mentor, never wavered throughout their thirty-year association. He expressed his thanks to her so consistently and so warmly that he must truly have believed she was the greater artist, as he affirmed many times. "DH—Innovator/JL—Perpetuator," he characterized the sequence once in some notes on the successive generations of modern dancers. "There are certain things that one not only remembers but cherishes with all fervor, for they are indispensable allies in the cruel yet splendid battle which artists must wage for their survival. . . . One of these is the moral support and regard of certain persons. For me that of Doris Humphrey was the 'magnum desideratum,'" he wrote. He knew her exacting standards from past experience, and her reaction when he showed her the *Chaconne* for the first time was so gratifying that he memorized it. He had been working on the piece in the living room at 13th Street, building up material on a single "seminal dance phrase from which the entire work would flow," in an effort to capture the sense of the music, which he had grappled with twice before unsuccessfully. When Doris saw it she was silent for a moment. Then she said, in her quiet voice, "This is one of the most magnificent dances I have ever seen. It is that for a number of reasons, but chiefly because it is a man dancing." Pauline thought it was a good dance, but too long.

As José described Doris' *Four Chorale Preludes* they must have been related in feeling to her earliest Bach piece, *Air for the G String,* "She used a style evocative of medieval religious art." John Martin saw its theme as the survival of human idealism, with a "Gothic mysticism" mirroring the music. Like many of her previous works, the *Chorale Preludes* dealt with the question of sin and redemption in terms of pure dance. For instance, in the second section, Man's Fall from Grace, instead of depicting some drama of Original Sin, she made a duet for herself and José that elaborated on the idea of real falling. She called the *Preludes* "a naive and stylized miniature, greatly simplified and understated, of the respective rewards of unity and disunity in human behavior."

The *Partita,* a lighter piece, was a suite suggested by the six preclassic forms in the music: allemande, courante, sarabande, minuet, passepied, gigue. As she had done so many times before, Doris invented her own movement but preserved the spirit of her baroque source. "Formal dances with a thread of courtly play," was how the *Dance Observer's* critic George Beiswanger described the work.

The Bach program had originally been scheduled to run three weekends at Studio Theater, but it was so popular with audiences that five more weeks were added to the schedule. Yet the program generated controversy. John Martin, taking up again the inexplicable argument he had used to condemn the *Passacaglia* at its premiere, wrote several columns indicting the whole concept of dancing to Bach. Taking the indulgent tone of the critic who knows he's about to reprimand one of his favorites, Martin wrote, "Why Miss Humphrey, one of the most progressively minded of the modern dancers and one of the greatest choreographers . . . should have felt the necessity of turning to Bach must be clear to her; it must also be clear to the delighted spectators." To the critic, however, the use of Bach by these artists remained "an irreconcilable combination, and one which sends him away unmoved

Four Chorale Preludes. Photo by Marcus Blechman. (Dance Collection, NYPL)

and unnourished." The whole concert to him was "dry, remote, and generally unrewarding."

Martin's objections seemed to have to do with the credo to which he himself had given so much weight over the years, that modern dance by its very nature meant an independence from any other sources including musical scores, and a resolute freedom from any precedents or aesthetics except those of the contemporary world. Doris' failure to wave banners or act out her sentiments about the sufferings of war seemed to Martin a retreat from her responsibility as an artist. He persisted in his belief that theater was an alien form to Bach, whose works, he believed, were too complete and too formal to allow superimposition of any independent assertions from a dancer. Nor could he conquer his curious inability to see the music and the dance as one entity. Even though he could admit that the *Four Chorale Preludes* "is beautifully designed and contains some ravishing passages of movement," he insisted that "the music dominates in feeling and form." The *Partita* he thought "neatly enough made but quite inconsequential." As for José's piece, he considered the Chaconne "music unsuitable for dancing."

Doris was stung and understandably baffled by Martin's attack, and she wrote him a long letter, part of which he published in his column in the Sunday *New York Times.* Proudly she admitted that she loved Bach, but, as if she too thought that wasn't quite enough to protect her credentials as a modern dance choreographer, "I deny that this is my sole reason for composing with it as a base, or that self-expression, in the narrow sense, is the strongest motivation." She had higher aims, and went on to enumerate how she and José had tried to achieve them in the four pieces on the program. She defended the *Chaconne* in terms of José's nobility as a dancer and asked, "Do you want to see this man's contribution to the development of the human race [danced] to the music which happens to inspire him in this way . . . or do you want to listen to the music and behead the dancer?" In effect, the necessity of defending her position against Martin's musical intransigence forced her to minimize her musicality and instinctive danciness, which in that climate couldn't be accepted for their own sake.

Humphrey-Weidman musical director Norman Cazden also replied to Martin. This careful and musically informed rebuttal, published in the *Dance Observer,* placed Bach in direct correspondence with all the aims of modern art. Cazden cited the composer's ideals of "communal unity elevated to artistic formalization and integrated harmony and proportion" and the inherent democratizing effect of the chorales themselves, which were meant to be sung by congregations and to dramatize the gospels in terms that laypersons could understand. Cazden concluded that Bach's dedication to the advance of communal faith represented the very spirit the Nazis at that moment were trying to snuff out in Europe.

Before the program had finished its long run at Studio Theater, Doris and José were planning another evening, totally different in character. This was a bill of dances on American and folk themes. José revived his *Danzas Mexicanas* and made a new piece, the lively *Western Folk Suite*. Doris, who was not dancing, showed Desert Gods from *Song of the West* and a new work, *El Salon Mexico*. Billed as José Limón and the Humphrey-Weidman Repertory Company directed by Doris Humphrey, the concert opened March 11 and ran for four weekends at Studio Theater.

Though outlived by its 1937 Aaron Copland score, *El Salon Mexico* was nevertheless an interesting work, and it assumes even more importance when seen as a possible forerunner of Doris' two later dreampieces, *Night Spell* and *Ruins and Visions*. According to John Martin the dance was a "fantasy about a youth in a dance hall and his ideal partner." The program note explained that the title referred to the "Roseland Ballroom of Mexico." Doris' own scenario pictures a setting made of boxes and screens with a platform and ramp, which could suggest at different times "a room for a rendezvous, a garden, a winding street, a ballroom, an amusement park." The language of this description indicates that she was beginning to consider her locale more graphically and specifically than before. The Humphrey-Weidman boxes had always been adaptable to many different interpretations, but they had not, in her own mind, done much more than prosaically delineate a dancing-space—the street and the mother's house in *With My Red Fires,* the various arenas and stages and thoroughfares in *Theatre Piece, Race of Life, Decade.*

The action of *El Salon Mexico* was supposed to be taking place in the imagination of a Mexican peon (José), and it flowed from one situation to the next without the necessity of literal motivation. He meets first his ideal, a peasant girl (Florence Lessing), then a succession of other women in the guise of cheap dancing girls and carnival-goers. After he dances with them all, they begin to mix and dissolve together. The original lovers are "reunited in the midst of a swirling throng and lead the boisterous revel to an overpowering climax," according to reviewer Robert Lawrence. Then, said Doris, "the women vanish by twos and threes. He is left clinging vainly to his first love, who also disappears as the last notes sound."

This was the first of many dances in which Doris projected the inner longings of a central male figure, who was, of course, José. In *Night Spell* (1951),
which could be a simplified, more intense version of the same theme, the
dreamer manages to extricate his love from the fantasy world, and holds her
fast at the end. The necessity to choreograph around other personalities than
herself may have opened up not only the male sensibility to Doris but a
more dramatic and human way of presenting ideas. Abstraction probably
seemed natural and comprehensible to her as long as she was dancing herself, but perhaps, being completely outside the action, she began to see the
uses of a more literal approach.

In partial counterbalance to John Martin's disapproval, the two 1943 programs gained Doris a new, though unfortunately short-lived champion. Con-
ductor-music critic Robert Lawrence had taken over the dance responsibilities
at the *New York Herald Tribune* when Walter Terry went into the army, and
he was extremely sympathetic to Doris. With some reservations about the
Chaconne, he had thought the Bach program "rich in inventive spirit," and
he was even more impressed with *El Salon Mexico.* "All of the qualities demanded by theatrical dance were present: design, movement, color, vitality,
and—above all—the heroic integrity of purpose, the refusal to luxuriate in
easy appeal, that brand Miss Humphrey as a vital modern force." Two
months later Lawrence handed over the *Tribune*'s dance department to Edwin Denby, and in his farewell column he named *El Salon Mexico* as the
second best new ballet of the 1942–43 season, after Léonide Massine's
Aleko. Other works on Lawrence's list included Antony Tudor's *Romeo and
Juliet,* Agnes de Mille's *Rodeo,* George Balanchine's *Ballet Imperial,* and
Charles Weidman's *And Daddy was a Fireman,* which had premiered at Studio Theater on March 7. Lawrence's ultimate tribute to *El Salon Mexico* was
to include it as one of the few modern dance works in his 1950 *Victor Book
of Ballets and Ballet Music.* There he said it was "one of the most vital and
dramatically integrated of American ballets. Miss Humphrey's strength of design was nobly sustained by Mr. Limón in his performance of the leading
role."

The draft finally caught up with José, and shortly after the last of the folk
programs he was inducted into the army. After basic training he joined the
Special Services unit at Camp Lee, Virginia, where he worked on shows for
recruitment drives, war-bond rallies, and camp entertainments. He served not
only as dancer, choreographer, and director, but sometimes as designer,
backstage technician, and even composer of music. But throughout his two-

and-a-half years as a soldier he never stopped thinking about his interrupted career and planning what he would do when he could fully resume it. He wrote to Pauline, "I want to dance only about serious things—certainly I don't want to spend my efforts being gay or cute or ingratiating—the best music and painting is the serious kind—and I want to do only the best dancing."

For the rest of the spring at Studio Theater, Charles and the company gave mixed programs consisting of his and Doris' choreography, a bill drawn from his nightclub numbers, and a program of Americana with *Lynchtown, Bargain Counter, Shakers,* and a reading from Edgar Lee Masters' *Spoon River Anthology* by actor Dan Reed to music by Norman dello Joio. Doris apparently danced only once, in a performance of *Shakers* at the Needle Trades High School. Summing up the 1942–1943 season in a letter to the subscribers, Doris reported that Humphrey-Weidman—in various combinations of personnel—had given thirty-two performances at Studio Theater and nine on the road, and had sponsored sixteen evenings of concerts in its Guest Artist Series. The theater had operated from September 29 to April 24. This in a year when there was reduced activity all over the modern dance field.

Doris told Hay she needed a long rest after the season ended, but what she got was another summer of teaching in New York. Studio factotum Olga Frye left to do war work, and Doris tried to get longtime Humphrey-Weidman ally Eleanor Frampton to come in from Cleveland and manage the summer courses, but Framp was so busy teaching that she didn't even reply to Doris' letter until August. Charles had a seven-night-a-week nightclub job, and he also began work on a new show, *Star Dust,* produced by Michael Myerberg. Commercial work now seemed so dominant in his affairs that Doris told Pauline she thought he was bored with concert choreography and didn't care anymore. Doris' domestic life was even more troubled than it had been the summer before. Although she sent Humphrey to camp in New Jersey, she had invited her mother to come east, and Julia stayed in New York both at the beginning and the end of the summer, visiting other friends in New England in between. Hay made her annual pilgrimage from the end of July till Labor Day, and during this period Leo got a rare shore leave. They all spent as much time as they could at the farm, but relations were strained. Pauline meanwhile fretted about José and tried intermittently to be agreeable. While still admiring Doris, she felt displaced and out of sorts without her former "power."

As classes began again in early September, Charles was not to be found.

He had gone on the road with *Star Dust* on tryouts and kept assuring Doris he longed to come home and help out but just couldn't leave. In fact, he hoped she would find time to drop down to Philadelphia and look at the show; maybe she would have some suggestions about the choreography. But she was teaching his classes two nights a week as well as her own, and she had also decided to move, since her lease on 22nd Street was up. The move to a new apartment on 16th Street was accomplished somehow, and Charles was back at the beginning of October, only to become involved in another show, *Jackpot*, with music by Vernon Duke. And the new season held still more frustrations. Plans fell through for a company tour in December and a reprise of the Lillian Gish production of the Bach Christmas Oratorio that had been so successful in 1934. Later in the winter she had to swallow some bitter medicine when Hanya Holm mounted a version of *Orestes*, with music by John Coleman ("revoltingly German," Pauline called it), and she had a preview of sitting on the sidelines when José borrowed some of the costumes from *Square Dances* for one of his army shows. And, a reminder of the old days, there wasn't enough heat in the studio, even during performances.

In addition to her hip, Doris' back was bothering her during the fall. When Leo went back to sea after his summer break, he once more complained of feeling estranged from her, but this time he acknowledged that she had more on her mind than he could comprehend. "Fundamentally I am an egocentric, as you well know by now, and my interest has always been in direct proportion to your interest in me. . . . The waning of the one has resulted in a waning of the other, just as the two waxed together. . . . I know where the blows are striking, but I feel helpless." Doris' state of mind at this time has to be surmised; not only were her letters to Hay lost, but Leo destroyed those she wrote to him, because he said he didn't want them read by officials who censored the mail aboard ship. Besides being depressed and physically depleted, she at last began to see her situation realistically.

For the first time, the Studio Theater could not open before the New Year. Doris had been planning a new dance, *Inquest*, for months, and putting it off because she didn't have the dancers to rehearse it. Neither Charles nor José was on tap, and the men who had been spared from the draft were all dancing in shows, either Charles' *Jackpot*, or *Mexican Hayride*, or *Marianne*. (Doris had turned down an offer to work on the last of these shows, which closed out of town.) All of the strongest women had left the company too. By the time *Inquest* did get performed, in March of 1944, half the ensemble had joined within only a few months of the premiere, and not a single person was left from the great touring days of Humphrey-Weidman. Just before Christmas, Hay wrote Doris in disbelief: "It was only last year that you were turning people away. . . . It would be utterly impossible for the studio to remain in a state of coma and finally pass out IN ONE YEAR." But in fact, after one final triumphant production, that is just what happened.

10 FALL AND RECOVERY, 1944 – 46

Many people remember *Inquest* as one of Doris' finest works. It was also the last time she danced and the last gasp of Humphrey-Weidman, so memories of it have undoubtedly been colored by a knowledge of the personal tragedy that lay behind it. Once again she chose a social theme, the most literal she had ever used, but through an imaginative choreographic design she was able to transcend the factual content of the material. The dance was slow in getting to the stage, but she persisted, as always when the idea meant a lot to her.

She had long wanted to make some statement about the wartime distress all around her, but she always drew back at the magnitude of the tragedy. "People were getting killed by the thousands in the war," recalled composer Norman Lloyd, "and Doris said the only thing to concentrate on was the individual." In her mind there was a strong connection between poverty and individual suffering, and the cost of fighting a war. Early in 1941 she saw a movie about a pellagra epidemic in the South, and felt a sense of outrage that the government could find money to build armaments and train soldiers but could not cure a widespread disease. "I would like to make as scathing a drama as I could—a *j'accuse* in my medium. I will too," she wrote to Leo. Around the same time she was browsing through the library at home and came across the volume *Sesame and Lilies* (1865) by the English essayist John Ruskin. This contains "Of Kings' Treasuries," one of Ruskin's many exhortations to the lower classes to better themselves through reading the great books. "Do you ask to be the companion of nobles? Make yourself noble, and you shall be," Ruskin admonished the half-schooled laborers who attended his lectures. The story of *Inquest* came from a footnote Ruskin inserted to illustrate the nobility of the poor, the persistence of their finer instincts in spite of the most desperate privation. It was a newspaper report of a shoemaker in London who had literally starved to death rather than take his family to the workhouse.

Fusing the techniques of Living Newspaper and her own epic choral dance, Doris constructed *Inquest* in two parts. First, a reading of the story just as it appeared in Ruskin, with Doris, Charles, and Peter Hamilton as the pathetic family, acting out the scenario in what John Martin described as "rhythmic mime that is a high abstraction of actual gesture." Then there was a group dance which used the gestural movement as thematic material for a more impassioned comment on the story. "In stormy crosscurrents, their angry, twisted bodies and violent gestures bespoke their wrath and despair," as Margaret Lloyd saw it. Martin thought, "It is as if the sparse and humble actuality had been heroically magnified into its true dimensional value." With its stirring, conscience-arousing words, its naturalistic settings and action, and its lyrical embodiment of pathos, *Inquest* was extremely effective with audiences in those wartime days. George Beiswanger compared it to the anguished portraits of Gorki and Van Gogh. "This was suffering 'out of the hurt heart' of humanity," said Lloyd. "It opened our hearts to the homeless, the cold, the hungry people everywhere." In the story of Mary and Michael Collins Doris had found a more objective and dramatic way of venting her personal despair—one must assume that she felt herself kin at this time to the oppressed principals in Ruskin's example, stymied in all directions despite her most valiant efforts.

Perhaps it was inevitable that Doris should draw on Ruskin as a choreographic source at some point. She could see flaws in his aesthetic and social philosophies, but she believed totally in the Ruskinian ethic that decreed the moral responsibility of art and the artist. She shared Ruskin's confidence that the individual's higher, finer instincts—as exemplified in the artist—would overcome the depersonalizing effects of an increasingly industrialized world. To the Victorians, the artist became the secular priest of the coming machine age—and if he would accept the duty to uplift and beautify life, no one could accuse him of indolence or decadence. This sense of mission underlay the arts-and-crafts movement in England, the theory of form-follows-function in architecture, the Bauhaus' attempts to reconcile craftsmanship and creativity, and many other aspects of modernism in the arts. It permeated the thinking of the early modern dancers in this country, from Isadora Duncan onward. And it certainly persisted into the World War II period. That spring Pauline sent José a clipping from an article by *New York Times* music critic Olin Downes, "A day . . . is coming fast when artists and other men of creative thought, whose sphere has been commonly supposed to be outside that of practical accomplishment, will be recognized as indispensable agencies of a progressive society for its constructive development and clarification of purpose." Doris not only believed this was her role, she of all the modern dancers was able to translate it into particularly strong, convincing dances.

It also, however, placed a restraint on her ambitions, a damper on her imagination. In reviewing *Inquest,* Edwin Denby went straight to what was in the long run a central flaw in almost all her works with a moral intent. "The piece has pointed out that poverty destroys humane values we all believe in. We applaud it as a sincere and eloquent sermon on the theme of the freedom from want. . . . *Inquest* is a piece that appeals to our moral sensibility, it aims to be clear and its esthetic appeal is secondary." Denby pointed out that in propaganda pieces, the intellectual idea often became apparent to the viewer long before the dance material had run out. "One grasps the moral implications quickly and agrees with them. But the full rhetorical exposition of these ideas in dance form takes a good deal longer. The result is that one's response is complete before the dance is finished. . . . Intellectually speaking, an interesting dance is a continuous discovery. The ideas it presents do not precede it, they are formed after one has perceived the movement. And because an interesting dance creates new ideas it is often not at all easy to understand nor in accord with what one would reasonably expect. This, of course, does not do for propaganda." Denby's aestheticism represented the other great stream of modern art, the one which didn't demand that the artist take a reformist social position. Even when she was not delivering a sermon, Doris was seldom able to relinquish her ingrained commitment to clarity, to form, and to moral uplift. Her dance, for some viewers, never transcended the serviceable.

The Studio Theater audience loved *Inquest,* and Doris' mostly-mimed performance in it. The piece premiered March 5, 1944, after a February premiere for subscribers. In June, summing up the season, John Martin gave it his "invisible gold medal" as the finest composition of the season. For the March opening Doris had also tossed off *Canonade,* a dance of canons and variations for four women; and Charles premiered a second part of his autobiography, *And Daddy was a Fireman.* Another new work of Charles', *The Heart Remembers,* was postponed from March to April 2, received bad notices, and was given only once or twice. Doris had been trying to revive *Red Fires,* with former Graham dancer Dorothy Bird in Katherine Litz' part, but it never reached the stage. The spring program—*Inquest* and *Canonade,* with *Partita, Daddy,* and *On My Mother's Side* in alternation—ran for twenty performances, eighteen at Studio Theater, one at the High School of Needle Trades, and one at Swarthmore College. In increasing pain, Doris danced in all of them. The Swarthmore concert, May 26, was her last performance.

In early May she was considering giving up the studio, having been told by the doctor to take a complete rest. She needed painkillers to sleep. Charles was having one of his busiest seasons in the commercial theater. Although classes were scheduled at the studio from mid-May to the end of June, it must have been Doris who taught the bulk of them, because Charles was choreographing an operetta, *The New Moon,* with Dorothy Kirsten and Earl Wrightson, for an opening at City Center on May 15. He then went to restage and dance in *School for Husbands* which was given July 12–15 at the Cain Park Theater in Cleveland. Doris had offers, of course, and she was working with José in the spring; he had been transferred to the New York area and took up his career again on weekends and during furloughs from the army. Hay was trying to help Doris become reconciled to not dancing: "Musicians seldom appear in their compositions and other creative artists never do. Do you remember how you said it felt all right to sit in the wings and play the drum while Beatrice did your part in the *Shakers?*" (She probably detested it, but had to endure it.)

Once while touring in Texas in 1940, Doris was taken to the chapel at Texas State College for Women, where a set of stained glass windows was devoted to great women of accomplishment. She and Graham, Duncan, St. Denis, and Pavlova were pictured on one of them. On another window, she found what she said would be the motto of the soon-to-open Studio Theater, in the words of Marie Curie: "Life is not easy for any of us but what of that? We must have perseverence and above all confidence in ourselves. We must believe that we are gifted for something and that this thing at whatever cost must be attained." In the August-September 1944 issue of the *Dance Observer* there appeared a brief announcement that Studio Theater was closing its doors.

Euphemistic to the last, the directors said they were planning to "expand their activities as dancers, teachers, and choreographers." What this really meant was that Charles would give classes at City Center and Doris was to institute a composition class at the 92nd Street YM-YWHA; then the two of them became absorbed for the fall in the Theatre Guild production of *Sing Out, Sweet Land.* But for the moment dance repertory was finished. Within months Doris was drafting another plan for something called The Dance Theater. Humphrey-Weidman would open Christmas week in a 900–1,000 seat theater and play every Friday and Sunday for six months of the year, alternating with other dance companies including small ballet groups. There would be nights for little-theater groups and musical concerts. There would be money for publicity, production, and salaries. Like so many other schemes, this one never left the drawing board. Humphrey-Weidman as a repertory company was ended.

For many months Doris suffered agonies of inactivity and paralyzing bitterness. Her physical condition precluded even heavy teaching, with which she had always been able to fill her time and earn a living. Between the summer of 1944 and the summer of 1946, the only major project she could complete was the dances for the Theatre Guild's Americana show *Sing Out, Sweet Land.* Always careless of her appearance, she developed a fierce vanity about her increasing limp. She tried to conceal it, as she did any other sign of weakness. A snapshot taken on a New York street when one of Hay's daughters paid a visit in the summer of 1945 shows her looking drawn and old but walking sturdily forward, almost as she had in more vigorous days. But it was getting harder for her to move around, and demonstrating for classes and choreography sessions soon became impossible.

While she tried to patch together some new working alliances out of the shreds of Humphrey-Weidman, her domestic support system slackened too. Leo had become an American citizen. He applied for his ship's masters license, and finally—just after the end of the war in Europe—was given his own command, a United Fruit Company boat which was being operated as a cargo vessel by the U.S. Navy. Delivering supplies around Mediterranean ports in the summer of 1945, he was appalled by the devastation left by the war but curiously exhilarated to have a ship under his own control at last. In his letters to Doris, he delivered homilies on the condition of the human race in the aftermath of the atomic bomb. But he had less compassion, apparently, for what his wife was going through. In 1945 he forgot her birthday, forgot to send Christmas presents, and missed seeing her on the one weekend in the fall when he was in port because he couldn't get her on the telephone from Baltimore and didn't want to risk going all the way to New York if she wasn't there. He mused at the end of the year on "how simple and easy a thing it is for normal people to be together if they wish it and I would go nuts with frustrations if I did not recall that most normal folk spend a good deal of their time scheming how to get the hell away from each other. Or do they?"

Doris' mother suffered a stroke in early 1945 and spent the next eight months severely disabled in a nursing home. She died in October, a few days before Doris' fiftieth birthday. The relatives with whom she had been living arranged the funeral, for which Doris made a hasty trip to Oak Park.

Professionally Doris' life, always so committed and clearly focused, grew indistinct. It is difficult to trace her activities during these transitional years. She started projects; they didn't work out. She spent a lot of time tidying up for Charles—teaching his classes when he didn't appear, fixing his shows. Ideas and offers came, but nothing suited her. She may have consulted a psychiatrist at this time. Added to the enormous burden of her physical condition and the studio's collapse, she now had to recognize that the whole evolution of dance was turning away from what she had worked so long to establish. The popular acclaim that eluded the modern dance was now converging on its two arch-rivals: ballet and musical comedy.

At war's end the resources for lavish, expert entertainment that the nation had rallied to the service of morale-building surged into a tide of celebratory shows. Rodgers and Hammerstein's *Oklahoma!* (1943) for the Theatre Guild, choreographed by Agnes de Mille, touched off an era of musicals that were truly unified in theme and style. *Oklahoma!* revolutionized the form by using a book with a thoughtful story and integrated musical numbers, rather than the standard assortment of dances and songs draped on a rickety plot. It also demonstrated to the audience and the Broadway producing world that classically trained dancers and professional choreographers could have an equal role in the success of a commercial venture. Agnes de Mille takes credit for upgrading the dancing quality—and the moral fiber—of the Broadway gypsy, "The chorus girl and the chorus boy of the past, corrupt, sly, ruthless and professionally inept, gradually disappeared. And in their place came singers and dancers, trained and self-respecting. Rehearsal halls began to lose their overtones of boudoir bargaining." Of course, Doris' and Charles' dancers among others had been appearing in shows for over a decade, but somehow the colossal success of *Oklahoma!* became a watershed for the whole profession.

Doris still could not reconcile Broadway work with her notion of independent, artistic choreography. *Sing Out, Sweet Land* was as onerous to her, and the product as unrewarding, as all the other shows she had grudgingly worked on, even though it was a success; the dances were praised, and she received a royalty for the entire run.

Sing Out, Sweet Land originated in a May 1944 student production at Catholic University in Washington, D.C., with a book by Walter Kerr, who was a professor of dramatics there at the time. The following fall the Theatre Guild put it into rehearsal with Doris and Charles as choreographers. An Americana revue, it set out "to show how music went hand in hand with labor and struggle throughout the history of our country, helping by its very existence to lighten labor and raise the heart," according to the *Boston Herald's* Elinor Hughes. Alfred Drake played an Everyman character, Barnaby Goodchild, pursued down the years by the puritanical Parson Killjoy. Burl Ives invariably stole the show singing composer Elie Siegmeister's adaptations of folk ballads, and the dances were generally commended. The co-choreographers apparently split up the work, with Doris doing a twenty-minute ballet eventually called *Five O'Clock Whistle* and Charles setting everything else. But given Charles' increasing undependability, she probably doctored his work as well as directing her own.

The scenario Doris prepared for the ballet—she called it *Building of the Cities*—demonstrates once again that she had an eye for total theater. As construction workers putting up a skyscraper, actors build a set onstage. A park is engulfed to make way for the building, but it will provide the towns-people with a new place to live. The men are called off to war and the women take their places on the job, "solid, heroic, and without sadness."

Doris traveled with the show for its tryouts in Boston and Philadelphia during the month before Christmas 1944. She was pessimistic about its prospects, though she thought her ballet was good and asked for separate credit on the program. The show did well, and was even more successful on the road after its New York run. But in May, it was Agnes de Mille who won the New York Drama Critics Circle Award as the best dance-director/choreographer, for *Bloomer Girl* and *Carousel. Sing Out, Sweet Land* and Jerome Robbins' *On the Town* got one vote apiece. De Mille was queen of the Theatre Guild. She gave interviews, bought expensive hats, posed for glamour pictures with her chorus dancers, and loved being the most sought-after choreographer of musicals, even though she too wanted desperately to succeed as a serious choreographer. But Doris didn't have the knack for self-promotion, nor at this time could she have mustered the self-esteem.

In any case she had what she thought would be an ideal project in the works with the Theatre Guild. Her connections with them went back to 1933 (*School for Husbands*), and directors Lawrence Langner and Theresa Helburn knew her as a serious if demanding artist. The spring before *Sing Out* went into rehearsals they had begun thinking about a series of Ballet Plays. "It won't compete with the ballet," Langner told the press, "as it will be combining short plays with special dances. There will be three or four such plays making up the performance which we hope will play for the season." The idea of the Ballet Plays was all that really sustained Doris during the months after the collapse of Studio Theater. Here, in a protected environment, almost a laboratory situation, dancers would be paid to develop a new dance-drama form that wouldn't be subject to the commercial whims of Broadway. She thought of *Sing Out, Sweet Land* as a meal ticket for the Ballet Plays. With her royalties she could pay for studio rent and dancers' salaries during developmental work.

She considered several story ideas. One, derived from Edgar Allan Poe stories, was finally produced in 1953 as *Poor Eddy* by a college group at Columbia University. She developed one script, based on James Thurber and E. B. White's spoof of Freudian sexology books, *Is Sex Necessary? or Why You Feel the Way You Do.* The action was to be mostly mimed, as accompaniment to a slide-illustrated "lecture" tracing the human race's irresistible urge to unite, from the time the one-celled organism separated itself into two halves. The play ended with a mass dance, "the showdown between men and women," in which the sexes, evenly matched, squared off against each other and battled until an equal number of men and women prisoners were taken and everyone was once again paired up in couples.

But Helburn and Langner procrastinated. Doris knew from experience that they liked to start ambitious, high-minded projects but, in her case at least, seldom carried them through. By the summer of 1947, Doris apparently still had gotten nothing for her trouble, and Langner agreed to meet with her to "settle this matter." Finally, in December, the Theatre Guild paid her $500, calling it an "award . . . in connection with the ballet play *Is Sex Necessary?*" They never produced this or any other Ballet Play of hers. Though Doris vastly admired Thurber, it was Charles who had the most enduring success in staging the crusty but affable humorist. Not only did he choreograph several of Thurber's *Fables for Our Time,* but he also did *The War Between Men and Women* (1954) and even *Is Sex Necessary?,* two years after Doris' death, using her script.

Although Doris had turned Studio Theater over to Charles when it became impossible for her to run the business herself, she still depended on teaching for a large part of her living. In the fall of Humphrey-Weidman's breakup she instituted a class in composition at the 92nd Street YM-YWHA. She had acted as an advisor and sometime organizer for that institution ever since it had opened its Dance Center in the mid-1930s. Under the direction of William Kolodney, it now sponsored not only a thriving school for modern and other dance classes, but also an important concert series. Kaufmann Auditorium, a modestly scaled theater, suited the needs of modern dancers, and was booked for concerts throughout the season whenever the schedule wasn't occupied by companies presented by the Dance Center itself. Doris, of course, served on the audition committee for these, along with the other leading modern dance choreographers and critics.

Oriented to professionals, her composition class began with the unassuming intention of teaching and analyzing dances from the Humphrey-Weidman repertory. She always preferred this kind of teaching to technique, and by the next year (1945–46), she had developed a full-fledged program of teaching choreography to advanced students. This course, together with the teaching of her own repertory, became the vehicle by which she imparted sound, clear principles of dance-making to hundreds of students through the years.

But somehow she had to keep making dances herself. When Walter Terry returned from the army to his old job at the *Herald Tribune,* she admitted to him that she wouldn't be dancing anymore—no formal announcement had yet been made. Terry paid her the compliment of devoting a whole Sunday column to her. "Great as she was in the role of dancer," Terry wrote, "she is even greater in the role of choreographer, ranking as one of the best, and perhaps the very best, that America has ever produced."

Sometime in 1946 Doris started working with Pauline Koner on an unusual project they called "choreographic direction" of a dance for Koner. The work pointed the way to Doris' method of choreographing from then on. Koner, another of the great individualists of modern dance, had built a career as a soloist after studying Spanish and Oriental dance, and ballet with Michel Fokine. As she remembers it, Doris sent her a congratulatory note after one of her concerts at the Y, and Koner suggested they work together. Koner needed advice and stimulation at that point in her career. She knew that Doris was interested in young dancers and that she wasn't dogmatically attached to any one technical approach. Koner rented a studio and arranged to pay Doris a fee. Doris showed up at the first session with a piece of music, Lukas Foss' Song of Anguish, and some cloth, which they began to use as a costume element. Doris thought the Biblical theme of Foss' music might work for Koner. "She didn't give me steps . . . she didn't choreograph. What she really did was trigger me with images. She'd say 'I see something like this' and I would find the movement for it."

The dance they evolved was first called *Woe Unto Them* (later *Voice in the Wilderness*). It was premiered by Koner on a concert at the High School of Needle Trades in November of 1946. The *Dance Observer*'s critic, Marie-

Anne Phelps, commended Doris' role in "clarifying choreography and . . . using space more freely than Miss Koner does in her own dances." After its initial performances, Koner thought the dance would be more dramatic if the baritone who had sung the text from the wings could be onstage and interacting with her to some degree. Doris endorsed this idea and Koner revised the dance with that in mind.

During this period of desolate reorientation, the ballet itself was another burgeoning field where Doris might logically have applied her skills. The foundations of American ballet had been laid before the war. Lucia Chase had steered the Mordkin Ballet through its metamorphosis into the Ballet Theatre, an evolution completed by 1940. Lincoln Kirstein and George Balanchine, having established the School of American Ballet as an incubator of dancers in 1934, were biding their time until a permanent organization could be sustained to present them. In 1946 they set up the Ballet Society, which presented independent evenings of Balanchine's work and later served as the structure under which the New York City Ballet was incorporated. The stream of expatriate Russians which had trickled into the United States after the Revolution was augmented by other refugees from Europe. As soon as wartime restrictions on travel were lifted, touring companies began coming to America again, and with the help of promoters like Sol Hurok, ballet became a major attraction in opera houses in New York and the provinces.

Throughout the 1940s, the ballet scene was lively, volatile, and very visible. The cast of characters—great international stars like Léonide Massine, Alexandra Danilova, Alicia Markova, Anton Dolin, and Igor Youskevitch—floated from one company to another. Balanchine worked for anyone who would provide him with the resources. Antony Tudor was imported from England to choreograph for Ballet Theatre. American choreographers and American themes were given a boost into acceptability by Kirstein's Ballet Caravan. During his very brief tenure at the *New York Herald Tribune* (1943–45), Edwin Denby wrote constantly and penetratingly about ballet, the first American critic to combine a receptiveness to the new with a sensibility for the classical. Denby's writing aimed at encouraging the New York public to sample ballet; his finely tuned instinct for rhythm, style, and effect put something into his reviews that went far beyond Martin's earnest chauvinism, Terry's instinct for theatricality, or the average reviewer's susceptibility to stars.

Denby wasn't a fan of modern dance, and he was never aesthetically sympathetic to Humphrey-Weidman's work, although he thought its themes morally commendable. Denby's comment on the dances in *Sing Out, Sweet Land* are perhaps subtle beyond their time, but they locate what might have been Doris' greatest liability in attracting a popular audience: she tried too hard, he thought.

> *Sing Out, Sweet Land* wants to make you feel at home, not here and now, but in our historic customs. Doris Humphrey and Charles Weidman have furnished historical steps (from "squares" to Charleston). . . . But as for the rest, if you begin to compare the heavy accents and strained postures of the dancing with the limpid, relaxed, and delicately elastic rhythm by which Burl Ives, the balladist, sings his songs, you notice how "unauthentic" the dance effects are. You will notice it, if you enjoy our country folklore straight and appreciate its inherent modesty and unassertive spaciousness. But it takes a unique artist like Ives to put across such mild and sweet effects.

Critic George Beiswanger, on the other hand, had called as early as 1941 for the Ballet Theatre to absorb Doris' and Charles' dances into its proposed "modern repertory" of American works. In January 1945 Hay was urging Doris to consider working with the company; her works could stand up beside those of Tudor and de Mille, Hay thought. Doris had already anticipated that the dancers wouldn't be able to manage her movement style, and Hay argued that most of the dancers in *Sing Out* hadn't been Humphrey-trained either, yet they had executed her needs.

In March 1947, Valerie Bettis became the first modern dancer to choreograph a ballet, for the Ballet Russe de Monte Carlo. Her *Virginia Sampler* was not a success—critics felt it failed to reconcile the two dance mediums— and Doris predicted, "now all the balletomanes will point a triumphant finger." Nevertheless, an opening wedge had been driven. That summer the Ballet Theatre, chronically in need of choreographers, was embarking on a determined and fairly adventurous search for fresh material, and Lucia Chase acceded to suggestions that modern dance should be a part of its repertory. Chase wrote graciously to Doris to make a formal bid for *With My Red Fires*. She said that the fall rehearsal period would begin in September; the company would leave on tour September 27; and they could open the ballet in Philadelphia September 30. This would have allowed a scant three weeks to prepare the dance, and some of that time would be on the road, when little serious rehearsing ever got done. Doris responded that she would be interested in the project, but she envisioned a minimum of fifty hours rehearsal time, and rather than set a definite premiere, she preferred to schedule that date when the dance was "ready."

Considering Ballet Theatre's hasty, pressured schedules of the time, Chase's reply was almost excessively accommodating. She noted that in order to avoid overtime the company was allowed only seventeen days of rehearsal at five hours per dancer for preparing the whole repertory. But even though all nineteen of Doris' dancers might not participate in every rehearsal, "We shall see that you get at least fifty hours all told." If the end of September was too early an opening date, Chase proposed Boston in November, or they could premiere the piece during the second week of their City Center season in New York, which was to begin November 17. Balanchine had been commissioned to do a work for this season (it turned out to be the classic *Theme and Variations* for Igor Youskevitch and Alicia Alonso), and "I think yours will make a good balance with it and should be very successful at City Center."

They met to discuss it further, but Doris still hesitated. She had insisted from the start that the three platforms running across the back of the stage were essential to her choreography, and this became a final insurmountable problem. Not only were the levels expensive to construct and heavy to ship around the country on tour, but setting them up and striking them during performances would be a big job. Though otherwise quick to revise or adapt her choreography to suit a situation, Doris this time offered no solution.

Yet Chase persevered. Maybe they could think of something else. They discussed *Inquest*, which Doris had considered too intimate for the Metropolitan Opera House, where Ballet Theatre would play in the spring, but perhaps it would work at the smaller City Center. Or would Doris consider doing something new for the company's dramatic ballerina Nora Kaye?

Having her work in the repertory of Ballet Theatre at this time would have gained Doris access to a public far greater than any she had yet reached, and one that was especially receptive to contemporary serious works. She had acquired a broad enough theatrical background by then to solve choreographic problems with taste and originality, particularly in the area of dance-drama which Chase was trying to secure her for. José offered to rearrange his plans for the fall to make himself available to her in any way she could use him, tactfully not mentioning outright that she would need someone to demonstrate at rehearsals. She would have the top American dancers to work with, and her ballet would be showcased in major theaters in New York and across the country on Ballet Theatre's touring schedule, which that year was to be booked by Sol Hurok. Yet she let the opportunity go.

Unlike many other modern dancers at that time, she would not in principle have opposed her works being done by a ballet company. But after all her unsatisfactory experiences with Broadway producers and sponsors whose efforts to include her work resulted in unacceptable compromises, she was immoderately wary of any situation where she might have to lower her standards. Margaret Lloyd supported her decision not to pursue the Ballet Theatre negotiations, "I am thankful that you will make no compromises but insist on showing your works as they should be or not at all." But in any case, it must have seemed to her at that moment that the job would mean diverting her attention, and long ago she had decided that she must concentrate her energies and consolidate her style. By this time she was once again working on home ground and didn't need any new direction. She had become partners with José, who was now assuming a public role to suit the commanding nickname the women of the family had given him: The Eagle.

After finally succumbing to the draft, José had pulled every string he could to get released from the army, or at least to do his service in some capacity that wouldn't uproot him totally from dancing. At war's end he was stationed in Brooklyn and managed to get into the city often enough to maintain a visible presence in the concert world, with performances of a trio consisting of himself, Bea Seckler, and Dorothy Bird. The group made its New York debut in May 1945 at Studio Theater. Doris was listed as director of this program. She did not officially choreograph anything on it, but she contributed two numbers (*If I Had a Ribbon Bow* for Bird and *True Love* for Seckler) to a divertissement called *Three Ballads,* which also included José's *Charlie Rutlage* from his *Western Folk Suite.* According to John Martin, this made "an enchanting little suite of folksongs, given an ingenious formal unity and most unusual presentation. The dancers themselves speak the verses as they dance." Doris probably considered them throwaways, but they served the trio in its touring programs, and they later came in handy for Doris as casual concert pieces.

For one choreographer to direct another's performance was an unusual working setup in the choreographer-centered modern dance. Precedent was further shattered when José formed his permanent company two years later and named Doris artistic director. Until her death, she not only choreographed regularly for this company as she had for Humphrey-Weidman but also served as José's editor, advisor, and sounding board.

As a choreographer José lacked discipline. His ideas invariably sprawled beyond the bounds of sensible form and theatrical conciseness. His humanistic sights were even loftier than Doris', verging at times on the histrionic. He was less interested than she in experimenting with movement or finding new ways to stage things. He had neither Charles' gift for whimsy nor Doris' ironic wit. Perhaps without Doris' tutelage he would have attained more compositional range on his own, but in the 1960s, when he was forced to go on without her, he had to confront crises of a kind that artists normally struggle with when they are younger and less established. The same, in fact, might be said of Charles after Doris allied herself with José.

The transition from Humphrey-Weidman to Limón Company took time to accomplish. While José was sweating out the army and Doris was trying to keep a grip on the Ballet Plays, Betts Dooley, her friend and literary collaborator, came up with some lines of the Spanish poet-playwright Federico García Lorca about a bullfighter's death. She thought it would make a vehicle for José, and gave the poem to Pauline; it may have originally been dedicated to the Spanish dancer La Argentinita, with whom Lorca was associated. Beginning in March 1944, they all turned the idea over in their minds. Doris probably visualized it as a Ballet Play, with its possibilities for dancing, acting, and speaking. At one point José thought he might do it alone, prompting Doris to ask Pauline guardedly whether he planned to undertake a solo "with no girls and no direction." But, she added, "any way he wants it, if he has a real conviction, will be all right with me." She suggested an actress from *Sing Out, Sweet Land,* Ellen Love, to speak the lines, and later urged José to try to get an introduction to the composer Heitor Villa-Lobos, who was giving concerts in New York. (Norman Lloyd was the eventual composer.) At last, early in 1946, José received a commission to do a presentation at Bennington during the summer, and *Lament for Ignacio Sánchez Mejías,* choreographed by Doris, became the centerpiece of the José Limón Company's debut. It was an auspicious moment not only for José but for Doris, because it proved that she could still choreograph magnificently despite her inability to demonstrate what she wanted.

The final script for *Lament* was a compilation of several translations of the poem, condensed from its original length into a few pages of striking death images and impassioned tributes to the fallen bullfighter Ignacio. Doris said the keynote to the dance was found in the concluding lines. "For you are

Lament for Ignacio Sánchez Mejías. Letitia and José. (Dance Collection, NYPL)

dead forever, like all the dead of the whole earth who are forgotten." She was thinking not only of Lorca's hero but of those who had died in the recently concluded world war. Two women, a Guardian of Destiny (Letitia Ide) and a Witness and Mourner (Ellen Love), spoke the words, and José danced the hero whose "drama . . . is intended to signify the struggle of all men of courage who contend in the ring of life and who meet a tragic end."

The dance is a discontinuous series of descriptive solos—the bullfighter's courage, his death agony after his fatal encounter in the ring, and his memory apotheosed by the Mourner. The action, apart from Ignacio's intense solos, is spare and suggestive, the women moving just enough to keep the dance flowing and make the poetry seem an integral rather than a separate element. Doris wanted the three figures bound by a red thread, symbolic of blood and bloodletting, which she thought was a central idea in Spanish poetry. This potent prop implemented some of the dance's richest imagery. As the dance developed, several scenic possibilities were considered. José pictured a "solid and palpable" bullring that would be almost like a prison and would merge into a painted backdrop. Doris thought curtains could be drawn across various parts of the space, to conceal Ignacio's coffin and the platform where his spirit would appear. Finally, the decor was simplified to a few boxes, and Michael Czaja's lighting did the rest.

Compared with some of Doris' danciest early works, *Lament* had a formal, almost static quality. The women stood nearly immobile when they spoke Lorca's eloquent, visceral images, "Death laid its eggs in his wound." "Now the moss and the grass / Open with sure fingers / the flower of his skull." and Letitia intoned the refrain "At five in the afternoon." like a funeral bell. But there were also strange, evocative movement sequences. Letitia stalked José, holding the rope high with one hand and wrapping the other arm in it with a series of vicious thrusts like the striking of a snake. Rattling the rope over her head and bending back in a cold fury, she resembled the demonic Matriarch in *With My Red Fires*. Then she chased him slowly around the arena, thrashing the rope and finally whipping it around his waist; and after he fell backwards with his back arched off the floor, she stabbed one end of the rope to his chest. José did a long solo to uneven rhythms, agonizingly beating one foot behind him and dragging himself sideways on the other. Decelerating and collapsing at last, he crawled up the steps to where the Guardian waited to cradle him on her lap and simultaneously lower him into his coffin. The Mourner then spoke her eulogizing lines, and he reappeared to revolve slowly with his arms raised in triumph.

As proof of Doris' continuing viability as a choreographer, *Lament* was a pivotal work. It was also the last and perhaps the most completely realized of the dance-and-spoken-words pieces that she had been experimenting with since *American Holiday* in 1938. Had she been able to discharge her talents fully outside of modern dance, she might have contributed much to the search for the perfect amalgam of dance, words, and music that has beguiled idealists of the American musical theater. But *Lament* did more than put an end to one phase of Doris' work. It opened up a more dramatic possibility for her, one that she took great advantage of in later years. And it provided José with the first of many heroic roles, choreographed by both Doris and himself, where he focused his particular qualities as dancer and star into a series of noble character portraits, and some ignoble ones too. Margaret Lloyd summed up the dance's poetic effect: "The impressions of visual and aural beauty reach farther than eye can see or ear can hear, opening secret vistas on the universal mysteries. It is a dance of transfixing splendor."

In comic contrast Doris made *The Story of Mankind*. This duet for José and Bea Seckler was based on Carl Rose's *New Yorker* cartoons about a couple's ascent from living in a cave to the sophistication of an urban apartment. At this point a newspaper headline announces the splitting of the atom, and the couple are blasted back to the Stone Age, or a bomb shelter. Doris used the device of a Dance of the Ages, a standby scenario similar to one Ted Shawn had filmed as early as 1913, to weave together a quick history of dance styles and behavior. Michael Czaja provided a mobile, boxlike construction which was upended and pushed around in different ways to represent the successive domiciles of the couple.

José had trouble with the dance. "Comedy is something he endures," Doris remarked. But "this particular piece has a bitter message, which sweetens it for him." To José, she thought, comedy "is something for relaxation . . . and a man's work must be a powerful expression of his immortal soul. We just happen to differ on a little point like that." The dance was a crowd-pleaser, and José eventually grew easier with the role. Both *Lament* and *The Story of Mankind* were choreographed and premiered at Bennington, and later given with José's *Vivaldi Concerto* [*Grosso*] at the Belasco Theater (January 1947), for the Limón Company's New York debut. These two successes and the culminating achievement of launching a company for José put an end to Doris' long crisis of transition. "Accomplishing these two works has given me a happier feeling than I've had in a long time," she told Hay. "Not composing was very hard on me."

The Story of Mankind. José and Pauline Koner. Photo by Dwight Godwin. (Dance Collection, NYPL)

Without the regular working apparatus of a company, she had also been tempted once again to move into more conventional social surroundings. She and Leo grew more anxious about whether Humphrey had the right kind of friends and influences as the boy entered adolescence. Early in 1946 she had been seriously house hunting on Long Island, with a vague notion of using the place only in the summers and on weekends should she continue to work in the city. After many trips to look at property, buying a house proved financially out of the question: neither she nor Leo had any savings, and their ability to carry a mortgage was minimal. Years later she admitted that, though she knew how much Humphrey loved the country, "Mothers have to be people too. I couldn't give up my life for my son." She did rent a house at Fire Island after the Bennington period was over in 1946, a holiday that turned into an extravagance when Leo was stranded for several weeks by a postwar shipping strike.

The summer was costly to her health too. Keeping house on Fire Island did her no good, and she complained about her hip and her back. Eleanor Frampton, learning how hard up she was, sent her $100 in the fall to see a new doctor. She went once, reporting dutifully to Framp, but it was the same old story now: the arthritis would not get any better. Some treatments might help but little was really known about this disease, and it would be expensive even to try what the doctor advised. As always, she diverted her miseries into work, and by the beginning of 1947 her work was cut out for her. There was never any more talk about moving to the country or giving up making dances.

11 THE EAGLE, 1947–51

Day on Earth, which Doris began early in 1947, appears to have had few if any literary precedents. It sprang out of the music as if in a flood of gratitude. She had solved her two most desperate problems—how and where to choreograph. In modern dance there was not yet a demand for the itinerant choreographer as there is today. The artist who wished to make dances had to have her or his own company, and not only for economic reasons. By the 1940s it had become mandatory for modern dancers to have a "style"; the selfless, nunlike allegiances of the early days had evolved into conscious choices. Young dancers didn't expect to be discovering the secrets of the universe, but after shopping around among teachers, they would find a technique that "felt right" to them. Ruth Currier showed up at the studio one day to take a technique class with José and, she says, "It was like going home. It was like: this is where I belong." She remained a member of the company from 1949 until the 1960s. Betty Jones, another mainstay, "felt comfortable" in José's classes, and when she was asked to join the company after dancing in *Oklahoma!* and other shows, "I felt I had found the right home. And I've never, ever thought otherwise."

Modern dance techniques and aesthetics were still highly individual, and this was the source of whatever popular recognition the medium attained. In this period before eclectic, ballet-based training reduced most modern dancing to stylelessness, great dancing personalities could be accepted as interpreters of particular points of view. During the 1950s José was probably the greatest of these, but he was by no means the only one: Pearl Lang, Daniel Nagrin, Bella Lewitzky, and Sybil Shearer were some others. Perhaps none of them could have mastered the niceties of technique and placement that today's dancers achieve, but their goals were entirely different. Modern dance was going through a transition from personal witness to objective professionalism. The problem for both interpreters and creators was to retain what was strongest and most individual in their dance philosophies, yet present something with enough scope to reach beyond a small loyalist audience.

Day on Earth. José. Photo by Carmen Schiavone. (Dance Collection, NYPL)

One of the most traumatic aspects of Doris' disability was that, denied her own expressive presence in bringing her ideas to the audience, she could not even invent her own movement physically as all modern dancers up to that time expected to do. She was fortunate in that she had never been vain or possessive about her performing and her working process was very organized, so that she was used to devising imagery, movements, and spatial and rhythmic patterns in her mind before coming to rehearsal. But it probably took the experiment with Pauline Koner, an experienced dancer totally untutored in her technique and aesthetic, to satisfy her that she still had the ability to get her ideas onto the stage. She did it by trusting the dancers to translate her verbal and gestural cues into action. If she didn't like what they showed her, she would make adjustments, and sometimes she had the dancers go off in corners to work on their own ideas, which she would then shape again and integrate into the whole.

Aaron Copland's 1941 Piano Sonata was a complex piece, quite unlike the romantic and deliberately folksy Americana of his better-known ballets *Billy the Kid* (1938, Eugene Loring), *Appalachian Spring* (1941, Graham), or *Rodeo* (1942, de Mille). To Copland's rhythmic dissonances Doris set a simple, almost abstract character study of a man who works, two women he loves, and his child. Without even the minimally specific regional coloration of the *Lament*, *Day on Earth* seems free of all pettiness or ego and somehow pertinent to the experience of every viewer. John Martin said it was "almost as if she had looked from some other planet and seen things telescoped into a simple, arduous pattern of dignity and beauty." The whole dance seems less a celebration than a resigned acceptance of whatever is inevitable: work, love, pain, and rebirth. After seeing a performance Eleanor King wrote Doris that it was "the most perfect work of dance I ever experienced."

The movement, beautifully developed from simple sources, gives each character a distinct expressive quality—the young girl (Miriam Pandor) is airborne, elusive; the man (José) deliberate, steady, tied to his work and also solaced by it; the woman (Letitia Ide) dependable and strong as he is, but more yielding; and the child (Melisa Nicolaides) awkward, inquisitive, formed by her parents but engrossed in her own private world of games and wonder. It's interesting to note how many of Doris' dances centered on family relationships and how well she met the challenge of giving characters of different generations appropriate dance movement, not simply mime or gestures.

Breath rhythm was especially effective in *Day on Earth*, both in establishing the bonds between characters and in underscoring the rupture of those bonds. A Humphrey duet, of which there are many in *Day on Earth,* has a distinctive look not found in most other choreography. The dancers seldom do strict unison movement, but their counterpoint shows them to be in the closest accord, because rather than answer an outside imperative like a musical cue, they dance on the inner impulse that they create together. The breath rhythm also infuses the body shape with emotional tone, so that the dancers don't have to act out what the characters feel. Near the end of the dance, after the child leaves, the parents storm across the space, their bodies wrenching open lopsidedly, spreading taut, then collapsing or retreating spasmodically, all on uneven, sobbing rhythms. The dynamic sequence of the whole dance is shaped by the fluctuating rhythms Doris drew from Copland's music and transferred into the life cycle of her characters.

Another key element in *Day on Earth* is a large cloth that serves different purposes, practical and metaphoric. When the dance opens, the man begins making a kind of furrow, diagonally across the space, with movements suggestive of farming or other physical labor. The woman sits on an upstage box with the cloth spread over her lap and onto the floor. After his early, passing relationship with the young girl, the woman rises to join him, carelessly dropping the cloth like a cast-off apron. They reach accord quickly, and together they turn upstage and draw the cloth up like a blanket. Under it lies the child, whom they coax and cradle to life. Later, after the child leaves, the mother takes the cloth and folds it against her body, the simple domestic action becoming extraordinarily tender and intimate in the context of a parent's sorrow. She puts the folded cloth on the bench and slowly lowers herself onto it, like a very tired, very old person. The man has one more paroxysm of grief at her loss, then all four characters join in a procession and a ritual transfer of generations: the three adults lie down on the floor, spreading the cloth over themselves and leaving the child seated on the box. This affecting image is a remarkable demonstration of how far Doris had evolved from her windblown, decorative scarf dances of the 1920s.

Day on Earth previewed in the spring of 1947 at the Beaver Country Day School near Boston. Then José began a summer teaching residency at the Duncanbury School in Boston, assisted by Miriam Pandor, with Pauline to accompany his classes. Doris, looking for an inexpensive way to get to the country, accepted a job at Green Mansions, a resort in the Catskills. She was to direct a dance group assembled for the summer to put on weekly shows—a popular revue and a dance concert—for the hotel patrons. "Leave it to Doris Humphrey to bring concert dance to the Borscht Belt," Joe Gifford congratulated her in August. And indeed, for once she had things as she liked them. In addition to Dorothy Bird and Bea Seckler, the young dancers included Herbert Ross, Mark Ryder, Emily Frankel, and several others. She didn't make anything new but revived *Shakers, Square Dances* (retitled *Party Dances*), her old Tcherepnine *March,* and the *American Ballads* she had done for José's trio in 1944. There were also pieces by Anna Sokolow and members of the company. She packaged this lightweight but skillful repertory into three programs that rotated through the eleven-week season.

Leo took a dim view of the venture though he visited Doris and Humphrey there in August. He had sour memories of the rich, rude patrons on his cruise ships before the war. But Doris thoroughly enjoyed herself. She had no housekeeping to take care of, and no rival dance personages were on the scene. "I liked it much better than trying to have a vacation," she told Hay. Both Martin and Terry came up to attend the final performance, and both praised her success at insinuating some art dance into the entertainment fare of the unsuspecting vacationers. After this positive experience, she was receptive to a revival of the Bennington idea, then in the discussion stage.

Since the demise of the Bennington School of Dance, the indefatigable Martha Hill had been searching for another place to hold a summer program. Connecticut College in New London, a convenient two-and-a-half hour train ride from New York, had many advantages: an attractive country campus, a fully equipped theater, and most important, a sympathetic president. Rosemary Park, a remarkable and far-sighted intellectual, undertook what was then a very unusual mission for a women's liberal arts college. Though modern dance was still a developing art form, President Park argued in her annual report for 1949,

> The ability and discipline of performers would soon convince an open-minded observer that here is an art worthy to stand with any of the other great expressive media, but because it is never destined to have the repeatability of the other arts, it is more like a phenomenon of nature, less absolutely controllable, more dependent on memory than record, and so perhaps never to be studied or classified in the satisfying manner of the other arts. But today it has a vitality and evokes from a student generation greater response than do other art forms.

The college at that time had no separate dance department—an undergraduate major and a program leading to the Master of Fine Arts degree were finally established in 1973—but it was looking to convert a summer school that had been engaged in accelerated wartime and postwar training, to more pertinent uses. Through Ruth Bloomer and Ruth Thomas of the college's Physical Education faculty, arrangements were made with the New York University School of Education to offer academic credit, and the Connecticut College School of Dance, co-sponsored with New York University, was opened in 1948 under Martha Hill's direction. Although the session was, like Bennington, principally a school, during the last weeks of each summer resident and guest companies presented performances at Palmer Auditorium under the title of the American Dance Festival. After three years, Connecticut College took over full sponsorship of both the school and the festival.

The plan worked out differently from Bennington, and distinctly in Doris' and José's favor. The first year, the Graham and Limón companies were both in residence, as well as the trio William Bales had formed with Sophie Maslow and Jane Dudley. This made for a spectacular Festival debut, but in subsequent years it was the Limón company that remained a permanent fixture. Graham technique was always taught, and Graham's company often appeared at the Festival, as did nearly every major modern dance group over the next thirty years. But it was José and Doris who dominated the Connecticut College summers until the entire structure of the project began changing, late in the 1960s. They taught in the school and, with the company in residence for the entire six-week session, were able to choreograph new works regularly. The Festival also afforded premiere opportunities, and sometimes separate concerts, for Limón company members Ruth Currier and Lucas Hoving and guest artist Pauline Koner.

From the beginning Doris was treated with great respect and deference at Connecticut College. In this community at least, she was seen as a founder and lawgiver, and a source of continuing energy. She taught her now-customary courses, advanced composition and repertory, staging student revivals over the years of *Passacaglia*, (in 1951), *Song of the West* (1952 and 1956), *With My Red Fires* (1953), *Soaring* and *Water Study* (1954), and *Shakers* (1955). Many of these were the subject of notation and filming projects, which helped to preserve a much greater proportion of her creative output than any other individual's choreography of her time. She gave her classes in a ballroom on the ground floor of one of the dormitories; Louis Horst's preclassic and modern forms classes were given down the hall in the dining room. Ruth Lloyd later recalled there was "no way to describe the pleasure of playing for Doris' composition classes at Connecticut. They were mostly why

I went . . . She taught her students to be supremely aware of life as it's going on. A dancer should never be bored."

The school ran along the same lines as Bennington, with basic technique and composition classes, augmented by the specialized techniques of different guest teachers each year. The curriculum also included courses in dance education, notation, music, and stagecraft. Each week at eagerly attended workshops, the composition teachers would present student pieces to demonstrate what problems they had been working on. An early publication described the "close collaboration of artist, educator, administrator, and student in an active working relationship for study and new production of student and professional work. . . . The student works for six weeks as apprentice to a group of artists and teachers responsible for the main developments in contemporary dance." While professionalism was increasing in modern dance, the school continued to serve a large constituency of teachers from college dance departments around the country, who would be training the next generation of dancers. By the time the Festival moved to Duke University in 1978, the emphasis had shifted to professional performance and direct preparation for performing. At Connecticut, the division between company members and students was still somewhat flexible, and the presence of José and the company, always at work on a new piece during part of each teaching day, stimulated great excitement all over the campus. Everyone seemed to share in an experience of intense learning and creativity. As Doris told Hay in 1952, "People ask me if I enjoyed it. . . . It's like being slightly delirious."

At the first American Dance Festival, which also saw the world premiere of Graham's *Diversion of Angels* (under its original title *Wilderness Stair*), José and the company gave three programs consisting mostly of Doris' works. *Day on Earth, Lament, Story of Mankind* and José's *Vivaldi Concerto Grosso* comprised one bill. Doris' and Koner's *Voice in the Wilderness* and two of José's works to Bach, *Chaconne* and *Sonata no. 4* for organ, were on the second bill, along with *Day on Earth* and the premiere of Doris' *Corybantic*. A third program included repeats of the *Sonata, Lament, Day on Earth,* and *Corybantic*. It was the first time the Limón company offered such a substantial showing of its work in a nationally prominent setting. The strong choreography, the dancing, and José's commanding stage presence immediately established the group in the forefront of modern dance.

Doris had been slightly apprehensive about the public's reception to *Day on Earth*, remarking that with "no murder, suspicion, neurosis or bitterness or guilt," it would be bucking the current anguished trend in modern dance.

Corybantic, which did have a gloomy outlook, fared much less well. Still fascinated with ancient Greece, Doris had been working on a dance about the Oedipus story, a contemporary treatment with a script by Lynn Riggs, when Martha Graham's *Night Journey* premiered in New York (May 1947). With that dance, a psychological study of Oedipus and Jocasta, Graham took possession of Greek heroic legend as source material for dance-drama, and Doris dropped her project. Instead, she reverted to the more primal and ritualistic possibilities in ancient Greek dancing. *Corybantic* got its title from the

Corybantic. José with Ruth Currier and (on floor) Betty Jones. (Dance Collection, NYPL)

word *Korybant,* "a celebrant of a rite given to wild and destructive dancing."
As usual, Doris visualized the dancers as archetypes, who could have either
contemporary or universal meaning. Doris meant the dance to offer a hope-
ful resolution to a strife-torn world, but most viewers saw only its darker side.
Doris Hering, writing in *Dance Magazine,* thought, "Doris Humphrey has
forsaken the mellow and the heroic and has set José Limón and the company to grappling with the fierce, the jubilant, the violent, and the harsh—
spearheads of Here and Now. . . . a choreographic gesture of defiance."

As Doris sketched the work, it was to have five dancers: The Defender
(José), The Antagonist (Miriam Pandor), The Innocent (Betty Jones), The Fa-
talist (Pauline Koner), and The Compassionate (Letitia Ide). The three sections
of the music, Bartók's Sonata for Two Pianos and Percussion, were devoted
to Agon, or conflict; Pathos, a ritual of survival and communion; and Satyric,
a celebration of the group's ability to withstand strife. Superficially, the dance
dealt with her old refrain about the benevolent power of group action. But,
as she revealed in some notes for a radio interview, she had her doubts
now. The initial group is ridden with difference. Two of its members "agree
on destructive action," and the others can't get together on how to combat
the crisis. "Hysteria of panic engulfs all." Finally, exhausted and "apparently
lifeless," they slowly come to their senses. "They learned through suffering to
be wiser, more tolerant." But even their celebration of restored unity gets out
of hand. "Innocence brings tidings of peace, no more to fear from unknown
enemy. Joy of celebration excessive. . . . Defender guesses that peace not so
simple." Betty Jones felt the dance was not completely accepted because it
was ahead of its time, and one of the few works Doris made that "didn't
have a positive resolution. So little sense of progress—the lesson wasn't
learned, after all that death and destruction." Doris' son now considers *Corybantic* "the ultimate in fatalism." He feels it had to do with atomic destruction and also reflected a pessimism about her declining health that influenced many of her later works.

Walter Terry was unreservedly impressed with the piece; he said it "captures the troubled, even terrified, spirit of modern man seeking progress,
peace, and honor." But the *Dance Observer's* Nik Krevitsky thought initially it
was unclear and perhaps unfinished. After Doris made revisions for the New
York premiere, Krevitsky reviewed it again and still felt it was muddled. He
also suggested that the group was too small to express all the ideas Doris
intended.

The company was now taking a clearer shape, and along with it José's choreography gained focus. Beginning with his two major works of 1949, *La Malinche* and *The Moor's Pavane*, he concentrated his passion, his sense of dramatic conflict, and his ability to convey character through abstract movement into a series of small but highly charged dance-dramas. Koner had become a more or less permanent guest artist with the company, and in Lucas Hoving José found a strong, contrasting male dancer to offset his own presence. Hoving, a native of Holland, had danced with the Jooss Ballet, been stranded in North America during the war, served in the Dutch Exile Army, and in 1949 was doing shows and nightclub dancing in New York when José asked if he would like to work on a new piece. *La Malinche* became the first in a long succession of parables based on historical and literary sources, in which the three dancers duelled and teamed up in different relationships, often supplemented by other characters.

La Malinche as a subject had been on José's mind for years. As early as 1942, Pauline had suggested Bea Seckler for the part of the Mexican peasant girl who was first seduced by the hated Cortez and who then repented and betrayed him by leading her people in the revolution against the Spanish conquistadors. In 1944 José applied, unsuccessfully, for a Guggenheim Fellowship, planning *La Malinche* as a duet, the first part of a trilogy on themes from Mexican history. In 1949 the piece—now a trio—premiered during the same season at the Ziegfeld Theater that saw the New York debut of *Corybantic*. José set the dance as a folk play, perhaps remembering Graham's 1941 *El Penitente*, and it was very successful, with Koner as the heroine, Hoving as the haughty Conquistador, and himself as El Indio, the oppressed peasant.

The same triumvirate, with the addition of Betty Jones, consolidated José's position at the 1949 American Dance Festival with *The Moor's Pavane*. Doris found the music that set the tone so brilliantly for what was to be José's most acclaimed dance, his meditation on *Othello*. Modern music wouldn't do, she thought, and she scoured the music stores, sampling records, until she discovered Henry Purcell's The Gordian Knot Untied. This suite for a forgotten Restoration comedy, together with excerpts from the same composer's The Moor's Revenge, was made of formal dances in the English style. The dance José constructed was also formal, suggesting the rituals of a royal court, but the characters kept lapsing from stately protocol into the seething jealousies and terrors of Shakespeare's famous tragedy. Doris was responsible for the ending too. When José showed her the finished dance, she came up with the idea of having the two conspirators, Iago and Emilia, conceal the Moor's murder of Desdemona by stepping between them and the audience, and spreading out Koner's opulent orange velvet skirt like a curtain across the scene.

With the end of the war, the revival of summer sessions at Connecticut College, and the clear emergence of new companies under a mature second generation, modern dance entered a new phase of its history. Margaret Lloyd was assembling her recollections and observations into a landmark document, the *Borzoi Book of Modern Dance* (1949), in which Doris and Charles were to have a preeminent place. Lloyd sent Doris a draft chapter in 1947 for her additions and corrections, telling her: "Yours is the longest chapter, the peak chapter. Everything must fall away from that." Walter Sorell was compiling an anthology, *The Dance Has Many Faces,* and at his request Doris contributed the entry on Dance-Drama. In the fall of 1948, Doris applied for a Guggenheim Fellowship to work on her own book. She received the award, a grant of $2,500, but didn't actually complete this lifetime project until ten years later, when illness stopped her from doing anything else.

This could have been the moment for modern dance to make its breakthrough to popular recognition, and the millennium seemed to have arrived in 1949, when the New York City Dance Theater was organized to present a two-week season at City Center in the end of December. According to John Martin, the idea was "to create a pool of dancers for those choreographers who do not have companies of their own." In effect, however, the Dance Theater was modern dance's perennial answer to its crisis of individualism: a season of repertory by three companies and several soloists, all doing their own thing. The managing directors were Richard Pleasant, a publicist who had been involved in the establishment of the Ballet Theatre, and his partner, Isadora Bennett. The usual parental figures served on the advisory board: Martha Hill, Louis Horst, Norman Lloyd, and lighting designer Jean Rosenthal. According to Graham biographer Don McDonagh, Bethsabee de Rothschild quietly underwrote the expenses. The companies were Dudley-Maslow-Bales, Weidman, and Limón; and soloists included Valerie Bettis, Bea Seckler, Katherine Litz, Merce Cunningham, and others, but Graham disdained to take part. Doris and José had no new works for the season (*The Moor's Pavane* had its New York debut in November, opening the 92nd Street Y Dance Series), but their repertory was very strong, with *Lament, Day on Earth, La Malinche,* and the *Pavane,* Doris' 1949 lyric trio *Invention, The Story of Mankind,* and a revival of *Shakers,* rescored for a vocal chorus, not a happy experiment.

Doris was generally pleased with the season: "for José and me it was a

success." There were rumors that City Center director Morton Baum was
pleased with the project too and wanted to continue it as a regular part of
the City Center's programming. "This is greatly to be desired," Doris wrote
Hay, "as the modern dance desperately needs a home and support. At the
City Center we have been offered these things for the first time in New York.
José couldn't get over being handed a salary instead of a crushing bundle of
bills." John Martin thought that the season had given a good account of itself despite the handicaps of being put together somewhat late and having
to play during the Christmas season. The biggest drawback, though, and
one the modern dancers never solved, was that to present real repertory, the
project needed "a single unified company of dancers with a number of
gifted choreographers to compose for them and a strong directorial hand to
guide its policy artistically." Martin reported, however, that Morton Baum
was making plans to continue the project the next year. But there it ended.

Invention. Ruth, Betty, and José. Photo by John Lindquist. Courtesy of Stephan Driscoll. (Dance
Collection, NYPL)

The balance of power in the dance world was shifting radically. Forces stronger than the modern dancers' coalition were in motion, forestalling its bid to install itself inside the structure of the City Center organization, where it would have been assured long-term public visibility. The City of New York had taken over the Mecca Temple on 55th Street for nonpayment of taxes from the fraternal order which built the auditorium. In 1943 the City Center of Music and Drama was incorporated so that the building could be used for performances of good quality at prices low enough for middle-class citizens to afford. After many difficult years, Lincoln Kirstein and George Balanchine had formed the Ballet Society to present Balanchine's work, and Morton Baum was so impressed with its offerings that in 1948 he invited it to become a constituent of the City Center and change its name to the New York City Ballet. Late in 1949 the new company was just beginning its long struggle to develop an audience and the financial backing to produce on a large scale. Probably at no time in its grueling history was the Balanchine / Kirstein enterprise more embattled, or more keyed up for a fight.

Ballet was its major enemy. The fall 1949 season in New York had seen "a stupendous diet of ballet," according to Walter Terry, with the Sadler's Wells from Britain in its American debut, the Ballet de Paris, and the Ballet Russe de Monte Carlo all giving seasons. Ballet Theatre was in its heyday. Balanchine was the outsider in this avalanche of spectacle and stars, considered too cerebral and eccentric for the popular taste. His main rival was Léonide Massine, who made exceedingly popular descriptive and character ballets. The powerful John Martin had not yet developed an appreciation for Balanchine's rarefied musicality, his spare and athletic approach to dancing. When the Ballet Society was adopted by City Center, Martin had reservations: the company would not be "inherently a strong box office attraction," the ensemble was young and inexperienced and in need of stronger male dancers, and the repertory contained "too many of Balanchine's musical abstractions." Nevertheless, the critic endorsed the experiment—and suggested a showcase season for modern dance as well.

Martin's failure to comprehend Balanchine, as well as his preference for modern dance, infuriated Kirstein. He had written, reviewing Martin's book *America Dancing:*

As for the contemporary American figures Mr. Martin so signally honors . . . what can one say in dispraise that will not sound like ill-tempered carping? After his . . . enthusiastic encouragement, his brave hopes for an indigenous and healthy art . . . only the answer of audiences can be a satisfactory answer . . . a few thousand people in New York City who religiously crowd a moderate-sized theater even ten times a winter is [not] mass support. . . . It merely is testimony to the persuasiveness of a single dominant voice in a newspaper which has a large metropolitan circulation.

Kirstein truly detested modern dance and took every opportunity in his prolific writings to "dispraise" it in the most caustic terms. To him, it violated the basic principles of dancing by being too literal, by opposing the ballet as a matter of principle, and by placing individual expression above the time-proven verities of the academy. He grudgingly accepted Graham as an original artist of great theatrical presence, but all other modern dancers were dangerous and presumptuous upstarts. The slightest notion that modern dancers might be installed as the New York City Ballet's equal at City Center must have been anathema to him on aesthetic grounds alone, besides the threat it would pose to his new mission of capturing a popular audience for ballet.

The New York City Ballet followed up its fall season with four weeks in February–March 1950, and this proved its turning point with both the public and John Martin. Several dancers moved over from Ballet Theatre that year, to add the spice Martin thought the ensemble lacked, and a strong young choreographic voice was added when Jerome Robbins was appointed associate artistic director. Robbins danced in a revival of Balanchine's *The Prodigal Son* and choreographed *Age of Anxiety* by Leonard Bernstein, which, together with Frederick Ashton's *Illuminations* and some lesser novelties, appealed to the critic's taste for dramatic dance. Martin covered the season breathlessly, and at its conclusion he gave the company his full endorsement, making no further report on rumors that the City Dance Theater would be following the ballet for a return engagement.

The tide had turned away from modern dance. New York City Ballet's fall 1950 season was received even more enthusiastically by Martin and his colleagues. "The ballet," he wrote, taking in the whole revitalized field, "has suddenly become an irresistibly ingratiating art." City Center announced another post-ballet season for the City Dance Theater, but Bennett and Pleasant insisted on putting it off until spring. They were miffed at being put into the box-office-poison week before Christmas again, and they wanted "the go-ahead on the larger new things or the important revivals" that were needed for a second season. These included *Passacaglia,* which Doris was

rehearsing with a repertory class, and *With My Red Fires,* for which Nora
Kaye had been cast as the Matriarch. Two weeks were blocked into the
schedule in April, but Baum was unwilling to commit funds to bring the repertory about. Isadora Bennett wrote to Baum in February complaining that
the City Center board was hanging back on the modern dance commitment,
while finding "huge" budgets for the City Ballet. In fact, by this time the
Board was producing not only City Ballet's seasons, but its new ballets as
well. Bennett was afraid that if the spring season were allowed to founder, it
would finish the modern dance project for good, and it did. So while Graham and Balanchine, through shrewd management and powerful connections, were able to gain footholds at this crucial juncture, the independent
modern dancers could not mobilize enough political or financial clout to play
in the big leagues. Graham, with her own school, housed in a building on
East 63rd Street purchased for her by Bethsabee de Rothschild, and Balanchine, with the company and a performance base at City Center, would be
able to function from day to day in spite of ongoing financial problems. For
the other dancers the struggle would not let up, and the gains would be
much more temporal.

But José's star was rising, and in 1950 he had his first international successes.
Chicago-based Ruth Page, another American dance maverick, invited José to
share a season with her during the month of May at the Théâtre des
Champs-Elysées in Paris. Billed as the Ballets Américains, the company included José, Lucas, Betty Jones, and Pauline Koner, with conductor Simon
Sadoff and a pickup group led by Page and Bentley Stone. The Limóns performed *The Moor's Pavane* and *La Malinche** and also took roles in the Page
repertory.
    Beginning with the opening night, the season was a scandal and a disas-
ter, although José's works were treated with some respect. Page's *"mauvais
goût"* and her flamboyant temperament incited scathing reviews from the ar-
biters of French culture, and the dance community was especially hostile.
There were old grudges to settle. When the Paris Opera Ballet had played
City Center in 1948, antifascist pickets had demonstrated against its director,
Serge Lifar, who had been accused of being a Nazi sympathizer during the

---

*Negotiations had been undertaken for Doris' *Story of Mankind* and it was included in a souvenir program book of the season, but it may not have been given. Neither Ruth Page in her collected "scribblings" nor her biographer, John Martin, mentions it in accounts of the season.

war. Other French dancers and choreographers had not been accorded especially good reviews on their visits to New York either. On the Ballets Américains' Paris opening night, rude demonstrations—probably organized—broke out during the first piece and continued throughout the evening. The next day Lucas Hoving ran into a French dancer friend in a café and was told, "We will make it impossible for any American ballet troupe to appear in Paris." Ruth Page thrived on controversy, and throughout the three-week engagement accusations and denials flew back and forth in the press. *Dance News* called the affair "probably the biggest scandal in ballet history" since the premiere of Nijinsky's *Le Sacre du Printemps* at the same theater in 1913.

Walter Terry noted that the French press liked Limón but didn't pay him as much attention as the melodramatic Page. He thought Page invited the bad criticism by calling her dances ballets, thus violating the sacred terrain of European classicism, while José's work was more tolerable because it "represents a way of dance indigenous to America." José's was the first appearance in Europe by a major American modern dance company, and Doris had been prepared for any reception. "They'll either think he's a crude Indian, or they'll throw roses in his path." José tried to take it philosophically, "It has been a dismal and valuable lesson to us—even if our things have gone well." He hoped he could go back again independently and present Doris' work as well as his own. When a group from the Comédie Française came backstage to congratulate him, he wrote Doris, "I was moved by all this great praise—and I want to pass it on to you because it belongs so largely to you and what you have given us all these years, and because you have done more than anyone else, I think, to give the dance great stature and power."

At Connecticut College that summer, in addition to preparing his new Adam and Eve piece, *The Exiles,* and another premiere, *Concert,* to Bach, José was getting ready for his debut in Mexico. This long-awaited return to his native country was arranged by the composer Carlos Chavez, head of the Instituto Nacional de Bellas Artes, and Miguel Covarrubias, head of its Academia de la Danza. Two weeks of performances at the Palacio de Bellas Artes in Mexico City were to begin on September 19. José and Pauline left by train at the end of August, right after the Festival in Connecticut, and Humphrey went with them until it was time for him to return for school. The Limóns had always been surrogate parents to Humphrey, and after they bought some property with a barn in New Jersey in 1948, he frequently spent weekends and holidays with them. Doris thought the trip to Mexico would be a good experience for him, and she paid his expenses. Although Doris' works were prominent in the repertory, José couldn't get the Mexicans to bring her down, so he did some extra teaching and paid for her trip himself. It was brief; she arrived about a week after they did and left right after the opening.

She went straight to Washington, D.C., apparently to bail Charles out of trouble again. He had been choreographing *The Barrier,* a music-drama by Jan Meyerowitz with a libretto by Langston Hughes. Initially done at Columbia University, the show was headed for Broadway as a production of Michael Myerberg and Joel Spector, with Lawrence Tibbett and Muriel Rahn as the stars. Charles had started out as sole choreographer when the show played Ann Arbor early in the summer, but by the time of the Washington tryout he and Doris were both listed. Doris, in fact, ultimately staged the show, and was credited as director by many reviewers although she did not take billing for it on the program. The show was difficult to place, with its downbeat theme of miscegenation and murder in the South and its operatic score, which some critics classed with Menotti and Blitzstein but considered too arty for the subject. Gershwin's jazzy treatment of Negro themes in *Porgy and Bess* was a better model, thought John Chapman of the *New York Daily News.* After some false starts out of town, *The Barrier* finally opened at the Broadhurst Theater on November 2, and ran only three performances. It got sixteen reviews—far more than any dance premiere—but none of the critics was enthusiastic, and according to Doris there wasn't enough money to keep the show running long enough to find an audience. José had disapproved of the adventure anyway, and she told him she'd write it off as a mistake.

The Mexican trip was a great success for José. Although other modern dancers had worked in Mexico before, "apparently it took Mr. Limón ... to lead Mexican audiences toward a genuine enthusiasm for modern dance," in the opinion of Walter Terry. The repertory included everything Doris and José had done for the company in the past five years. *Day on Earth, Invention,* and *The Moor's Pavane* were the most popular pieces, and the Lorca was done in Spanish by a Mexican actress. Doris was gratified by José's good reception. She reported to Hay: "You can't imagine what a stir José made ... he was treated like a national celebrity, and audiences responded the way we've always dreamed they might. With such appreciation you'd

Doris, Humphrey, and Leo at José's farm, around 1952. Collection of Charles H. Woodford.

Pauline Lawrence Limón and Doris in Mexico, about 1950. Collection of Charles H. Woodford.

wonder why he ever comes back, but strangely enough he doesn't feel as much at home there as he does here."

After this first residency, José was invited by the Mexican government to make the country his permanent headquarters, but he declined, preferring to visit for only part of each year. In January 1951 he returned for a long period of teaching and choreographing, which was to end in a spring season of works by himself and other choreographers. He was doing big works on Mexican themes, including *Los Cuatro Soles* (*The Four Suns*), to music of Chavez and decor by Covarrubias; *Tonzanintla,* a baroque piece in Mexican angel style according to Pauline; and *Dialogues,* a duet for himself and Lucas on the theme of two pairs of antagonists from Mexican history: Juarez and Maximilian and Cortez and Montezuma.

Koner and Betty were brought down along with conductor Simon Sadoff to do *The Moor's Pavane*—Lucas had been assisting José during the residency, as well as choreographing a piece for himself and Lupe Serrano, then a ballet teacher at the Academia. The Institute officials were generous this time; John Martin and Walter Terry were invited for the opening. So was Lincoln Kirstein, according to a rumor Doris heard. José wanted Doris to come too, but she hung back. Koner wired Pauline from New York that she "does not feel she could come just for social purposes but would make the effort if wanted." She complained that she didn't have the right clothes and had to save money for Humphrey's tuition at college the following fall. She needed to know she was needed. Finally her ticket was provided and she agreed to fly down for a week.

Doris had spent her whole career at the physical as well as the spiritual center of all her dance activities. Now her status was changing. All travel now was painful and difficult. She avoided it, and simultaneously grew more self-conscious about her public appearances. She would not give in to her handicap unless it was absolutely necessary. Betty Jones remembers her laboriously climbing stairs to the studio in New York. José would offer to carry her, but she always refused. She preferred to take herself out of action rather than appear weak or infirm. It was natural for her to stay in New York while the company toured; natural, after ten years of Pauline's managing José's career, for Doris to be less involved with advance planning and projects. But more and more, her absence from the scene led to forgetfulness, unintentional slights. Critics didn't always mention her name when they raved about the company's performances. Doris might have withdrawn from the stage by this time even if she hadn't been disabled—she was fifty-five. And, as she

well knew, in dance those who are young and in the public's eye receive
the most attention. All these circumstances were drawing the company
away from her, separating its identity from hers. It must have been increasingly difficult for her to see José's success as a fulfillment of her own ambitions.

Life was becoming more stable for her, and narrower in scope. In the spring
of 1951 another source of institutional support materialized when the Juilliard School of Music announced the opening of a Dance Division under the
leadership of Martha Hill. That fall Doris began giving composition and repertory classes there in addition to her teaching at the 92nd Street Y and Connecticut College. José and the company were teaching too, with every accommodation being made for their touring schedules, and the Juilliard
building on Claremont Avenue and 122nd Street (now occupied by the
Manhattan School of Music) became their winter working quarters. With a
core quintet of dancers—José, Lucas, Betty, Ruth, and Koner—the company
also included musical director Simon Sadoff; lighting designer-technical director Tom Skelton; business manager and costumer Pauline Lawrence; and
additional dancers as needed. Company rehearsals were usually held at the
Dance Players Studio on West 56th Street, but the Juilliard theater was the
scene of many Limón and Humphrey premieres in the next years.

While José was doing his spring 1951 residency in Mexico, Doris held the
fort in New York, getting dancers ready for the City Dance Theater season
that never materialized. There was a flurry of interest in dance films. The phenomenal success of *The Red Shoes* (1948) caused a reassessment of the possibilities for making an impact with serious dancing through a mass medium.
Filmmaker Walter Strate had done highly theatrical versions of the *Lament*
and *Moor's Pavane*, with voice-over narrations, and these opened at the
55th Street Playhouse in February on a bill with Strate's movie of Valerie Bettis' *The Desperate Heart* and an English film called *The Little Ballerina* with
Margot Fonteyn. Doris told José she didn't think the films would do him any
harm, but "I'll never like them until they give me the excitement and satisfaction the dances do."

She was not indifferent to history, though, and she permitted cinematic records to be made of her dances whenever the opportunity presented itself.
She also became the first modern dancer to participate in the writing of a
score in Labanotation. This took place during one of her repertory classes in
1948–49. The Dance Notation Bureau, the first American center for the writ-

ten recording of dance, had been in existence for eight years, working the snarls out of Rudolf Laban's system of dance script, and the time had come to test it. Doris' response was immediate and supportive. Ann Hutchinson and Els Grelinger started work on *The Shakers,* attending rehearsals and making the meticulous notes that would later be put into a standardized script. Hutchinson reported in the *Dance Observer* that Doris' way of teaching a dance was ideal for notators, beginning with a general blocking out of the floor plan and overall idea of the dance, and proceeding to rhythm, steps, body and arm movement, and finally the subtler details. At least eight subsequent scores were started in Doris' repertory classes and rehearsals, in addition to those which have been made from posthumous revivals.

In the summer of 1951 she completed one of her most evocative and introspective dances, *Night Spell.* Originally called *Quartet* after Priaulx Rainier's music (String Quartet no. 1), the dance was about a Dreamer (José) and the creatures of his fantasy (Lucas, Betty, and Ruth). A program note reads, "Things of the night, riding the wind, beset the sleeper. Before terror can entirely take him, he gropes toward waking, tries to reorder the menace of nightmare into remembered love and comfort." At another point, the piece carried this note, "The one asleep cries out: 'What is in me, dark—illumine.'" The dance is related in theme to Matthew Arnold's "Dover Beach," which Doris had encountered in 1943 by way of Samuel Barber. Hoping they might collaborate on a dance, Barber had played her some of his music, including the work he based on the Arnold poem. Doris was struck by the nineteenth-century English poet's imagery, which seemed to foretell the war that occupied her thoughts at that time. The dance with Barber never materialized, but *Night Spell* retained the mood of "Dover Beach," especially the last stanza:

Ah, love, let us be true
To one another! for the world, which seems
To lie before us like a land of dreams,
So various, so beautiful, so new,
Hath really neither joy, nor love, nor light,
Nor certitude, nor peace, nor help for pain;
And we are here as on a darkling plain
Swept with confused alarms of struggle and flight,
Where ignorant armies clash by night.

José danced the first movement as a solo, with movement suggestive of sleeping, falling, fear, floating, and flight, according to Doris' notes. A simple

Night Spell. Betty and Lucas. Photo by Walter Strate. (Dance Collection, NYPL)

boxlike bench, the only decor, was situated downstage left and served as his home-base. Doris found ingenious ways for him to perch, lean, and balance on it that were neither literal nor acrobatic but communicated the precarious emotional state of a dreamer. The three night creatures enter, wrapped in a large tie-dyed cloth. Prancing and gesturing together, they seem like a single menacing organism, but by dashing between them José separates Ruth from the other two, who retreat momentarily while they dance a duet. This dance begins antiphonally, as a series of exclamations and responses, and as it unfolds the two characters from different worlds gradually find a common rhythm. After they achieve unison, he sinks to the floor and she revolves around him with slow, surging steps. They sit on the bench spoon-fashion, rocking back and forth. The nightmare creatures return and, with increasingly forceful wrenching jumps and turns, try to recapture their former cohort. The struggle doesn't involve any bodily contact, but the spatial patterns are in-fused with prying-away and tearing-apart energies. Finally the Dreamer suc-ceeds in breaking the creatures' power. He banishes them, and the woman runs across the width of the stage to where he's standing on the bench. He pulls her up and they embrace tightly as the lights black out. Doris had two endings for the dance—in the alternate one, the woman slipped out of the embrace and "dissolved into a puddle at his feet," as Currier describes it. Eventually, either because this image didn't work or because of her basic op-timism, Doris chose the happy one.

Most people saw psychological implications in the dance, though Doris repeatedly denied that any were intended. One critic said it "suggested both the eeriness and the erotic striving of Schönberg's Verklärte Nacht," and Cur-rier thought it might have some relationship to Carl Jung's four parts of the psyche. In any case, audiences liked it from the first, and it continues to be an appealing piece in revivals. Its direct narrative line is very clear, and its ro-mantic idealism seems unimpeded by polemical demands. But the juxtaposi-tion of real and fantasy characters, and the climactic moments when the "real" character snatches the "fantasy" character out of her element, are puz-zling, especially for so rational a choreographer as Doris. John Martin initially found the dance inferior to her "top achievements." The expressionistic look of it—well suited to Rainier's music—seemed grotesque to him, and he of-fered suggestions on how Doris could tidy it up. Lucas Hoving recalled that he never liked his part, though he admired José's solo and the duet. He al-ways felt that he and Betty were "playing at being scary." Nevertheless, since Doris' dances so often were, at least in part, meditations on her personal situation, *Night Spell*'s ambiguity could be an indicator of her feelings at this time—feelings of loneliness, threat, and a longing for someone to screen her from loss.

Night Spell was premiered in New London at what was the American Dance Festival's most successful summer to date. Attendance had been poor the year before, so the number of performances was cut back from eight to five. The big event was a gala Mexican night on which José showed two of the pieces he'd made during the spring residency. He had arranged for four Mexican dancers to have scholarships at the School of Dance, and they appeared with him in *Tonzanintla*. *La Malinche*, *Moor's Pavane*, and *Dialogues*, with José and Lucas, were also done on this program, which was attended by the Mexican Consul General from New York. José's new piece, *The Queen's Epicedium*, had to be cancelled when Letitia Ide was injured. There were shared programs with Dudley-Maslow-Bales and with Charles Weidman, who was on the teaching faculty that year. Koner and Hoving also showed pieces of their own.

But it was Doris, according to Walter Terry, who was "perhaps the key figure" in the success of the festival. She was, of course, mentor to three of the choreographers, José, Charles, and Koner, and her new work, the *Quartet*, Terry thought "an utterly fascinating dance, rich in movement invention . . . exciting and beautiful." She staged a revival of *Passacaglia* for her repertory class of twenty that year, and after being shown on the student workshop it was added to one of the festival programs (perhaps in place of *Epicedium*). John Martin finally recanted about the piece he had attacked so often, "The real surprise . . . was the emergence of . . . *Passacaglia* as head and shoulders above everything else on the program," he enthused, praising its "formal beauty and its profound sensitiveness."

After New London, Doris saw Humphrey off for his freshman year at Lafayette College. She then had to deal with the agonizing job of closing the former Studio Theater. Despite everyone's attempts to cover for Charles' lapses, he had become so advanced in alcoholism that he could no longer keep up his regular classes or company rehearsals. The studio ceased operations, and Doris went there day after day, supervising the removal of the old Humphrey-Weidman props and costumes, the physical dismantling of what had disintegrated in spirit long before. As usual when she was depressed, she talked of moving; she wanted to be closer to Juilliard, the Dance Players Studio, and the Y. But work intervened; she suspended her apartment hunt and continued to make the long taxi ride uptown from her 16th Street walkup until 1955, when she moved to the Ruxton Hotel on West 72nd Street.

In late October Doris left for Mexico City, where she was to have a major role in another Limón residency. José was choreographing *Antigona*, to music Carlos Chavez had based on the Cocteau play about Antigone, and *Redes* (*Nets*), a big work Doris thought was "very symbolic and mystical" based on the "struggle between positive and negative forces." Doris taught the *Passacaglia*, encountering some trouble because she felt the dancers didn't have enough technique to do it. But the dance impressed the critics when it was given during a three-week series of concerts that included José's pieces and the works of local choreographers. Doris also acted as artistic advisor to all nine productions for the season. Despite her problems, she praised the hard-working Mexican dancers and in general enjoyed herself. She was far better off than Pauline, who was, she reported to Hay, "just Mrs. Limón in Mexico. . . . All the costumes for José are designed by other people and she can only chew her fingernails." Pauline meanwhile told Humphrey, "Your mother is having a big time, as all the new ballets from the academy are coming up and she is putting on endings, and bolstering up middles, and asking for *'mas luz'* and counting up to six in Spanish like mad. What do you mean it doesn't agree with her?"

That fall, when they were all in Mexico, a curious article entitled "The Theater of José Limón" appeared in the influential magazine *Theatre Arts Monthly*. The writer, Beatrice Gottlieb, began with the assertion that the "highbrow" dance had not realized its full theatrical value under the domination of women, and that José's masculine contribution for the first time "proves that a dance theatre may be as comprehensive as any other theatre." Having said that, Gottlieb went on to enumerate a long list of reasons why José had not yet surpassed his first important choreographic works, *La Malinche* and *The Moor's Pavane*. She felt above all that he needed "a clear external organizing principle, both when he dances and when he composes." This could be provided for him by a formal composer like Bach or Vivaldi, or by another structure like a story or a court dance form—or by Doris, when she choreographed for him. Gottlieb felt José had a limited dramatic range, of which "pathos is his chief ingredient." While he could portray suffering, he was not hostile or destructive; for example, the bullfighter in Doris' *Lament* was "a man who is great in defeat rather than in triumph." Gottlieb thought that José's "limited sense of tragic action reduces drama to a struggle between two people" and that he ran the risk of sentimentality, which Doris' greater natural sense of form could curb. She puzzled over why the works commissioned in Mexico had not been more successful, given all the resources that had been placed in José's hands, and she concluded that his Mexicanism reflected "something he feels he *should* be instead of something he naturally *is.*"

Finally, though, the writer went on to extol the Limón company as "complete theatre," with the sensual appeal of color and sound as well as skill and performing ability. She praised the dancers as individualistic and strong performers, with no decorative mannerisms such as she found in Graham. Limón, she said, "reminds us that we go to the theatre *both* to revel and to perceive."

In retrospect, Gottlieb seems to have been right in her assessment of José's strengths and weaknesses and in locating the differences between his talent and that of Doris. At the time, however, the piece must have seemed capricious and divisive—heaping great honor on his head only to uncover serious flaws in his abilities. The most telling parts of the article did emphasize what had always been José's greatest asset, his virile style. Outside the dance field, to theater people, academics, and writers, it came almost as a relief to find a "real man" dancing about "real male" subjects—that is, José was taken to conform to traditional male-dominant stereotyping of the time, and he himself believed he was restoring dignity to a debased profession. In "The Virile Dance," his contribution to Walter Sorell's *The Dance Has Many Faces,* he excoriated the "diluted trivialities" of popular dancing, the "arrogant, mincing, graceful" image of ballet's father-figure, Louis XIV, and called for "men of caliber and dedication . . . to affirm man's sanity and dance it." A young admirer remembered José's saying once, "It has been and is the duty of myself, Ted Shawn, and others like us, to make sure the people realize that [the male dances], and has, for thousands of years. Dancing is *not* something weak and effeminate."

José didn't return to Mexico the next year; changing leadership at the Bellas Artes and accompanying internal politics shifted attention away from the visiting-artist idea. Rosa Covarrubias told José that some people considered him the likely choice to take over the Academy, but he had already realized that his artistic home was the United States, so he probably would not have been prepared to accept such an offer. During the next year or two the company toured America extensively, while Pauline, in New York, worked with their booking agents, the firm of Musical Artists, on various unsuccessful schemes to put together an international engagement. In early 1952, there were difficulties within the company too: Simon Sadoff had left to tour Europe with the New York City Ballet, and Koner and Lucas weren't happy about having to go on the road.

Nevertheless, the Limón Company was the top modern dance company of the time. Graham had disbanded her company and gone into what John Martin called "creative limbo," making infrequent solo appearances. The rest of modern dance seemed to be in decline, and Martin pictured Doris and the "stalwart José Limón" carrying on all alone in a languishing field. Early in 1952, Walter Terry devoted another Sunday column to eulogizing Doris, exhorting her to live for another 150 years, as an inspiration and example to young choreographers. Modern dance was no longer an open field where freewheeling experimentation could be sampled and discussed by benevolent critics. With so much local and imported ballet occupying major theaters, Martin especially began to limit the places he would go to review dance. This made most of the modern dance spaces off-limits to the *Times*. Even the sites of major dance events, the 92nd Street Y, Hunter College, Cooper Union, and the High School of Needle Trades, now lay on the fringes of his territory. When Merce Cunningham's company had its first season at the Theatre de Lys in Greenwich Village in December 1953, Martin didn't even give it a Sunday column's reflection.

Now that the expressive appeal of modern dance was acknowledged, each ballet season brought forth important works that borrowed liberally from modern dance ideas. Jerome Robbins' *The Cage,* premiered by the New York City Ballet in the fall of 1951, was only the most dramatic example; Roland Petit's *Le Jeune Homme et la Mort,* Todd Bolender's *Miraculous Mandarin* and *The Still Point,* Herbert Ross' *Caprichos,* and even Balanchine's *Tyl Eulenspiegel* all depended on character created by a nonclassical use of dynamics, space, and the body rather than on balletic display. Terry said *The Cage* proved that modern dance and ballet could be integrated successfully, and by the end of 1952 he felt he had to defend the continuation of modern dance as a separate entity. "There are some adamant balletomanes who feel that modern dance has served its purpose through the influences it has exerted upon the movement range, the performing style, the choreography, and the thematic materials of the ballet . . . but it boasts independent as well as contributory purposes." Terry thought that as long as there were individual artists as powerful as José, the dance medium could keep on expanding.

The Limón hegemony didn't last long. Graham reorganized her company and gave a successful season at Juilliard in the spring of 1952. It was the first Juilliard-sponsored series of concerts by a member·of the dance faculty, and six performances by José and the company followed in December. Doris' Mozart *Fantasy and Fugue,* premiered the previous summer in New London, was her newest work for that season, which also included *Lament, Night Spell, Day on Earth,* and a revival of the Variations and Conclusion from *New Dance.* When the newly formed Bethsabee de Rothschild Foundation for Arts and Sciences announced a forthcoming two-week Broadway season of modern dance, it was taken for granted that Limón and Graham would be prominent participants. The others were Graham alumni Nina Fonaroff, Pearl Lang, Helen McGehee, and May O'Donnell, and the enigmatic Merce Cunningham. Following the season, which took place at the Alvin Theater at the end of April 1953, the foundation sponsored an additional week of Graham.

Doris' new work, *Ritmo Jondo (Deep Rhythm),* was the only world premiere on the Alvin season. (Graham saved her new dance, *Theatre for a Voyage,* for her own season in May.) However, all the participants boasted so-called Broadway premieres, first showings on the critics' official turf of works that had been seen elsewhere at theaters without the Broadway prestige or overhead. *Ritmo Jondo* was perhaps the only fully commissioned work of Doris' career. She and de Rothschild had heard a six-minute chamber piece by Carlos Surinach at a Museum of Modern Art concert, and they asked the composer if he would expand it for the stage. Using Doris' general suggestions as to the character of the dance sequence, Surinach produced a twenty-two-minute piece for small orchestra, and he himself conducted the premiere. Jean Rosenthal, who acted as lighting designer for the season and subsequently for the Graham company, did a set meant to suggest a park on the outskirts of a town. With no apparent promptings other than the Flamenco-influenced music, Doris made a three-part dance on the simplest of premises: the presentation of a group of men, then a group of women, and their subsequent meeting, courting, and parting.

Using no story, characters, or even any appreciable dramatic gesture, she drew an inventive movement vocabulary and vibrant performances out of the eight dancers. The men dominate the space with big traveling jumps, commanding arm, leg, and upper-body attitudes, and motifs of greeting and bonding. The women are more low-key. Koner distributes branches to them and they dance a sort of summoning ritual, their beautiful spiraling and curving upper bodies accentuated by the ultrafeminine costumes of Pauline Lawrence—long black skirts and white blouses with deep ruffles on the sleeves. The two groups pair up in a folklike dance, the men always the more active partners, often catching the women and bending them in a low embrace, or standing apart and showing off with fancy foot-dancing. There's a colorful scarf-play as the men unwind the cummerbunds from their waists and wrap them, shawllike, around the women. The pace and the excitement mount steadily and the couples grow more passionate. Suddenly José whips his scarf away from Koner, slings it casually over his shoulder, and summons his comrades, who desert their partners with equal abruptness. José gives a courtly bow, and the men go off. The women, stunned, sink to the floor as the curtain falls.

The dance is formal but not impersonal, as John Martin noticed, commenting on its "deftly suggested mood and human interplay." Today's liberated dancers and audiences may object to the conventional male and female roles—unusual for Doris. Possibly she was more intent on exploiting what she saw as the principal dancers' innate dance qualities—the quickness and delicacy of Koner's movement, her diminutive stature in contrast to José's imposing size. The whole men's section is influenced by José's personal style: his characteristically urgent baby-steps, like ballet bourrées, often taken in place with the legs spreading into second position; the almost exaggeratedly strong and spatial upper-body gestures; the explosive emphasis of his total changes of mood, like his farewell bow to the women, a courtesy almost brutal in its effect. *Ritmo Jondo* was often spoken of as a "peasant" piece, but the costumes and the semiurban setting overtly contradict this. The *Dance Observer's* Lois Balcom astutely saw the dance as an "evocation of the emotional currents of simple folk as felt and projected through a sympathetic but sophisticated insight." This seems correctly to describe Doris' distance from her subjects—including the dancers who helped realize them—as well as her admiration for them. Balcom saw *Ritmo* as "a distillation—delicate even when most vigorous, deft with the true Humphrey touch, spirited—tender—gay—and wistful by turns."

The Alvin season seemed calculated to prove the continuing importance of modern dance as an art, and to Walter Terry it did indeed signal a "renascence." But John Martin thought the choice of choreographers and programming odd, the evenings "miscellaneous and competitive in feeling." The producers' determination to showcase the strongest works of each participating artist resulted in what seemed to Martin like benefit performances rather than a "normal and orderly season." In fact, at the end of the 1952–53 dance season, Martin concluded that the modern dance was "still in a serious condition," and without Graham and the Humphrey-Limón alliance, "we would have nothing." One might wonder to what extent these dire turning points are created by the critics who report them, for in the spring of 1953, besides the American Dance-Graham seasons at the Alvin, there were programs by several choreographers on a series sponsored by the New Dance Group Studio, and the Lester Horton Dance Company from Los Angeles made its New York debut, in addition to many individual noteworthy events.

Both Martin's assessment and the events at the Alvin had the effect of intensifying Graham's predominance in the public eye, for she was not only the author of extraordinary works—*Night Journey, Dark Meadow, Appalachian Spring, Letter to the World* were some of the dances on at the Alvin—but still a riveting performer. Doris' new work was very well received but was given less space in the critics' appraisals than the season itself. As a new attempt to consolidate the intractable modern dance, it elicited their commentary on how this elusive goal ought to be reached. Despite the great respect in which critics held Doris, her personal impact was now always filtered through the performances of the dancers, and with José, Koner, and the company in top form, the unseen choreographer moved imperceptibly a little further into the background.

Between José's Juilliard season in December 1952 and the Alvin performances, Doris also managed to oversee the birth of another company, the

Merry-Go-Rounders, and to coax the long-deferred *Poor Eddy* into a brief, unfortunate life. Probably one reason she did the *Poor Eddy* project was to help Charles. In this period of his life—he later admitted that his worst drinking years were from 1950 until after he joined Alcoholics Anonymous in 1955—Doris passed on what jobs she could to him, and the role of the tormented poet Edgar Allan Poe, who transmutes the misfortunes of his life into fantastic tales, seemed suited to his talents. In Elizabeth Dooley's script, biographical interludes alternated with danced or mimed renditions of eight famous Poe stories. Produced by the Columbia University Theater Association, the show employed a mixed cast of students and professionals and had a limited run beginning March 11, 1953. Most of the dance and theater critics who reviewed it approved of its experimental scheme of blending fact and fantasy, acting, music, and dance. But they felt the central role was seriously flawed by having the dialogue in the "real life" sections spoken offstage while Charles, left onstage, "can only smile, nod, and gesture when spoken to, so that he seems to be a complete ninny," according to Douglas Watt of the *Daily News.* Louis Horst, reviewing the piece for the *Dance Observer,* thought the book far inferior to Doris' "masterful choreography." Her staging of "The Masque of the Red Death" was particularly admired, and more than one critic thought some of the tales could stand on their own as independent choreography.

Doris' involvement with the Merry-Go-Rounders was a by-product of her role as director of the Dance Center at the 92nd Street YM-YWHA. Children's classes at the Y had grown to such proportions that in 1952 there were 200 little darlings to be herded into the June recital, and Bonnie Bird, who was on the Y teaching staff, felt that this had become an unmanageable situation. In the fall, together with Doris and Y director William Kolodney, she developed a plan for an adult company that would do special performances for children. All the dancers were to be members of the Y staff, and outside choreographers were invited to provide the repertory. Bird was named administrative director, and Doris artistic director.

The first performances were given at the Y in February 1953, with a repertory of pieces by Bird, Alwin Nikolais, and Fred Berk. It also included *The Goops,* suggested by Doris from a popular story of her own childhood and choreographed by former Humphrey-Weidman dancer Eva Desca, which became a signature piece for the company. With a variety of story dances, mime and circus entertainments, and movement games that its young audiences could play, the Merry-Go-Rounders developed a successful format that soon spread outside the Y into school programs around the city and beyond.

Doris remained artistic director until her final illness. Although she never choreographed for the company herself, she provided constant guidance, and worked with the group to maintain its high standard and imaginative programming.

Soon after the Alvin season, Doris was deep into plans for another big work, *Ruins and Visions*. There was to be a British Festival of dance and music at Juilliard the next season, with several contributions from the English choreographer Antony Tudor, who was on the ballet faculty. Doris selected the first movement of the String Quartet no. 1 by Benjamin Britten, followed by the whole of his Second Quartet. The Juilliard administration, always scrupulous about musical matters, wondered "if Juilliard will be criticized for cutting up a long work" and asked Doris for some justification. In fact, the choice was accidental. According to Ruth Currier, Doris heard the music first on records, not realizing where the break between the two compositions lay. By the time she discovered it, she was too far along in composing the dance to change music. The dance premiered at the 1953 American Dance Festival instead of at Juilliard.

Doris used a text by the contemporary poet Stephen Spender, returning to themes she had pondered before, but setting them in an entirely new way. The themes were war and human insensitivity, overprotective mothering, the blending of reality and pretense, and the redemption of society through an acceptance of brotherhood. Doris dramatized these ideas through a montage of incidents: three sets of people, mutually unaware of each other, gradually recognize their commonality through suffering and the mediation of an artist.

A mother and son (Koner and Lucas), enclosed in a private world, float above the ground in a garden swing. The mother seems to dominate the son, drawing him back when he seems momentarily attracted by the world outside. They go to the theater, where a pompous actor (José) makes love to his paramour (Lavina Nielsen). Later he returns to find her in another man's arms, and he kills them both. The mother and son walk home, disdainfully avoiding some rowdy youths on the street. The actor visits the cemetery and undergoes a conversion in remorse for his killings. The son, now married, is lured off to war, and as his wife and mother lament for him, the actor tries to comfort them. The son's corpse is dragged in, and all the characters gather in mourning recognition of their common tragedy. Then, in Doris' words, "With the artist as catalyst and leader they take the first tentative steps toward a united destiny."

A comparison of two scene-by-scene abstracts Doris made of the dance

Ruins and Visions. Koner and Lucas. Photo by Peter Basch. (Dance Collection, NYPL)

with the corresponding lines by Spender reveals that her outlook was far more optimistic than his. In "The Fates" and "At Night," from Spender's 1942 volume *Ruins and Visions,* the poet speaks about self-deception and the way social conventions help shield people from the fearsome questions of death, loneliness, and barbarity. "The Fates," which provided both the narrative and the poetic substance of the dance, tells of a family in which the mother is obsessed with keeping her son from learning about "the real." She stage-manages life so that "nothing happens that can matter / Except that we look well produced and bright." Spender asks whether these characters are any more real than "those on the stage who open ribs like doors, / To show their hearts." With savage irony he traces the son's emergence into a smug, her-metic manhood. Abruptly the language and tone of the poem change, and in a few even more bitter lines we see the son's inevitable end as a victim of war, fallen into the dust, "Staring at the sun, the eyes at last cut open."

Doris paraphrased Spender in some notes she sent to Pauline, who was designing the costumes, and in several cases the words she chose to key each scene in the dance were softer than the originals. (These notes were also used on the program.) For example, when Spender tells of the family's awakening to reality, "The walls fall, tearing down / The mother-of-pearl in-laid interior." Doris remembered these lines as "The walls fall, tearing down / The fragile life of the interior." Where the poet suggests a brittle artificiality, the choreographer is more sympathetic. Adopting a quotation from "At Night," a searching but not devastating poem, Doris added a final Litany of Survival after the son's death. The characters finally give up their isolation and try to comfort one another, then ritualistically step forward into "an opening out of spaces." This last scene reduces the son's death—an immense irony in Spender's telling—to not much more than a device for effecting the rec-onciliation of the factions.

Doris was manipulating several important ideas here, and if the dance was unclear to some of its viewers, the complexity of her message may be the reason. Her overall perspective was the one with which "The Fates" be-gins, "Which are the actors, which the audience?" All the characters in the dance are at first immune to what the others deem of paramount impor-tance, being preoccupied with the "unreal" façades they present to the world. The actor's crime of passion touches his own humanity and prepares him to sympathize with the others when they are overwhelmed by war. But Doris also said, "The theme is the attainment of tolerance and understanding through mutual suffering in a catastrophe," and for this the dance shifts styles midway, from the pantomimic clarity of the narrative scenes to a more impersonal and abstract denouement rather reminiscent of Kurt Jooss' *The Green Table,* in which archetypal persons rather than individuals act out grand ideas. Doris made a similar shift at the end of *Day on Earth,* when, the man's work over, he and the three female characters become depersonalized actors in the ritualistic completion of one generation and transferral of life to the next.

The switch was intentional in both cases; she told Pauline about *Ruins,* "Nobody will care what it is about as each scene will have such a style of its own and contrast to other scenes that it might be just interesting to watch this element." Even the early, more literal scenes are purposefully different in feeling. The mother and son, rocking on the swing, have an elegaic stillness between them, and an intuitive accord in their actions. The actors' scenes are melodramatic, overdone in the size, intensity, and vulgarity of the movement. Two of this section's most brutal images—the actress' taunting of the actor with her skirt pulled over her head, and his grotesque attempts to dance with her lifeless body—are apparently borrowed from Herbert Ross' ballet based on Goya etchings, *Caprichos,* produced by the Ballet Theatre in 1950. The street urchins have the most dancey parts. Their action seems speeded up and exaggeratedly physical; their play can turn into violence or, later, quick commiseration. Although the three groups are completely self-contained in the first part of the dance, they cross each other's paths in various ways. After the actor's conversion, however, they all impinge directly on each other's lives. Some of the dancers assume different roles. The urchins and the second actor become a sort of enlistment parade, using long poles and ribbons to whip up a miniature spectacle that has a hypnotically alluring effect on the son. Throughout the long last scene, not only do the distinctions between the groups drop away, but the personal identity of even the leading characters becomes submerged until they all take their first faltering steps together toward the future. *Ruins* is thus a variation on the thesis of *New Dance:* the group acknowledges the need for unified action, but here the individual is pictured as destructive and detrimental to the ideal society rather than that society's supreme product.

After seeing the dance twice in New London, Margaret Lloyd appreciated what Doris was trying to do. "We see more clearly the silken boy, the silver cord, the actor in us all, the leveling of war, the final triumphant theme of brotherhood, of understanding through experience." Doris Hering of *Dance Magazine* remarked that "although Miss Humphrey has used war as the leavening experience . . . she implies that art can also draw people from their self-created isolation and give them understanding."

Today nearly all of Doris' associates consider *Ruins and Visions* one of her greatest works. Yet it was performed rarely and, except for a memorial program at the 1959 American Dance Festival, has not been fully reconstructed since her death. Its usefulness in repertory was curtailed because of a technical flaw. This was the swing designed by Paul Trautvetter and used in the first scene. The working prop was extremely cumbersome. It had to be flown on battens above the stage and took up so much room that it required careful maneuvering by the dancers onstage and by the crew in order to clear the lighting instruments and other technical equipment. With practice, this drawback could be surmounted in New London's Palmer Auditorium, but there was rarely enough time and space to struggle with the problem on tour. When the Limóns played Jacob's Pillow that summer, only one of Doris' dances was on the program, the plotless 1949 trio, *Invention*.

Throughout the demanding 1952–53 season Doris had once again been experiencing serious pain in her leg. As usual, she was too busy to look after it, and other people explored ways of getting help for her. Early in 1953 Pauline and José found out through Ted Shawn the names of two surgeons who could perform a relatively new operation to replace the hip joint. Shawn warned that the operation would entail "excruciating pain," but if Doris were conscientious about exercising afterward, she could have excellent results. Hay also told her about the operation around this time. But it wasn't until November 2 that she entered Polyclinic Hospital in New York to have it done. She found it less painful than she had anticipated and was able to go home on crutches in three weeks. Humphrey was studying in England that year, but Leo came home to take care of her while she recovered. She felt optimistic about the prospects, and for a while she was able to walk without a limp, although the condition worsened again in a year or two. She told Hay after the operation: "My general attitude . . . is a fury. After being master of my body all these years, it finally turns on me and I am the prisoner of it." During the next five years, as the bonds of illness tightened their grip, her determination not to submit grew stronger.

Doris won the Capezio Award for outstanding contributions to dance in 1954. She was only the third recipient, following Zachary Solov (1952), who had revitalized the Metropolitan Opera Ballet, and Lincoln Kirstein (1953). Doris was cited for "her creative leadership in modern dance and for the repertory of high distinction with which she has enriched it." Martha Hill, John Martin, Walter Terry, and *Dance News* editor Anatole Chujoy served as the selection committee. On March 9, she was given a luncheon with about 100 guests at the St. Regis Roof, and William Schuman, president of the Juilliard School, presented her with the award, which included a check for $500. Reflecting on the award, Martin noted that Doris had never choreographed "primarily for the exploitation of her own gifts as a performer," and that this transcending of individual style, which he considered unique in the modern dance, gave her dances the independent stature of "genuine work of the theater."

In spite of her acknowledged preeminence, when Connecticut College decided to award the first American Dance Festival commission, for the summer of 1954, it was José who got the honor. President Rosemary Park wrote him in January that the $1,500 was being awarded as a "gesture of friendship to one who has contributed so much to the school." The male contingent of the Limón company had been gradually expanding since *Ritmo Jondo*, and to fulfill the commission José decided to do an all-male ballet. *The Traitor* was based on the betrayal of Christ, and, reversing the good-evil roles of the *Pavane*, Lucas played the Christ figure and José was the Judas. The dance, to Gunther Schuller's Symphony for Brasses, was a great hit and became one of José's major creations. Both Martin and Terry initially applauded its dramatic gesture, its use of visual devices such as a cloth that the group manipulated in a series of Last Supper tableaux, but "movement in space" was not one of its attributes according to Martin. He observed that there was a difference between speech and song, suggesting that *The Traitor* was "a passionate oration, but it fails to sing." However, it proved a durable success for José, and touched off a string of men's dances: *Scherzo* (1955), *Emperor Jones* (1956), and *The Unsung* (1970).

Doris' new piece for the festival, *Felipe el Loco*, did not succeed. Although she had initially thought she would do a "dance piece" for the company to balance the many dramatic works in the repertory, she later decided on an interpretation of a true story with a dance setting. Felix Fernandez, an extraordinary flamenco dancer and an innocent, had been taken up by Diaghilev in Madrid in 1918. Brought to London to coach Léonide Massine, who was to choreograph a Spanish ballet (*Le Tricorne*), Fernandez suffered a nervous breakdown with delusions and had to be institutionalized. Probably Doris' chief reason for choosing this theme was to make another Spanish-flavored role for José, but this turned out to be a bad miscalculation. To most critics, the semblance of gypsy movement that she gave José was a poor substitute for real flamenco dancing, which, of course, José had never been trained to do.

The dance had an effective opening scene which Louis Horst, reviewing for the *Dance Observer,* commended for the feeling of "great tenderness and pathos" the characters created as they wandered through an impressionistic fog of draperies. Then there was a "battle of misunderstanding" between the naive Felipe and the ballet dancers he was supposed to instruct. Here Doris had to simulate ballet movement for the nonballetic Limón dancers. Finally Felipe went mad—Horst found this "too naturalistic"—but then, "with a great show of showmanship rather than choreography, she whipped up a tremendously climactic and surefire finale." In another one of her escapes into fantasy, Doris made an apotheosis for the unhappy story, in which the imprisoned Felipe sees a vision of his homeland in the person of Pauline Koner dancing. Koner had the technique to do an accomplished Spanish number, and this undermined whatever credibility José's pseudo-Spanish movement had managed to project. Though dissimilar in its details, the choreographic plan of *Felipe el Loco* resembled other dances in which Doris created a free-flowing interplay between the literal and the idealized or abstract, causing the potential for confusion in her audiences. John Martin thought the piece should be done over for a little ballet company, with a flamenco dancer as its star.

As always, there were partisans. *Felipe*—or Doris herself—got a "frenzied ovation" in New London, and friends wrote to tell her how moved they had been by the piece. In view of the poor press, Doris called the company together and asked if they would give her a vote of confidence to rework *Felipe.* According to Betty Jones, the dancers didn't like the piece either but "nobody would dare say they didn't want to do it." After revisions, the dance still didn't work, and it went out of the repertory the next spring. It is one of the few pieces Doris did for the Limón Company that was not filmed or recorded in any form.

In the fall of 1954 the Limón Company received another important commendation when it was named as the first overseas ambassador of dance under the State Department's new ANTA-administered International Exchange Program in the Performing Arts. For the next two decades, this was to be the sponsoring agency for United States cultural organization tours abroad. The Limóns were to visit South America for a week each in Rio de Janeiro, São Paulo, Montevideo, and Buenos Aires at the end of 1954. Performances would be in major theaters, with an orchestra and good technical support. The tour came up on very short notice, and the company had only three weeks to prepare the repertory of fourteen dances and "extricate everybody from other commitments," for as usual when not expecting to be on the road, the dancers had arranged their own outside teaching and performing dates. Nevertheless, they got off with a company of ten dancers, Simon Sadoff to conduct the local orchestras, and a technical crew. Neither Pauline nor Doris went along.

The tour was a great success "both artistically and diplomatically," as José told John Martin when they returned. In every city, he had been careful to ward off the expectations that had sabotaged *Felipe el Loco.* Despite his Hispanic heritage, he would tell the press, he did not know Spanish dancing or even Mexican dancing; he had been reared in the United States and "thought like a North American." The dances, naturally, weren't universally liked, and José theorized to Martin that reactions in the four cities depended partly on a European cultural orientation and an exposure to American dance limited to the Balanchine and Ballet Theatre approaches. José's baroque-style *Vivaldi Concerto Grosso,* which he regarded as a very old piece, was the most popular number. Doris' best-liked pieces were *Night Spell,* with its score expanded for a chamber orchestra, and the Variations and Conclusion from *New Dance. Day on Earth,* so admired by the Mexicans, was considered "grim and drab." José thought this was because its imagery was too spare and earthy for South Americans; the Mexicans, on the other hand could appreciate these qualities, which were basic to their own folk artists and to modern painters like José Clemente Orozco.

The company's touring successes kept them on the road so much of the time that Doris complained they were "almost impossible to catch anymore for new works." She had them in New London during the summers, and she still found her repertory classes rewarding. *Water Study* and *Soaring* were reconstructed at the 1954 American Dance Festival; and she mounted *Red Fires* twice, in 1953 at New London and the following year at Juilliard. This revival prompted John Martin to reflect on the scarcity of a modern dance "literature" for students to work on. Doris herself had admitted, in introducing the Juilliard performance, that "its rhythms and counterpoint were perhaps more complex than she would now employ," and Martin concluded that "it would have been a privilege to see [*Red Fires*] even if it were not one of the masterpieces of our time." But teaching established masterpieces had never satisfied Doris' choreographic needs, and in 1954 a new outlet was created to put a more-or-less permanent ensemble of bodies at her disposal.

The Juilliard Dance Theater was initiated in the fall of 1954 with Doris as artistic director, and its chief purpose was to produce new and repertory works that would give gifted young dancers the training and experience to prepare them for professional careers. Its members included Juilliard students and other young dancers who paid a fee or were given scholarships to work under Doris though they were not enrolled in Juilliard classes. A small one-time grant from Bethsabee de Rothschild helped get the company started, and Juilliard maintained it thereafter. The sixteen-member company made its debut April 19 and 20, 1955, at the Juilliard concert hall with a program consisting of new works by Doris and Anna Sokolow, and a revival of *Life of the Bee*. In addition to annual performances at Juilliard, the company did some modest touring under the name of the Doris Humphrey Dancers—this was because the famous music school didn't want its name attached to a company that danced to recorded music. In all, Doris choreographed three ballets for the Juilliard dancers, and sketched on them her last work, *Brandenburg Concerto no. 4*.

All three of the finished pieces represented an attempt not only to choreograph especially for the skills of the young dancers but also to articulate the feelings of adolescence and transition that she thought they were experiencing. The themes were ideas Doris had returned to again and again: the rebellion of youth and its emergence into adulthood, the importance of nature's beauty as an antidote to the dehumanization of the urban world. But in each piece she tried something new. Critics might complain that her dances were unsatisfactory for one reason or another, but she was never accused of resorting to formulas.

The Rock and the Spring (1955) looked at a young girl torn between a matriarchal tradition and the independence of her contemporaries. *Descent into the Dream* (1957) traced a young girl's growing up to join a mature sisterhood. *Dawn in New York*, perhaps the most interesting of the three, was premiered in April 1956 as part of a festival of American music that Juilliard staged to celebrate its fiftieth anniversary. Doris used a score by Hunter Johnson and based the dance on some bleak lines of Lorca about the oppressiveness of city life. The critics differed drastically about it—Martin thought it a masterpiece while the *Dance Observer*'s Robert Sabin asserted it was definitely not one. But everyone liked the central duet danced by Joyce Trisler, symbolizing spring, and John Barker, as a young man struggling to escape the frantic, mechanized bustle of the urban crowd. Trisler was one of several outstanding dancers to emerge from the Juilliard Dance Theater; others included Lola Huth, Patricia Christopher and many other future members

of the Limón Company, Jeff Duncan, critic Deborah Jowitt, and Melisa Nicolaides, the original child in *Day on Earth,* now a teenager and still devoted to
Doris.

Hard on the heels of the Juilliard Dance Theater's debut followed another
season of American Dance sponsored by Bethsabee de Rothschild. This one
lasted for three weeks beginning May 3, 1955, and took place at the ANTA
Theater—formerly the Guild and later the Virginia—where so many of the
cornerstones of modern dance had been put in place. Unaccountably, the
ANTA repertory consisted of only one Limón piece, *The Traitor,* with *The
Moor's Pavane* added in the last week. The rest of the dances were Doris':
Ruins and Visions, Felipe el Loco, Night Spell, Ritmo Jondo, Variations and
Conclusion, *Day on Earth, Fantasy and Fugue,* and *Lament.* The company
had been on the road, returning at the end of March, which gave Doris only
the month of April to rehearse all these pieces including the revised *Felipe* at
the same time that she was preparing the Juilliard Dance Theater's debut.

The ANTA series was a showman's dream and a critic's nightmare. Besides
the Graham and Limón companies, it featured group works by John Butler,
Pearl Lang, Anna Sokolow, and Valerie Bettis, plus soloists Pauline Koner, Iris
Mabry, Janet Collins, Daniel Nagrin, Ann Halprin, and tap dancer Paul
Draper. The programs, eight a week, were indigestible feasts, often encom-
passing four major works or three big pieces interspersed with solos. A typical bill offered Graham's *Diversion of Angels, Day on Earth, Night Spell,* and
Graham's *Theatre for a Voyage.* For the Limón company the only New York
premiere was the ill-fated *Felipe el Loco,* while Graham boasted three novelties including the splendid *Seraphic Dialogue.* John Martin excoriated the
entire undertaking. "Better three days of consistent values," he recommended, "than three weeks of miscellany assembled for virtually every reason except the all-important one of presenting the art at its unquestionable
best." He considered the mixture of theater styles, some of them frankly
meant for entertainment, with older recital pieces "irrelevant in the extreme"
and thought the season as a whole "ineffectual and maladroit, and [it] may
have done more harm than good." The *Dance Observer's* Robert Sabin
thought the season's diversity and quantity demonstrated the richness of the
modern dance field rather than what Martin felt was a quiescent state with
the same few leaders providing most of the creativity. To Martin's mind "only
two works stood out as complete and unquestionable masterpieces": *Day
on Earth* and *The Moor's Pavane.*

The tremendous exertions of the spring were overlaid by Humphrey's impending graduation from Lafayette and the worrisome question of what he would do for a living. He had been unable to make up his mind about a career and now, with the draft reinstituted because of the Korean War, had put a decision aside until he completed his military service. Doris had also been having extensive dental work and sometime in the spring was momentarily halted by appendicitis. All this took its toll. Her walking had become labored again, and during the ANTA season she had refused to take any bows except if she came onstage while the curtain was down, to be discovered by the audience standing in place. Then, in the brief respite before summer school in Connecticut, she developed severe pains in her leg and was hospitalized for a week in early July. No clear cause of this problem was apparent, other than the fact that she had driven herself to a breakdown, and as often before the doctors were amazed when she pulled herself together so quickly.

She went to New London on crutches, in a car the college sent for her. Again she was furious at her infirmity and set herself to the summer's tasks as though nothing had happened to impair her ability to do them all. But in fact, that summer she was a semi-invalid. She taught and rehearsed in a living room that had been cleared out, in the same dormitory where she was living. Her meals were sent to her on a tray so that she would not have to leave the building. She spent most of the time between classes and rehearsals lying down, listening to the music she was choreographing and planning the new dance, which was behind schedule. She had no time and no strength for socializing, and even asked the faithful Hay not to come for a visit.

In these last years, Doris was reduced by pain and her own concentration to a kind of intense shadow. In pictures she looks drawn, her eyes are haunted, and she is seldom smiling. Steadily she eliminated everything from her life that would take energy away from work. Ruth Lloyd remembered that in the summer of 1955 she could hardly move at all; her body was "sort of frozen," probably from a combination of pain, weakness, and fear of doing further damage to her leg. But, she told her classes, there was nothing the matter with her mind.

In addition to reviving *Shakers* for her repertory class, she now fled from the dramatic, as she had intended to do the year before. Her new piece, *Airs and Graces* (Locatelli), was a light, even frivolous series of visual puns on the antiquated terms for baroque musical figures: Double Relish, Quaver with Four Tails, Passing Shake, and more. Lucas clowned his way through it with

Betty, Ruth, and Lavina, but it came off as trivial even to those, like Louis Horst, who appreciated its wit. Martin hit it hard, "There is no eighteenth century (or any other) style, the humor is so heavy as not to be humorous, and Miss Humphrey's hand is nowhere evident." The festival was almost overloaded with light and plotless novelties that year, with José's five-man dance to drum rhythms, *Scherzo;* his *Symphony for Strings* (William Schuman); and Koner's *Concertino of Pergolesi;* so the Locatelli's failure to take wing is doubly understandable.

Back in New York, Doris admitted her handicaps to the extent of moving into an apartment hotel at 72nd Street and Columbus Avenue, where she would not have to climb stairs. The Ruxton had maid service and convenient restaurants, and was much closer to her work. Leo helped her find it and move in, clearing out the accumulated junk at 16th Street and buying some new furnishings. He then left again on a long trip. He was now assigned to a ship that went to the Mediterranean and was away from home up to six months at a time. Since his United States port was usually in the South, Doris began to think of him as little more than "a voice on the telephone." Humphrey moved in with her for a while, then was accepted at the navy's officer candidate school in Newport.

With neither her son nor her husband around for assistance or companionship, she felt isolated and withdrawn. Even getting dressed was a time-consuming labor. "The failure of the mechanism is an enemy to outwit, to defeat, which takes all my strength and will to conquer," she told Hay. In the fall she was reading Virginia Woolf's biography, and found it depressing, "If your heroine is going to have difficulties and frustrations and finally commit suicide it's more dignified and grander and more worthy of her to be defeated by something bigger than a headache." Doris was growing intolerant, short tempered. People who knew her only in these later years thought of her as impersonal, mercilessly demanding. But the struggle she had to wage with herself precluded much sympathy for others; privately she must have often been lonely and in despair.

Ironically, for the first time, there was some space in her life. She was making enough money, not that her fees had become enormous, but she no longer had to pour every extra penny into supporting a company and mounting a repertory. Her personal responsibilities had also diminished. For several years Humphrey had been spending weekends and summers at the Limóns' farm, and with Leo gone and the company so often on the road, her accustomed social apparatus had dissolved. She filled her time with more work; she had no hobbies or outside interests. For the first time in her career she took to writing letters to critics, defending dancers she thought they had misunderstood. In the fall of 1956 she wrote an extraordinary series of letters to radio and television producers suggesting a whole battery of ideas for programs on dance. She served on the selection committee for the ANTA-International Exchange Program. And during these years she would make her way to walk-up studios and threadbare lofts where eager young choreographers giving concerts had begged for her feedback. Leo disapproved of her tiring herself out on these chores that didn't seem imperative, but to her it was a lifeline, one of the few ways to be useful that she had left.

When she did have the company at her disposal, she continued to experiment. The idea for the dance that became *Theatre Piece no. 2* had been in her mind at least since 1953. That fall she wrote to the composer Vincent Persichetti outlining a work about the "oneness" of dance, music, words, and other stage elements. The opening scene, she thought, should have "something of the attitude of primitive man," a sense of being "at one with air, light, trees, animals. Here the light would swell and burst into music, followed by ecstatic movement of the dancers, and then by voice—inarticulate, like cries in rhapsodic mood." This would develop into a ritual scene, in which the "elements are still combined, but consciously." They would then become fragmented in three short, comedic motifs, which she visualized as: a play with obscure, pseudo-sophisticated words and stilted acting; a dance that would be "linear, intellectual, deadly serious"; and a modernistic musical interlude she described as "eye music—dry, dissonant, and unpleasant." Then there would be a return to unity using a very brief selection from the text in Ecclesiastes beginning "To every thing there is a season, and a time to every purpose under the heaven."

Theatre Piece no. 2, which premiered at Juilliard in April 1956, followed this scheme almost identically, although the text for the final section had become "Poem of Praise" by May Swenson: "O light, the spirit that leaps from the eye of the sun to every living eye / O light, dwell in us . . ." The first and second parts were to suggest the origins of theater and "the lighting of the fires at the altar of ritual," followed by satirical distortions of the theater arts, in acting (Koner and Lucas), dancing (Betty), and singing (Lavina). The dance had been commissioned by the Juilliard School for its American music festival, and it was repeated the next summer in New London. In the event, it wasn't Persichetti who did the music but the pioneer electronic music composer Otto Luening, who made an innovative score for voice, orchestra, and tape recorded sound. According to Luening, both Doris and Martha Graham had attended his first concert in the new medium, in 1952 at the Museum of Modern Art. "I had no reaction from Martha about it," he reported, "but Doris was very interested and got me to do a ballet. . . . We used everything. . . . It was fairly successful too, probably a little premature, but she had the right idea. . . . Doris wasn't afraid to take on musical ideas and then work with them."

Critics found the dance intriguing, ahead of its time, "a free fantasy," said Robert Sabin. Most of them felt it lacked unity of style—something Doris had intended—but John Martin, after thinking it over, decided it was not just a miscellany but was "treating with insight and passion that all-inclusive art, the theater itself." The May Swenson poetry that replaced Ecclesiastes, re-cited by Carl White, was considered banal by Sabin, "chintzy imagery" by Doris Hering.

For the same Juilliard festival José appropriated the Ecclesiastes theme and choreographed all eight verses in a literal, romantic work with music by Norman dello Joio. First called *Variations on a Theme*, later *There is a Time*, José's dance struck Doris Hering uncannily as the actual flowering of the premise of *Theatre Piece*. "It was as though Mr. Limón had caught the romanticism inherent in Miss Humphrey's idea and expanded it in his own terms." This is probably very close to what happened.

In its ninth year the American Dance Festival must have appeared established enough to withstand a severe attack, and this John Martin administered in his season review. Walter Terry in 1954 and Doris Hering in 1955 had already suggested that the festival suffered from domination by the Limón company, but in 1956 Martin declared he didn't know what purpose the whole thing served. If it was to be a showcase for new and rare works that couldn't be seen elsewhere, it "must be pronounced a failure." Aside from *Kaleidoscope* by Alwin Nikolais—whom Martin had "discovered" the previous year doing mixed-media theater-dance pieces at the Henry Street Playhouse—he had little use for the festival repertory. Though many of the works seen in 1956 became modern dance classics—*There is a Time*, *Ritmo Jondo*, and Anna Sokolow's *Rooms* and *Lyric Suite*, for example—Martin found the only item with a "quality of greatness" to be a revival of *Song of the West*, although that too displeased him because it was performed by Doris' student repertory class, not a professional company. Martin was now nearing his thirtieth year as the *Times'* dance critic, and his disaffection with the modern dancers he had promoted for so long is understandable as a product of satiation if nothing else. Six years later he retired and moved to Los Angeles, convinced that nothing new was happening. Even though the dancers must have understood, they felt betrayed by this treatment from their former champion.

13 DESCENT INTO THE DREAM, 1957–58

By the summer of 1957 critical opinion was the last thing on their minds. The Limón company was about to achieve its long-desired goal of performing in Europe. At the end of 1956 the announcement had come from ANTA that the International Exchange Program would sponsor the tour, which an overseas booking agent, Anatole Heller, had been setting up for years in anticipation of government funding. In New London Doris choreographed *Dance Overture* (Paul Creston), a dancey, joyous piece meant to introduce the company. During its brief ten minutes, it showed off the thirteen dancers in small ensembles and large groups, through the manipulations of scale, counterpoint, and sequence at which Doris excelled.

It was the American Dance Festival's tenth anniversary year, and Connecticut College printed a handsome book of photographs and excerpts from press notices, with lengthy opening tributes to Doris and Louis Horst. "Doris Humphrey has made dance history as unselfconsciously as history has ever been made, and simply as the result of an inborn creativeness that was not to be denied," the article about her began. (Though uncredited, it was probably written by Ruth Bloomer of the Physical Education Department, who had become director of the School of Dance.) Despite the celebration, John Martin skipped the festival entirely that year, and Selma Jeanne Cohen, reviewing it for the *Times,* found *Dance Overture* "the happiest" of the premieres.

But Doris called the summer the hardest yet, with "many shocks, alarms, emergencies, worms-to-be-found-and-fed-to-the-young, choreographic, personal and organizational problems to be met." Besides her own dance, she was helping José with *Blue Roses,* a long, complicated piece based on Tennessee Williams' *The Glass Menagerie,* which—despite her hopes for its eventual consolidation—didn't survive the summer.

The tour began immediately after New London and lasted the entire autumn. More than a year before it was launched, Doris had been hedging about whether she would go along. "If they ever do go," she told Hay in

June 1956, "I've promised to show up in the key places . . . but Spain is the
only country I really want to go to." She thought six to eight weeks would
be strenuous enough, and she was concerned about her commitments at
home. Certainly she was in no condition to endure one-night stands and
constant traveling through nine countries, many of them still recovering from
wartime disruptions. In the event, she stayed with the tour for three of its
four months. After a season in London, where the company opened at Sadler's Wells Theatre on September 2, and Paris (beginning September 16 at
the Marigny Theatre), she went to Spain with Leo while the company played
in Berlin and toured for two weeks in Poland. After Leo left, she rejoined
them in Bonn on October 23 and accompanied them through Germany, Bel-
gium, and Holland, returning home via London on November 23, when they
were preparing to go to Yugoslavia. But her reasons for departing early
weren't only physical.

The English dance press was condescending as only it can be when confronted with the unfamiliar. It had been the same a few years before to Martha Graham, and soon would be again on Merce Cunningham's first visit.
The critics were especially unkind to *Night Spell;* they tried to like *Ruins*—for
Benjamin Britten and Stephen Spender's sake, apparently—but failed. José's
works were hardly more popular, though his dancing was appreciated as
"forceful" and "athletic." Paris was worse, if anything—José reported that
the press "disliked us intensely and wrote of us with derision and mockery."
Houses in both cities were only fair, sometimes poor; later it was thought
that the tail-end of summer vacation had kept people away, especially the
modern dance community. Only after these first two defeats did the tour
start to take hold, first in Berlin, then in Poland, and almost everywhere after
that.

From the beginning José's pieces were more successful than Doris' with
the press and the public, especially those based on well-known literary
themes, like the *Pavane* and *Emperor Jones.* Doris' stories were less conventional, less linear, and her nonnarrative pieces eluded the Europeans, who
were conditioned to balletic grace and couldn't cope with any degree of
compositional rigor. Soon Heller, the impresario, began to press for elimina-
tion of the problematical works and abridgement of the repertory down to
the box-office favorites. Of the seven Humphrey dances in the initial lineup,
Ruins and Visions was dropped because of its unwieldy set, *Lament for Ignacio* was dropped because of language difficulties, and *Dance Overture,* her
brave and generous gift to the company, was withdrawn after only twelve

performances because Paul Creston's royalty fees were higher than any other composer's and the dance seemed on its way to being a hit. For *Day on Earth* a child had to be recruited and taught the part in every location because of prohibitive labor laws. For this role, which Doris saw as made for a starry-eyed little girl, they located a suitable thirteen-year-old ballet child in London. Then they had to hold auditions again in France. The replacement turned out to be oversophisticated, which was exactly wrong for the delicate, nearly nondancing part. Doris remarked acridly, "This is a very capable and skillful performer. I believe she will be quite able to give a fine impersonation of an innocent child." Finally, *Day on Earth* was abandoned.

By the second half of the tour the repertory had boiled down to a single program, with one or two infrequent variations: *Ritmo Jondo, Moor's Pavane, Concerto Grosso, Emperor Jones,* and Lucas and Lavina's comic duet, *Satyros.* "We all felt so awful for Doris," Hoving says. Pauline Koner remembers that "José started getting all the reviews and they started leaving her out or saying she wasn't that important, and José was the big choreographer. This shocked her to death."

Doris had not been on tour with José in years. At their performances in New York and New London, she was always surrounded by admirers, reassured and complimented even when the critics were negative. She had never had to tax her native reticence in order to get credit for her accomplishments. But in Europe, handicapped and depleted by the unaccustomed efforts of travel, she was not known or deferred to, while José, vigorous, charismatic, and outgoing, captivated everyone from the diplomatic corps to the press. Always adept at social niceties, José had become a master at charming the public. He could push beyond any amount of fatigue to smile at fawning lady fans, enthuse over local treats and attractions, explain his work patiently. In short, he was everyone's pet star. At the exuberant postperformance sessions, when friends and well-wishers would come backstage, Doris would sit unnoticed on the sidelines. "People would not even get to know her," Hoving recalls. "She'd sit backstage and nobody'd go to her because they didn't know who she was."

By the time the company left Paris at the end of September, Doris saw herself as a minor player. When she came back from Spain, without Leo to help her get around, she withdrew even more. Says Ruth Currier: "It was hell, this thing that was going on between Doris and José. Because Doris obviously was very much hurt by the reception, and was feeling that she wasn't needed. But she was still artistic director of the company and still conducting rehearsals, and she absolutely worked us to death." Currier remembers Doris calling a rehearsal in Germany when the dancers were all exhausted, simply to restage the bows for *Concerto Grosso.* Some kind of blowup occurred, and Currier tried to resign and go home. She said she had practically nothing to do anyway, with *Day on Earth* and *Ruins* cancelled, as well as her duet with José, *The Exiles,* which had been scratched because the orchestra couldn't handle the Schönberg score. Doris accused her of "leaving the company in the lurch," and a day or two later she was persuaded to reconsider.

Only five days after Doris rejoined the company and a day after the Currier crisis had blown over, Doris decided to pull out. Pauline reported to Humphrey: "Your mother flies home. . . . It's pretty tough for her this sort of travel. As you can imagine she is cross as a bear because she must go home—she could *never* stand the strain in Yugoslavia." This became the accepted rationale for Doris' leaving the tour. She still had to grit her teeth and get through another three weeks of rehearsals, press conferences, and the televising of five dances in Brussels. She must have been desperate to get away, because the company's departure for Yugoslavia was still five days off when she fled Holland, leaving herself with a week to kill in London before a planned lecture for the British society of dance notators. However reasonable they all tried to make it look, a catastrophic rift had occurred between her and José that altered their relationship permanently. Writing to Humphrey from London, Doris hinted that something serious had gone wrong: "The company is going to Yugoslavia and I decided not to go with them. There's nothing more for me to do in my capacity as choreographer and artistic director anyway."

The tour continued through five cities in Yugoslavia, and ended December 21 in Lisbon. After a brief holiday in Spain, the Limóns returned to New York on January 3. The tour had affected José profoundly. He had been perceived all over Europe not only as a star performer but also as a major choreographer and director in his own right. With his fiftieth birthday approaching on January 12, he must have felt it was time to establish his artistic independence from Doris. And she, normally so generous toward her protegés, was less prepared than she had ever been to let go; for perhaps the first time, she had to confront the possibility that in furthering someone else's career, she had pushed herself into the background. Neither one of them would openly admit that there had been a quarrel or even a quiet decision to separate, and nobody at Juilliard or in the company detected a serious change.

But on the day of his return, in one of the pocket calendars that served as José's telegraphic diaries and appointment books, he noted the title of a popular song, "*Me Canse de Rogarle*" (I get tired of begging), in which a man whose lover wants to leave him says he can't live without her. The next day José urged himself to have courage and not be afraid. On January 5 he had dinner with Doris and Humphrey, then noted in Spanish that life was unbearable. Whatever passed between them in those first days of 1958, their differences were neither negotiable nor publishable. Looking back, most people felt it was José who had cut the tie.

Doris had to keep up a good front when José received the *Dance Magazine* award three weeks later for "steadfastly maintaining a high professional standard of modern dance in performances with his company throughout the United States and, this season, in Europe." At the reception at the Plaza Hotel, Sarah Lawrence College president Harold Taylor was the guest speaker, and Agnes de Mille presented the awards to José and the other winners, Alicia Markova, Jerome Robbins, and Lucia Chase. Doris made an appearance at the party but contrived to leave for a rehearsal before the speeches. In his acceptance, José was gracious as always, insisting that the honor must be shared among all his colleagues and mentors. He listed Doris in both categories, but nothing more than that. He had seldom referred to her publicly in such disaffected terms.

José's inner turbulence continued through the spring. He was choreographing a tremendous work, and he was doing it alone. The European tour had not only exposed the tragic necessity of freeing himself from Doris, it had revealed to him the devastation wrought on Europe by the war. José was deeply affected by the still-bombed-out cities they visited, particularly in Poland, and by the gallant spirit of the people who survived. He began a tribute to these people in the form of a choral dance to Zoltan Kodaly's Missa Brevis in Tempore Belli. Using his own company and dancers from Juilliard Dance Theater, about twenty in all, he pictured a community and their leader, in somber street clothes, surging and soaring in waves of disbelief, pain, and finally affirmation. Ming Cho Lee's skeletal silhouette of a bombed-out church was the backdrop.

Missa Brevis owed a lot to Doris, even though she wasn't intimately involved in its creation. Like so many of José's works, it drew on her choreographic techniques, especially in its shifts of scale from large to small ensembles and its swift, dramatic alternations between the broad, driving assertion of the group and its moments of meditative stillness. In his groups of peasants, clustering together and ritualistically acting out the events of the Mass, he skillfully drew on the possibilities of counterpoint and architectural patterning to illustrate unity and divisiveness. He himself played a sort of secular pastor, who could comfort his flock and suffer for them, but who stood apart from them finally, a humble yet stubborn figure of doubt.

Doris attended a rehearsal a month before the premiere, which took place at Juilliard April 11. According to Deborah Jowitt, who was one of the augmented group from Juilliard Dance Theater, José was quite nervous about showing it to Doris, and after the rehearsal she dismissed the dancers, saying that she would give him comments in private. At the next rehearsal, José made some changes she had suggested—they weren't extensive, Jowitt says, but they improved certain designs greatly. Doris may also have seen some of the solo and small-group work José was doing separately with the company dancers and may have come to one more big run-through later on, but her contributions to *Missa Brevis* were hardly of a collaborative nature.

Romantic, fervent, and monumental in scope, *Missa Brevis* was an immediate hit with the audience. It was probably the most successful symphonic work José ever made. Without Lucas, who had been captured by an adoring band of German and Dutch dancers for several months of teaching in Europe after the tour, or Koner, who was taking some time off and didn't like big group works anyway, the piece had no characters and no dramatic interplay. José's own role, a focal point, of course, carried no story or psychological portents. John Martin called the dance "surely one of the finest works of art of our time . . . relying altogether on the essential power of emotional vision to operate through the transparency of the inspired artist."

For the April series at Juilliard, Doris revived the Bach *Partita* and let Anna Sokolow and Donald McKayle do the other new works. "I did not knock myself out as much as usual," she reported to Hay. Physically and psychically, Doris had begun to run down. She decided not to do a new work at Connecticut College, and by summer she had begun work again on her theory book. Writing to Ernestine Stodelle, she mentioned accumulating "difficulties and disappointments . . . not only personal ones but in the modern dance field in general." This time she was finding her escape in laying out the principles of dance composition which she had been exploring for thirty-five years and which she had tested in so many ways. "I find writing is a very lonely business—no music, no people, no movement, but rather fascinating once you're in it," she told Stodelle.

Doris hated to leave loose ends; she would push herself and her coworkers unrelentingly and against terrible handicaps to achieve some exemplary goal. Perhaps she was already feeling ill in the spring when she arranged for a typist and set to work on the book; she didn't give any hints to others until the summer in New London. She may have had a premonition of death. Or she may simply have decided to let time sort out the difficulties between her and José and to finish the long-deferred wrap-up of her choreographic teachings in the meantime.

She had a fairly light summer.planned for New London: a revival of *Life of the Bee* for the repertory class and rehearsals of *Ritmo Jondo,* the only piece of hers that the Limón company did on the festival. José, still working through his European experience, produced *Dances* (to Chopin mazurkas) and dedicated it to four Polish cities. He also made *Serenata* to music of Paul Bowles. Whether by her choice or José's, Doris' visibility at the festival had diminished, and by the time the summer was over she had let people know she didn't plan to return in 1959. She agreed with the critics who were accusing the school of inbreeding, and she told the final faculty meeting she might travel out West the next year. Again, perhaps she was really determined to explore new fields for herself, or perhaps, with second sight, she was preparing people for her not being there.

By then, in any case, she knew she was ill, and immediately after returning to the city she went into the hospital for tests. On August 28 the doctors did an exploratory operation and found a massive and inoperable stomach cancer. Doris was not to be told, and for the next four months everyone maintained the fiction that no one could figure out what was wrong with her, and the only treatment was total rest. Leo phoned José at the farm to tell him the news; "*Sentencia de muerte para Doris,*" José wrote in his day book. The shock seemed to activate all José's old feelings of devotion for Doris, and probably considerable guilt as well. Within a week he and Pauline had given up their room at the Laurelton Hotel, where for years they had stayed between weekends and vacations in the country, and had taken an apartment at the Ruxton on the same floor as Doris'.

Leo was momentarily stunned, and in near-hysteria he wrote to Humphrey, who was stationed with his ship in Scotland. He urged their son to come home immediately, saying that Doris was "desperately ill" and that they must both be prepared to lose her, though whether it would be in a few weeks or a year the doctors couldn't be sure. Humphrey took this frantic signal with a curious detachment, writing to Pauline to ask if things were really serious, and to Doris hoping that she was feeling better. Within a week Leo had gotten control of himself and reassured Humphrey that there was no immediate emergency, while Pauline explained that the operation had been for "diverticulosis and gall bladder."

Even if she suspected what was happening—the doctors told her she definitely did not have cancer—Doris was not going to start giving in to physical disability at this stage. When she got home again at the end of September, José and Pauline took up a daily visiting pattern, and he wrote in his
diary: "We are pretending that we don't know, and if she does, she's the
best actress in the world. She appears to be very happy and serene—and
gay. Full of life and projects." Doris thought—or said she thought—it was
simple coincidence that the Limóns had found an apartment right in her
building, but she was very happy to have their company. She got busy arranging for people to take over for her at Juilliard. She asked Lucas to do the
composition classes, and Ruth began rehearsals with Juilliard Dance Theater.
She pictured herself as "directing the battle from well behind the firing line."
    Almost totally immobilized, increasingly sedated, and enduring calamitous
pain, Doris went on working. With great satisfaction, she finished her book,
The Art of Making Dances, which was published posthumously the following spring by Rinehart & Company. In a brief and personal introduction
dated October 11, she admitted that she probably would have "preferred to
be a composer of music." Then she thanked those who had helped her visualize her ideas, "the hundreds of students and professional dancers who
have served as guinea pigs . . . and who, I hope, were rewarded then, and
will also now be able to see some of the results of their labors in this book.
But my deepest gratitude goes to my husband, Charles Francis Woodford,
who stood by me in famine and in feast, and who always believed that I
could make more dances, think more creative thoughts, and write this book."
She then began her autobiography, which remained unfinished and was
published first by Selma Jeanne Cohen as a *Dance Perspectives* monograph
in 1966; it later formed the opening section of Cohen's biography, *Doris
Humphrey: An Artist First* (1972).
    At the same time, she was directing a new dance. Late in the previous
spring she had made a start on choreographing Bach's fourth Brandenburg
Concerto on the Juilliard dancers. After she became ill, she asked Ruth Currier to finish it. Currier thinks now she probably had sketched out the whole
dance in her mind although she executed only part of the first movement
with the dancers. During the fall of 1958 Currier was teaching at Bennington.
On weekends she would come into New York for rehearsals, then go to see
Doris to report on the dance's progress and get her notes and suggestions.
The completed dance wasn't premiered until May 1959. Doris never saw it.
    Late in the fall Doris grew worse. On December 8 José recorded, "Doris is
dying." Leo sailed for the Far East on December 11 but Doris expected to be

with the Limóns and Humphrey for Christmas. She had a lot of pain when trying to get out of bed, though, and told José, "I know I'm getting worse." He noted the next day, "The strong ones don't ask for love, they give it." The Limóns were planning a party for her on Christmas, with a showing of all the films of her dances they could gather together. As usual she wrote over a hundred Christmas cards and letters to her friends, and then, on December 24 she went into the hospital. On the 29th José recorded her death in his diary, with a line from the Lorca *Lament.* "'How tremendous with the last banderillos of darkness.' Doris died at 9:08 P.M. How beautiful is the end of the agony."

Doris Humphrey was the most persistent humanist in modern dance. She took dance to be an expression of society: the dancers were its flawed, aspiring citizens; the dance work a sublimated reflection of how they lived their lives, or a prospectus for living better. As choreographer she thought she should depict not her own desires and dreams but those of a bigger, more noble entity. Her own life was marked by defeat, financial hardship, and extreme physical suffering. Her dances outsmarted the hazard and neglect, with images of cooperative groups, physical resilience, and labor as its own reward. These dances of affirmation, so devotedly put together, so evanescent, can stand, as long as we remember them, for the transfiguring joy of hope, courage, and work.

CHRONOLOGY

A summary of important events and dances in Doris Humphrey's career. For dances not listed in the Chronology, see Index.

1895   Doris Humphrey born, October 17 in Oak Park, Illinois.

1913   Humphrey graduates from the Francis W. Parker School and begins teaching dance classes in suburban Chicago, with her mother as accompanist.

1917   Enrolls for summer classes at Denishawn School in Los Angeles.

1918   Joins Denishawn Company, where she becomes a principal dancer, teacher, and co-choreographer with Ruth St. Denis. Meets her future partners, Pauline Lawrence and Charles Weidman.
Dances include *Valse Caprice (Scarf Dance)*, *Bourrée*, and, with St. Denis, *Soaring* and *Sonata Pathétique*.

1921–2   With Pauline Lawrence, runs a small independent company touring in vaudeville.

1923   Rejoins Denishawn.
Dances include *Sonata Tragica* (later called *Tragica*), *Scherzo Waltz (Hoop Dance)*, *At the Spring*, *Whims*, and, with St. Denis, *A Burmese Yein Pwe*.

1925–6   Denishawn tour to the Orient.

1927   Runs Denishawn school in New York with Weidman and Lawrence while main company is on tour in Ziegfeld Follies.

1928   Student performance at Little Theater, Brooklyn, March 24, with works from Denishawn repertory and new works by Humphrey: *Air for the G String* and *Color Harmony*.
Humphrey, Weidman, and Lawrence leave Denishawn and form their own school and performing group.
First independent concert of Humphrey-Weidman group, October, including premiere of *Water Study*.

1929   *Life of the Bee* premiere, Guild Theater, New York, March 31.

1930   First season of Dance Repertory Theatre at Maxine Elliott's Theater, New York, January. Premiere of *Drama of Motion*.
Choreographs Schönberg's *Die Glückliche Hand* for League of Composers, April. Dances in the production with Weidman and members of the company.
Co-choreographs *Lysistrata* with Weidman, for production directed and designed by Norman Bel Geddes. With Humphrey-Weidman dancers. Opens April 28 in Philadelphia.

1931   Second season of Dance Repertory Theatre, at Craig Theater, New York, February. Premieres of *The Shakers* and *Dances for Women.*
Other 1931 dances include *Two Ecstatic Themes.* Work begun on *Orestes* and continues until around 1935, when the dance is abandoned without a production.
Humphrey does the choreography for Irene Lewisohn's dramatic interpretation of the Ernest Bloch String Quartet, given at the Library of Congress and the 92nd Street YM-YWHA in April.
Moves studio to 151 West 18th Street.
On a vacation to the West Indies, Humphrey meets Charles Francis Woodford in May.

1932   Concert at Guild Theater, New York, March 13. Premieres of *Dionysiaques* and the first section of *The Pleasures of Counterpoint.*
Humphrey marries Woodford on June 10.
September 17, opening of Shuberts' *Americana,* with dances from Humphrey-Weidman repertory, including *Water Study* and *The Shakers,* and a special arrangement of the Blue Danube Waltz by Humphrey.

1933   Choreographs *Run Little Chillun* for Bahamian dancers, Lyric Theater, New York, March.
Birth of Charles Humphrey Woodford, July 8.
Roussel Suite at Lewisohn Stadium and Robin Hood Dell, Philadelphia, in August.
Dance family moves into 31 West 10th Street.
School for Husbands, co-choreographed with Weidman, for the Theatre Guild. Opens Empire Theater, New York, October 16, with Humphrey, Weidman, and twelve company dancers in the cast.

1934   Guild Theater, New York, April 15: *Rudepoema,* two more parts of *Pleasures of Counterpoint,* and *Alcina* (with Weidman).
First summer of Bennington School of Dance, Vermont.

1935   Humphrey-Weidman makes first national tour by a modern dance company, January, establishing the "college circuit."
92nd Street YM-YWHA forms Dance Center under William Kolodney. Humphrey invited to be on the faculty.
Bennington premiere of the first sections of *New Dance.* New York premiere, with Variations and Conclusion, Guild Theater, October 27.

1936   Premiere of *Theatre Piece* at Guild Theater, January 19.
With My Red Fires premieres at Bennington, completing the *New Dance Trilogy.*

1937   Teaching and touring.

1938   *American Holiday* and *Race of Life* premiere during concerts at the Guild Theater, January.
Passacaglia and Fugue in C Minor created at Bennington workshop. Premiered August 5.

1939   Bennington School of Dance held at Mills College, Oakland, California. José Limón's first major choreography.

Square Dances premieres at Washington Irving High School, New York, November 25.

Humphrey sustains leg injury in a fall while on tour in Virginia, December. Apparently the event that precipitated arthritis of the hip, which forced her retirement from dancing five years later.

1940   Limón leaves company to work with May O'Donnell on the West Coast after teaching for the summer at Mills College.

First two parts of *Song of the West* premiere, Mary Washington College, Fredericksburg, Virginia, November 8.

Humphrey-Weidman Studio Theater opens at 108 West 16th Street, on December 26.

1941   *Decade* premieres at Bennington, a revue of Humphrey-Weidman work from 1930–40.

Dance family breaks up as members move into separate apartments. Pauline Lawrence joins Limón in San Francisco and they marry October 3.

1942   Final section of *Song of the West* premieres, Studio Theater, January.

Limón breaks with O'Donnell and returns to New York in the summer.

Joint Humphrey-Limón concert of all Bach works opens at Studio Theater in December. Premieres of *Partita in G Major, Four Chorale Preludes,* and Limón's *Chaconne.*

1943   Weidman and Humphrey-Weidman dancers alternate weekends at Studio Theater with Humphrey-Limón during winter and spring.

El Salon Mexico premieres in folk program of Humphrey and Limón works at Studio Theater, March 11.

Limón is drafted into the army in April.

1944   Premiere of *Inquest,* Studio Theater, March 5. Humphrey's last dancing role. Runs with Humphrey-Weidman repertory works at Studio Theater throughout the spring, and is given for the last time at Swarthmore College, May 26.

The August / September issue of *Dance Observer* announces the closing of Studio Theater. This marks the de facto dissolution of Humphrey-Weidman. Studio continues to be used by Weidman for classes and performances for the next seven years.

Humphrey and Weidman co-choreograph *Sing Out, Sweet Land* for the Theatre Guild, opening November 13 at the Colonial Theater in New York.

1945   Debut of Limón's trio at Studio Theater in May, with Humphrey as director.

Limón is discharged from the army in December.

1946   *Lament for Ignacio Sánchez Mejías* and *The Story of Mankind* premiere at Bennington College. This marks the debut of the José Limón Company, with Humphrey as artistic director.

Pauline Koner begins performing as a guest artist with Limón in October. Humphrey "directs" Pauline Koner in *Woe Unto Them* (later *Voice in the Wilderness*) with premiere at High School of Needle Trades, New York, November 30.

1947   *Day on Earth* premieres at Beaver Country Day School, Brookline, Massachusetts, May 10.

1948   Connecticut College School of Dance is established in summer. *Corybantic* is premiered there at the first American Dance Festival.

1949   Humphrey receives Guggenheim Fellowship for work on a book about dance theory.

1950   Limón Company appears in Paris with Ruth Page in the spring. They make their first trip to Mexico that fall.

1951   *Night Spell* premieres at Connecticut College, August 16.
        Juilliard School of Music opens a dance division. Humphrey and Limón are invited to be on the faculty.
        Humphrey teaches *Passacaglia* to Mexican dancers during a Limón company residency in December.

1953   Debut of the Merry-Go-Rounders dance company for children, with Humphrey as artistic director, at 92nd Street Y, in February.
        Humphrey directs and choreographs *Poor Eddy,* based on Edgar Allan Poe stories, for Weidman and dancers, at Columbia University, March 11.
        Ritmo Jondo is commissioned by Bethsabee de Rothschild for the season of American Dance at the Alvin Theater in April.
        Ruins and Visions premieres at Connecticut College, August 20.

1954   Humphrey wins Capezio Award for her outstanding contributions to modern dance.
        Premiere of *Felipe el Loco* at Connecticut College.
        Limón company inaugurates State Department/ANTA International Exchange Program in the Performing Arts with tour to four South American cities.
        Juilliard Dance Theater is formed in the fall under Humphrey's direction, a semiprofessional company for which she subsequently choreographs three works.

1956   Limón company premieres *Theatre Piece no. 2* at Juilliard Concert Hall, April 20.

1957   *Dance Overture* premieres at Connecticut College, August 15. The tenth anniversary year of the American Dance Festival.
        Limón company including Humphrey leaves on four-month European tour.

1958   After the summer at Connecticut College, Humphrey diagnosed with stomach cancer. During the fall she is bedridden, but finishes her theory book, *The Art of Making Dances,* and begins her autobiography (published in 1966 by Dance Horizons and in 1972 as the first section of Selma Jeanne Cohen's *Doris Humphrey: An Artist First*). She also consults regularly with Ruth Currier, who is carrying forward her plans for *Brandenburg Concerto no. 4.*
        Doris Humphrey dies December 29.

1959   *Brandenburg Concerto* is premiered in May at Juilliard by the Juilliard Dance Theater in a series of memorial concerts, which include works by Humphrey, Limón, Tamiris, and Valerie Bettis.
        In spring *The Art of Making Dances* is published by Rinehart & Company.

FILMOGRAPHY

Films are listed in approximately chronological order according to the dates of the choreography. *The titles and dates are those of the films, not the choreography.* All films are silent unless otherwise noted.

Most of the films and videotapes are located in the Dance Collection, Library and Museum of the Performing Arts at Lincoln Center. Some restrictions may apply for general viewing there. The catalogue of Dance Films, Inc., 241 East 34 Street, New York, N.Y. 10016, lists films in general circulation which may be rented or purchased.

A considerable number of Humphrey reconstructions have been filmed or video-taped privately by the producing organizations. I have not included these work-films in this listing unless they represent the only viewable version of a given dance.

Denishawn 1915—Documentary footage originally produced as a newsreel, show-ing students and classes at the Denishawn School in Los Angeles.

Hoop Dance and *Scarf Dance* 1924—The earliest known films of Doris Humphrey dancing. Included on the Denishawn film with Shawn's *Death of Adonis* and *Cuadro Flamenco.*

Spirit of Denishawn 1976—Joyce Trisler's Danscompany in a program of revivals in-cluding *Sonata Pathétique, Soaring,* and *Scarf Dance.* Directed by Klarna Pinska. This program was also taped on subsequent occasions. (sound)

Air for the G String 1934—Doris Humphrey and group. Filmed as a commercial short subject by Westinghouse. (sound)

Life of the Bee 1958—Repertory class directed by Humphrey at Connecticut College.

Choreography by Joyce Trisler Part III 1975–76—A program on tape, with a revival of *Life of the Bee* staged by Trisler. (sound)

Water Study 1976—Summer workshop at New York University, reconstruction di-rected by Eleanor King. (sound)

Water Study 1980—Group directed by Ernestine Stodelle.

Repertory Dance Theater 1980—A program with narration, "Then: The Early Years of Modern Dance," taped in performance at Riverside Church, New York City, by the Utah group. Includes *Water Study* and Variations and Conclusion from *New Dance.* (sound)

Doris Humphrey Dances ca. 1930—Home movies of Humphrey in two solos, probably excerpts from *The Call / Breath of Fire* and *Quasi-Waltz,* and directing students in exercises.

The Shakers 1940—Filmed in the Humphrey-Weidman studio by Thomas Bouchard. Not available for viewing, it is, nevertheless, a strong, impressionistic performance by the company at that time.

The Shakers 1955—Repertory class directed by Humphrey at Connecticut College.

The Shakers 1967—Students at Ohio State University, directed by Lucy Venable. (sound)

Charles Weidman: A Celebration 1975—Members of the José Limón company in *Shakers,* taped in performance at this memorial program. (sound)

Two Ecstatic Themes 1980—Nina Watt and Carla Maxwell of the José Limón company give successive performances of the dance as reconstructed by Ernestine Stodelle. (sound)

The Libation Bearers 1966—Eleanor King's reconstruction of *Orestes,* with students at the University of Arkansas.

Charles Weidman and Doris Humphrey 1935, 1938, and 1939—Films made at Bennington School of Dance and Mills College, with excerpts from *New Dance* and exercises. Documentary footage and film clips have been put together under various titles.

New Dance 1972—Performed by Charles Weidman's Theater Dance Company. (sound)

New Dance 1972—Reconstruction supervised by Charles Weidman, partly from Labanotation, on a company of professional dancers at Connecticut College, with Linda Tarnay and Peter Woodin in the leading roles. (sound)

With My Red Fires 1972—Reconstruction supervised by Charles Weidman, on a company of professional dancers at Connecticut College, with Dalienne Majors in the role of the Matriarch. (sound)

Humphrey-Weidman Company ca. 1938—Films made in performances at Chicago's Auditorium Theater by Ann Barzel, with brief excerpts from *New Dance, Race of Life.*

The Modern Dance ca. 1938—Demonstration of exercises from Doris Humphrey technique, with Beatrice Seckler, Katherine Manning, Letitia Ide, Edith Orcutt, and Katherine Litz.

Dance: Four Pioneers 1965—Documentary film on Bennington School of Dance, with a complete performance of *Passacaglia* directed by Lucy Venable on a company headed by Chester Wolenski and Lola Huth. (sound)

Song of the West 1956—Desert Gods section, by Humphrey's repertory class at Connecticut College.

Song of the West 1965—Desert Gods section, by students at the High School of Performing Arts, New York, directed by Odette Blum. (sound)

Lament for Ignacio Sánchez Mejías 1948—Excerpts filmed at Jacob's Pillow with José Limón.

Lament for Ignacio Sánchez Mejías 1951—Filmed by Walter Strate, with the original cast. (sound)

Lament for Ignacio Sánchez Mejías 1959—Filmed at Juilliard with José Limón, Letitia Ide, and Meg Mundy.

Day on Earth 1959—Filmed at Connecticut College with José Limón, Letitia Ide, Ruth Currier, and Abigail English. (sound)

Day on Earth 1972—Revival by Juilliard students Peter Sparling, Janet Eilber, Ann DeGange, with Elizabeth Haight. (sound)

Day on Earth 1975—Taped by Daniel Lewis' Contemporary Dance System, with Matthew Diamond, Carol Rae Kraus, Teri Weksler, and Julie Miele, directed by Peter Sparling and Letitia Ide. (sound)

Invention 1951—Nearly the complete dance, filmed at Jacob's Pillow by Carol Lynn, with the original cast.

Creative Leisure 1951—Clips from Connecticut College School of Dance, including excerpts from *Invention* with the original cast. (sound)

Night Spell 1952—Excerpts filmed at Jacob's Pillow by Carol Lynn, with the original cast.

Night Spell 1960—Dwight Godwin's film, with the original cast. (sound)

Night Spell 1975—Videotape, with Daniel Lewis, Laura Glenn, Leigh Warren, and Teri Weksler, directed by Lewis with Risa Steinberg and Laura Glenn. (sound)

Fantasy and Fugue 1953—One section, probably the last, of this three-part work, filmed with the original cast.

Ritmo Jondo 1956—Limón company headed by Limón and Pauline Koner, filmed at Connecticut College.

Ruins and Visions 1957, 1959—The dance is virtually complete on these two work films made by the Limón company, with Limón, Pauline Koner, and Lucas Hoving.

Dance Overture 1957—José Limón company, filmed at Connecticut College.

Brandenburg Concerto no. 4 1959—Danced by Juilliard Dance Theater.

Brandenburg Concerto no. 4 1962—Members of the Limón company filmed in rehearsal at Connecticut College.

Brandenburg Concerto no. 4 1963—Members of the Ohio State University dance group in the first movement only. (sound)

NOTES

The narrative substance of this book has been drawn largely from three types of documentary material: letters, films, and memorabilia such as programs, articles, company records, and working notes for dances. Most of this material is housed in the Dance Collection of the Library and Museum of the Performing Arts at Lincoln Center in New York.

In particular I have studied the following collections of letters, grouped and titled by the manuscript librarians as they were acquired by the Dance Collection. They comprise thousands of letters extending from Doris Humphrey's nineteenth-century ancestors through her parents' courtship, her own professional and personal life, and the careers of her close associates. Several containers of Charles Weidman's letters have been deposited at the library but have not been made available to researchers. In the notes, numerals after the collection code letters refer to specific folders in the series.

DHC Doris Humphrey Collection
DHL Doris Humphrey Letters
DHP Doris Humphrey Papers
JLP José Limón Papers
PLC Pauline Lawrence Limón Collection
EFC Eleanor Frampton Collection

In quoting from these letters, I have regularized some of the more eccentric spellings and punctuation, for the sake of readability.

In addition to the collections mentioned above, I was granted access to two important oral-history collections. Selma Jeanne Cohen's interview tapes made prior to her book *Doris Humphrey: An Artist First* are located at the Dance Collection at Lincoln Center. The Bennington School of Dance Oral-History tapes (BOH), a series of interviews made by Theresa Bowers and Nancy Goldner in 1978–79, are housed in the Oral-History Archive at Columbia University.

The following Humphrey dancers and associates were generous in giving me personal interviews or sharing their recollections informally: Rosemary Park Anastos, Sidney and Joan Levy Bernstein, Bonnie Bird, Ruth Currier, Els Grelinger, Martha Hill, Lucas Hoving, Letitia Ide, Betty Jones, Deborah Jowitt, Eleanor King, Pauline Koner, Helen Mary Robinson, Beatrice Seckler, Janet Mansfield Soares, Nancy Spanier, Ernestine Stodelle, Thomas and Lois Watson, Chester Wolenski, David Wynne.

For critical commentary, feature articles, and contemporary background, I have consulted pertinent clipping files in the Dance Collection and the following magazines: *American Dancer, The Dance, Dance Magazine, Dance News, Dance Observer, The Director, The New York Scrapbook.*

The principal books referred to are listed below. For complete citations, see Bibliography.

SJC	Cohen, *Doris Humphrey. An Artist First*
TAMD	Humphrey, *The Art of Making Dances*
EK	King, *Transformations*
SAK	Kriegsman, *Modern Dance in America: The Bennington Years*
Borzoi	Lloyd, *The Borzoi Book of Modern Dance*
Richards	"A Biography of Charles Weidman"

NOTES

1. WHAT DO YOU CALL YOUR WORK, MISS HUMPHREY?

1:1   "What do you call . . ." DHC C285.4.
1:2   "hoidenish romping . . ." Mr. and Mrs. Vernon Castle, *Modern Dancing,* p. 39.
1:5   "an evolution . . ." Genevieve Stebbins, *Delsarte System of Expression,* p. 398.
1:6   "I wanted each girl . . ." Quoted in Mildred Spiesman, "American Pioneers in Educational Creative Dance—The Natural Dance Program," *Dance Magazine,* June 1951, pp. 42–45.

2. PALACE HOTEL, 1895–1917

2:8   "a new woman" DHC C86.1–3.
2:13   "a new woman" DHC C86.1–3
2:17   "an unnaturalized German . . ." DHC C108.20.
2:20   "A man should learn . . ." Ralph Waldo Emerson, "Self Reliance", *Emerson's Essays,* p. 32.
2:21   "Parker did not want . . ." Jack K. Campbell, *Colonel Francis W. Parker,* pp. 238–239.
2:22   "She showed you how . . ." SJC, pp. 11–12.
2:25   Santa Fe tour descriptions . . . uncat. Weidman collection, Dance Collection, Library and Museum of the Performing Arts at Lincoln Center.
2:27   "The only aim I *can* have . . ." DHC C240.
2:29   "It is so full . . ." DHL 39.1.

3. DENISHAWN, 1917–26

3:31   "presenting the dance as an art . . ." Denishawn brochures.
 :31   "the most effective . . ." Denishawn brochures.
3:32   "These people were on the stage . . ." SJC, p. 32.
3:34   "You'd better add somebody . . ." DHC C243.
3:35   "Of course I'm thinking . . ." DHC C243.8
 :35   "After all even such a chance . . ." DHC C243.12
 :35   "No point in staying . . ." DHC C243.

3:36   "very pagan of course . . ." DHC C245.2.
:36   "one of the most artistic . . ." Ibid.
:36   "the lead and management . . ." DHC C245.3.
3:37   "the dull business of earning . . ." Ruth St. Denis, *An Unfinished Life,* p. 161.
3:38   "the scientific translation . . ." *Denishawn Magazine,* 1924.
3:39   St. Denis denies being influenced by Dalcroze . . St. Denis, *An Unfinished Life,* p. 216.
:39   "the first symphonic dancing . . ." Ibid., p. 216.
3:40   Trying out movements . . . SJC, p. 41.
3:42   "casting the body's vest . . ." Parrish, In David Larkin, ed., *The Fantastic Kingdom,* unpaged.
3:44 $100 in her savings . . . DH speech at Juilliard School, 7 November 1956.
3:47   "There was fresh interest . . ." *New York Times,* 4 April 1924.
:47   "The Ensemble . . ." DHC M26.1.
3:50   He acquired what training . . . Richards.
:50   "humiliation . . ." DHL 90, undated.
3:51   "resentment and self-pity . . ." SJC, p. 48.
:51   Jane Sherman witnessed . . . Jane Sherman, *Soaring,* p. 143.
:51   "with me the unpleasant . . ." DHC C261.1.
:51   "As I think of us . . ." DHC C261.2.

4. A NEW DANCE, 1927–28

4:53   *Whims* puzzled viewers . . . Jane Sherman, *The Drama of Denishawn Dance,* p. 150.
:53   "This year for the first time . . ." DHC C265.2.
:53   financing Shawn's plan . . . DHC C261.7.
4:55   "My emotions were mixed . . ." DHC C266.2.
:55   "Miss St. Denis was materially assisted . . ." *Denishawn Magazine,* vol. 1, no. 2.
:55   "swamped" DHC C265.10.
:55   "I'm so tired of dinky . . ." DHC C266.12.
4:56   "I feel more free . . ." DHC C267.7.
:56   "I'm putting some . . ." DHC C267.9.
4:57   She was working on . . . DHC C268.10.
:57   "avoid upholding . . ." DHC C268.18
:57   Ronny Johansson's reaction . . . EK, p. 2.
4:58   She thought it would be impossible . . . draft letter, DHC C272.1.
4:59   Doris suspected that Ruth . . . DHC C269.8.
:59   "Ted made such a fuss . . ." DHC C269.11.
:59   "Every spark of life . . ." Ibid.
:59   Follies tour "devastating" Sherman, *Soaring,* p. 266.
:59   "I'd like to snatch . . ." DHC C269.11.
4:60   "I have at last . . ." DHC C270.2.
:60   "Our ideas of values . . ." DHC C270.5.
:60   "he is most interested . . ." DHC C270.6.
:60   "I knew how . . ." DH speech at Juilliard School, 7 November 1956.

4:61   "I think the only hope . . ." DHC C270.6.

:61   "instead of [Ted's] . . ." DHC C270.8.

:61   "polluted water" Ibid.

:61   "Theoretically they think . . ." Ibid.

:61   "stated and agreed" DHC C270.10.

:61   Account of the meeting at which DH association with Denishawn was ended . . . DHC C270.10 and SJC, pp. 61–65.

4:62   "the art is American . . ." SJC, p. 62

:62   "I thought of the very talented . . ." SJC, p. 62.

:62   "Let the immigration department . . ." SJC, p. 62.

4:63   . . . scattered appearances . . . Christena L. Schlundt, *The Professional Appearances of Ruth St. Denis and Ted Shawn,* pp. 65–73

:63   "Since Ted's and my . . ." St. Denis, *An Unfinished Life,* p. 322.

:63   "voted out . . ." SJC, p. 64.

:63   "I don't see how . . ." DHC C270.10.

:63   . . . inevitable loss of their "children" . . . St. Denis, *An Unfinished Life,* p. 323.

:63   St. Denis and Humphrey's subsequent relationship . . . Suzanne Shelton, *Divine Dancer,* p. 222.

:63   St. Denis' message about *Color Harmony* . . . SJC, p. 86.

:63   Years later, Doris . . . DH speech at Juilliard School, 7 November 1956.

4:64   "held onto the idea . . ." DHC C268.12.

:64   "to give that sustained . . ." Ibid.

:64   "a long, golden ray . . ." *Borzoi,* p. 78.

4:65   *Kuan Yin* and *White Jade* . . . DHC C245.2.

:65   "coming up there . . ." DHC C266.12.

4:67   "For the audience . . ." *TAMD,* pp. 26–28.

:67   . . . after the first inexplicable . . . Ibid., p. 32.

:67   . . . experiments with the synchoric orchestra . . . St. Denis, *An Unfinished Life,* p. 216.

:67   "The Color Dancer" *Denishawn Magazine,* vol. I, no. 2.

4:68   Rudhyar's theories . . . Dane Rudhyar, *The Magic of Tone and The Art of Music,* pp. vii–xi.

:68   Working notebook on *Color Harmony* . . . DHC Z–21.

:68   Martin's comments on *Color Harmony* . . . John Martin, *America Dancing,* p. 215.

:68   King's comments on *Color Harmony* . . . EK, p. 4.

:68   "Following my theory . . ." DHC C266.

:68   "Just because color . . ." DHC Z–21.

5. ECSTATIC THEMES, 1928–31

5:73   "Beautiful one . . ." DHL 51.

5:74   "Darling . . ." JLP 33.

5:75   "With you I can be natural . . ." DHL 53.5

5:77   As early as 1926 . . . DHC C261.1.

:77   "the unique organ . . ." Maurice Maeterlinck, *The Life of the Bee,* p. 39.

:77   "of virgins" Ibid., p. 84.
:77   "the almost perfect . . ." Ibid., p. 32.
5:78   "In proportion as a society . . ." Ibid., p. 33.
:78   "Transition is called for . . ." Ibid., p. 394.
:78   "The hour of the great annual sacrifice . . ." Ibid., p. 44.
:78   "the wings were . . ." *The Dance,* June 1931.
5:79   . . . winner of the battle. . . EK, p. 25; JLP 458, p. 71.
:79   "The bees don't interest . . ." *The Dance,* June 1931.
:79   "the theme is never . . ." Ibid.
5:80   "Through the new conception . . ." program, Guild Theater, 31 March and 7
         April 1929.
:80   "The solo dancer . . ." *The Dance,* June 1931.
:80   José Limón noted . . . JLP 458, pp. 65 and 70.
:80   Description of *Speed* . . . EK, p. 26.
5:82   "A warrior . . ." Helen Caldwell, *Michio Ito,* pp. 20, 136.
:82   Angna Enters . . . Ginnine Cocuzza, "Angna Enters: American Dance-Mime,"
         Drama Review 88 (December 1980): 93–102.
:82   Horace Humphrey's advice on home movies . . . DHL 63.6.
5:86   "Nature moves in succession . . ." DHC M73.6.
:86   "Ocean roll . . ." DHC Z–21.
5:87   When Doris was making the dance she used to walk up and down hum-
         ming . . . EK, p. 22.
5:89   "I'm perfectly convinced . . ." DHC C271.9.
:89   "the most satisfying of all Humphrey works . . ." EK, p. 22.
:89   "The work with Doris . . ." Sherman, *Soaring,* p. 270.
5:90   "late in the year 1928" JLP 457, p. 1.
:90   March 13, 1930 . . . PLC 78.
:90   Sunday performance . . . JLP 457, p. 38.
:90   "I knew with a . . ." JLP 457, p. 39.
:90   Limón's debut in *Rhythmic Dances of Java* . . . Richards, p. 163.
5:91   "that they [the Guild] . . ." Harold Clurman, *The Fervent Years,* p. 24.
:91   "In our belief . . ." Ibid., p. 22.
:91   "make the actor face . . ." Ibid., p. 40.
:91   "to move and think . . ." SJC, p. 89.
5:92   "show me what . . ." Ibid.
:92   "the rich creative . . ." Ernestine Stodelle, *The Dance Technique of Doris Hum-
         phrey,* dedication.
:92   "it was the first . . ." Martin, *America Dancing,* p. 217.
:92   "A work done entirely . . ." JLP 458, p. 65.
:92   "it has three contrasting . . ." SJC, p. 91.
:92   "The first division . . ." H. T. Parker, *Boston Evening Transcript,* 8 March 1930.
:92   "The opening Processional . . ." EK, pp. 44–45.
5:93   "introduced by a brief dance . . ." program note, SJC, p. 91.
:93   "A transitional division . . ." Parker, *Boston Evening Transcript,* 8 March 1930.
:93   "She was joined . . ." EK, 44–45.

:93   "The third movement . . ." program note, SJC, p. 91.
:93   "From opposite sides . . ." EK, pp. 44–45.
:93   "a considered prose . . ." Parker, *Boston Evening Transcript,* 8 March 1930.
5:94   . . . it was misunderstood . . . EK, p. 47.
:94   "the couples break away . . ." EK, p. 48.
:94   "The two extricated . . ." JLP 458, p. 64
:94   "the joy arising . . ." DHC Z–21.
:94   "Any artist's struggle . . ." JLP 33.
5:95   The Shakers believed . . . E. D. Andrews, "Dance in Shaker Ritual," in *Chronicles of the American Dance,* p. 3.
:95   "war between flesh . . ." Ibid., p. 13.
:95   "seen or consulted . . ." *Dance Magazine,* September 1955.
5:97   "Who will bow . . ." E. D. Andrews, *The Gift to be Simple,* p. 114.
:97   . . . symbolic gestures that she drew upon . . . Ibid., p. 10.
:97   "Why I wonder . . ." Ibid., p. 121.
5:98   "wrestling with . . ." Labanotation score, p. 4.
5:99   "crude and possessed" JLP 458, p. 60.
:99   Andrews has noted . . . Andrews, in *Chronicles,* p. 4.
5:100   "random bizarre exercises . . ." Ibid., p. 7.
:100   "auto-intoxication . . ." Havelock Ellis, *The Dance of Life,* p. 39.
:100   "Pantomimic dances . . ." Ibid., p. 39.
:100   "All great combined efforts . . ." Ibid., p. 58.
:100   Ellis saw the group . . . Ibid., p. 60.
:100   "impassioned formalism" JLP 458, p. 61.
5:101   "all things at the moment . . ." DHC Z–15.
:101   "One thing I vow . . ." DHC C734.12.
:101   "enthralled" *Dance Magazine,* September 1955.
:101   "I loved *The Shakers* . . ." Helen [Gail] Savery in EK, p. 303.
:101   "This strikes Pauline . . ." DHC C284.16.
5:102   "our love dance" SJC, p. 128.
5:103   "a counterpoint . . ." Stodelle, *Dance Technique of Humphrey,* p. 261.
5:105   "The days go by . . ." JLP 33.

6. CONSOLIDATION, 1930–34

6:106   "I am first . . ." C280.1.
:106   "To be master . . ." EK, p. 12.
6:107   Graham spoke . . . Martha Graham, "Seeking an American Art of the Dance," in *Revolt in the Arts.*
:107   Ted Shawn . . . DHC C274.13 and JLP 34.
:107   Duncan disciples . . . "A Study in American Modernism," *Theatre Arts Monthly,* March 1930.
:107   "makes propaganda . . ." *New York World,* 31 March 1929.
6:110   Ted Shawn's solo recital . . . Ted Shawn, *One Thousand and One Night Stands,* p. 213.
:110   Lila Agnew Stewart . . . *New York Herald Tribune,* 28 April 1929.

:110 "Our dancing is beginning ..." *New York Times,* 10 February 1929.

6:111 "The best is to say ..." DHC C270.2.

:111 "great peril ..." *The Dance,* January 1931.

:111 "broken health ..." *The Dance,* June 1930.

:111 License for the Golden Theater ... DHC C270.2 and C276.4.

6:112 "There would be no ..." *New York Herald Tribune,* 3 March 1929.

:112 "Early in that morning ..." DHC M–48.

6:113 "By the time ..." DHC C274.8.

:113 Watkins account of genesis of Dance Repertory Theatre ... *New York Herald Tribune,* 5 January 1930. For other accounts see Christena L. Schlundt, *Tamiris,* p. 14; *Borzoi,* p. 137; Martin, *America Dancing,* p. 246.

:113 "Important and representative work ..." Watkins, *New York Herald Tribune,* 5 January 1930.

6:114 "Organization has come ..." DHC C275.10.

:114 "distressing conditions ..." DHC M–48.

:114 "she was more modern ..." Schlundt, *Tamiris,* p. 7.

6:115 "simply movement ..." Ibid., p. 10.

:115 Martin's account of first Dance Repertory Theatre season ... *New York Times,* 19 January 1930.

6:116 "walked away ..." *New York Herald Tribune,* 15 February 1931.

6:117 "Following reported squabbles ..." *Variety,* 18 February 1931.

:117 "If you happen ..." *New Yorker,* 18 January 1930.

:117 "Miss Graham, a serious student ..." anon. clipping, Dance Repertory Theatre scrapbooks.

:117 Martin's account of second Dance Repertory Theatre season ... *New York Times,* 15 February 1931.

6:118 "All I could present ..." DHC C283.12.

:118 Eleanor King remembers ... EK, p. 52.

6:119 "comradeship ..." Malcolm Cowley, *The Dream of the Golden Mountains,* pp. 36–37.

:119 ... dance tended to get smothered ... DHC C276.16.

6:120 Resolution of Sabbath Law question ... *Dancers Club News,* April 1932, and *New York Times,* 7 April 1932.

:120 "Actually I understood ..." Clurman, *Fervent Years,* pp. 46–47.

6:121 "Everybody has a right ..." DHC C470.10.

:121 Limón's assessment of Doris' and Charles' political disengagement ... JLP 461, pp. 166–168.

:121 "Miss Irene Lewisohn's ..." JLP 459, p. 85.

:121 "a dignified way ..." DHC C274.4.

:121 Bloch Quartet (*Quatuor a Cordes*) score and scenario by Irene Lewisohn, with interleaving cue sheets ... Neighborhood Playhouse Collection, Dance Collection, Library and Museum of the Performing Arts at Lincoln Center.

6:122 "Doris, costumed ..." JLP 459, p. 86.

6:123 Antheil opera for children at the Dalton School ... DHC C299.6.

:123 Advising League of Composers ... DHC C283.4.

:123 "The thing can't ..." DHC C276.16.
:123 Oliver Sayler asked a question ... *Revolt in the Arts,* introduction.
6:124 "so far no one ..." Robert Edmond Jones, "Toward an American Ballet," in *Revolt in the Arts.*
6:125 "Emancipation must come ..." Graham, in *Revolt in the Arts.*
:125 "Crystallization ..." *New York Herald Tribune,* 27 October 1929.
6:126 "Don't you know ..." DHC C324.16.
6:127 ... she said there were royalty problems ... DHC C302.14.
:127 She was probably apprehensive ... EK, p. 131.
:127 "cellophane set" DHC C303.2.
:127 José recalled a scene ... JLP 459, p. 113.
:127 King's version of the Shubert controversy ... EK, p. 131.
6:128 *Water Ballet* ... EK, pp. 66–67.
:128 "rehearse the daylights ..." SJC, p. 93.
:128 Shuberts' offer of a tour ... *Borzoi,* p. 138.
:128 "he wants to do ..." DHC C301.8.
6:129 "all great artists ..." DHC C362.2.
:129 "of course ..." DHC C329.11.
:129 She was supposed to get a royalty ... DHC C330.4.
6:130 "my first taste ..." JLP 459, p. 96.
:130 Radio City ... DHC C331.
:130 "dance of seductresses ..." JLP 459, pp. 102–03.
:130 "America's next ..." EFC.
:130 ... strained metatarsal arches ... DHC C335.2.
:130 "Beethoven and Brahms ..." *New York World Telegram,* 10 August 1933.
6:131 "much ado ..." JLP 459, pp. 102–03.
:131 "against the combined ..." DHC C305.
6:132 "try to include ..." DHC C279.6.
:132 "full of plant ..." *Borzoi,* p. 93.
:132 "comment about women ..." EK, p. 84.
:132 "metaphysical solace ..." Friedrich Nietzsche, *The Birth of Tragedy,* p. 50.
:132 "a Dionysiac chorus ..." Ibid., p. 56.
6:134 a book Charles had given her ... EK, p. 117.
:134 "I could make it ..." DHC C305.
:134 "by way of being ..." *New York Times,* 14 March 1932.
:134 Limón's description of *Dionysiaques* ... JLP 459, pp. 89–91.
6:135 "find individual ways ..." Eleanor King, "The Influence of Doris Humphrey," *Focus on Dance* 6 (1969).
:135 Doris' greatest work ... EK, p. 123 and *Borzoi,* p. 93.
:135 "one of the supreme ..." EK, p. 123.
:135 Although no records of *Orestes* survive, Eleanor King's *The Libation Bearers* (1950) was an approximate reconstruction. ... EK to author, October 1982.
6:136 "tried and true ..." *New York Times,* 14 March 1932.
:136 "The joke is ..." DHC C300.6.
6:137 "I wouldn't lose ..." DHC C329.12.
:137 "our artistic efforts ..." DHC C336.9.

7. MAKING DANCES, 1934–36

7:140   "a center for . . ." SAK, p. 11.
7:141   "To think . . ." DHC C390.2.
7:142   "I'm afraid will . . ." DHC C398.4.
7:143   "didn't smother people . . ." BOH-Bockman, 8.
  :143   "Now whether . . ." BOH-Beaman, 22.
  :143   He then asked the students . . . BOH-Beaman, 22.
  :143   Martin felt that . . . Martin, *American Dancing,* pp. 75–77.
7:145   "To compose . . ." Louis Horst and Carroll Russell, *Modern Dance Forms,* p. 23.
7:146   "You were beginning . . ." BOH-Wertheimer, 23.
  :146   "All of these teachers . . ." BOH-Murray, 65.
7:147   "disintegrating" DHC C353.10.
  :147   According to Stodelle . . . DHC C365.15.
7:148   "the increase of professional . . ." *New York Times,* 22 July 1934.
  :148   "protect the welfare . . ." EK, p. 184.
7:149   "in abstract form . . ." EK, p. 195.
  :149   "First was the elemental . . ." JLP 459, p. 119.
7:150   "That initial wave . . ." EK, p. 184.
  :150   "keeping the dancers out of shows . . . DHC C354.10.
7:150   The dancers would be taxed . . . EK, p. 191.
  :150   The dancers were paid minimum . . . DHC C354.14.
  :150   "happy" DHC C371.6.
7:151   "opened up the field . . ." *Christian Science Monitor,* 8 June 1935.
  :151   The vast Chicago Auditorium . . . EK, p. 200.
  :151   "on a bare stage . . ." *Chicago Journal of Commerce,* 21 January 1935.
  :151   "financially encouraging" *New York Times,* undated clipping.
  :151   "they would only . . ." DHC C374.4.
7:152   "I love to work . . ." DHC C371.6.
  :152   "overwhelmingly beautiful" EK, p. 205.
  :152   The premiere in February . . . DHC C371.8.
  :152   "the most enlivening feature . . ." Linton Mather, *Philadelphia Inquirer,* 23 February 1935.
  :152   The orchestra had first proposed . . . DHC C354.
  :152   Ernestine Henoch and Eleanor King capped . . . EK, pp. 212–213.
7:153   "whoops, bird cheeps . . ." DHC C371.16.
  :153   Norman Lloyd . . . Interview with Selma Jeanne Cohen, January 1971.
7:154   "Comment on our times . . ." SAK, p. 284.
7:155   Robert Farris Thompson . . . Robert Farris Thompson, *African Art in Motion* (Berkeley and Los Angeles: University of California Press, 1979), p. 27.
7:156   Lecture on *New Dance Trilogy* . . . SAK, pp. 284–286.
7:159   "square and oblong platinum . . ." *Christian Science Monitor,* 28 January 1936.
  :159   There she tells it . . . *Borzoi,* pp. 96–97.
  :159   "maintains a circular theme . . ." *Christian Science Monitor,* 28 January 1936.

:159   "condemnation . . ." *New Theater Magazine*, March 1936, p. 2.
:159   On the other hand . . . BOH-Bockman, 46–47.
:159   John Martin saw it . . . *New York Times*, 20 January 1936.
7:160   "great danger that . . ." "Trends in the Dance," WQXR, 7 April 1937.
7:161   "The Matriarch . . ." program, 15 January 1937.
:161   "a hymn to Aphrodite . . ." SAK, p. 140.
7:162   "primitive love-ritual" program, 15 January 1937.
:162   . . . the largest production . . . SAK p. 139.
7:163   "assuredly one of the great . . ." *New York Times*, 21 April 1936.
:163   In the original production . . . *Borzoi*, pp. 98–99.
7:164   "anti-Dionysiac . . ." Nietzsche, *Birth of Tragedy*, p. 106.
:164   . . . John Martin pointed out . . . *New York Times*, 23 August 1936.
:164   Lucia Chase tried to acquire . . . DHC C611.14 and C621.2.
:164   Matriarch as portrait of Doris' mother . . . DHL 73.5, SJC, p. 142.
7:165   "For the Divine Appearance . . ." William Blake, "Jerusalem II," SAK, p. 140.

8. ON THE ROAD, 1936–39

8:166   On these tours . . . BOH-Bales, 91.
8:167   These studies showed . . . JLP 462, p. 208.
:167   "an opening dance in which . . ." company brochure, 1938 or 1939.
:167   "unvarying mood" of *To the Dance* . . . *Dance Magazine*, July 1939, p. 8.
:167   "This sequence represents . . ." program note.
:167   "the most unnatural part . . ." *Dance Magazine*, July 1939, p. 8.
:167   "She completely . . ." JLP 459, pp. 71–74.
8:168   "the motivation . . ." DHC C533.
8:169   "She thought . . ." Norman Lloyd interview with Cohen, January 1971.
:169   "Take the Big Apple . . ." *San Francisco Examiner*, 11 March 1938.
:169   In Cleveland a society item . . . DHC C350.10.
:169   A picture spread . . . DHC C401.7.
8:170   "Years before Martha Weidman . . ." *New York Daily News*, 30 April 1937.
:170   "Oop! . . ." *New York Daily News*, 3 May 1937.
:170   "Pioneering exactly says it . . ." DHC C397.10.
8:171   "The reaction of a crowd . . ." program, 30 June 1936.
:171   "hysterical stage manager" DHC C388.12.
8:172   "social and ballroom . . ." program note.
:172   Even the staunch Margaret Lloyd . . . *Borzoi*, p. 106.
8:173   "celebrates the Death . . ." Humphrey-Weidman press book, 1938–39.
:173   "rhythmically intertwined . . ." *Christian Science Monitor*, 18 January 1938.
8:174   "might have pointed . . ." *Borzoi*, p. 106.
:174   "formal groupings . . ." *New York Sun*, 10 January 1938.
:174   "futile exhibition . . ." *New York Times*, 10 January 1938.
:174   "an experiment . . ." *New York Times*, 10 January 1938.
:174   "an abstraction . . ." SJC, p. 149.
:174   "my most mature dance" *Dance Magazine*, July 1939.

:174   "the ideal of that . . ." SAK, p. 181.

:174   In musical terms . . . John Mueller, "Notes for the film 'USA: Dances—Four Pioneers,'" pp. 14–15.

8:175   "man's reiteration . . ."*Borzoi,* p. 108.

:175   "It's time we go back . . ." BOH-Read, 97–98.

8:176   "moving powers . . ." *New York Times,* 4 December 1938.

:176   "It is theatrical . . ." *Boston Herald,* 28 November 1936.

:176   "Audiences expect . . ." Margery Dana, *Daily Worker,* 5 December 1938.

8:177   Design of the boxes . . . *Borzoi,* p. 82.

:177   Martha Graham recognized . . . *Christian Science Monitor,* 10 June 1939.

8:178   Rudhyar on Bennington 1937 season . . . *Dance Observer,* August/September 1937.

:178   "a new and definite . . ." DHC C403.12.

:178   "those who would turn . . ." *Dance Observer,* June 1939.

:178   Cushing had studied with . . . DHC C408.2.

8:179   . . . advance agent for Massine's Ballet Russe . . . *Seattle Times,* 3 February 1939.

:179   "A nightmare" Lincoln Kirstein, "Blast at Ballet," *Three Pamphlets Collected,* p. 42.

:179   He paid Doris . . . Ibid., pp. 87–88.

:179   "frightening originality . . ." Ibid., pp. 92–93.

8:180   What they needed . . . Beatrice Seckler interview with author, 13 March 1983.

:180   So the ill-advised . . . DHC C407.5.

:180   "several hundred . . ." DHC 407.7.

:180   "suffers badly . . ." DHC C407.3.

:180   Later that year . . . DHC C417.8.

:180   "I think there are . . ." DHC C408.2.

8:181   She even dreamed . . . DHC C407.5.

:181   "Bitter sweet . . ." DHC C407.3.

8:182   "bend every effort . . ." Ibid.

:182   She had no taste . . . BOH-Read, 87–88.

:182   "a venture which . . ." *New York Times,* 14 August 1932.

8:183   "if people work . . ." *Theatre Arts Monthly,* May 1934.

:183   Apparently it was John Martin . . . DHC R8 and R9.

:183   Two years later . . . SAK, pp. 48–49.

:183   Bogue requested a budget . . . DHL 70.2 and DHC C393.10.

8:184   By the end of the decade . . . DHC C424.2.

9. STUDIO THEATER, 1939–44

9:185   Around 1937. . . BOH-Bockman, 33.

:185   People like Eleanor King . . . EK, p. 277.

9:186   To a script by Humphrey-Weidman colleague . . . JLP 462, pp. 234–236.

:186   "I saw that my association . . ." JLP 462, p. 236.

9:187   "glowing reports" DHC C444.2.

:187 ... they had met a young man ... SJC, p. 160.
:187 Hamilton was impressed ... Hamilton interview with Marian Horosko, 19 June 1967, Dance Collection Oral-History Archive.
9:188 "She would be too honest ..." BOH-Nowak, 57–58.
:188 "like a five-word history ..." *Borzoi,* p. 203.
:188 José screamed as if ... BOH-Read, 131–133.
:188 "a distinctive contribution ..." *Borzoi,* p. 204.
9:189 Doris thought the Humphrey-Weidman students ... DHC C425.
:189 Charles was flighty ... SJC, p. 156.
9:190 "new profession" DHC C424.8.
:190 "I would like ..." DHC C442.
9:191 She scraped her shins ... DHC C426.18.
:191 "lame duck" DHC C407.1.
:191 "still far from perfect" DHC C408.1.
:191 ... and, if she didn't dance ... DHC C408.4.
:191 So was blotting out discomfort ... DHC C407.4.
9:193 "turning in the squirrel cage" DHC C446.6.
9:194 "disrobing himself ..." DHC C454.2.
:194 "from 31 West 10th Street" DHC C452.16.
:194 "I think it's hell ..." JLP 44.
9:195 "I miss her terribly ..." DHC C443.9.
9:196 ... against her impulse ... DHC C447.8.
:196 "an understanding" JLP 463, p. 261.
:196 "make a new man ..." JLP 8.
:196 "passion for reforming" JLP 44.
:196 "a rock to lean on" Ibid.
:196 "we are still living ..." DHC C448.11.
:196 ... she went to a sanitarium ... DHC C448.1.
9:197 Leo chose this time ... Ibid.
9:198 "The marvelous west ..." DHC C425.8.
:198 "The first dance ..." program note.
9:199 Somehow, *Song of the West* ... Harriet Ann Gray interview with Selma Jeanne Cohen, 21 October 1970.
9:200 John Martin described ... *New York Times,* 28 April 1941.
:200 A rather elaborate system ... subscription announcement, 1941.
9:201 "not attempting to open ..." *New York Times,* 20 October 1940.
:201 "have once again ..." Ibid.
:201 "the first year ..." DHC C470.6.
:201 "percentage of the profits" DHC C447.
9:202 ... faculty received only expenses ... DHC C471.8.
:202 "A Biography ..." program note.
:202 Script for *Decade* ... DHC M–152.
:202 "The artist, in his endeavor ..." SAK, p. 147.
:202 ... Doris approached Wilder ... DHC C494.11.
9:203 "kind of a wonderful failure ..." SAK, p. 218.

:203   Unsympathetic writers . . . SAK, p. 220.
9:204   . . . critics remembered it . . . *Borzoi*, p. 115.
:204   Hay later said . . . Helen Mary Robinson interview with author, 9 March 1981.
9:205   "being dumped" JLP 11.
:205   "I'm sure they'll both . . ." DHC C471.8.
:205   "It is at a tremendous price . . ." DHC C490.2.
:205   Doris went back to the studio . . . DHC C490.13.
:205   She told her mother . . . DHC C471.14
9:206   "the work had never seemed . . ." *New York Times,* April 1942.
9:208   "two beautiful dancers . . ." *Borzoi*, pp. 206–207.
:208   "my fling . . ." JLP 463, p. 275.
:208   "What I have . . ." DHC C501.15.
:208   Apprehensive over money . . . SAK, p. 116.
9:209   "I was once again . . ." JLP 463, p. 275.
:209   "DH—Innovator/JL—Perpetuator" . . . JLP 464.
:209   "There are certain things . . ." JLP 463, pp. 279–80.
9:210   "This is one of the most magnificent . . ." Ibid.
:210   "She used a style . . ." JLP 463, p. 276.
:210   "Gothic mysticism" *New York Times,* 17 January 1943.
:210   . . . in the second section . . . JLP 463, p. 276.
:210   "a naive and stylized miniature . . ." SJC, p. 255.
:210   "Formal dances . . ." *Dance Observer,* February 1943.
:210   "Why Miss Humphrey . . ." *New York Times,* 17 January 1943.
9:212   "dry, remote . . ." *New York Times,* 27 December 1942.
:212   "is beautifully designed . . ." *New York Times,* 17 January 1943.
:212   "neatly enough made . . ." *New York Times,* 27 December 1942.
:212   "music unsuitable for dancing." *New York Times,* 17 January 1943.
:212   "I deny that this . . ." SJC, p. 255.
:212   "Do you want . . ." Ibid.
:212   Cazden's rebuttal to Martin . . . *Dance Observer,* March 1943.
9:213   "fantasy about a youth . . ." *New York Times,* 12 March 1943.
:213   scenario for *El Salon Mexico* . . . DHP 55.
:213   "reunited in the midst . . ." *New York Herald Tribune,* 14 March 1943.
9:214   "rich in inventive spirit" *New York Herald Tribune,* 28 December 1942.
:214   "All of the qualities . . ." *New York Herald Tribune,* 14 March 1943.
:214   . . . he named *El Salon Mexico* . . . *New York Herald Tribune,* 23 May 1943.
:214   "one of the most vital . . ." Robert Lawrence, *The Victor Book of Ballets and Ballet Music,* p. 294.
9:215   "I want to dance . . ." JLP 2.
:215   Doris' letter to subscribers . . . *New York Times,* 27 June 1943.
:215   Doris thought Weidman was bored . . . PLC 26.
9:216   In fact, he hoped . . . DHC C548.
:216   But she was teaching . . . DHC C546.4.
:216   "Fundamentally I am an egocentric . . ." DHC C536.5.
9:217   "It was only last year . . ." DHC C547.18.

10. FALL AND RECOVERY, 1944–46

10:218 "People were getting killed . . ." Norman Lloyd interview with Cohen, January 1971.

:218 "I would like to make . . ." DHC C472.2.

:218 "Do you ask to be . . ." John Ruskin, "Of Kings' Treasuries," *Sesame and Lilies.*

10:219 "rhythmic mime . . ." *New York Times,* 12 March 1944.

:219 "In stormy crosscurrents . . ." *Borzoi,* p. 121.

:219 "It is as if . . ." *New York Times,* 12 March 1944.

:219 George Beiswanger compared it . . . *Dance Observer,* April 1944.

:219 "This was suffering . . ." *Borzoi,* p. 12.

:219 "A day . . . is coming . . ." *New York Times,* 27 April 1943.

10:220 "The piece has pointed out . . ." Edwin Denby, *Looking at the Dance,* p. 332.

:220 "invisible gold medal" *New York Times,* 4 June 1944.

:220 In increasing pain . . . DHC C566.4.

10:221 . . . told by the doctor to take a complete rest . . . DHC C565.

:221 "Musicians seldom appear . . ." DHC C565.10.

:221 "Life is not easy . . ." Richards, pp. 213–214.

:221 "expand their activities . . ." *Dance Observer,* August/September 1944.

:221 plan for The Dance Theater . . . DHC Z–22.

10:222 "how simple and easy . . ." DHC C583.14.

10:223 "The chorus girl . . ." Agnes de Mille, *And Promenade Home,* p. 36.

:223 "to show how music . . ." *Boston Herald,* 26 November 1944.

10:224 scenario for *Building of the Cities* . . . DHP 49.

:224 De Mille was queen . . . *New York Journal American,* 4 June 1945.

:224 "It won't compete . . ." *New York World Telegram,* 28 April 1944.

10:225 Script for *Is Sex Necessary?* . . . JLP 651.

:225 "settle this matter." DHC C618.4.

:225 "award . . ." DHC C618.8.

10:226 . . . full-fledged program of teaching . . . 92nd Street YM–YWHA brochure, 1945–46.

:226 "Great as she was . . ." *New York Herald Tribune,* 2 December 1945.

:226 As she remembers it . . . Pauline Koner interview with author, 4 April 1984.

10:227 "clarifying choreography . . ." *Dance Observer,* January 1941.

10:228 *Sing Out* review . . . *New York Herald Tribune,* 21 January 1945.

:228 Beiswanger called for Ballet Theatre . . . *Theater Arts Journal,* June 1941.

:228 . . . and Hay argued that . . . DHC C587.9.

:228 "now all the balletomanes . . ." DHC C611.7.

:228 Chase wrote graciously . . . American Ballet Theatre Collection, Dance Collection, Library and Museum of the Performing Arts at Lincoln Center, 1947 correspondence.

:228 Time on the road . . . de Mille, *Promenade Home,* chap. 10.

10:229 Chase's reply . . . DHC C616.4.

:229 They met to discuss . . . DHC C616.6.

:229 José offered to rearrange . . . DHC C620.6.

10:230 "I am thankful . . ." DHC C621.12.

   :230 . . . she must concentrate her energies . . . Paul Love Collection, Dance Collection, Library and Museum of the Performing Arts at Lincoln Center, interview from 1930s.

   :230 "an enchanting little suite . . ." *New York Times,* 21 May 1945.

10:231 "with no girls . . ." DHP 4.

   :231 She suggested an actress . . . Ibid.

   :231 Script for *Lament* . . . DHC M-23.

10:233 "drama . . . is intended . . ." Ibid.

   :233 "solid and palpable" DHP 5.

10:234 "The impressions . . ." *Borzoi,* p. 125.

   :234 Michael Czaja provided . . . *Borzoi,* p. 126.

   :234 "Comedy is something . . ." DHC C600.10.

   :234 "Accomplishing these two works . . ." Ibid.

10:236 "Mothers have to be . . ." Ruth Currier interview with author, 4 June 1984.

   :236 Eleanor Frampton sent her . . . EFC 31–11.

11. THE EAGLE, 1947–51

11:237 "It was like going home . . ." Currier interview with author, 4 June 1984.

   :237 "felt comfortable . . ." Betty Jones interview with author, 8 July 1984.

11:239 If she didn't like . . . Ibid.

   :239 "almost as if she had looked . . ." *New York Times,* 4 January 1948.

   :239 "the most perfect work . . ." DHC C641.5.

11:240 "Leave it to Doris Humphrey . . ." DHC C614.10.

11:241 "I liked it much better . . ." DHC C611.16.

   :241 Both Martin and Terry . . . *New York Times* and *New York Herald Tribune,* 31 August 1947.

   :241 The college at that time . . . Gertrude E. Noyes, *A History of Connecticut College,* (New London: Connecticut College, 1982), pp. 194–95.

11:242 . . . but it was looking to convert . . . Rosemary Park letter to author, 6 July 1983.

11:242 . . . Connecticut College School of Dance, cosponsored with NYU . . . Noyes, *History of Connecticut College,* pp. 167–68.

   :242 "no way to describe . . ." Ruth Lloyd interview with Selma Jeanne Cohen, 20 January 1971.

11:243 "close collaboration . . ." *A Decade of Dance 1948–57* (New London: Connecticut College, 1957), p. 4.

   :243 "People ask me . . ." DHC C677.2.

   :243 "no murder, suspicion, . . ." DHC C611.9 and .11.

11:244 *Corybantic* fared much less well . . . *New York Times,* 11 May 1947.

   :244 script for "origin: Oedipus" . . . JLP 660.

11:245 "a celebrant . . ." program note.

   :245 "Doris Humphrey has forsaken . . ." *Dance Magazine,* October 1948.

   :245 Notes on *Corybantic* for a radio interview . . . DHC M–147.

   :245 "didn't have a positive . . ." Jones interview with author, 8 July 1984.

:245 "the ultimate in fatalism" Charles H. Woodford letter to author, 13 April 1983.

:245 "captures the troubled . . ." *New York Herald Tribune,* 19 August 1948.

:245 . . . Nik Krevitsky thought . . . *Dance Observer,* August/September 1948 and May 1949.

11:246 Hoving's background . . . Lucas Hoving interview with author, 25 March 1981.

:246 As early as 1942, Pauline . . . JLP 15.

:246 Limón's Guggenheim application . . . DHC C577.6.

:246 . . . suite for a forgotten . . . Liner notes by Sidney Finkelstein for Fritz Mahler recording of Purcell, Vanguard SRV 155SD.

:246 Doris was responsible for the ending . . . Jones interview with author, 8 July 1984.

11:247 "Yours is the longest chapter . . ." DHC C621.2.

:247 She received the award . . . DHC C650.8.

:247 "to create a pool . . ." *New York Times,* 11 December 1949.

:247 . . . Bethsabee de Rothschild quietly underwrote . . . Don McDonagh, *Martha Graham,* p. 212.

:247 "for José and me . . ." DHC C645.2.

11:248 "This is greatly to be desired . . ." Ibid.

:248 John Martin thought . . . *New York Times,* 11 December 1949.

:248 "a single unified company . . ." *New York Times,* 8 January 1950.

11:249 "a stupendous diet of ballet" *New York Herald Tribune,* 18 December 1949.

:249 "inherently a strong box office attraction" *New York Times,* 28 November 1948.

:249 "As for the contemporary . . ." *New York Herald Tribune,* 13 December 1936.

11:250 Martin covered the season . . . *New York Times,* March 1950.

:250 "The ballet . . ." *New York Times,* 26 November 1950.

:250 Account of negotiations for second City Dance Theater season . . . Isadora Bennett Collection, Dance Collection, Library and Museum of the Performing Arts at Lincoln Center, pp. 22–112 and 178.

:250 These included *Passacaglia* . . . JLP 128.

11:251 . . . the Board was producing not only City Ballet's seasons . . . Anatole Chujoy, *The New York City Ballet,* pp. 210–11.

:251 Page's *"mauvais goût"* . . . *Journal de Dimanche,* May 1950.

:251 . . . antifascist pickets . . . *Dance Magazine,* June 1950, p. 6.

11:252 "We will make it impossible . . ." Ibid.

:252 "probably the biggest scandal . . ." *Dance News,* June 1950.

:252 He thought Page invited . . . *New York Herald Tribune,* 25 June 1950.

:252 "They'll either think . . ." DHC C655.

:252 "It has been a dismal . . ." DHC C660.5.

:252 "I was moved . . ." DHC C660.7.

11:253 . . . started out as sole choreographer . . . *New York Times,* 28 June 1950.

:253 . . . there wasn't enough money . . . DHP 6.

:253 Gershwin's jazzy treatment . . . *New York Daily News,* 3 November, 1950

:253 . . . "it took Mr. Limón . . ." *New York Herald Tribune,* 22 October 1950.

:253 "You can't imagine . . ." DHC C666.2.

11:256 . . . José was invited . . . *New York Herald Tribune,* 29 October 1950.
  :256 Koner and Betty were brought down . . . DHC C673.7.
  :256 "does not feel . . ." JLP 295.
  :256 . . . her ticket was provided . . . Ibid.
  :256 . . . laboriously climbing stairs . . . Jones interview with author, 8 July 1984.
11:257 . . . she didn't think the films . . . DHP 7.
11:258 . . . Doris' way of teaching . . . *Dance Observer,* January 1949.
  :258 Doris was struck by the nineteenth-century English poet's imagery . . . DHC C546.2.
  :258 "Dover Beach" lines . . . *Viking Book of Poetry of the English-Speaking World,* vol 2 (New York: Viking, 1958), p. 972.
  :258 José danced the first movement . . . DHC M–59.1.
11:260 Doris had two endings . . . Currier interview with author, 4 June 1984, and Els Grelinger interview with author, August 1983.
  :260 "suggested both the eeriness . . ." Cecil Smith, *Musical America,* September 1951.
  :260 . . . Currier thought it might . . . Currier interview with author, 4 June 1984.
  :260 "top achievements" *New York Times,* 2 September 1951.
  :260 . . . he never liked his part . . . Hoving interview with author, 25 March 1981.
11:261 "perhaps the key figure" *New York Herald Tribune,* 2 September 1951.
  :261 "an utterly fascinating dance . . ." Ibid.
  :261 "The real surprise . . ." *New York Times,* 28 August 1951.
  :261 Despite everyone's attempts . . . SJC, p. 201.
11:262 "very symbolic and mystical" DHC C665.15.
  :262 . . . impressed the critics . . . *Mexico News,* 2 December 1951.
  :262 Doris also acted as artistic adviser . . . *Dance Magazine,* February 1952.
  :262 "just Mrs. Limón . . ." DHC C677.1.
  :262 "Your mother . . ." DHC C673.10.
  :262 "The Theater of José Limón" *Theatre Arts Monthly,* November 1951.
11:263 "diluted trivialities" José Limón, "The Virile Dance,"in *The Dance Has Many Faces,* pp. 82–86.
  :263 "It has been . . ." PLC 10.

12. HARMONY AND COUNTERPOINT, 1952–57

12:264 José didn't return to Mexico . . . PLC 10.
  :264 . . . Simon Sadoff had left to tour . . . DHC C676.2.
  :264 "creative limbo" *New York Times,* 4 May 1952.
  :264 "stalwart José Limón" *New York Herald Tribune,* 20 April 1952.
  :264 . . . exhorting her to live . . . *New York Herald Tribune,* 3 February 1952.
12:265 Terry said *The Cage* . . . *New York Herald Tribune,* 9 September 1951.
  :265 "There are some adamant . . ." *New York Herald Tribune,* 21 December 1952.
  :265 Graham reorganized her company . . . JLP 298.
  :265 Surinach and *Ritmo Jondo* . . . Surinach interview with Katherine Matheson, 27 February 1979, Dance Collection, Oral History Archive, Library and Museum of the Performing Arts at Lincoln Center.

12:266 "deftly suggested mood . . ." *New York Times,* 3 May 1953.

12:267 "evocation of the emotional . . ." *Dance Observer,* June/July 1953.

:267 "renascence" *New York Herald Tribune,* 26 April 1953.

:267 "miscellaneous and competitive . . ." *New York Times,* 26 April 1953.

:267 "still in a serious condition" *New York Times,* 28 June 1953.

12:268 . . . his worst drinking years . . . Richards, p. 282.

:268 "can only smile . . ." *New York Daily News,* 12 March 1953.

:268 "masterful choreography" *Dance Observer,* May 1953.

:268 Founding of the Merry-Go-Rounders . . . Bonnie Bird interview with author, 8 April 1983.

12:269 There was to be a British Festival . . . JLP 301.

:269 Choosing the Britten music . . . Currier interview with author, 3 June 1986.

12:271 "The Fates" and "At Night" lines . . . Stephen Spender, *Collected Poems 1928–1953,* pp. 129–133.

:271 Doris' notes to Pauline . . . JLP 46.

12:272 "We see more clearly . . ." *Christian Science Monitor,* 29 August 1953.

:272 "although Miss Humphrey . . ." *Dance Magazine,* October 1953.

12:273 Correspondence with Shawn about hip operation . . . PLC 12 and 66.

:273 Hay also told her . . . DHC C688.2.

:273 . . . she entered Polyclinic . . . JLP 663.

:273 She found it less painful . . . DHC C684.

:273 "My general attitude . . ." Ibid.

:273 "her creative leadership . . ." DHC C698.2.

12:274 "primarily for the exploitation . . ." *New York Times,* 7 March 1954.

:274 "gesture of friendship . . ." JLP 304.

:274 "movement in space" *New York Times,* 29 August 1954.

:274 Felix Fernandez/Diaghilev events . . . S. L. Grigoriev, *The Diaghilev Ballet* (Brooklyn: Dance Horizons #47, 1953), pp. 135–142.

12:275 "too naturalistic" *Dance Observer,* August/September 1954.

:275 John Martin thought . . . *New York Times,* 29 August 1954.

:275 "frenzied ovation" DHC C696.16.

:275 Reworking *Felipe el Loco* . . . Jones interview with author, 8 July 1984.

12:276 "extricate everybody . . . " DHC C692.5.

:276 Limón's account of South American tour . . . *New York Times,* 23 January 1955.

:276 "almost impossible . . ." DHC C700.2.

:276 This revival prompted John Martin . . . *New York Times,* 10 May 1954.

12:277 Founding of the Juilliard Dance Theater . . . Juilliard School Dance Department, announcement.

:277 . . . or were given scholarships . . . Deborah Jowitt interview with author, June 1985.

:277 A small onetime grant . . . DHC C703.5.

:277 Doris Humphrey Dancers . . . Martha Hill conversation with author, 12 May 1981.

12:278 "Better three days . . ." *New York Times,* 22 May 1955.

:278   . . . Robert Sabin thought . . . *Dance Observer,* June/July 1955.
:278   . . . quiescent state . . . *New York Times,* 5 June 1955.
:278   "only two works . . ." *New York Times,* 29 May 1955.
12:279   Doris' health in 1955 . . . DHC C699 and C700.
:279   "sort of frozen" Ruth Lloyd interview with Cohen, 20 January 1971.
12:280   . . . like Louis Horst . . . *Dance Observer,* August/September 1955.
:280   "There is no eighteenth century . . ." *New York Times,* 28 August 1955.
:280   "a voice . . ." DHC C707.2.
:280   "The failure of the mechanism . . ." DHC C700.
:280   "If your heroine . . ." DHC C708.
12:281   "something of the attitude . . ." DHC C685.2.
:281   "O light, the spirit . . ." program note.
:281   "the lighting of the fires . . ." program note.
12:282   "I had no reaction . . ." BOH-Luening, 56–57.
:282   "a free fantasy" *Dance Observer,* June/July 1956.
:282   "treating with insight . . ." *New York Times,* 6 May 1956.
:282   "chintzy imagery" *Dance Magazine,* June 1956.
:282   "It was as though Mr. Limón . . ." Ibid.
:282   "must be pronounced a failure" *New York Times,* 26 August 1956.

13. DESCENT INTO THE DREAM 1957–58

13:284   "Doris Humphrey has made dance history . . ." *A Decade of Dance,* p. 5.
:284   "the happiest" *New York Times,* 25 August 1957.
:284   "many shocks, alarms . . ." DHC C715.4.
:284   . . . didn't survive the summer . . . DHC C715.6.
:284   "If they ever do go . . ." DHC C707.4.
13:285   She thought six to eight weeks . . . DHC C715.2.
:285   "disliked us intensely . . ." JLP 569.
:285   Dances given on European tour . . . Oliver Nicoll correspondence with music
        publishers, PLC 160–164.
13:286   . . . starry-eyed little girl . . . Koner at rehearsal of *Day on Earth,* 14 April 1983.
:286   "This is a very capable . . ." JLP 569.
:286   . . . the repertory had boiled down . . . JLP 64.
:286   "We all felt so awful . . ." Hoving interview with author, 25 March 1981.
:286   "José started getting . . ." Koner interview with author, 4 April 1984.
:286   "People would not even . . ." Hoving interview with author, 25 March 1981.
:286   "It was hell . . ." Currier interview with author, 4 June 1984.
:286   Currier crisis . . . JLP 146.
13:287   "Your mother flies home . . ." JLP 64.
:287   "The company is going to Yugoslavia . . ." DHC C714.
:287   . . . title of a popular song . . . JLP 663.
13:288   "steadfastly maintaining . . ." *New York Times,* 16 February 1958.
:288   In his acceptance . . . *Dance Magazine,* March 1958.
13:289   According to Deborah Jowitt . . . Jowitt conversation with author, 8 October
        1984.

:289 Koner taking time off . . . Koner interview with author, 4 April 1984.

:289 "surely one of the finest works . . ." *New York Times,* 22 June 1958.

:289 I did not knock myself out . . ." DHC C721.4.

:289 "difficulties and disappointments . . ." Humphrey letter to Stodelle, 7 June 1958.

13:290 She agreed with the critics . . . SJC, p. 219.

:290 "*Sentencia de muerte* . . ." JLP 663.

:290 "desperately ill" DHC C724.2.

:290 "diverticulosis and gall bladder" DHC C725.

13:291 "We are pretending . . ." JLP 663.

:291 Doris thought—or said she thought. . . DHC C721.8.

:291 "directing the battle . . ." Ibid.

:291 "preferred to be a composer . . ." TAMD, foreword.

:291 Currier thinks now . . . Currier interview with author, 4 June 1984.

:291 "Doris is dying." DHC C721.10.

13:292 "I know I'm getting worse." JLP 663.

:292 "The strong ones . . ." Ibid.

:292 "'How tremendous . . ." Ibid.

BIBLIOGRAPHY

Amberg, George. *Ballet in America.* New York: New American Library, Mentor Books, 1949.

Andrews, E. D. "Dance in Shaker Ritual," in *Chronicles of the American Dance.* Edited by Paul Magriel. 1948. New York: Da Capo Press, 1978, pp. 2–14.

———. *The Gift to be Simple.* 1940. New York: Dover Publications, 1962.

Barnouw, Eric. *Documentary: A History of the Non-Fiction Film.* London: Oxford University Press, 1974.

Becker, Svea, and Joening Roberts. "A Reaffirmation of the Humphrey-Weidman Quality." *Dance Notation Journal* 1, no. 1 (January 1983): 3–17.

Bolitho, William. "Isadora Duncan." *Twelve Against the Gods,* 1929. Reprinted in *Chronicles of the American Dance.* Edited by Paul Magriel. New York: Da Capo Press, 1978.

Cafflin, Caroline and Charles H. *Dancing and Dancers of Today.* 1912. New York: Da Capo Press, 1978.

Caldwell, Helen. *Michio Ito: The Dancer and His Dance.* Berkeley and Los Angeles: University of California Press, 1977.

Campbell, Jack K. *Colonel Francis W. Parker: The Children's Crusader.* New York: Teachers College Press, 1967.

Castle, Irene. *Castles in the Air.* 1958. New York: Da Capo Press, 1980.

Castle, Mr. and Mrs. Vernon. *Modern Dancing.* 1914. New York: Da Capo Press, 1980.

Chujoy, Anatole. *The New York City Ballet.* New York: Alfred A. Knopf, 1953.

Clurman, Harold. *The Fervent Years.* 1945. New York: Hill & Wang, 1961.

Cocuzza, Ginnine. "Angna Enters: American Dance-Mime." *Drama Review* 88 (December 1980): 93–102.

Cohen, Selma Jeanne. *Doris Humphrey: An Artist First.* Middletown, Conn: Wesleyan University Press, 1972.

Cowell, Henry, ed. *American Composers on American Music.* New York: Frederick Ungar Publishing Co., 1962.

Cowley, Malcolm. *The Dream of the Golden Mountains.* 1980. Penguin, 1981.

Crowley, Alice Lewisohn. *The Neighborhood Playhouse: Leaves from a Theatre Scrapbook.* New York: Theatre Arts Books, 1959.

Davis, Martha Ann and Claire Schmais. "An Analysis of the Style and Composition of 'Water Study.'" *Research in Dance.* New York: CORD, New York University, 1968, pp. 105–113.

de Mille, Agnes. *And Promenade Home.* Boston: Little, Brown & Co., 1958.

————. *Dance to the Piper.* Boston: Little, Brown & Co., 1952.

Denby, Edwin. *Looking at the Dance.* New York: Horizon Press, 1968.

Dewey, John. "Francis W. Parker," in *Characters and Events.* New York: Henry Holt & Co., 1929.

Ellis, Havelock. *The Dance of Life.* Grosset Universal Library, 1923.

Emerson, Ralph Waldo. *Emerson's Essays.* Edited by Irwin Edman. New York: Thomas Y. Crowell Company, 1926.

Flanagan, Hallie. *Arena—The Story of the Federal Theatre.* 1940. New York: Limelight Editions, 1985.

Hayden, Dolores. *Seven American Utopias.* 1976. Cambridge: MIT Press, 1979.

Hinman, Mary Wood. *Folk and Gymnastic Dancing.* New York: A. S. Barnes, 1916–27.

Holloway, Mark. *Heavens on Earth: Utopian Communities in America 1680–1880.* 1951. New York: Dover Publications, 1966.

Horst, Louis. *Pre-Classic Dance Forms.* 1937. Princeton, NJ: Dance Horizons/Princeton Book Company. New edition with introduction by Janet Mansfield Soares, 1987.

Horst, Louis, and Carroll Russell. *Modern Dance Forms in Relation to the Other Modern Arts.* 1961. Princeton, NJ: Dance Horizons/Princeton Book Company. New edition with introduction by Janet Mansfield Soares, 1987.

Humphrey, Doris. *The Art of Making Dances.* 1952. New York: Grove Press, 1959.

————. *The Collected Works.* vol. I. Dance Notation Bureau, 1978. Includes Labanotation scores of *Water Study, Shakers,* and *Partita V.* Other Humphrey dances in Labanotation are listed in *Notated Theatrical Dances,* published by the Dance Notation Bureau, 1985, with addenda.

————. Manuscripts and drafts for articles, essays, and speeches are found in the Manuscripts folders of the Doris Humphrey Collection, Dance Collection at the Library and Museum of the Performing Arts at Lincoln Center. Published writings referred to in this text are cited in the endnotes.

Jaques-Dalcroze, Emile. *Rhythm, Music and Education.* 1921. London: Dalcroze Society, 1977 (Distributed in North America by Princeton Book Company).

Kagan, Elizabeth. "Towards the Analysis of a Score." *CORD Annual,* #9, 1978.

Kendall, Elizabeth. *Where She Danced.* New York: Alfred A. Knopf, 1979.

King, Eleanor. "The Influence of Doris Humphrey." *Focus on Dance* 6 (1969).

————. *Transformations.* Princeton, NJ: Dance Horizons/Princeton Book Company, 1978.

Kirstein, Lincoln. "Blast at Ballet." 1937. Reprinted in *Ballet: Bias and Belief* edited by Nancy Reynolds. Princeton, NJ: Dance Horizons/Princeton Book Company, 1983.

Koner, Pauline. "Working with Doris Humphrey." *Dance Chronicle* 7, no. 3 (1984).

Kriegsman, Sali Ann. *Modern Dance in America: The Bennington Years.* Boston: G.K. Hall & Co., 1981.

Larkin, David, ed. *The Fantastic Kingdom.* New York: Ballantine Books, 1974.

Lawrence, Robert. "El Salon Mexico," in *The Victor Book of Ballets and Ballet Music.* New York: Simon & Schuster, 1950, pp. 394–95.

Lindsay, Vachel. *The Art of the Moving Picture.* 1915. Revised 1922. New York: Liveright Publishing Corp., 1970.

Lloyd, Margaret. *The Borzoi Book of Modern Dance.* 1949. Princeton, NJ: Dance Horizons/Princeton Book Company, 1987.

McDonagh, Don. *Martha Graham: A Biography.* Westport, Conn: Praeger Publishers, 1973.

Maeterlinck, Maurice. *The Life of the Bee.* 1901. Translated by Alfred Sutro. New York: Dodd Mead & Co., 1914.

Marks, Joseph E., III. *America Learns to Dance.* 1957. Brooklyn: Dance Horizons, #81.

Martin, John. *America Dancing.* New York: Dodge Publishing Co., 1936.

———. *The Modern Dance.* 1933. Princeton, NJ: Dance Horizons/Princeton Book Company, 1965.

———. *Ruth Page: An Intimate Biography.* New York: Marcel Dekker, 1977.

Mueller, John. "Notes for the film 'USA: Dances—Four Pioneers' including Doris Humphrey's *Passacaglia,*" in *Dance on Film: Commentary,* University of Rochester, n.d., pp. 11–27.

Naylor, Gillian. *The Arts and Crafts Movement.* 1971. Cambridge: MIT Press, 1980.

Nietzsche, Friedrich. *The Birth of Tragedy.* 1872. Translated by Francis Golffing. New York: Doubleday, Anchor Books, 1956.

Odom, Selma Landen. "Chicago, 1913: Eurythmics Entering American Dance." *American Dalcroze Journal* 11, no. 1 (Fall 1983).

Page, Ruth. *Page by Page.* Brooklyn: Dance Horizons, 1978.

Payne, Charles. *American Ballet Theatre.* New York: Alfred A. Knopf, 1977.

Pischl, A. J. and Barbara Naomi Cohen, eds. "The Franchising of Denishawn." *Dance Data #4,* n.d.

Richards, Sylvia P. "A Biography of Charles Weidman with emphasis upon his professional career and his contributions to the field of dance." Ph.D. dissertation, Texas Woman's University, College of Health, Physical Education and Recreation, Denton, Texas, 1971.

Rudhyar, Dane. *The Magic of Tone and The Art of Music.* Boulder, Colo: Shambala Publications, 1982.

Ruskin, John. *Sesame and Lilies.* 1865. London: J. M. Dent & Sons, 1907.

Ruyter, Nancy Lee Chalfa. *Reformers and Visionaries.* Princeton, NJ: Dance Horizons/Princeton Book Company, 1978.

St. Denis, Ruth. *An Unfinished Life.* 1939. Reprint. Brooklyn: Dance Horizons, 1969.

Sayler, Oliver M. *Revolt in the Arts.* New York: Brentano's, 1930.

Schlundt, Christena L. "The Choreography of Soaring: The Documentary Evidence." *Dance Chronicle* no. 4 (1984), pp. 363–373.

———. *The Professional Appearances of Ruth St. Denis and Ted Shawn.* New York Public Library, 1962.

———. *Tamiris: A Chronicle of Her Dance Career.* New York Public Library, Astor, Lenox & Tilden Foundations, 1972.

Scully, Vincent. *American Architecture and Urbanism.* 1969. Westport, Conn: Praeger Publishers, 1976.

Selden, Elizabeth. *The Dancer's Quest.* Berkeley and Los Angeles: University of California Press, 1935.

Sergeant, John. *Frank Lloyd Wright's Usonian Homes.* New York: Whitney Library of Design, 1976.

Shawn, Ted. *Every Little Movement.* 1954. Second revised edition, 1963. Princeton, NJ: Dance Horizons/Princeton Book Company, 1974.

————, with Gray Poole. *One Thousand and One Night Stands.* 1960. New York: Da Capo Press, 1979.

Shelton, Suzanne. *Divine Dancer: A Biography of Ruth St. Denis.* New York: Doubleday & Co., 1981.

Sherman, Jane. *The Drama of Denishawn Dance.* Middletown, Conn: Wesleyan University Press, 1979.

————. *Soaring.* Middletown, Conn: Wesleyan University Press, 1976.

Siegel, Marcia B. *The Shapes of Change: Images of American Dance.* 1979. Berkeley and Los Angeles: University of California Press, 1985.

————. "José Limón (1908–1972)," in *Watching the Dance Go By.* Boston: Houghton Mifflin, 1977, pp. 160–65.

Sorell, Walter, ed. *The Dance Has Many Faces.* 2d ed. New York: Columbia University Press, 1966.

Spender, Stephen. *Collected Poems 1928–1953.* New York: Random House, 1955.

Stebbins, Genevieve. *Delsarte System of Expression.* 1902. Princeton, NJ: Dance Horizons/Princeton Book Company, 1978.

Stewart, Virginia and Merle Armitage, eds. *The Modern Dance.* 1935. Brooklyn: Dance Horizons, #27.

Stodelle, Ernestine. "Air for the G String." *Ballet Review* 11, no. 4 (Winter 1984): 86–87.

————. *The Dance Technique of Doris Humphrey.* Princeton, N.J.: Princeton Book Co., 1978.

Stott, William. *Documentary Expression and Thirties America.* 1973. New York: Oxford University Press, 1976.

Thurber, James, and E. B. White. *Is Sex Necessary?* 1929. New York: Harper & Row, Colophon Books, 1984.

Wentink, Andrew Mark. "The Doris Humphrey Collection—An Introduction and Guide." *Bulletin of the New York Public Library* 77, no. 1 (Autumn 1973): 80–142.

Youngerman, Suzanne. "The Translation of a Culture into Choreography: A Critical Appraisal of *The Shakers* Through the Use of Labananalysis." *CORD Annual* #9, 1978.

ACKNOWLEDGMENTS

Grateful acknowledgment is made for permission to reprint the following: to William Morrow & Co., Inc., for the passage from Lillian Faderman's *Surpassing the Love of Men*, copyright © 1981 by Lillian Faderman; to Random House, Inc., for lines quoted from Stephen Spender's "The Fates" and "At Night," *Ruins and Visions: Poems 1934–1942*, copyright © 1942, renewed 1970, by Stephen Spender; to Viking Penguin Inc. for a selection from *The Dream of the Golden Mountains* by Malcolm Cowley, copyright © 1964, 1965, 1975, 1978, 1979, 1980 by Malcolm Cowley. The lines quoted from Shaker hymns are reprinted from *The Gift to Be Simple* by E. D. Andrews (Dover Publications, Inc., 1962), copyright 1940 by E. D. Andrews; renewed 1967 by Mrs. Faith Andrews. Material from the Doris Humphrey Collection, Doris Humphrey Papers, and Pauline Lawrence Limón Collections in the Dance Collection, Library of the Performing Arts at Lincoln Center, is quoted with permission of Charles H. Woodford. Material from the José Limón Manuscript Collection in the Dance Collection, Library of the Performing Arts at Lincoln Center, is quoted by permission of Charles D. Tomlinson, José Limón Dance Company. The photographs on the jacket, frontispiece, and pages 41, 45, 58, 66, 71, 81, 133, 138, 144, 158, 168, 172, 173, 197, 211, 232, 235, 238, 244, 248, 259, and 270 are reprinted with permission of the Dance Collection, the New York Public Library at Lincoln Center, Astor, Lenox & Tilden Foundations.

Portions from chapter 6 appeared in *Dance Research Journal* 19/1 (Summer 1987).

INDEX